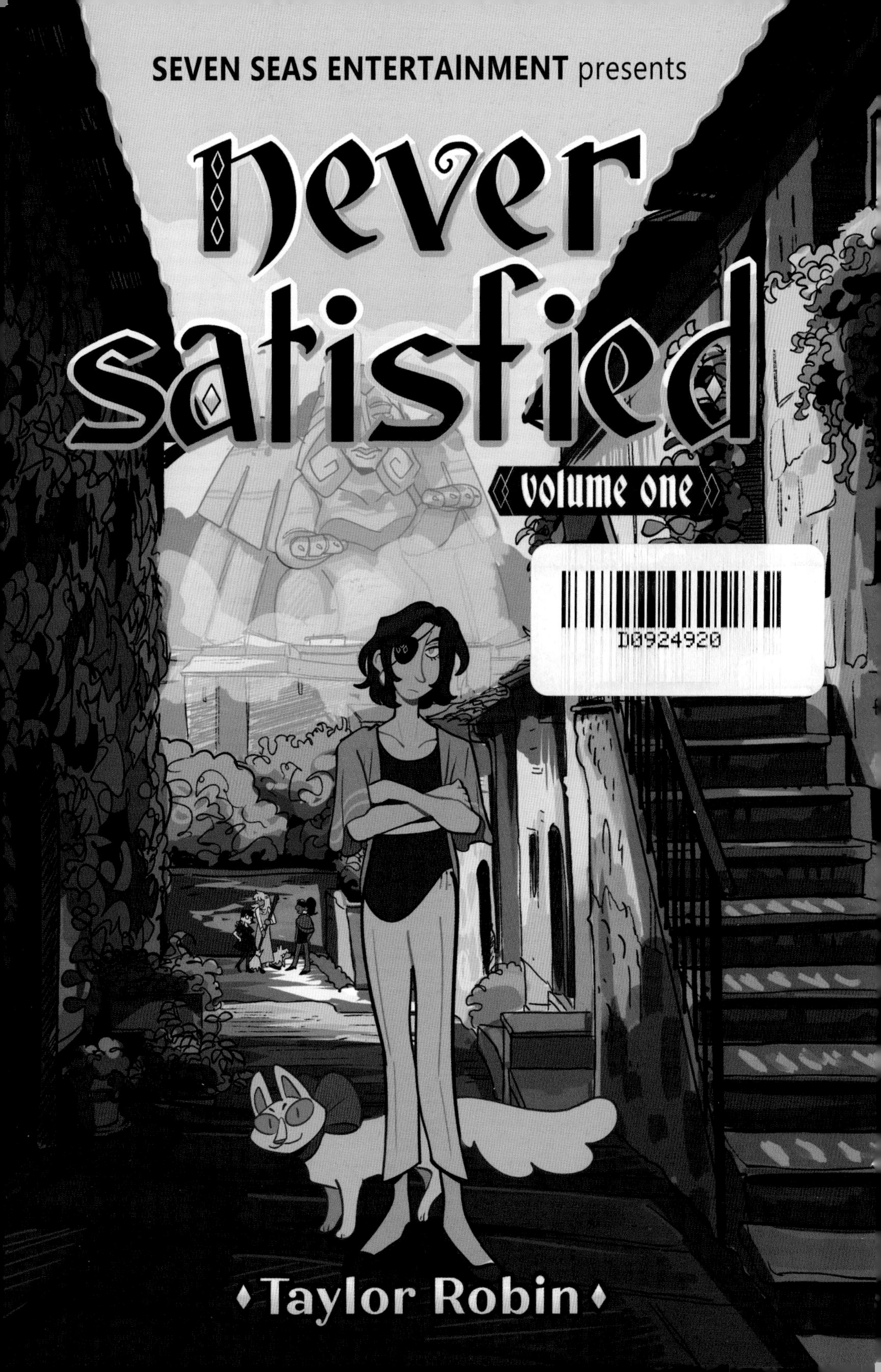
SEVEN SEAS ENTERTAINMENT presents
never satisfied
volume one
Taylor Robin

Art & Writing by Taylor Pendleton

Edited by Hiveworks Comics LLC
hiveworkscomics.com
neversatisfiedcomic.com

Seven Seas press and purchase enquiries can be sent to
Marketing Manager Lianne Sentar at press@gomanga.com.

Seven Seas and the Seven Seas logo are trademarks of
Seven Seas Entertainment. All rights reserved.
sevenseasentertainment.com

COVER DESIGN **Hannah Carey**
PRINT EDITOR **Robin Herrera**
PRODUCTION DESIGNER **Stevie Wilson**
PRODUCTION MANAGER **Lissa Pattillo**
PREPRESS TECHNICIAN **Melanie Ujimori, Jules Valera**
EDITOR-IN-CHIEF **Julie Davis**
ASSOCIATE PUBLISHER **Adam Arnold**
PUBLISHER **Jason DeAngelis**

ISBN: 978-1-63858-397-4
Printed in China
First Printing: February 2023
10 9 8 7 6 5 4 3 2 1

Names & Pronouns

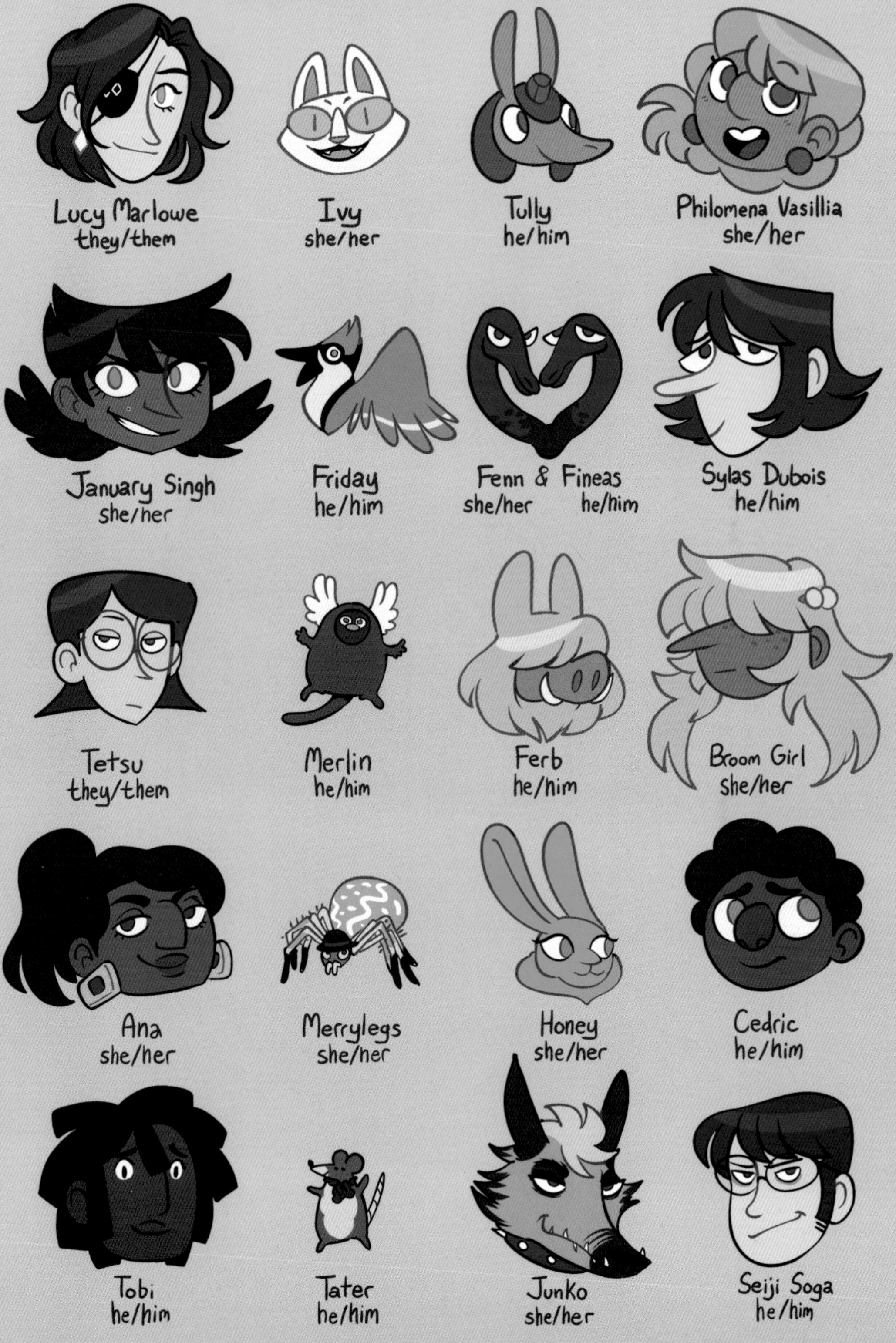

Lucy Marlowe they/them
Ivy she/her
Tully he/him
Philomena Vasillia she/her
January Singh she/her
Friday he/him
Fenn & Fineas she/her he/him
Sylas Dubois he/him
Tetsu they/them
Merlin he/him
Ferb he/him
Broom Girl she/her
Ana she/her
Merrylegs she/her
Honey she/her
Cedric he/him
Tobi he/him
Tater he/him
Junko she/her
Seiji Soga he/him

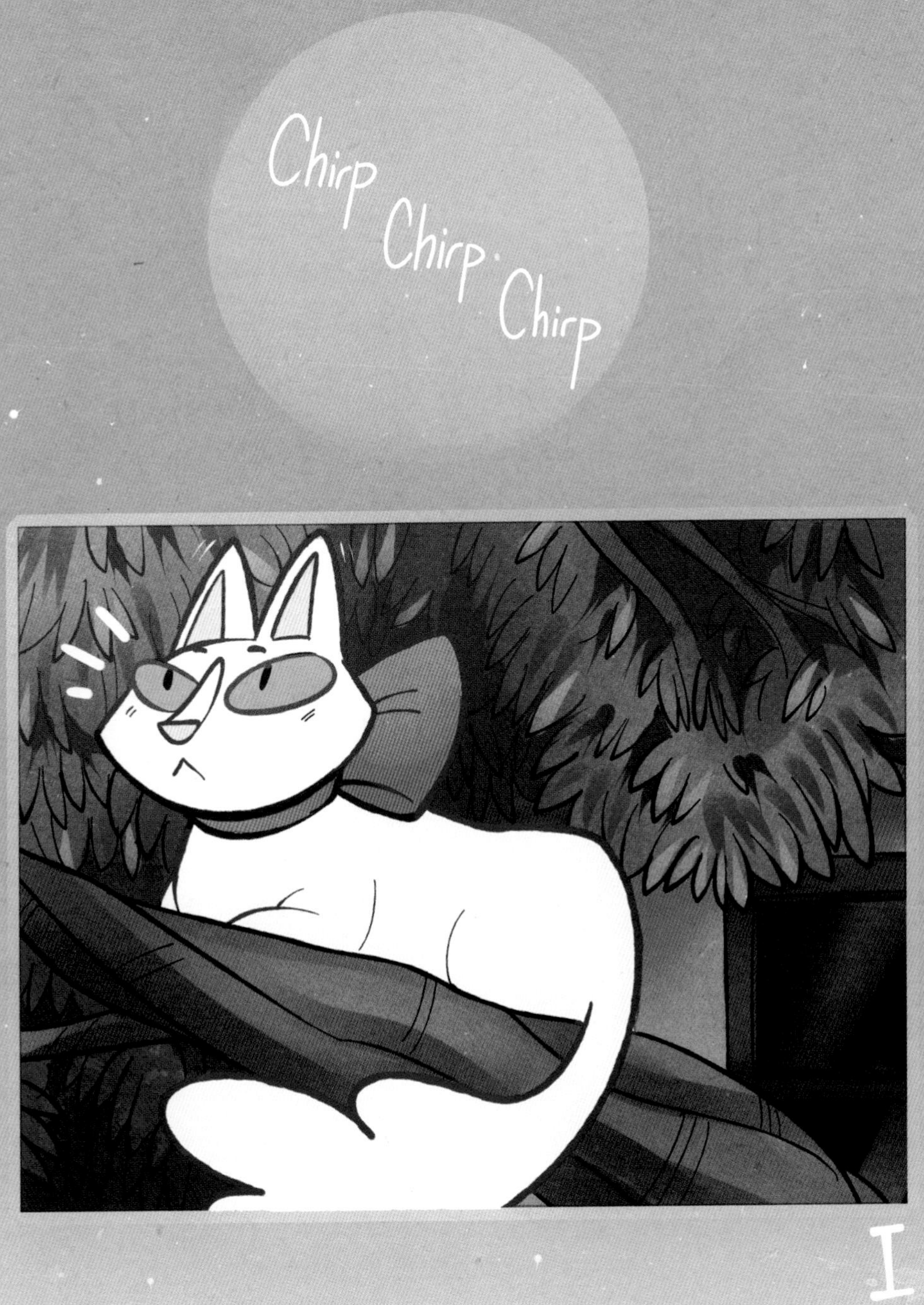
Chirp Chirp Chirp
I

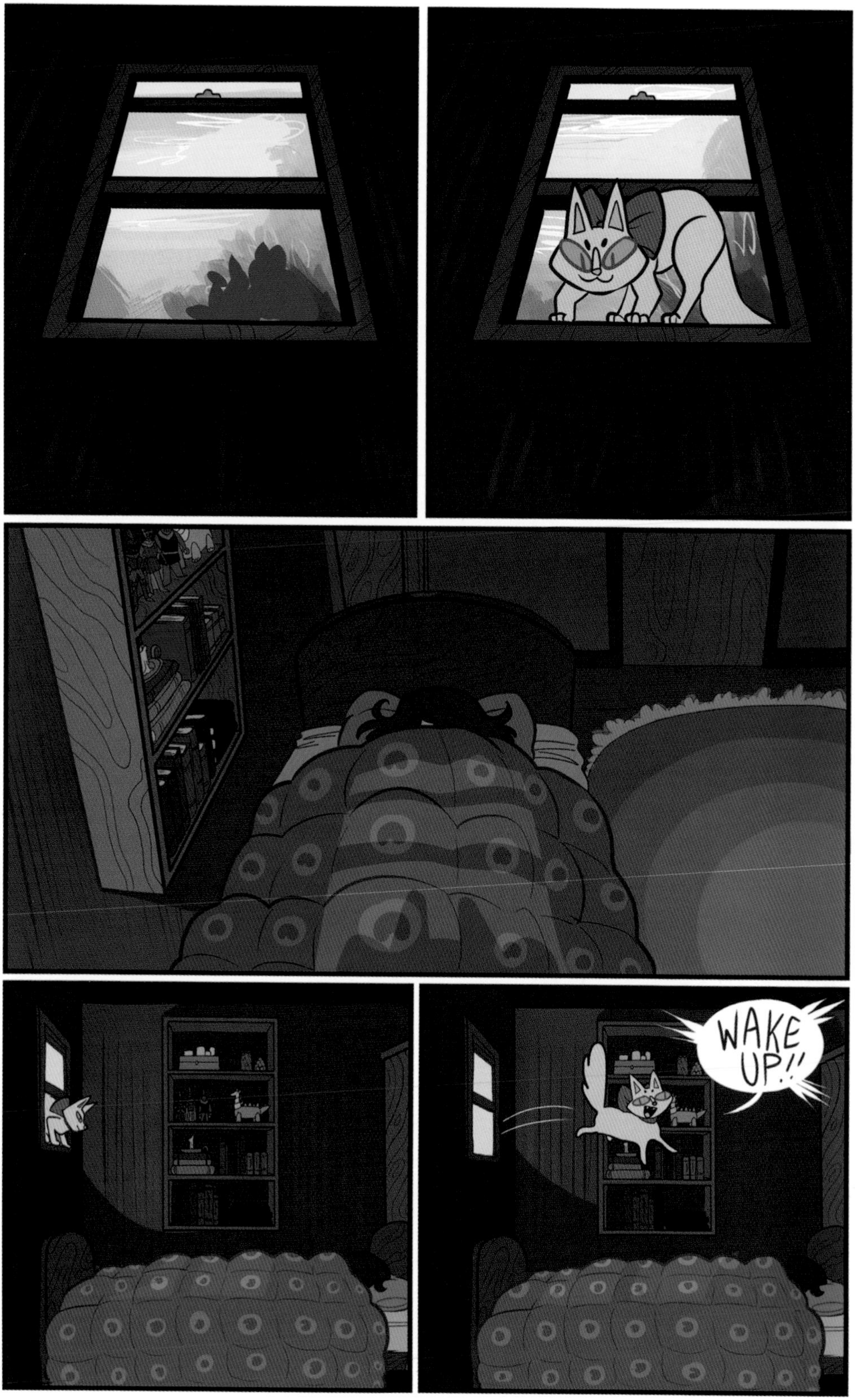
WAKE UP!!

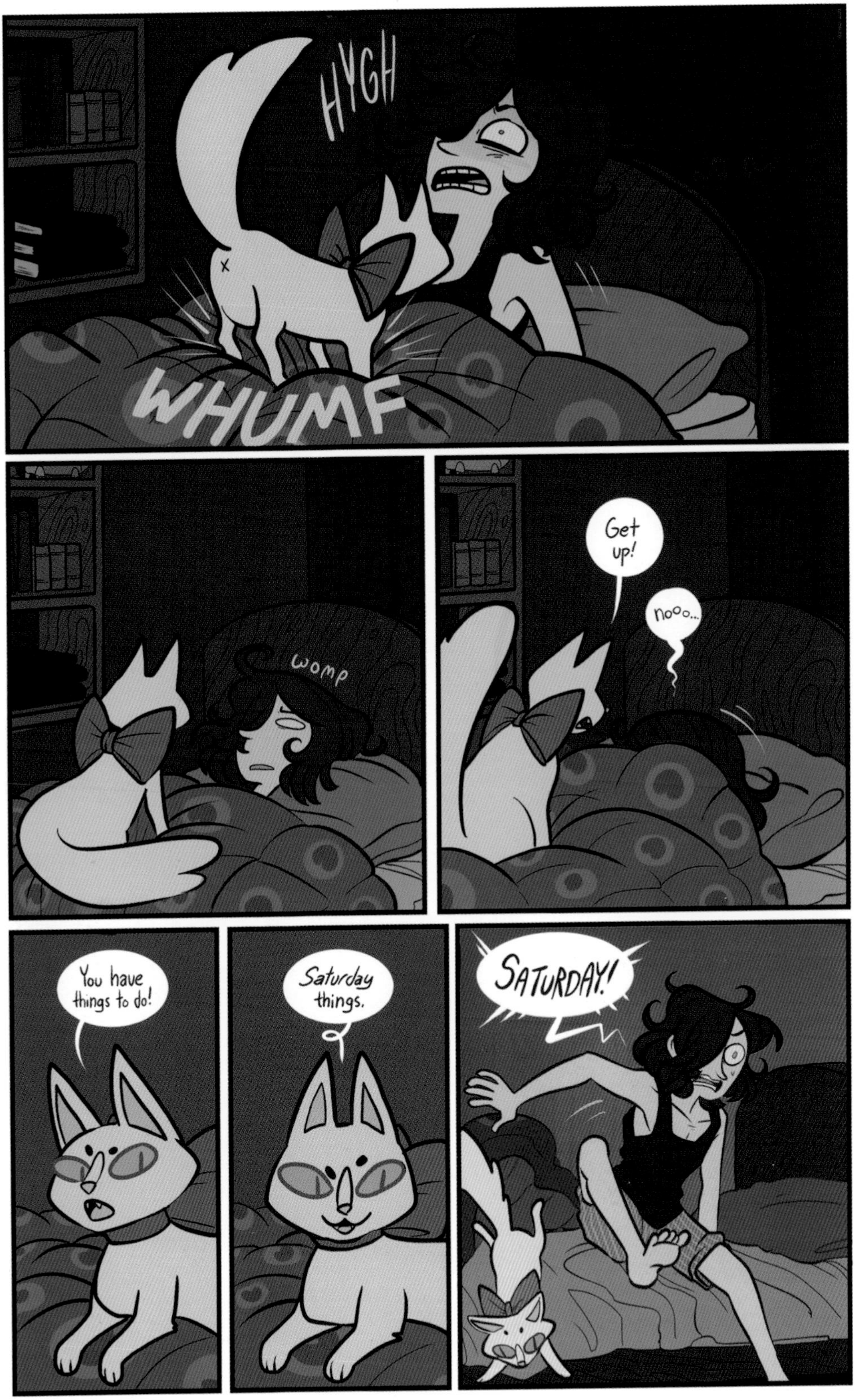
HYGH
WHUMF
womp
Get up!
nooo...
You have things to do!
Saturday things.
SATURDAY!

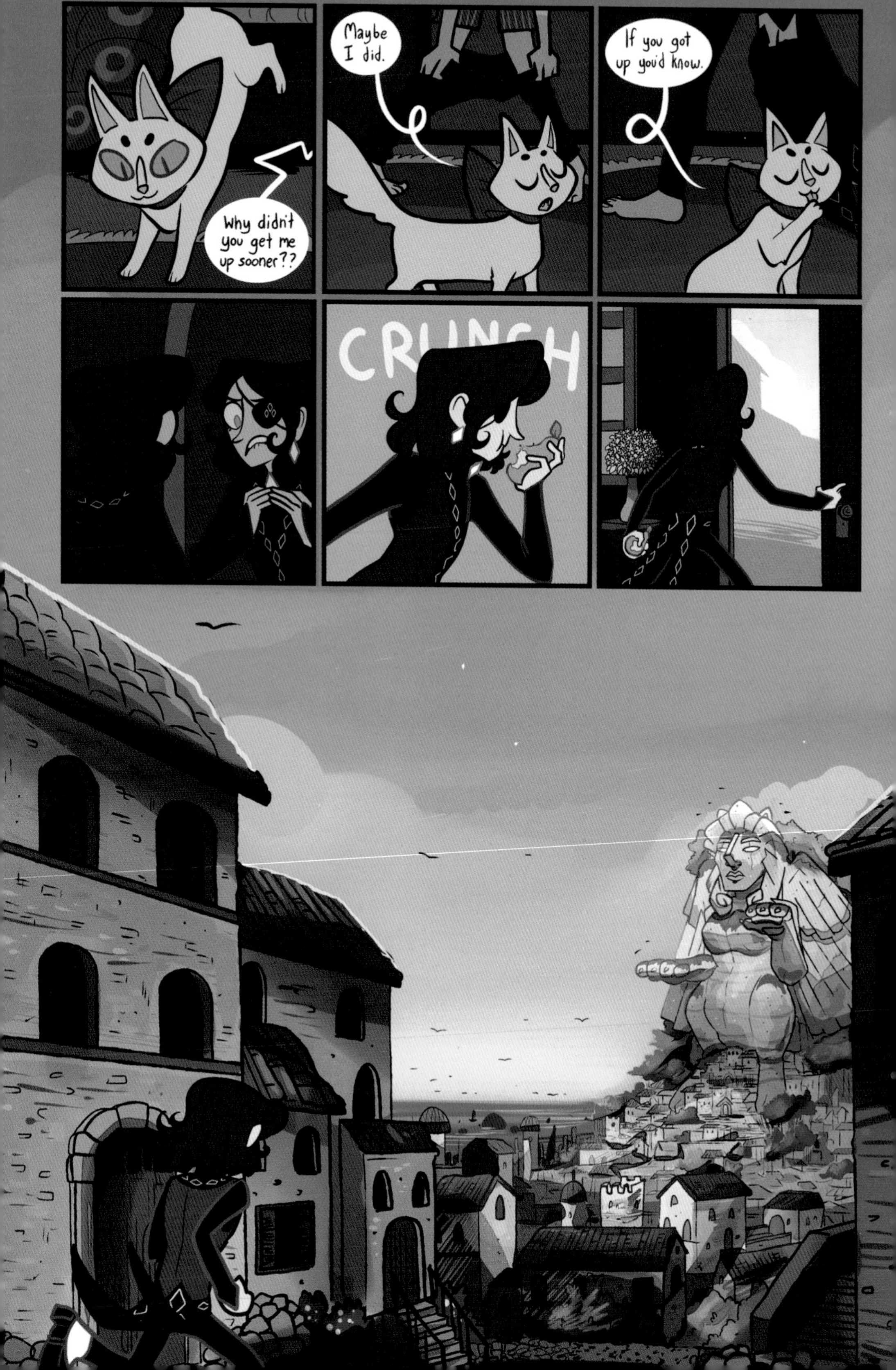
Why didn't you get me up sooner??
Maybe I did.
If you got up you'd know.
CRUNCH

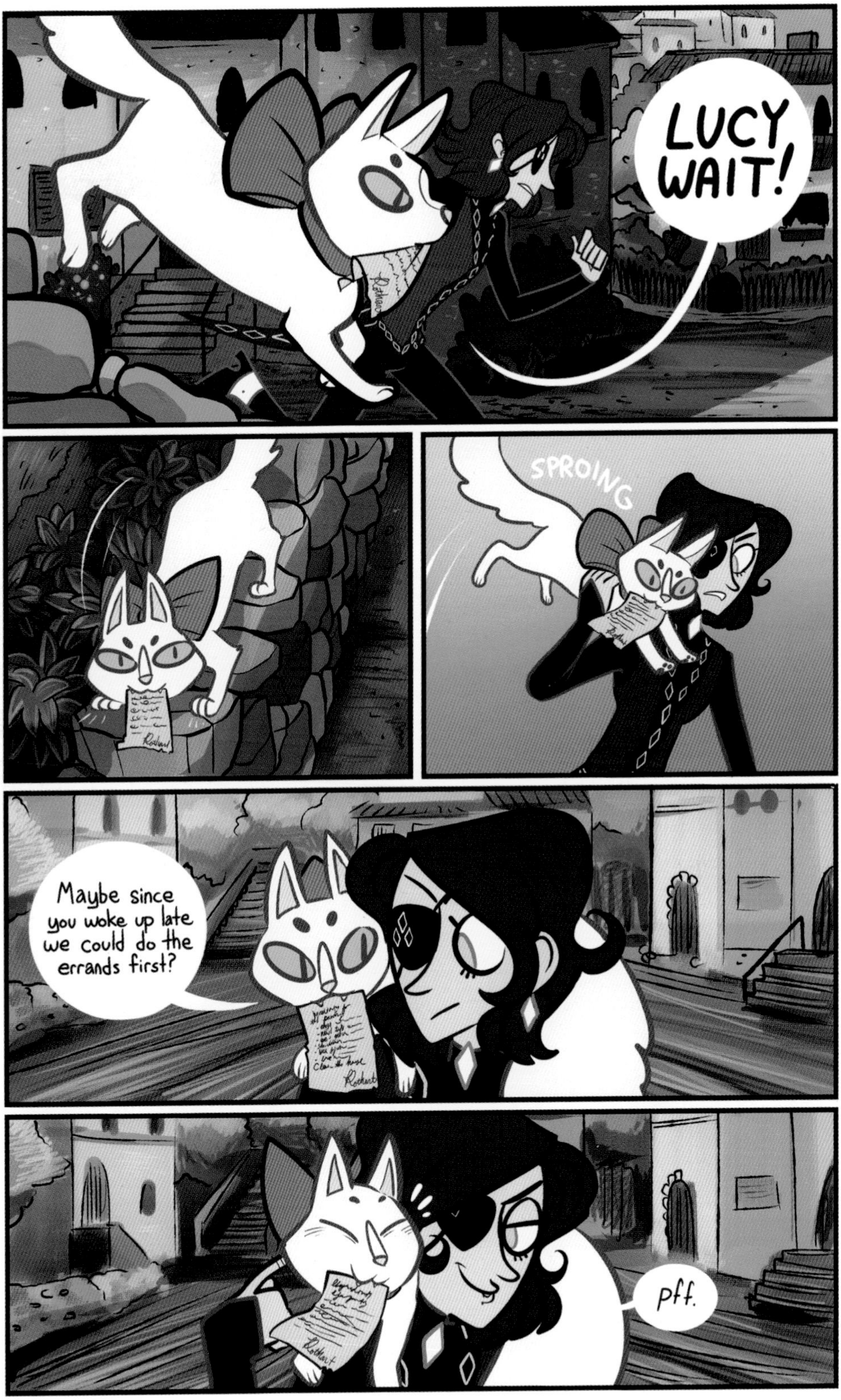
LUCY WAIT!
SPROING
Maybe since you woke up late we could do the errands first?
pff.

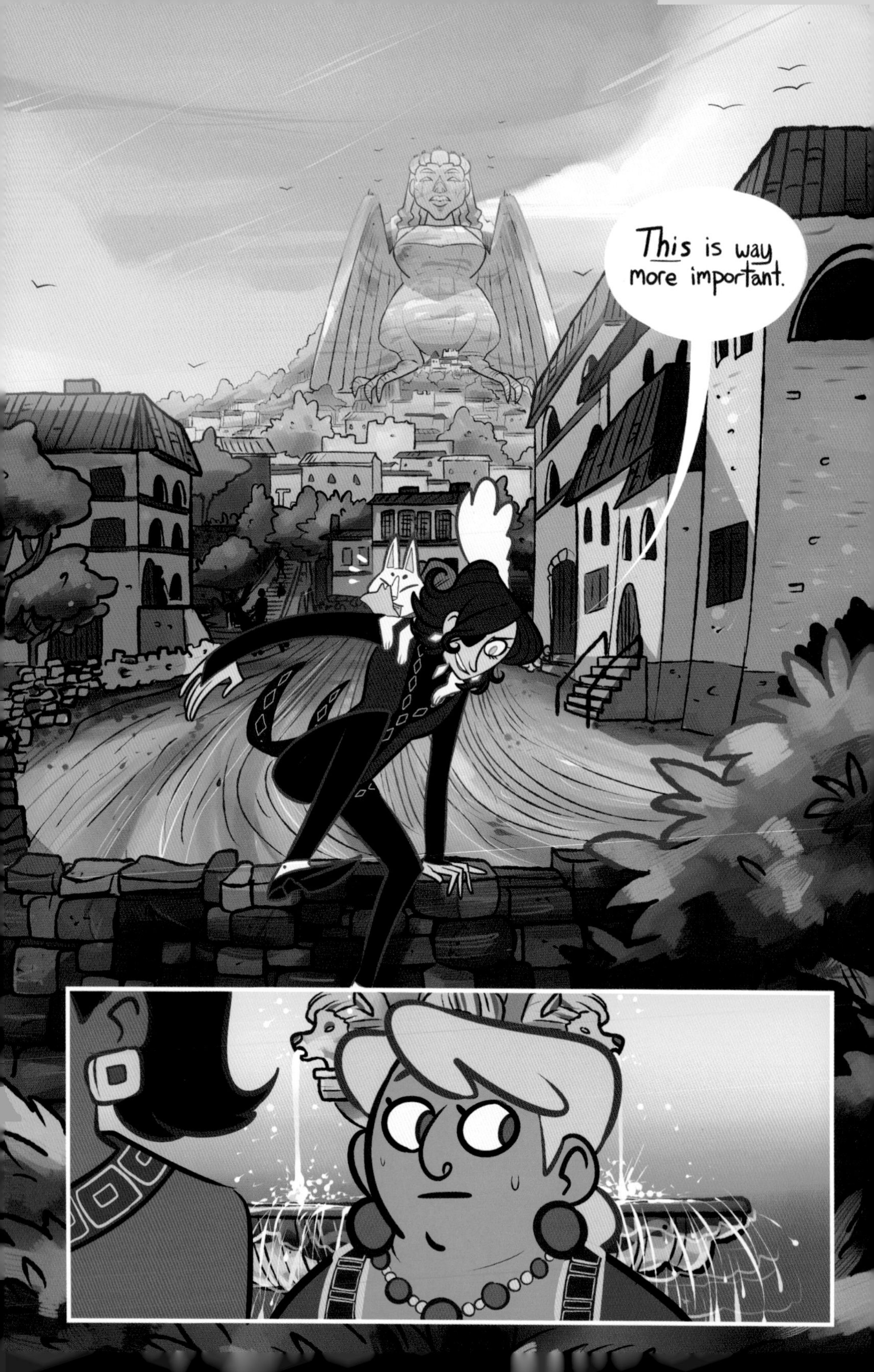
This is way more important.

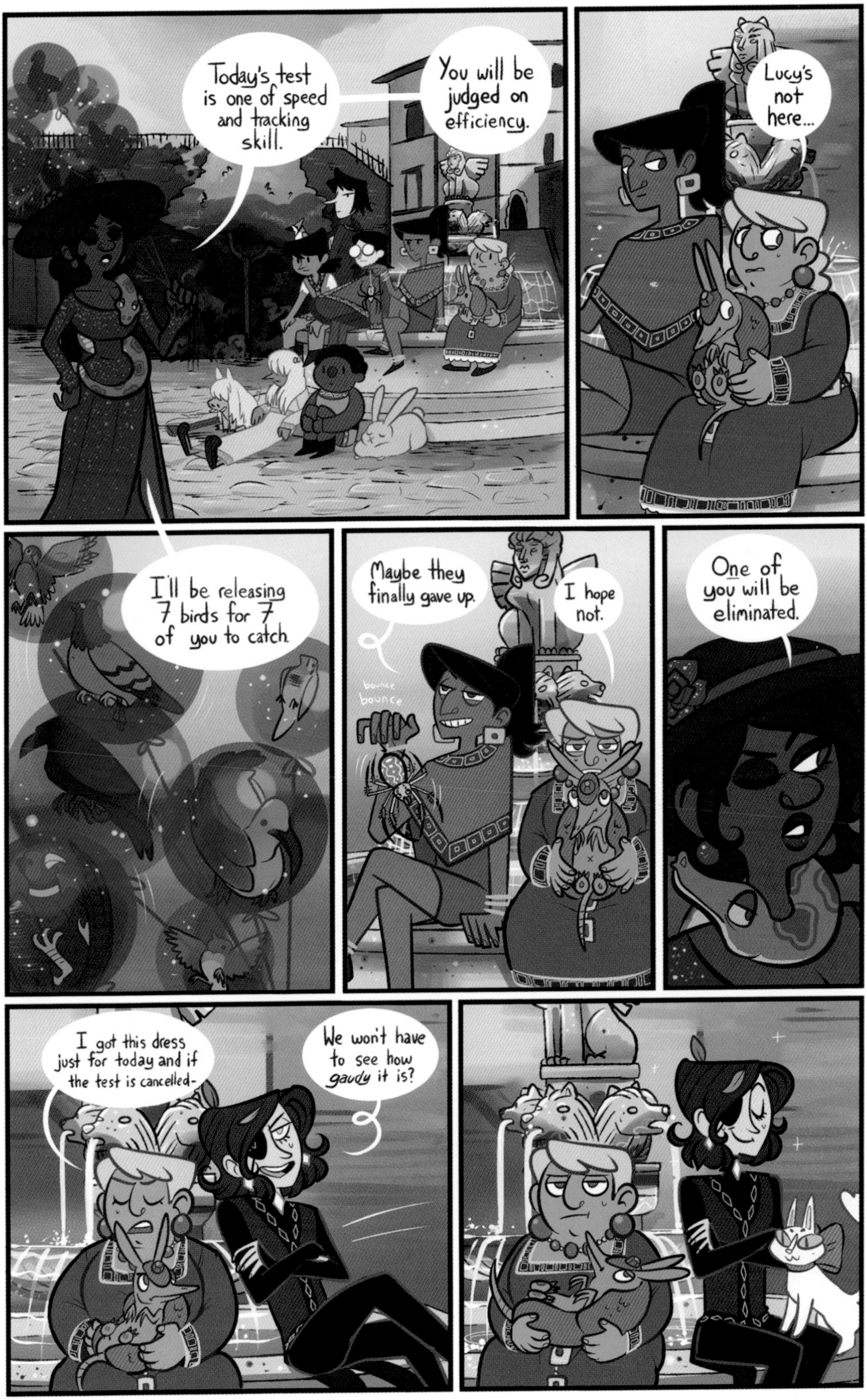
Today's test is one of speed and tracking skill.
You will be judged on efficiency.
Lucy's not here...
I'll be releasing 7 birds for 7 of you to catch.
Maybe they finally gave up.
bounce bounce
I hope not.
One of you will be eliminated.
I got this dress just for today and if the test is cancelled-
We won't have to see how *gaudy* it is?

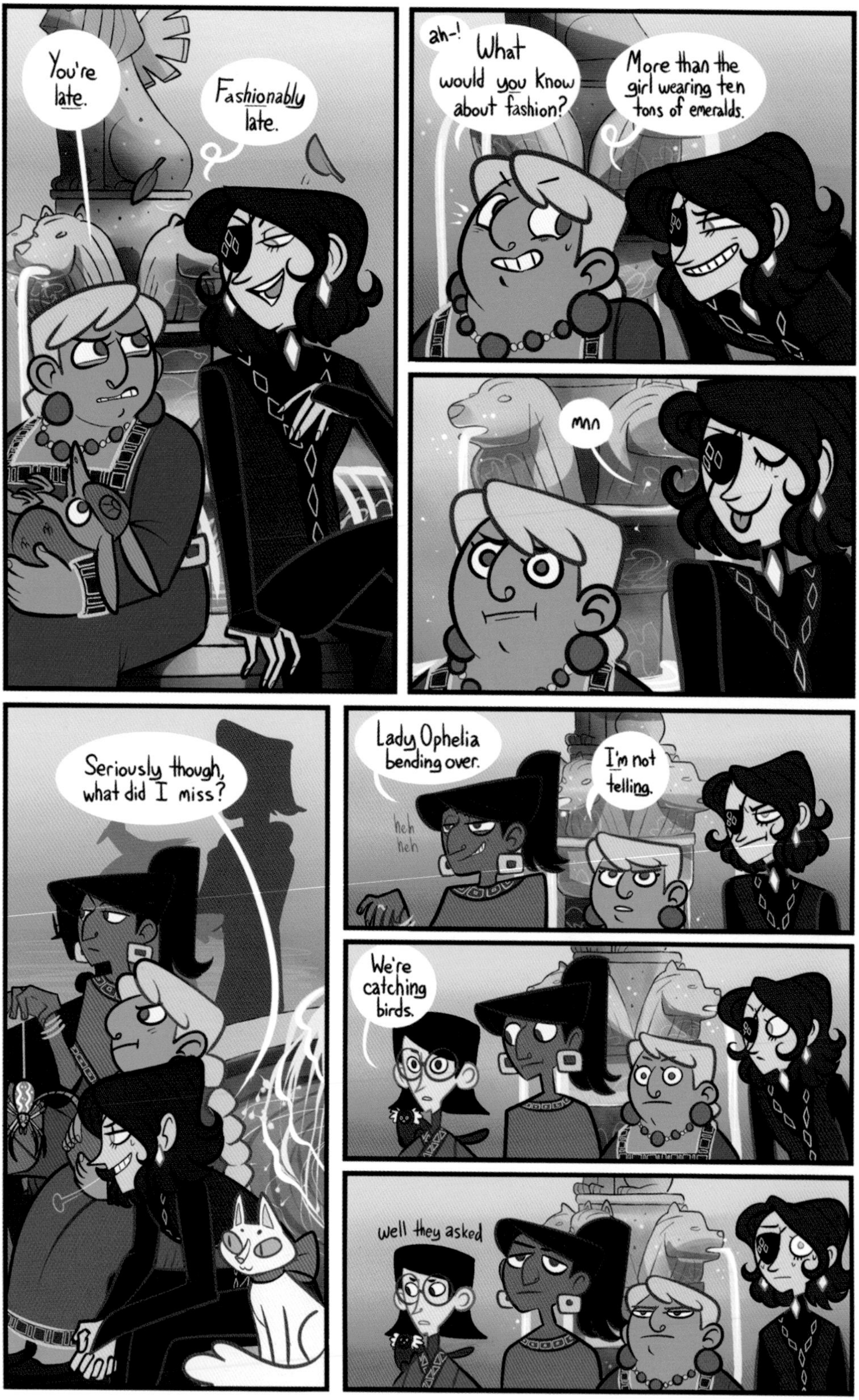
You're late.
Fashionably late.
ah-!
What would you know about fashion?
More than the girl wearing ten tons of emeralds.
mnn
Seriously though, what did I miss?
Lady Ophelia bending over.
heh heh
I'm not telling.
We're catching birds.
well they asked

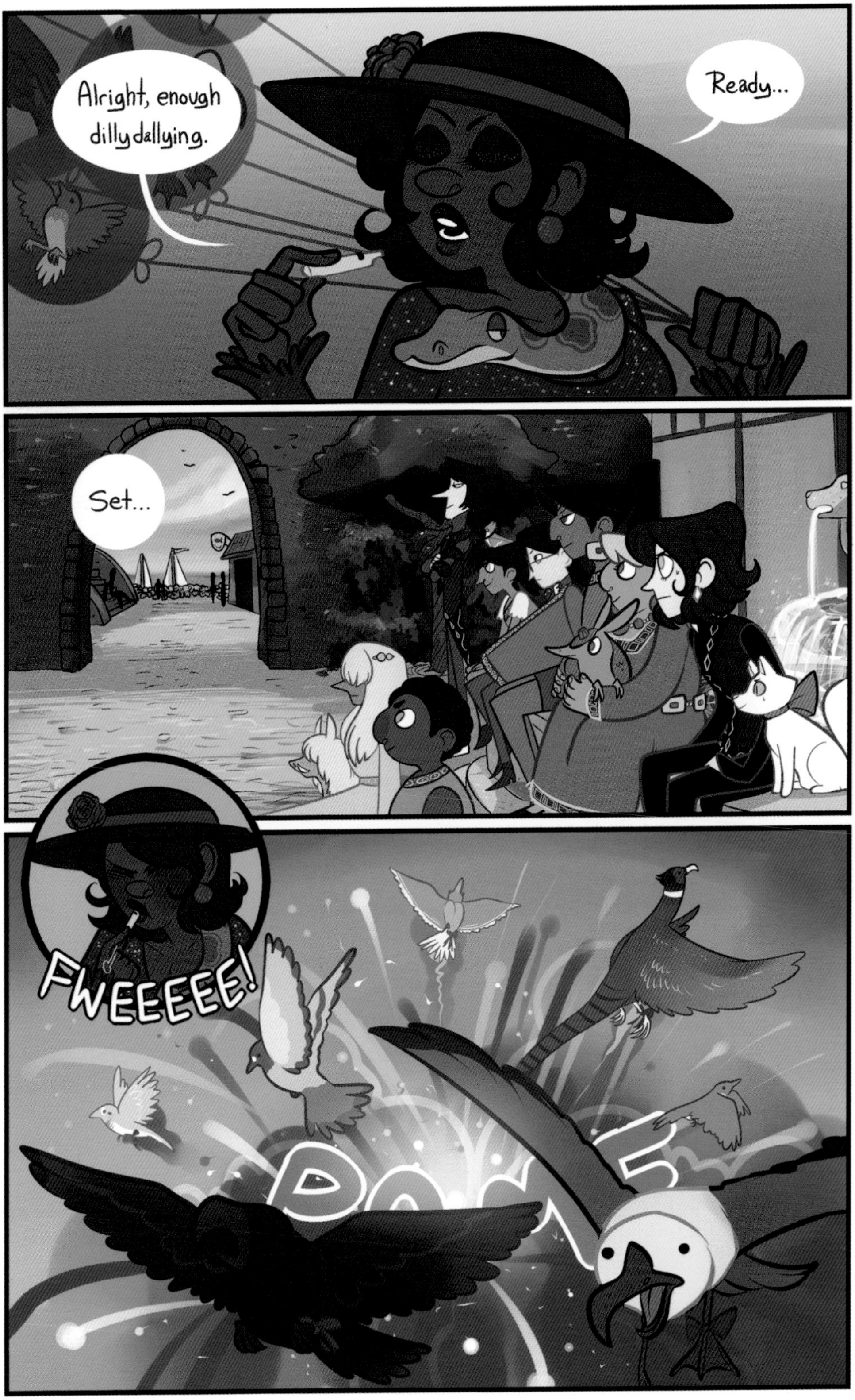

Alright, enough dillydallying.
Ready...
Set...
FWEEEEE!

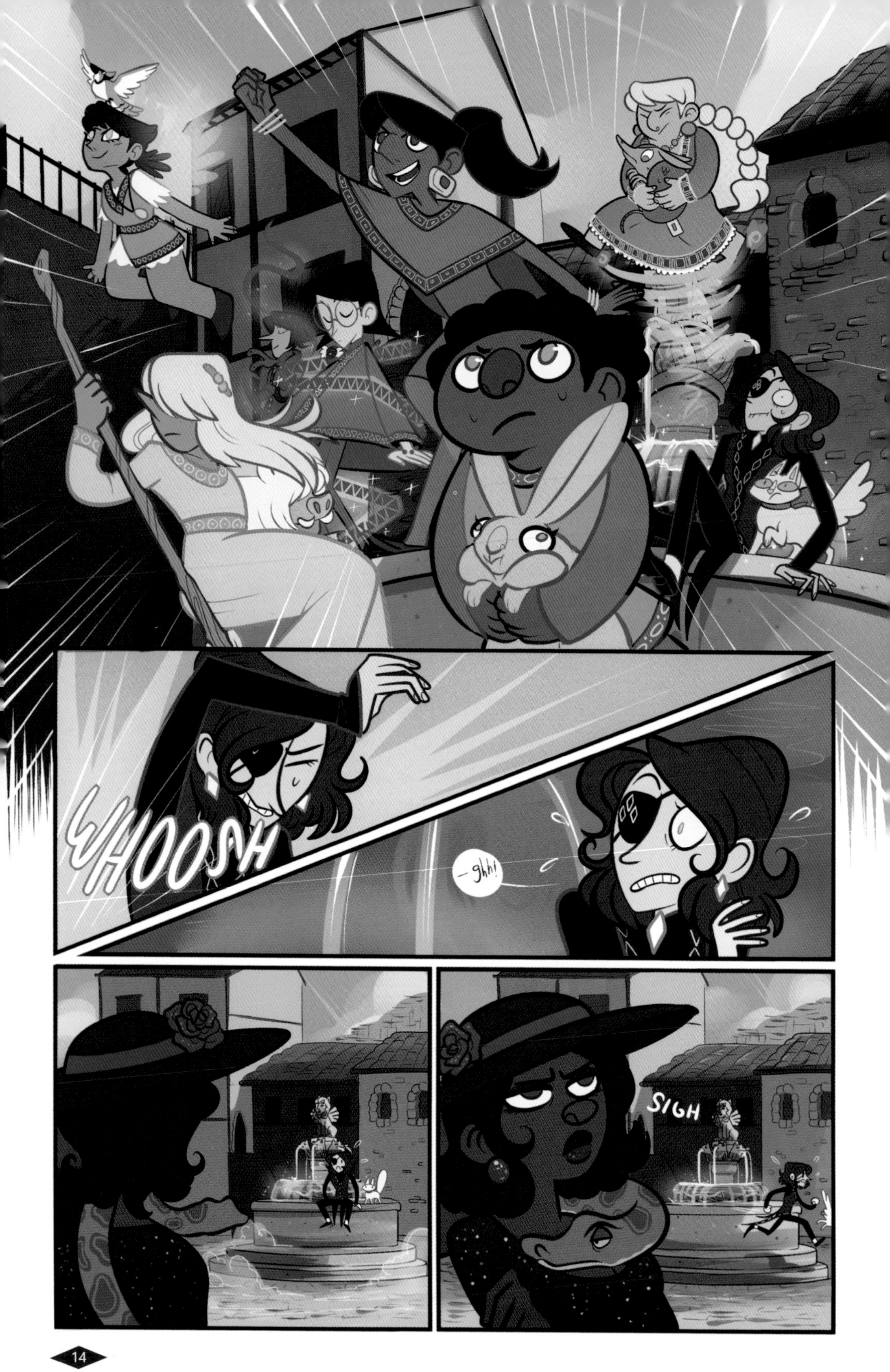
WHOOSH
—ghh!
SIGH

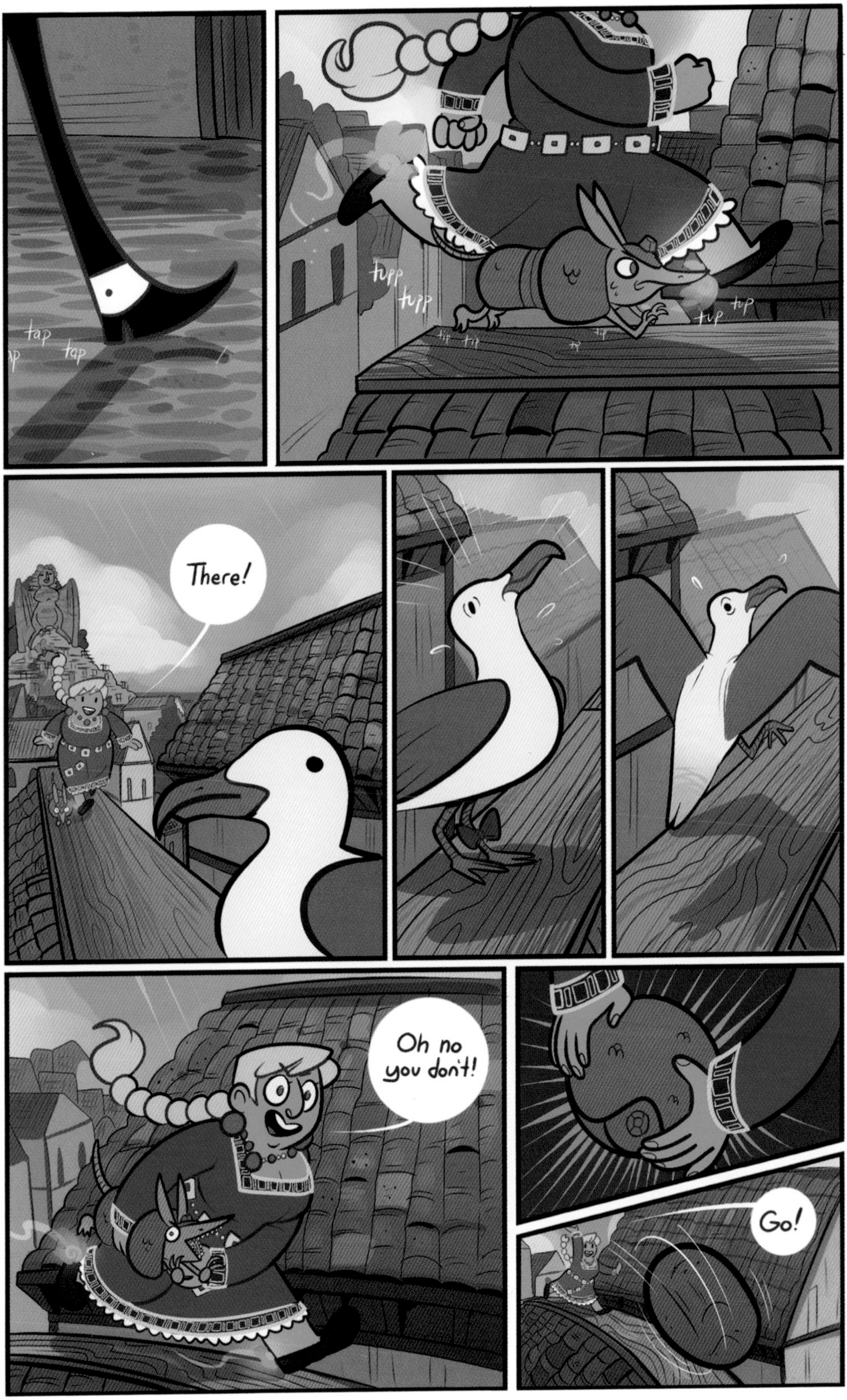
tap
tap
tap
tupp
tupp
tip tip
tup
tup
There!
Oh no you don't!
Go!

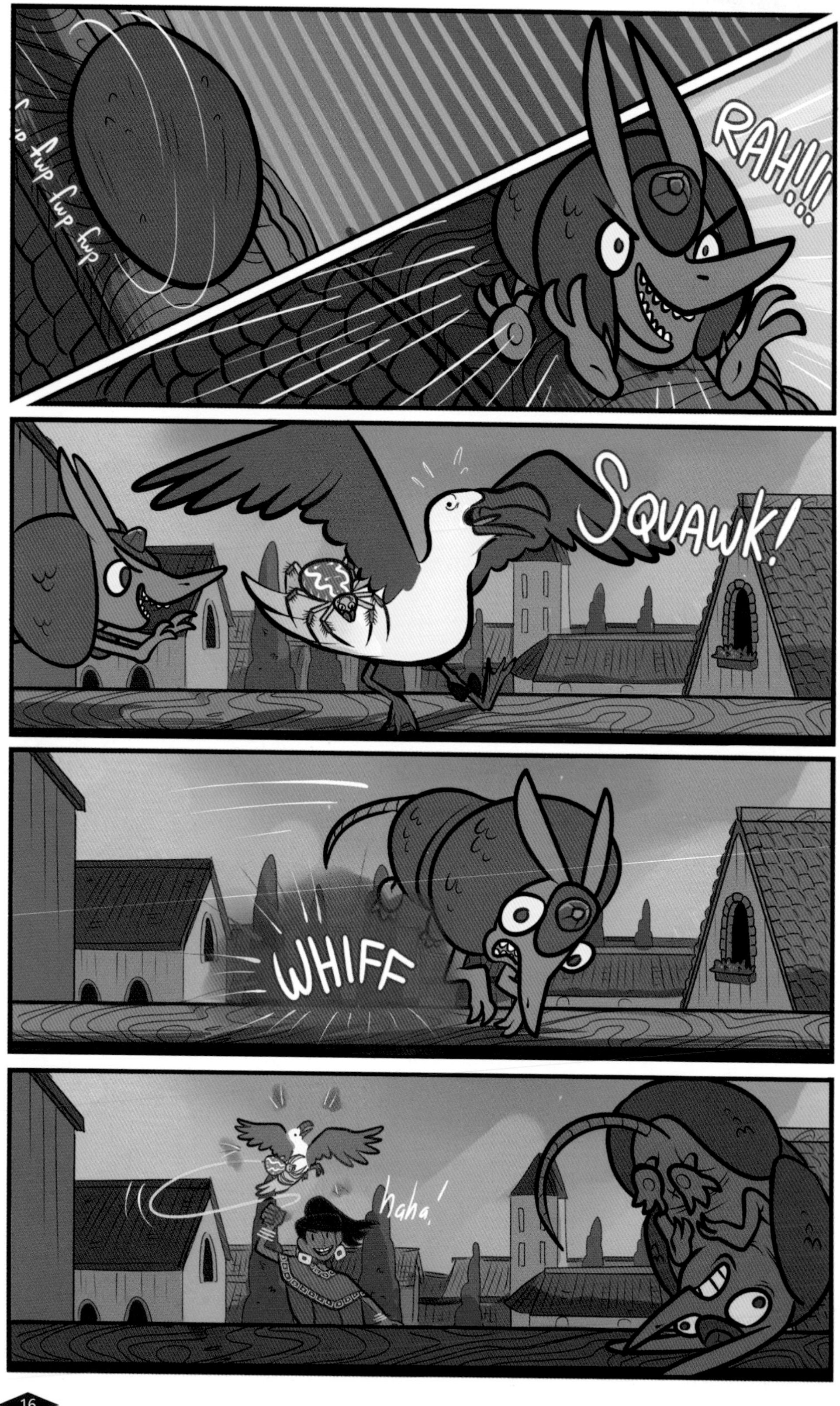
fwp fwp fwp fwp
RAH!!!
SQUAWK!
WHIFF
haha!

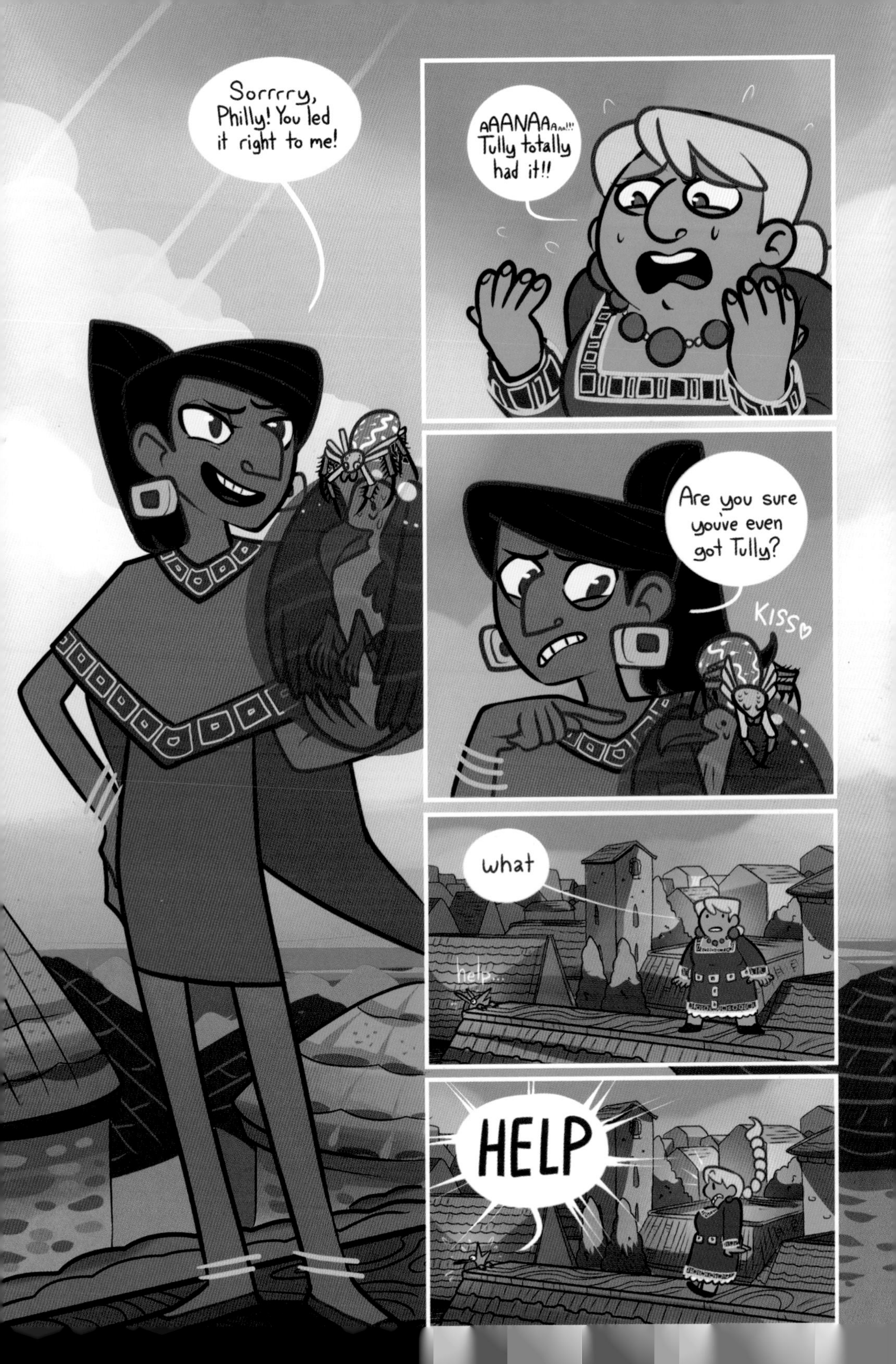
Sorrrry, Philly! You led it right to me!
AAANAAAaa!!! Tully totally had it!!
Are you sure you've even got Tully?
KISS♡
what
help...
HELP

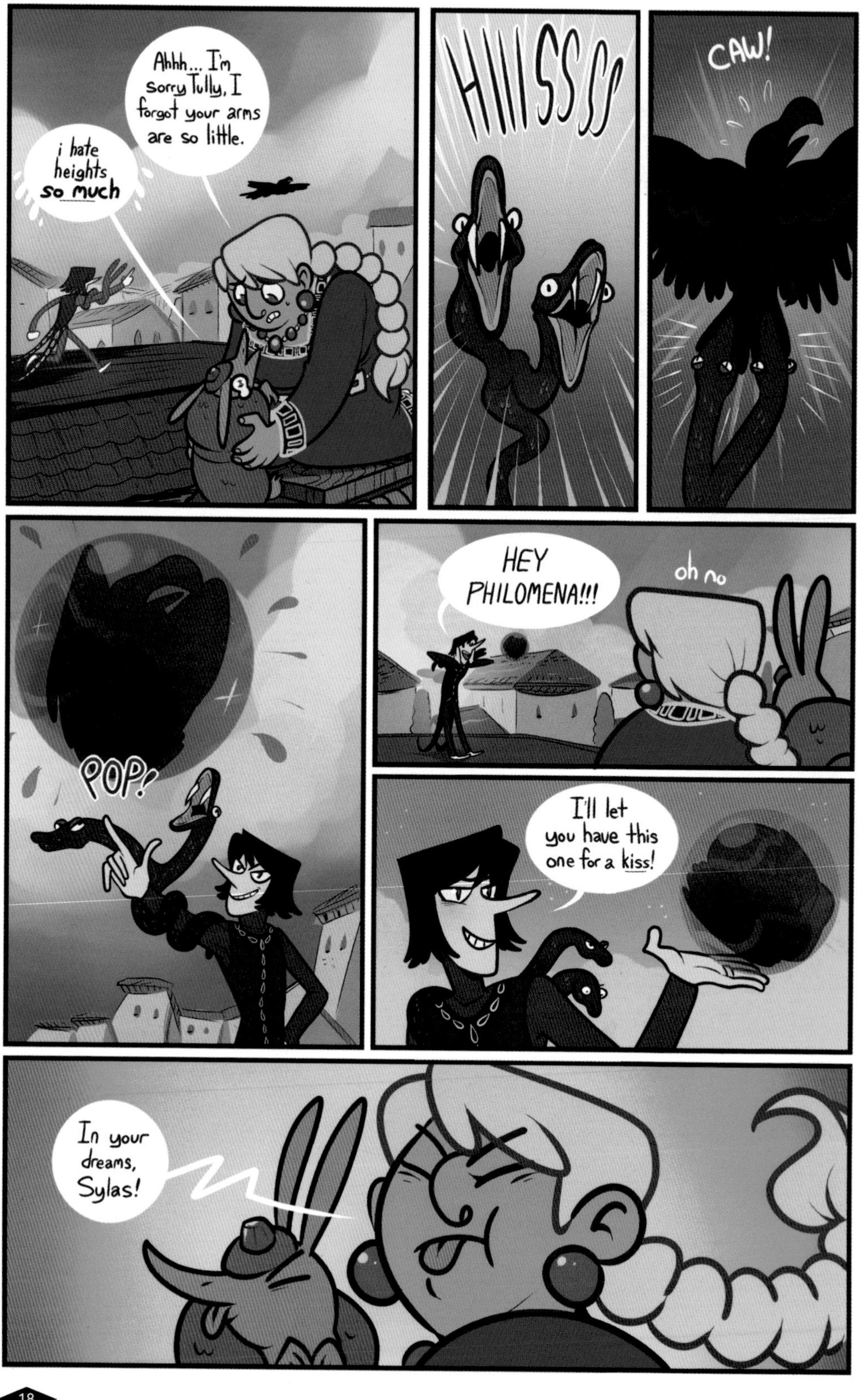

Ahhh... I'm sorry Tully, I forgot your arms are so little.
i hate heights so much
HIIISSSS
CAW!
POP!
HEY PHILOMENA!!!
oh no
I'll let you have this one for a kiss!
In your dreams, Sylas!

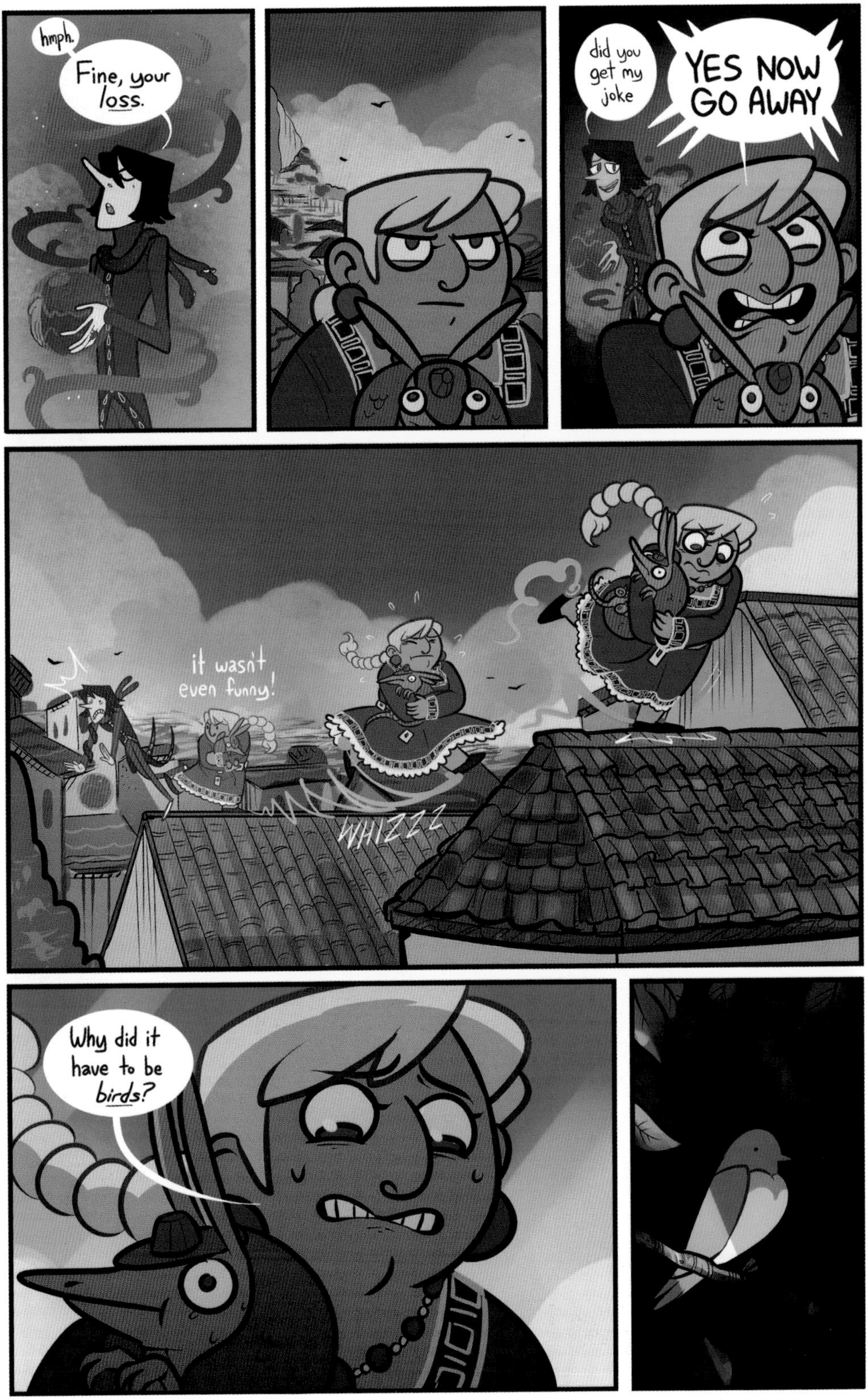
hmph.
Fine, your loss.
did you get my joke
YES NOW GO AWAY
it wasn't even funny!
WHIZZZ
Why did it have to be birds?

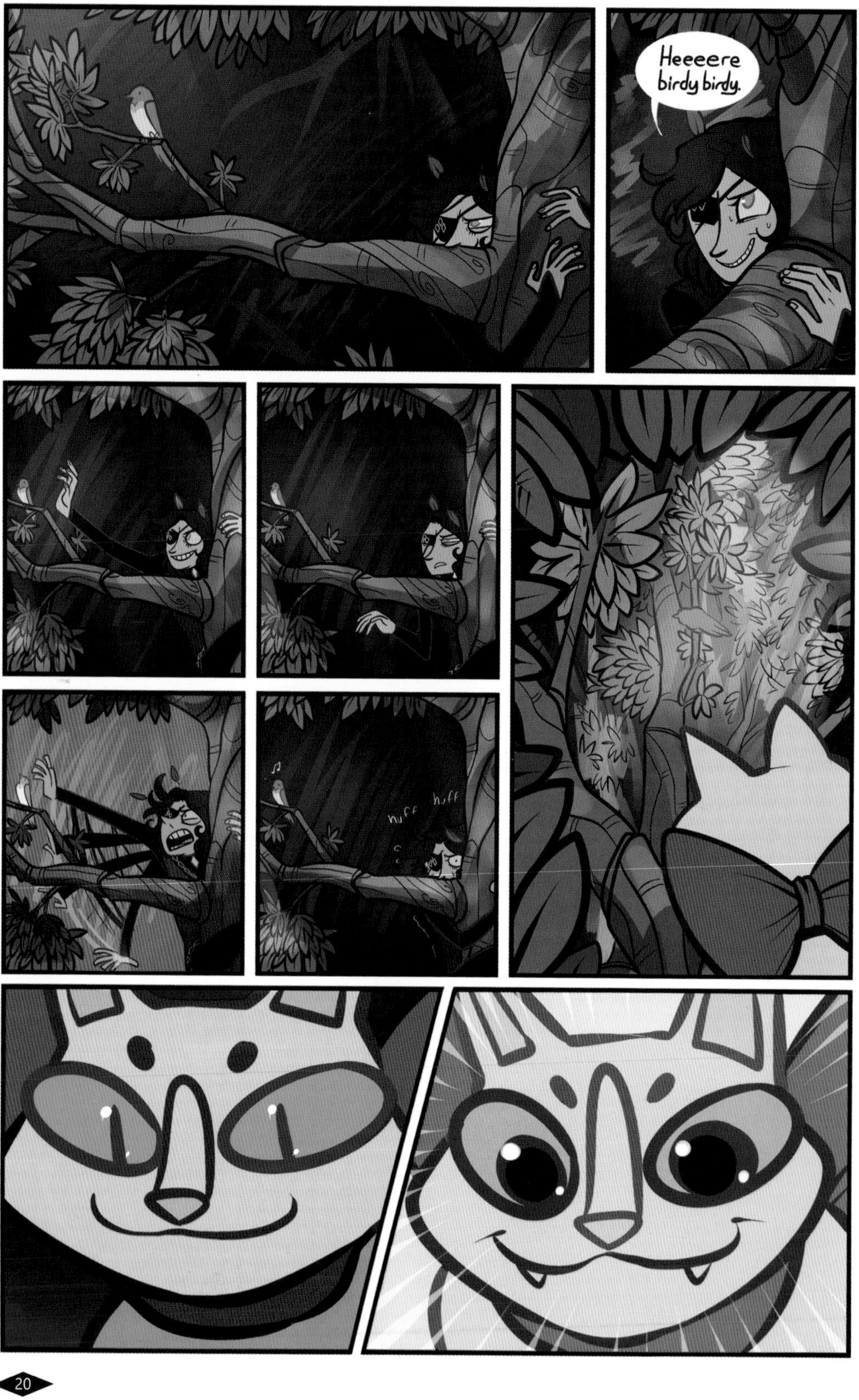
Heeeeere birdy birdy.
huff
huff

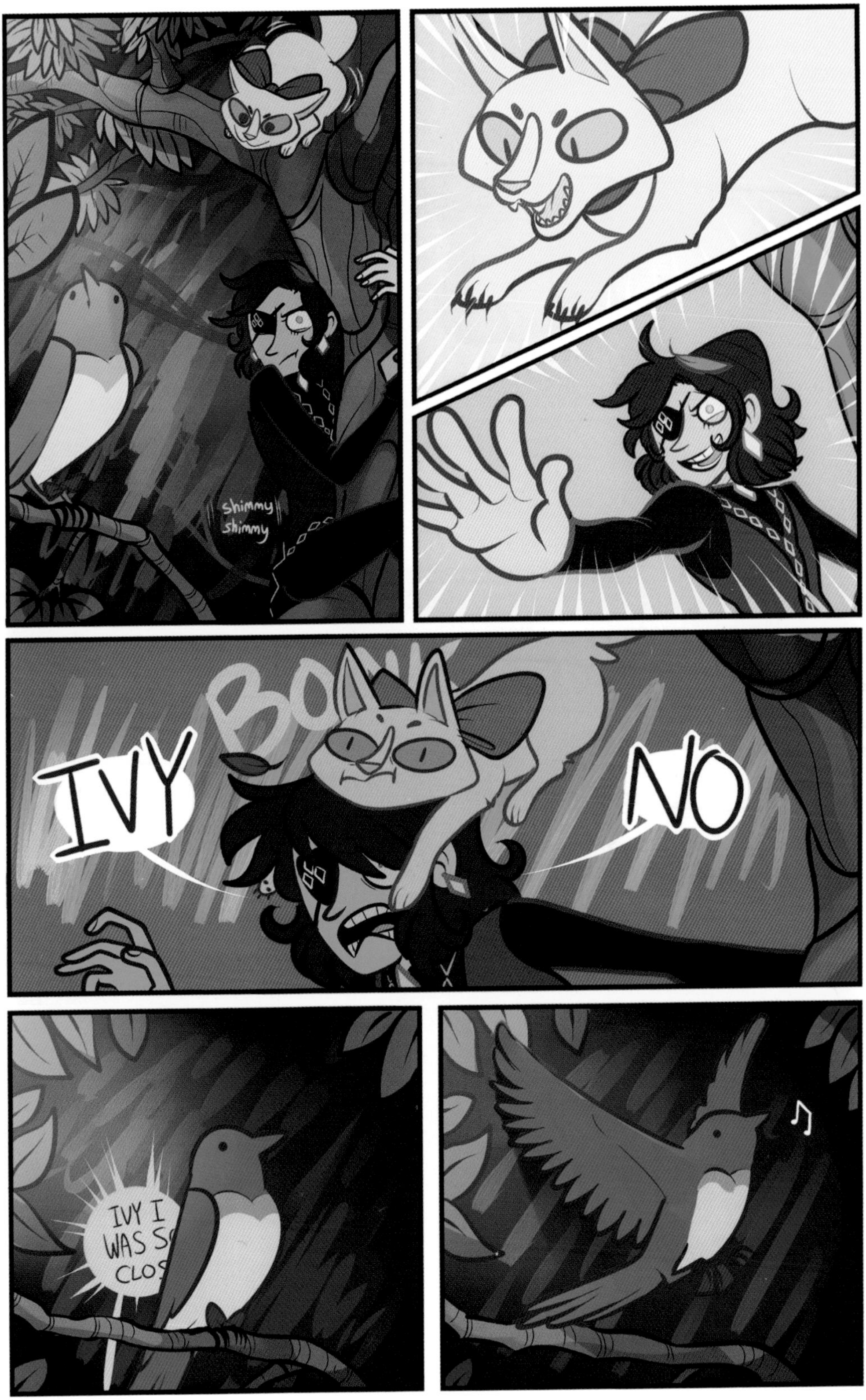
shimmy
shimmy
BON
IVY
NO
IVY I WAS SO CLOS
♪

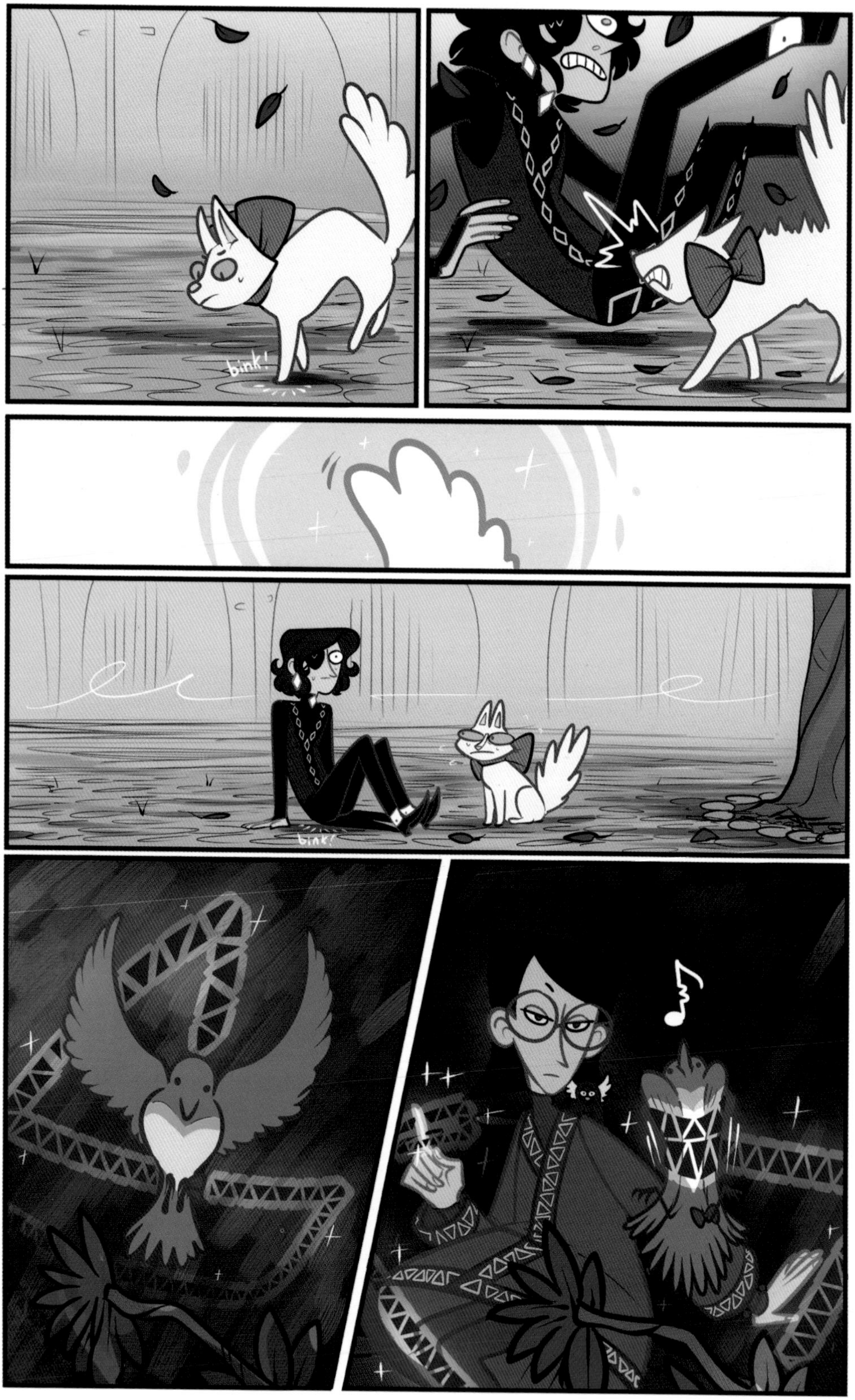
bink!
bink!

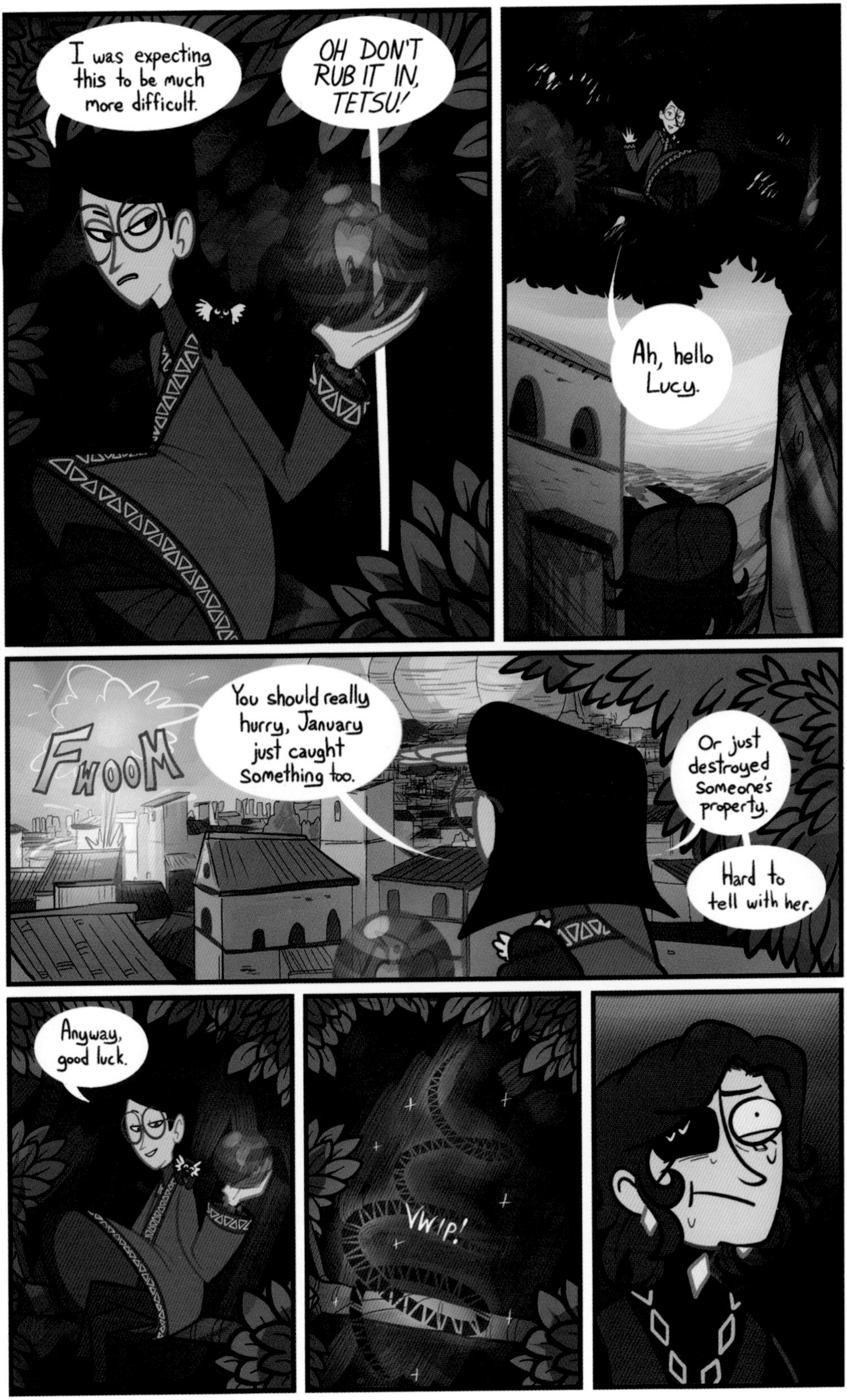
I was expecting this to be much more difficult.
OH DON'T RUB IT IN, TETSU!
Ah, hello Lucy.
FWOOM
You should really hurry, January just caught something too.
Or just destroyed Someone's property.
Hard to tell with her.
Anyway, good luck.
VWIP!

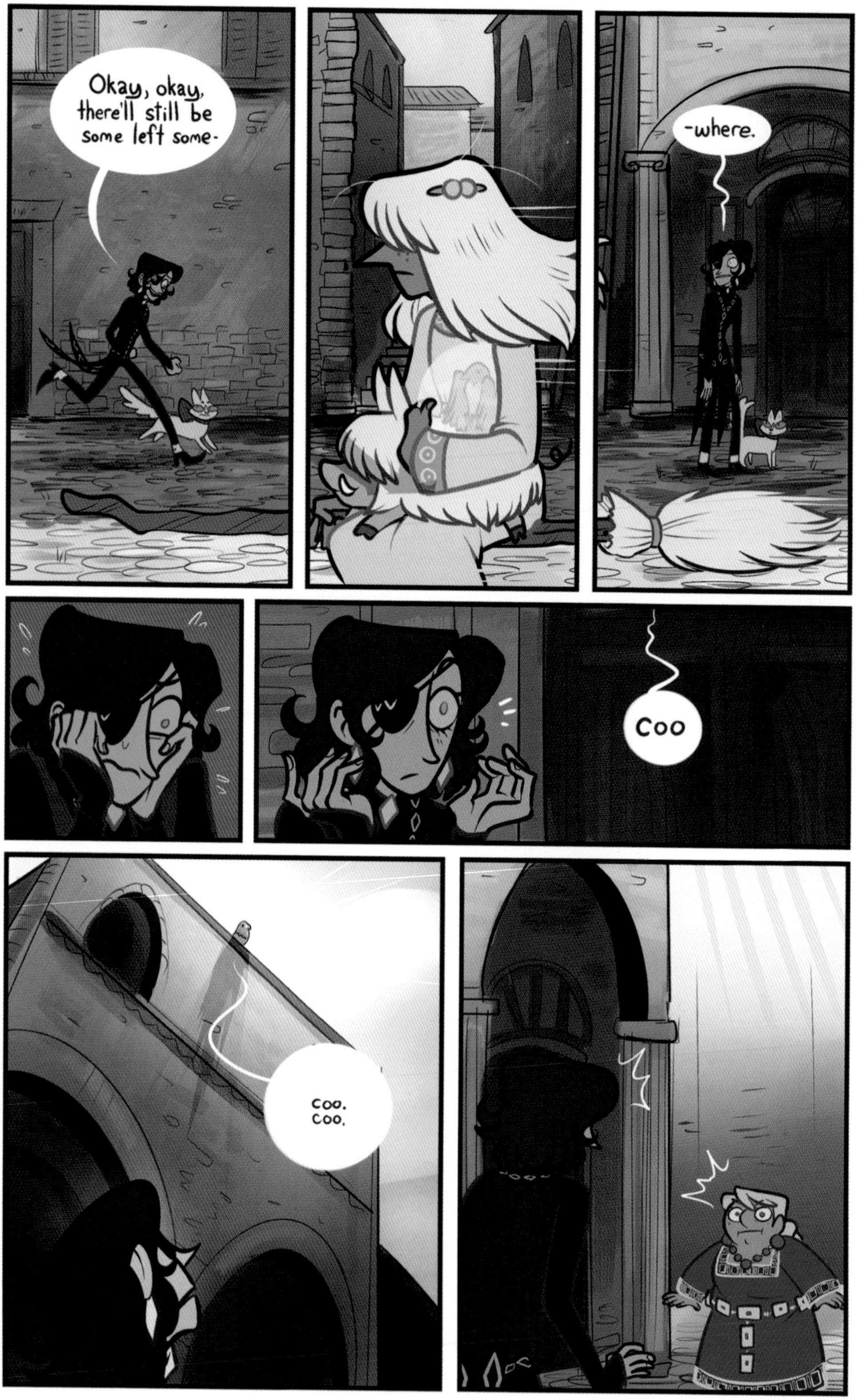
Okay, okay, there'll still be some left some-
-where.
Coo
Coo.
Coo.

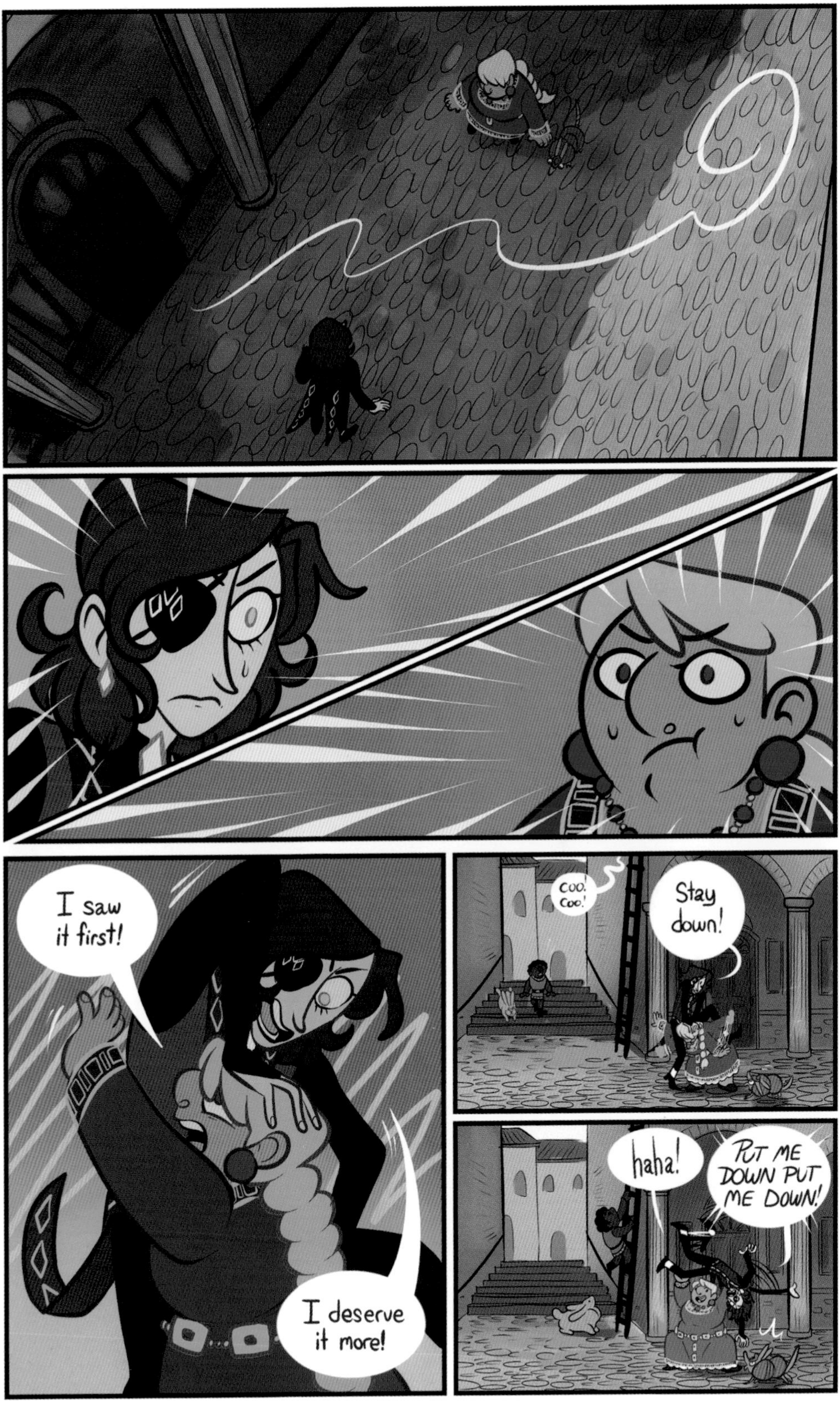
I saw it first!
I deserve it more!
COO! COO!
Stay down!
haha!
PUT ME DOWN PUT ME DOWN!

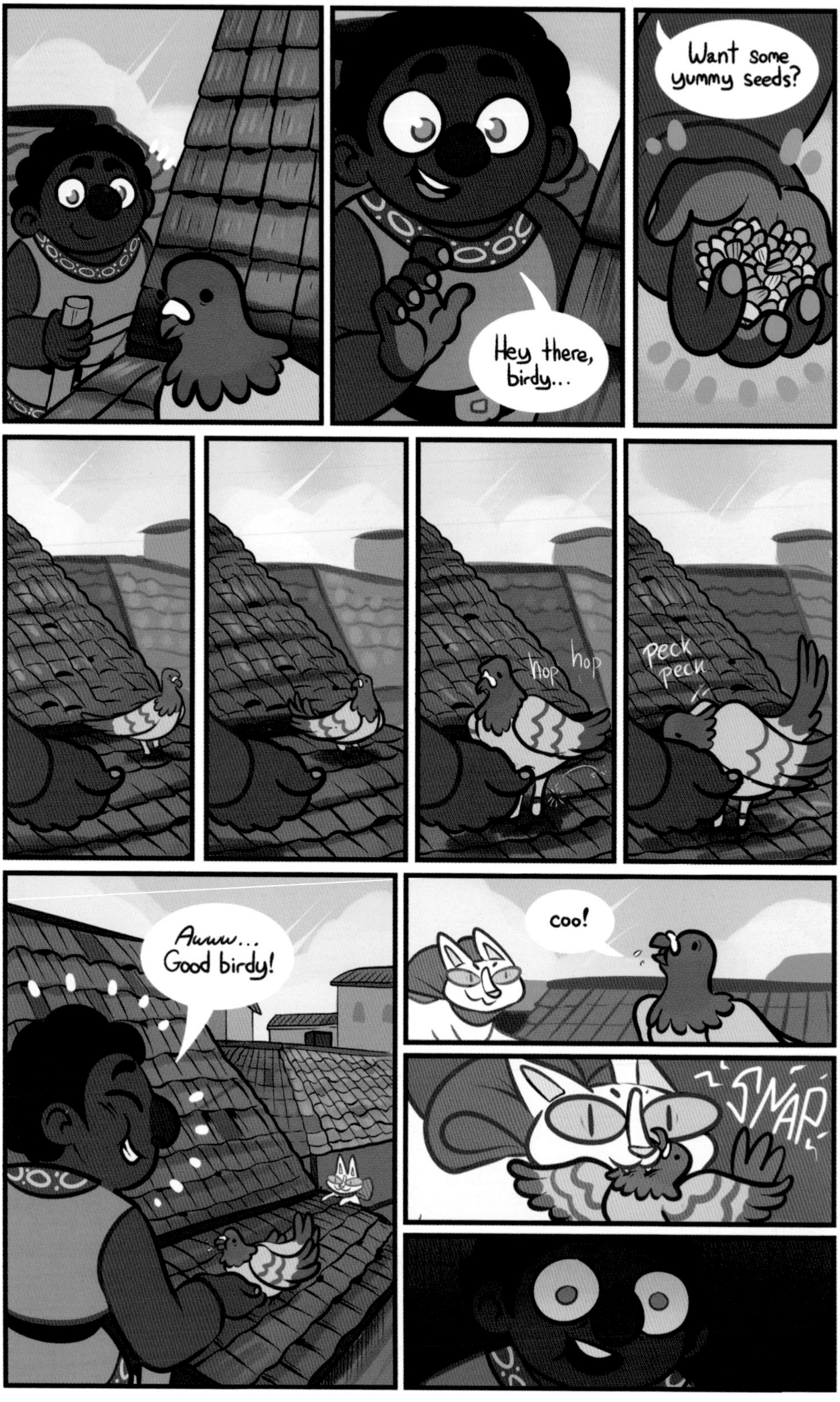
Hey there, birdy...
Want some yummy seeds?
hop hop
peck peck
Awww... Good birdy!
coo!
SNAP

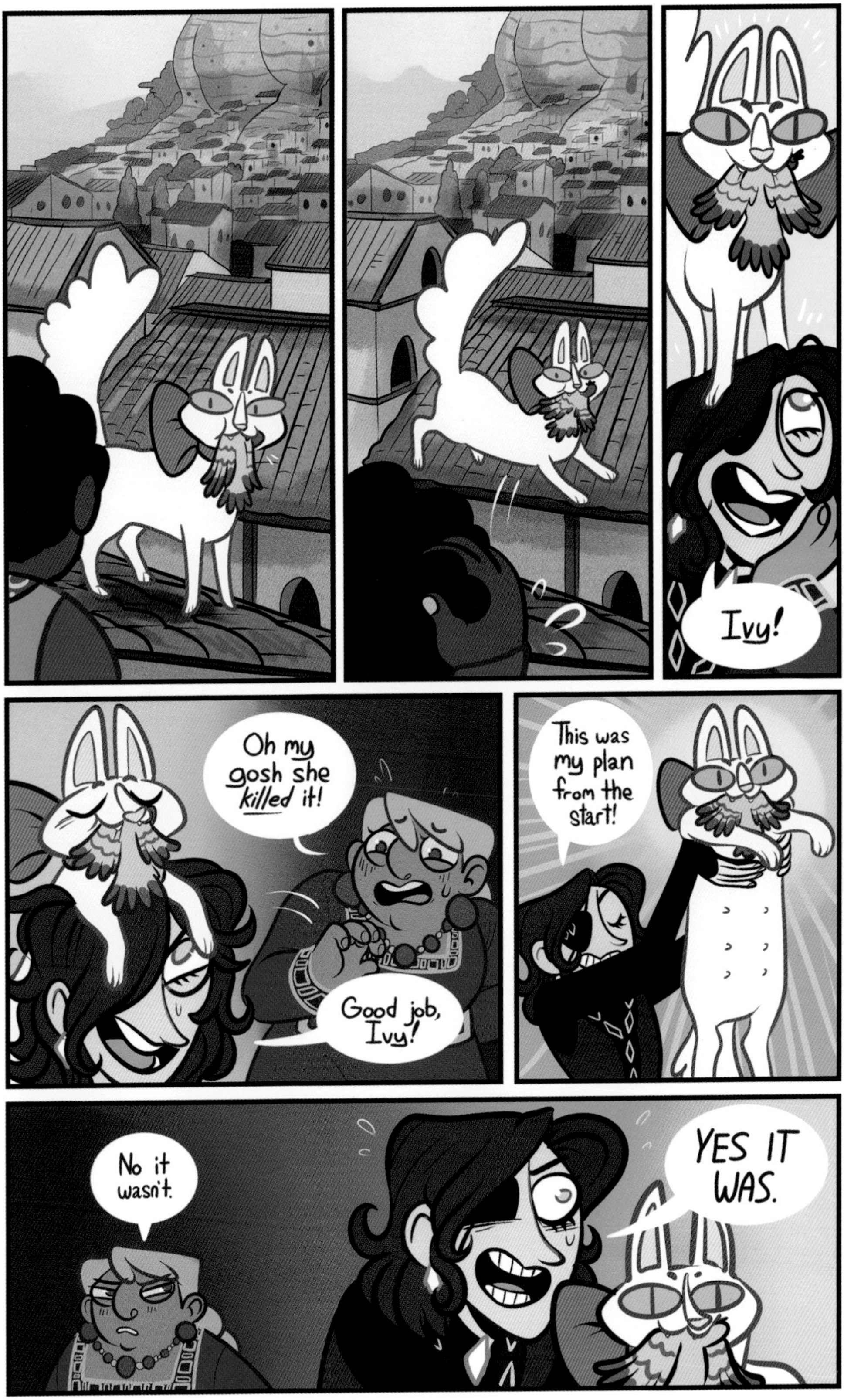
Ivy!
Oh my gosh she killed it!
Good job, Ivy!
This was my plan from the start!
No it wasn't.
YES IT WAS.

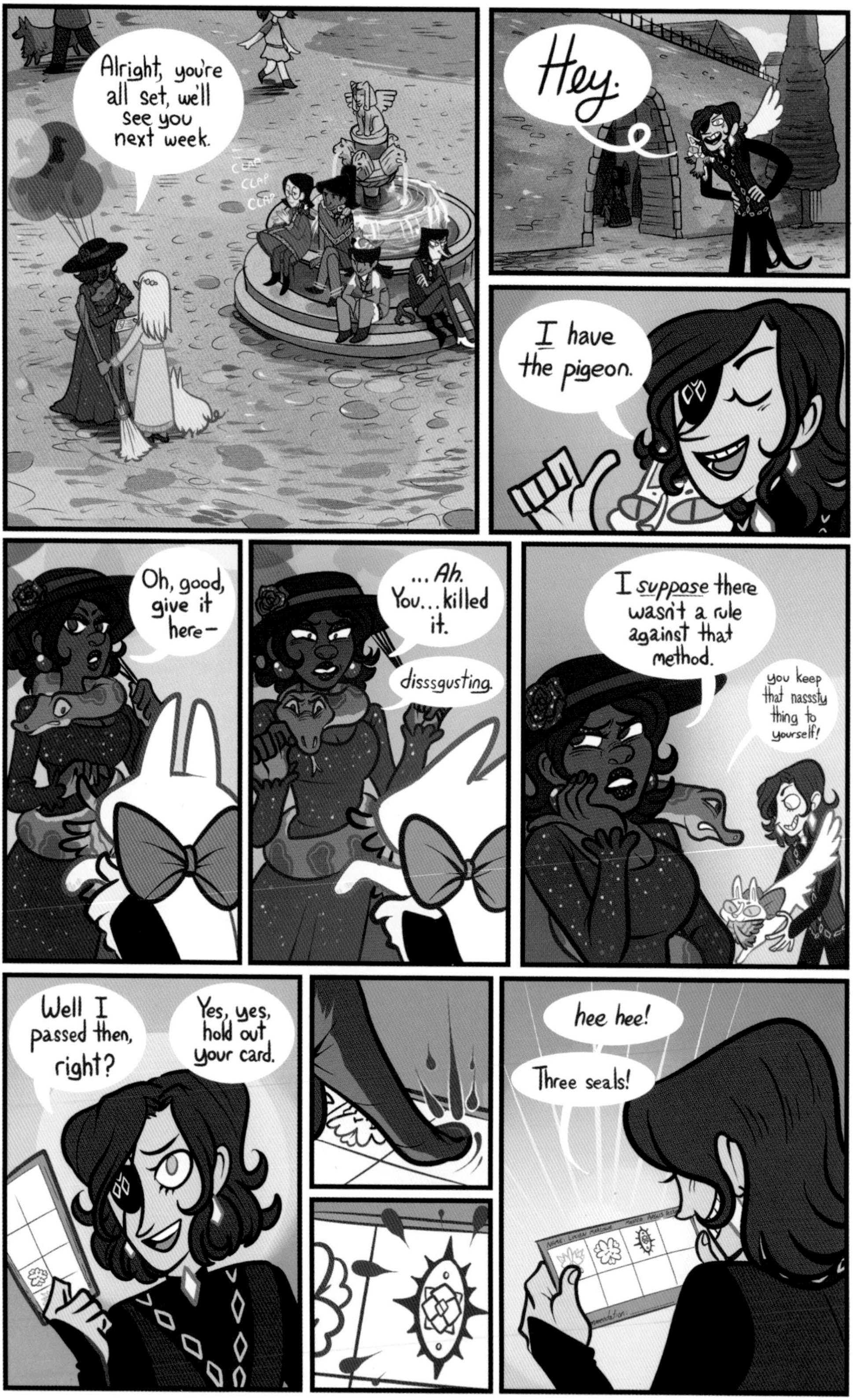
Alright, you're all set, we'll see you next week.
CLAP CLAP CLAP
Hey.
I have the pigeon.
Oh, good, give it here-
...Ah. You...killed it.
disssgusting.
I suppose there wasn't a rule against that method.
you keep that nasssty thing to yourself!
Well I passed then, right?
Yes, yes, hold out your card.
hee hee!
Three seals!

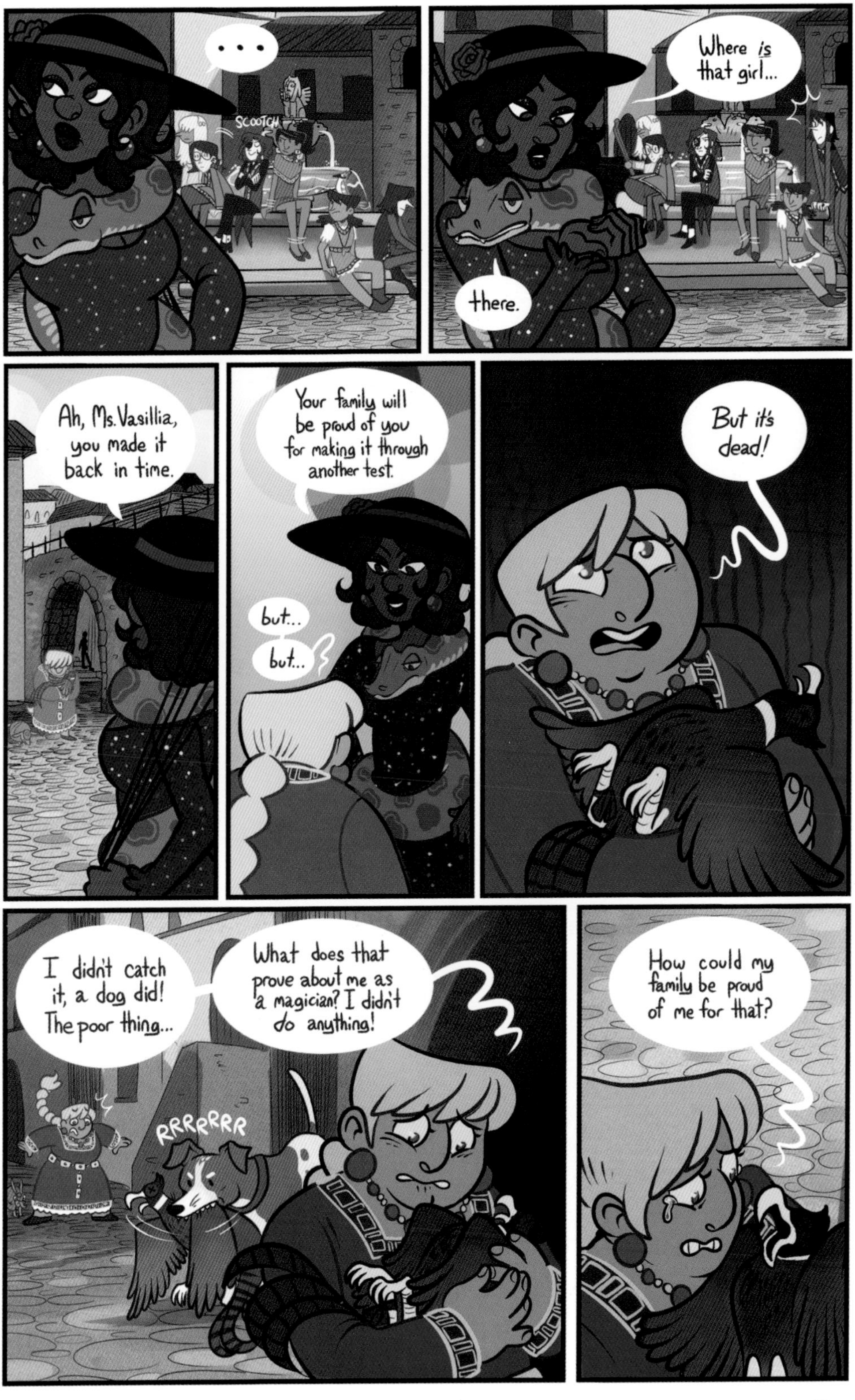
. . .
SCOOTCH
Where is that girl...
there.
Ah, Ms. Vasillia, you made it back in time.
Your family will be proud of you for making it through another test.
but...
but...
But it's dead!
I didn't catch it, a dog did! The poor thing...
What does that prove about me as a magician? I didn't do anything!
RRRRRRR
How could my family be proud of me for that?

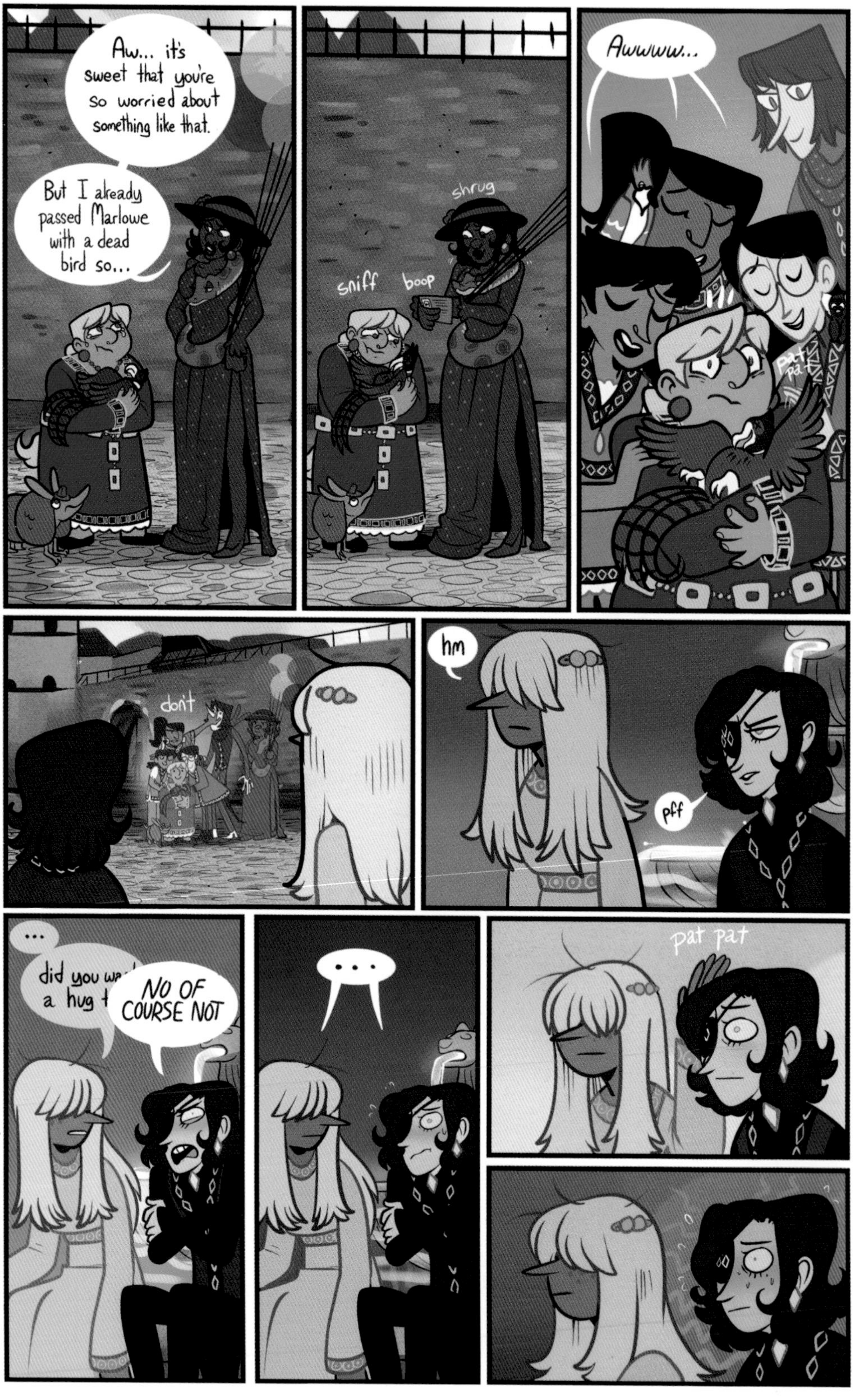

Aw... it's sweet that you're so worried about something like that.
But I already passed Marlowe with a dead bird so...
shrug
sniff
boop
Awwww...
pat pat
don't
hm
pff
...
did you wa a hug t
NO OF COURSE NOT
...
pat pat

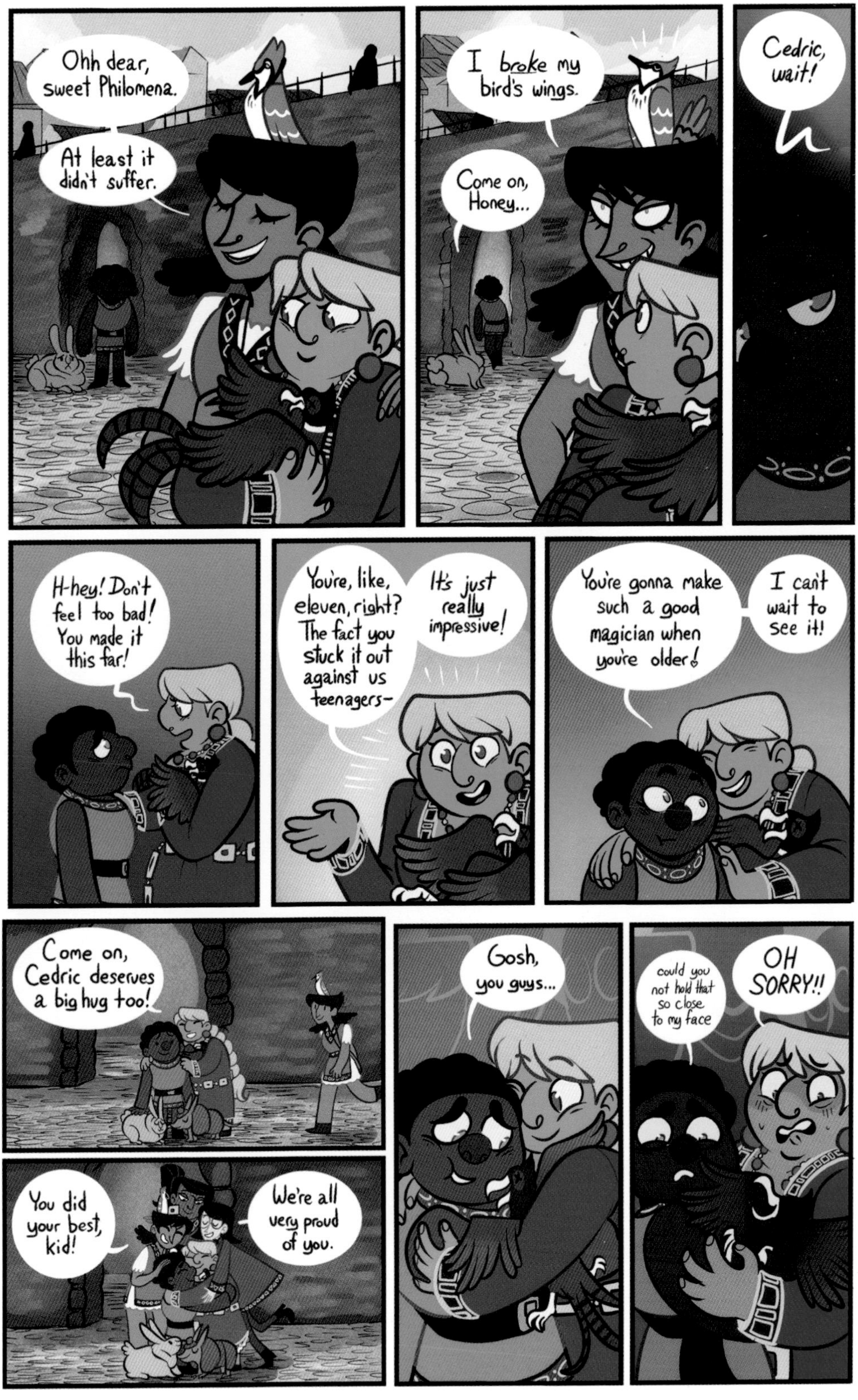
Ohh dear, sweet Philomena.
At least it didn't suffer.
I broke my bird's wings.
Come on, Honey...
Cedric, wait!
H-hey! Don't feel too bad! You made it this far!
You're, like, eleven, right? The fact you stuck it out against us teenagers-
It's just really impressive!
You're gonna make such a good magician when you're older!
I can't wait to see it!
Come on, Cedric deserves a big hug too!
You did your best, kid!
We're all very proud of you.
Gosh, you guys...
could you not hold that so close to my face
OH SORRY!!

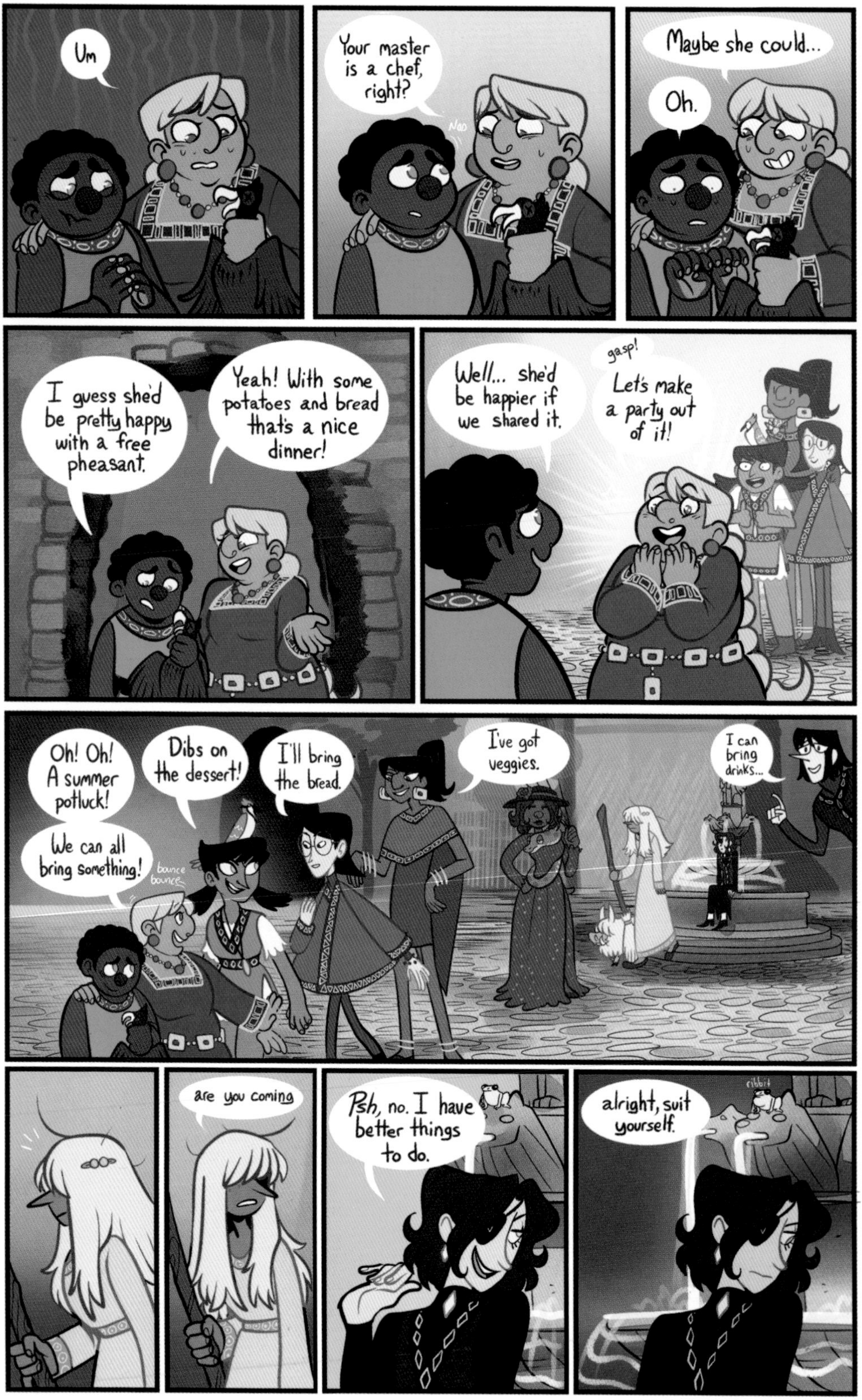
Um
Your master is a chef, right?
NOD
Maybe she could...
Oh.
I guess she'd be pretty happy with a free pheasant.
Yeah! With some potatoes and bread that's a nice dinner!
Well... she'd be happier if we shared it.
gasp!
Let's make a party out of it!
Oh! Oh! A summer potluck!
We can all bring something!
bounce bounce
Dibs on the dessert!
I'll bring the bread.
I've got veggies.
I can bring drinks...
are you coming
Psh, no. I have better things to do.
alright, suit yourself.
ribbit

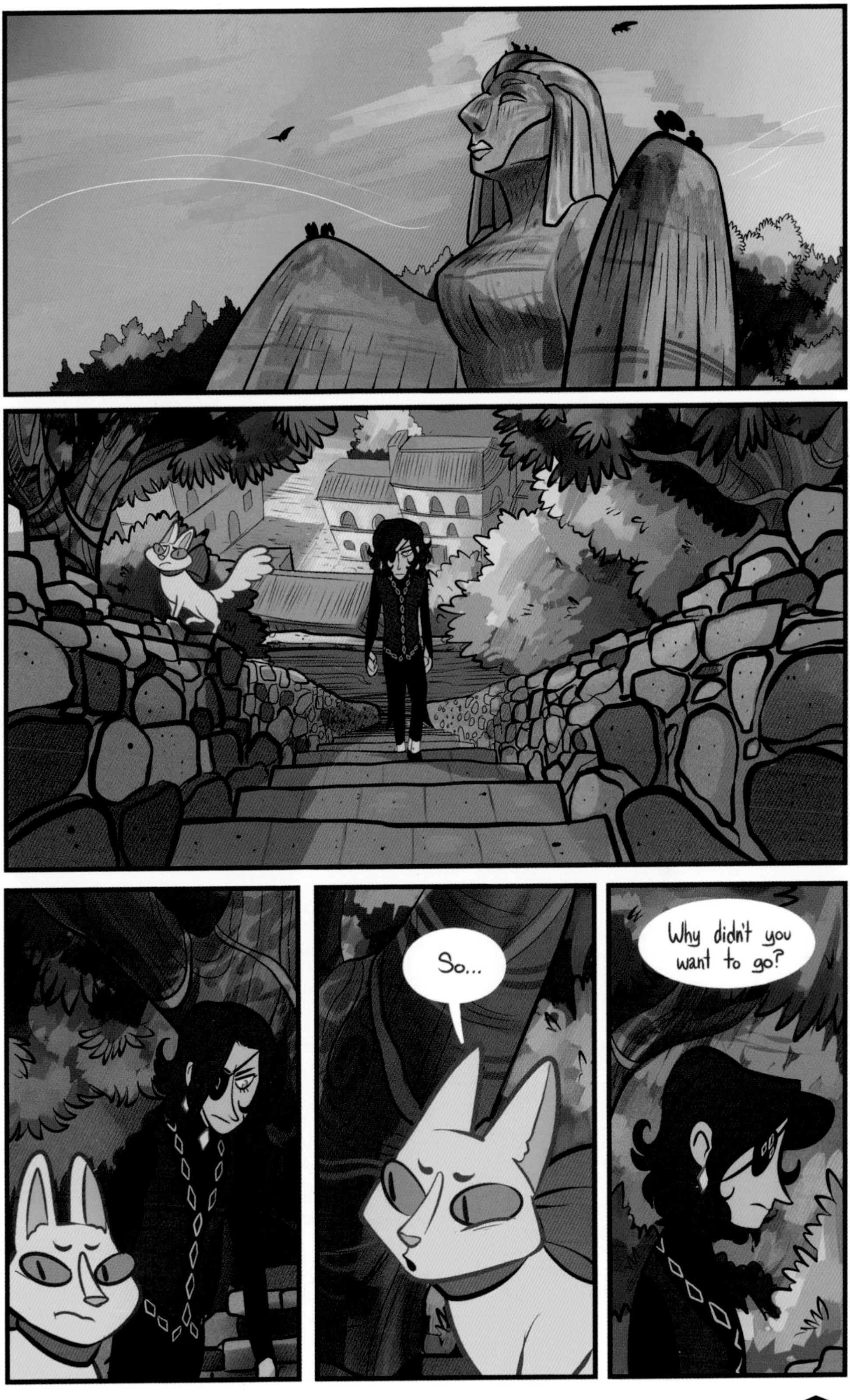
So...
Why didn't you want to go?

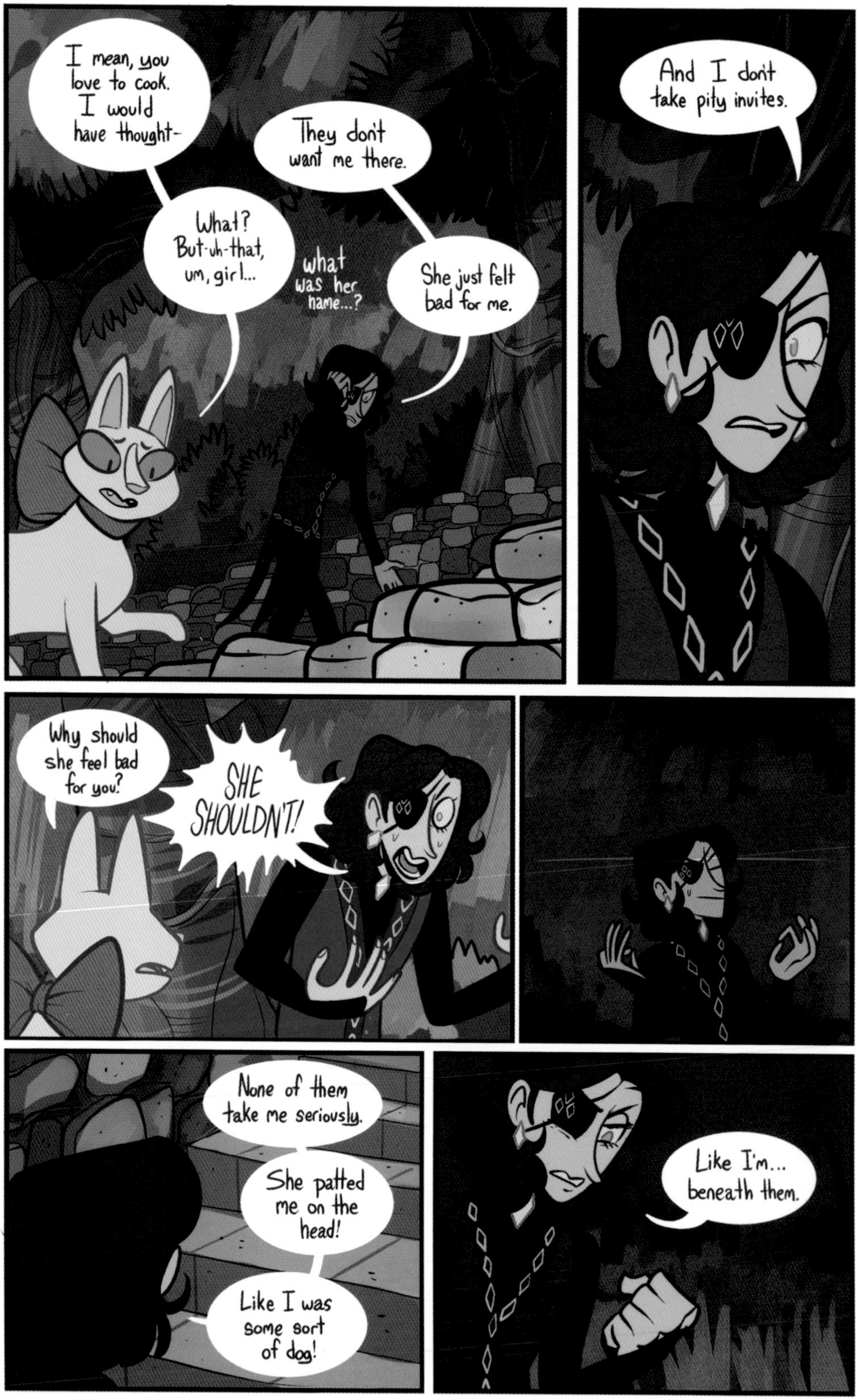
I mean, you love to cook. I would have thought-
They don't want me there.
What? But-uh-that, um, girl...
what was her name...?
She just felt bad for me.
And I don't take pity invites.
Why should she feel bad for you?
SHE SHOULDN'T!
None of them take me seriously.
She patted me on the head!
Like I was some sort of dog!
Like I'm... beneath them.

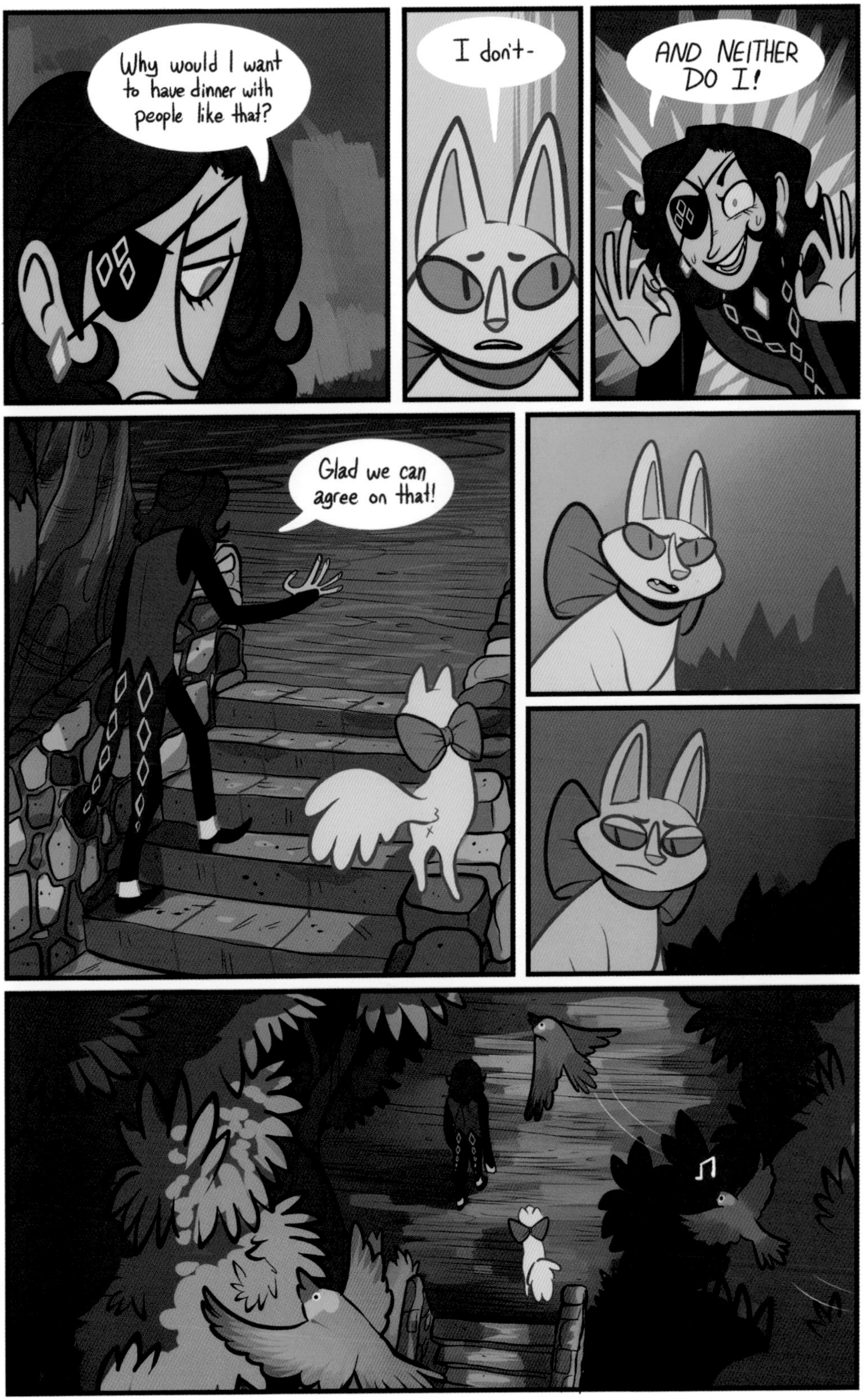
Why would I want to have dinner with people like that?
I don't-
AND NEITHER DO I!
Glad we can agree on that!

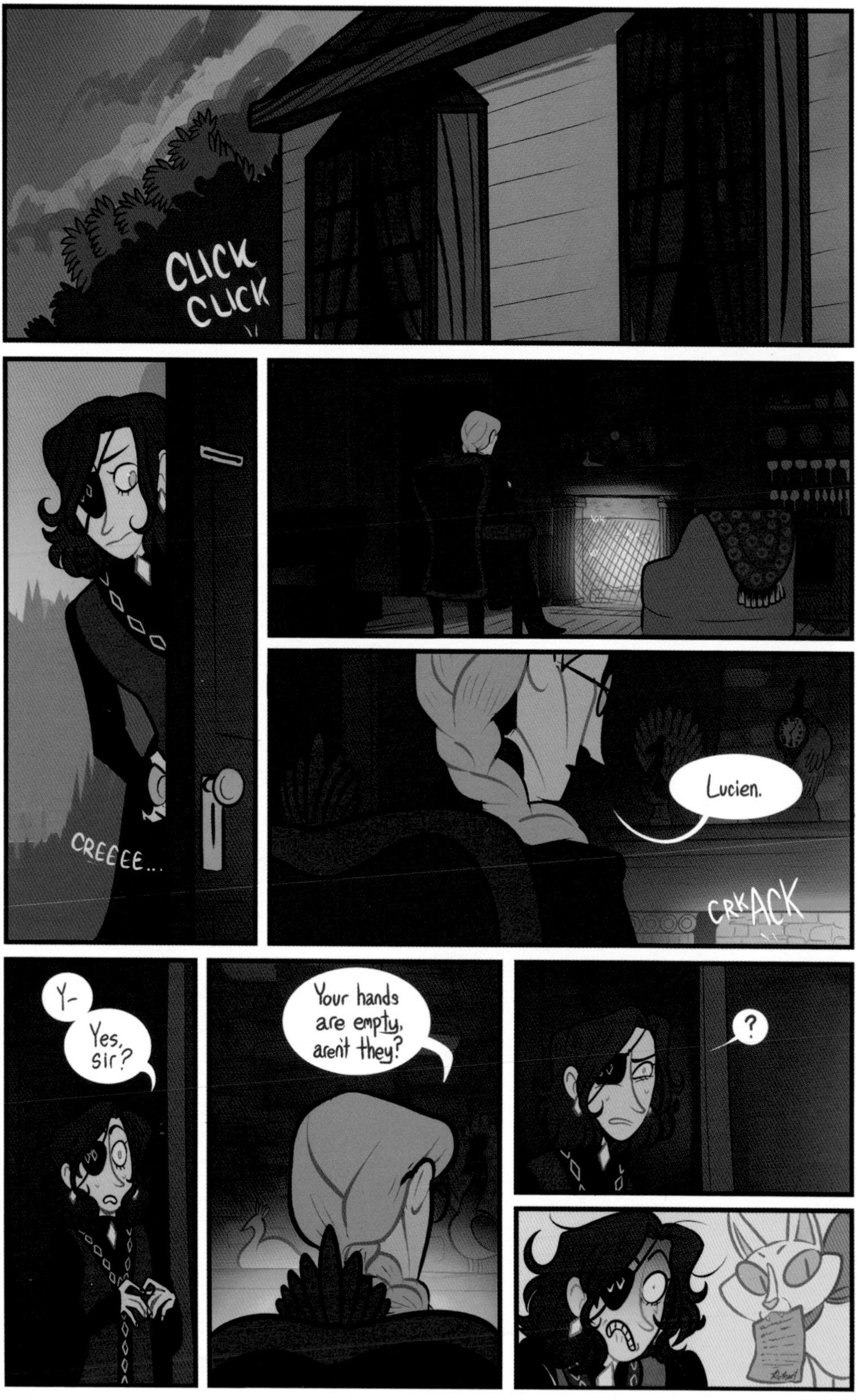
CLICK
CLICK
CREEEE...
Lucien.
CRKACK
Y-
Yes, sir?
Your hands are empty, aren't they?
?

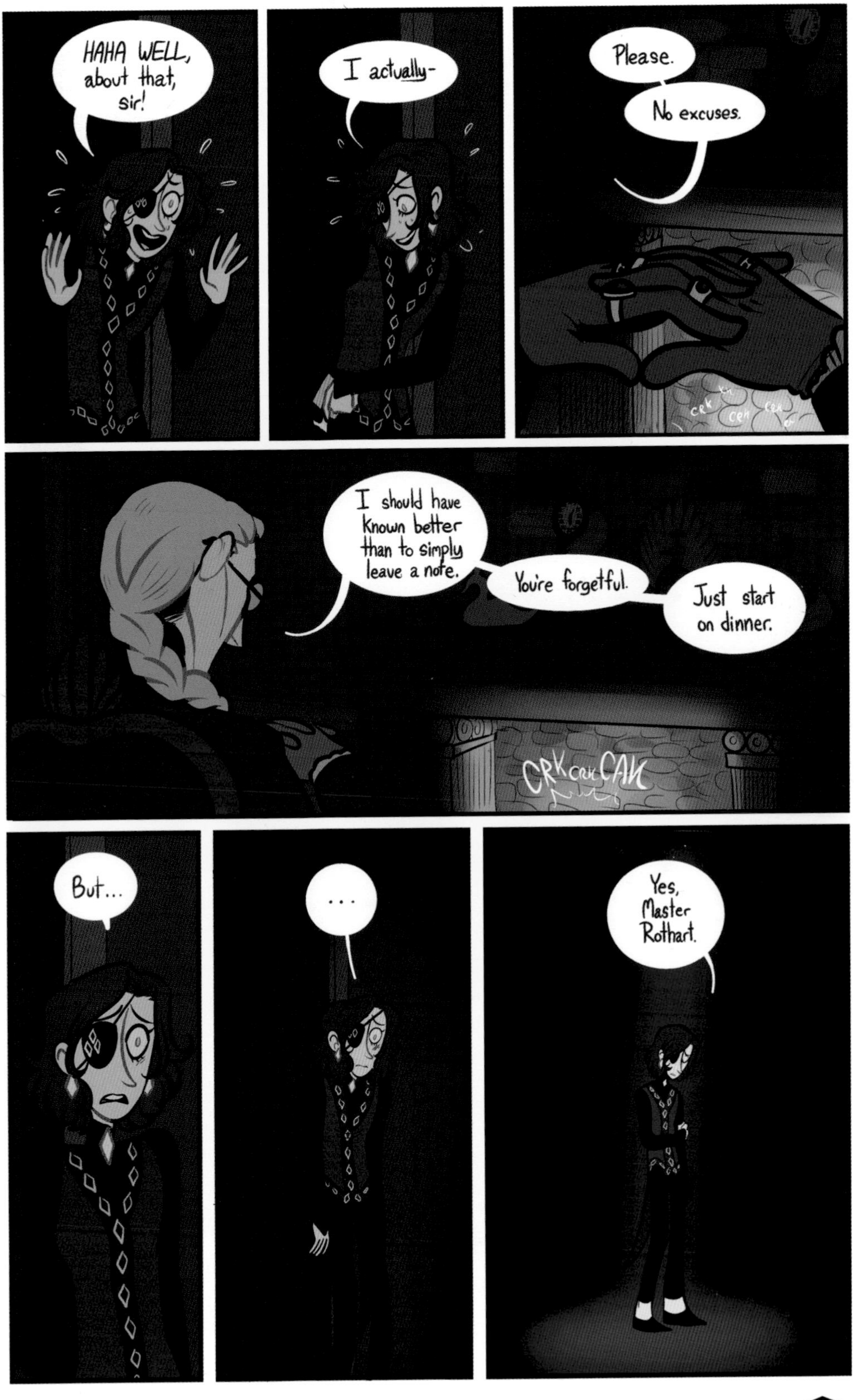
HAHA WELL, about that, sir!
I actually-
Please.
No excuses.
CRK
CRK
CRK
I should have known better than to simply leave a note.
You're forgetful.
Just start on dinner.
CRKcrkCAK
But...
. . .
Yes, Master Rothart.

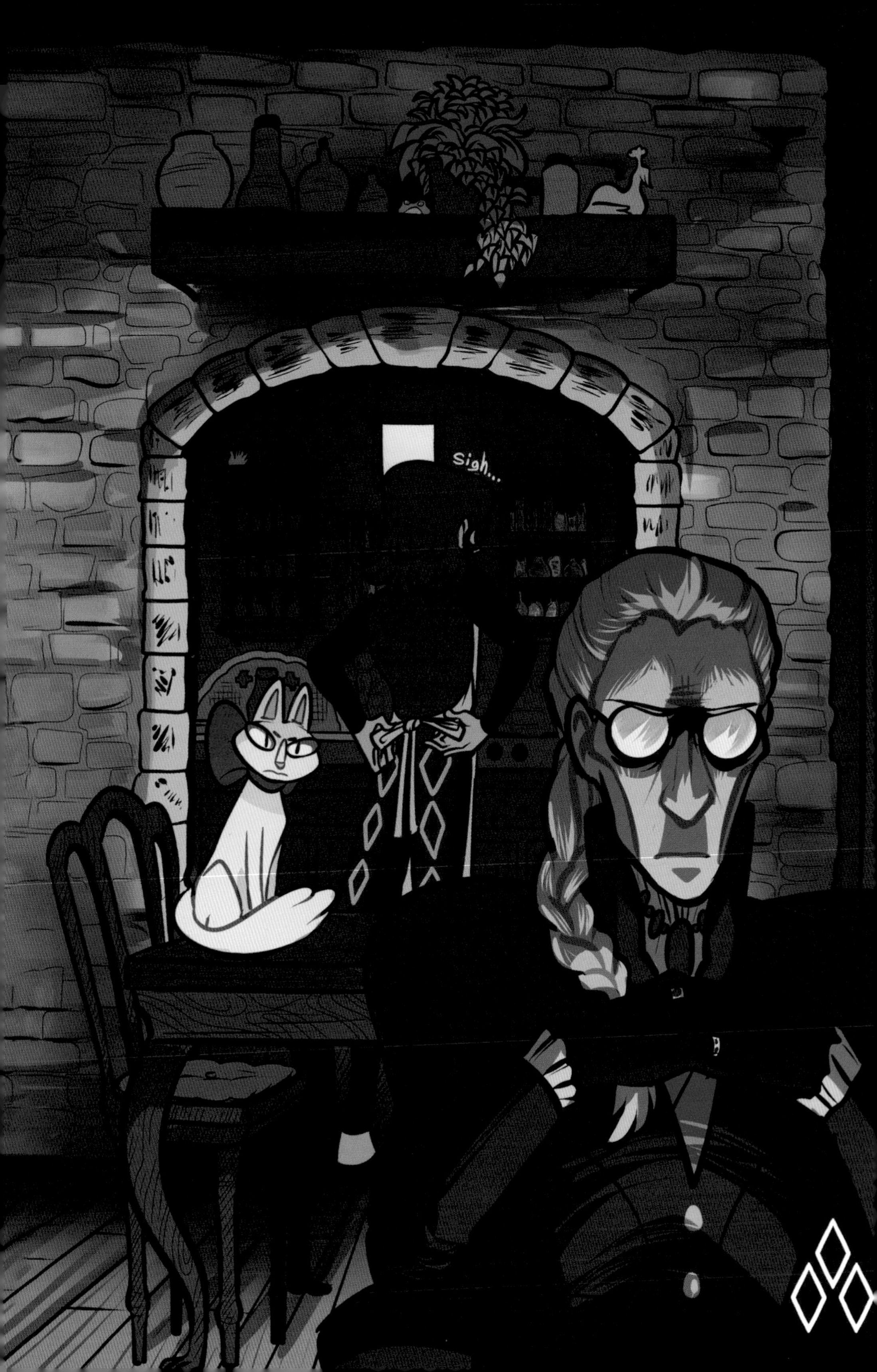
sigh...

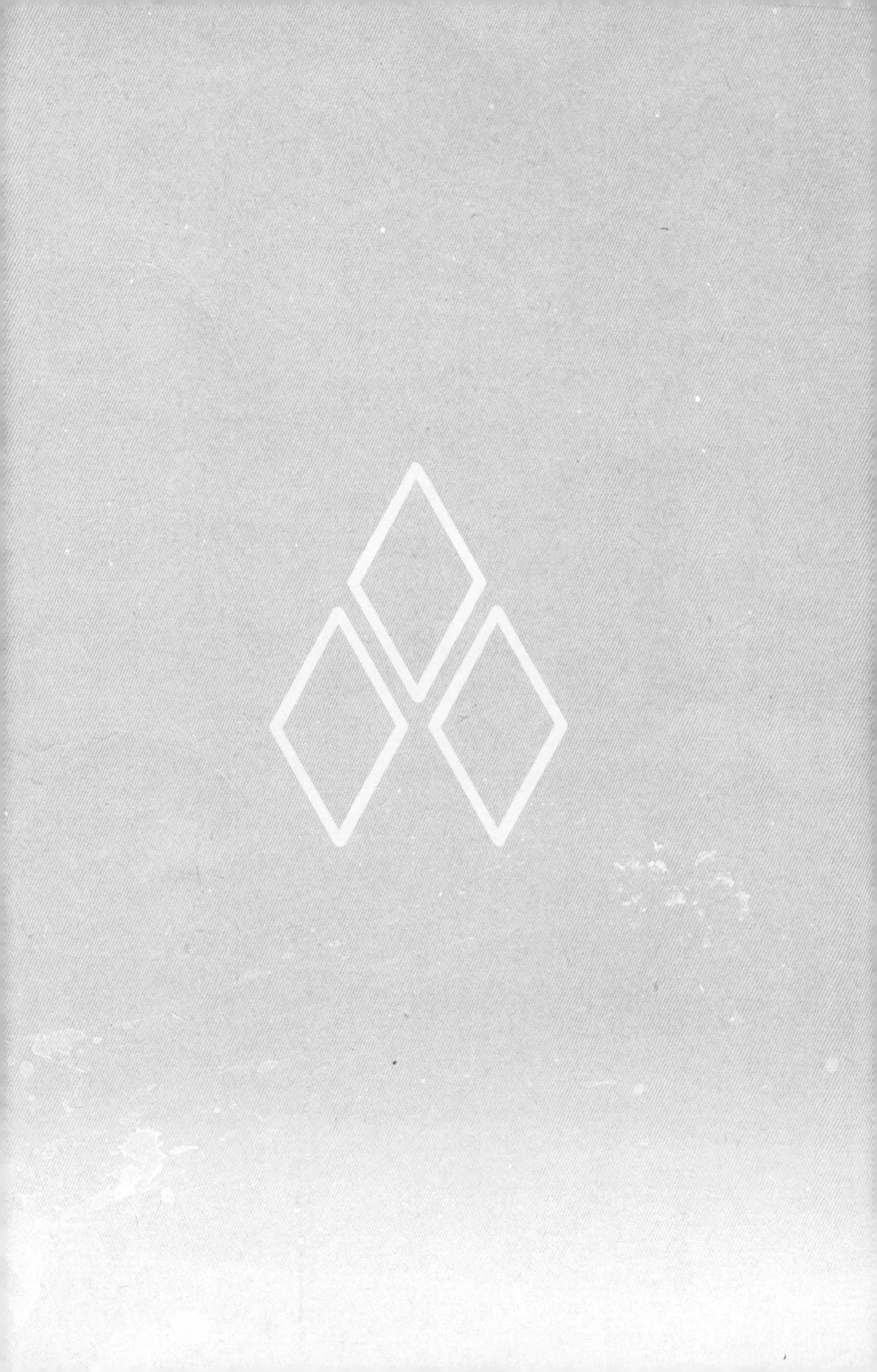

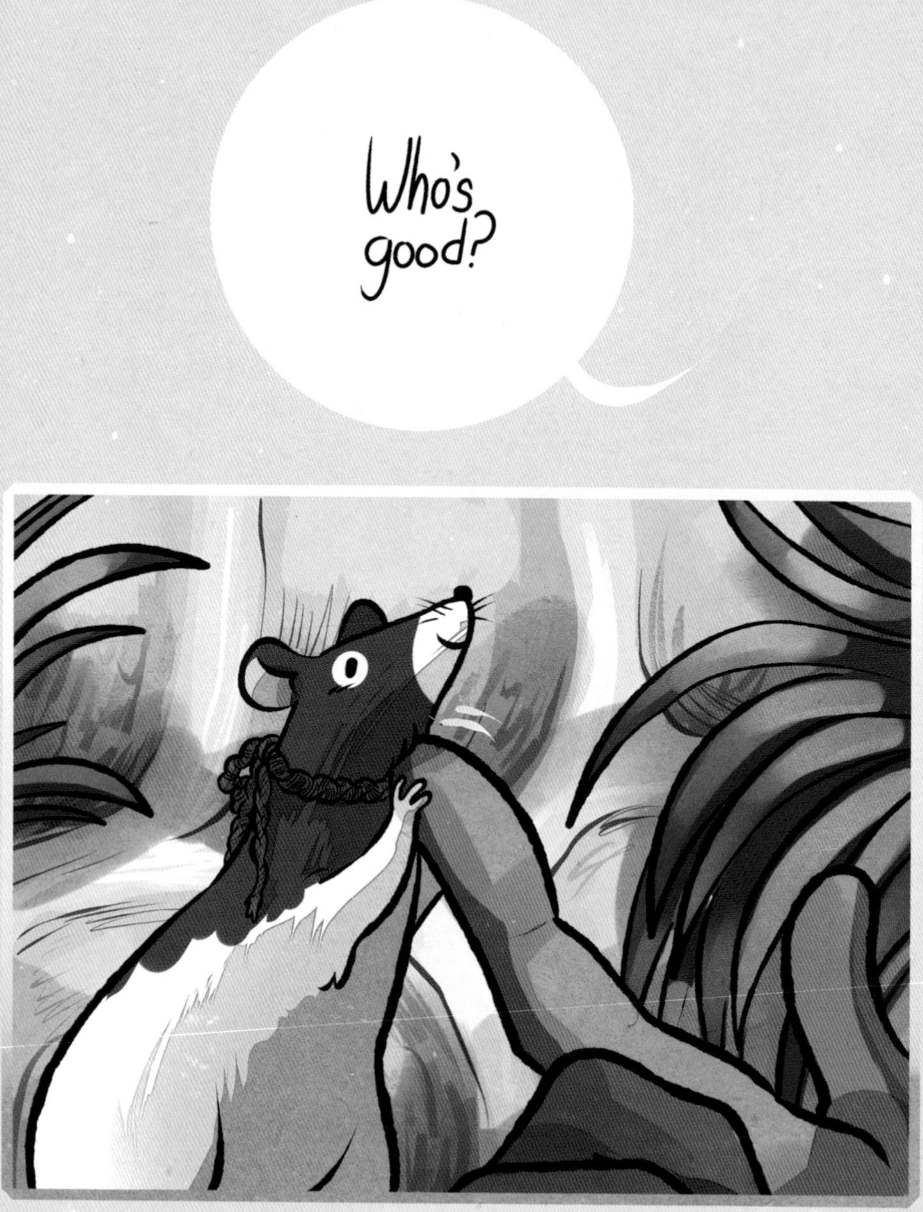
Who's good?

II

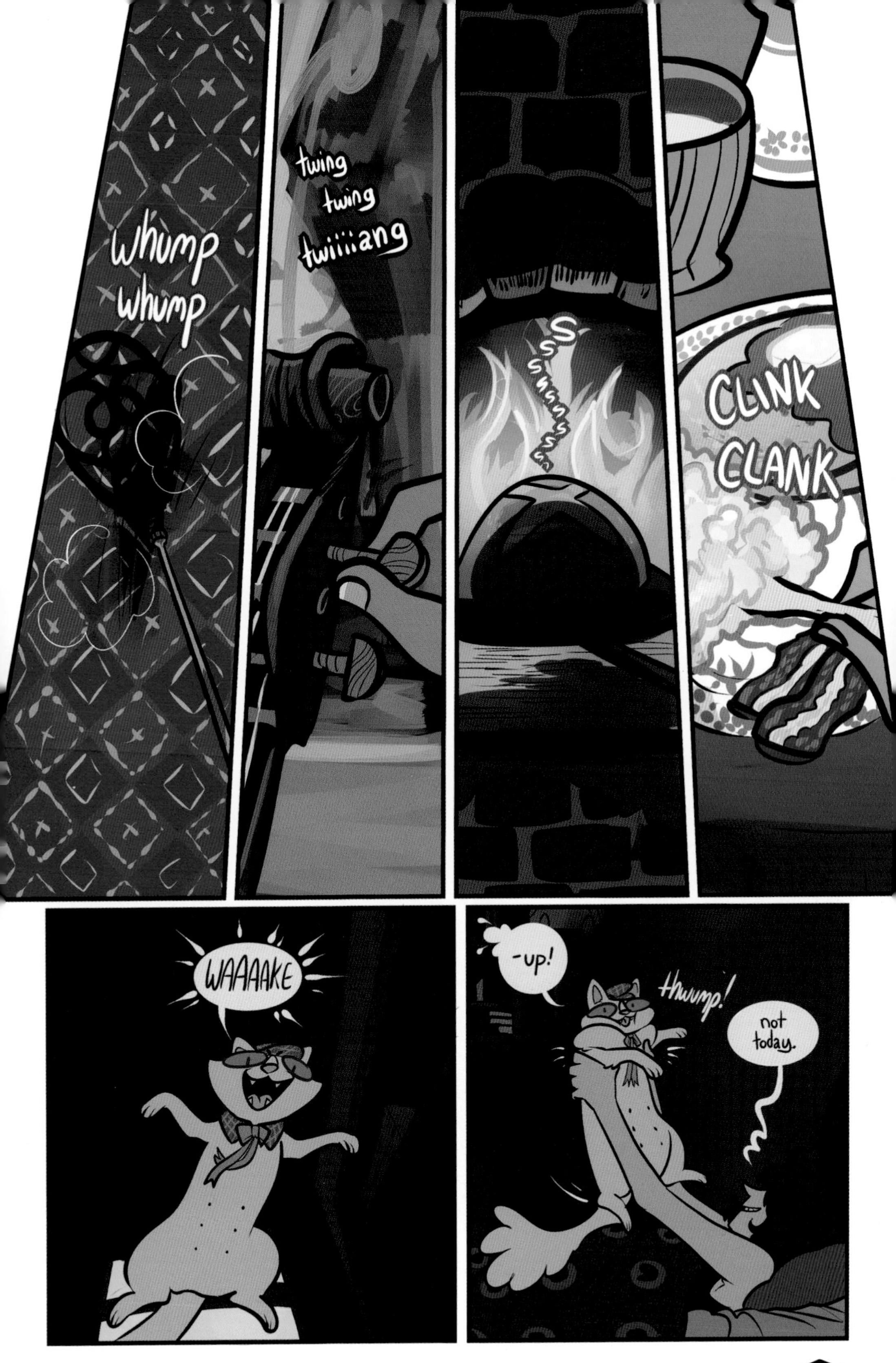
whump
whump
twing
twing
twiiiiang
SSsssssss
CLINK
CLANK
WAAAAKE
-up!
thwump!
not today.

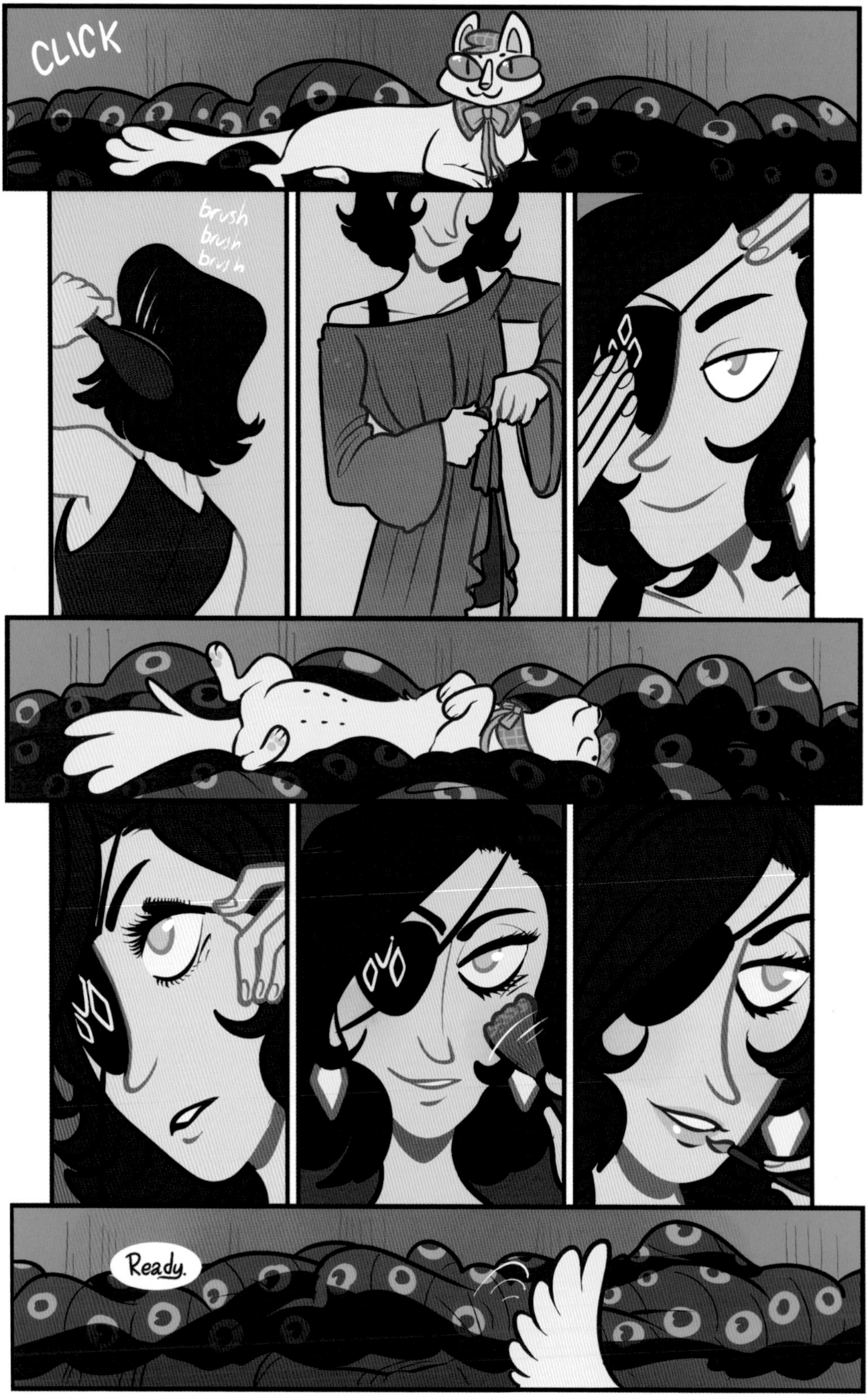
CLICK
brush
brush
brush
Ready.

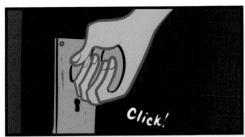

Click!

I'm going out!

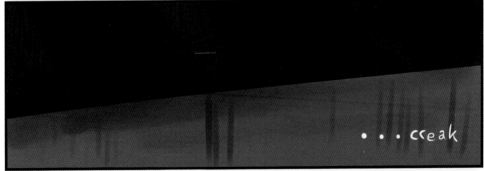

. . . creak

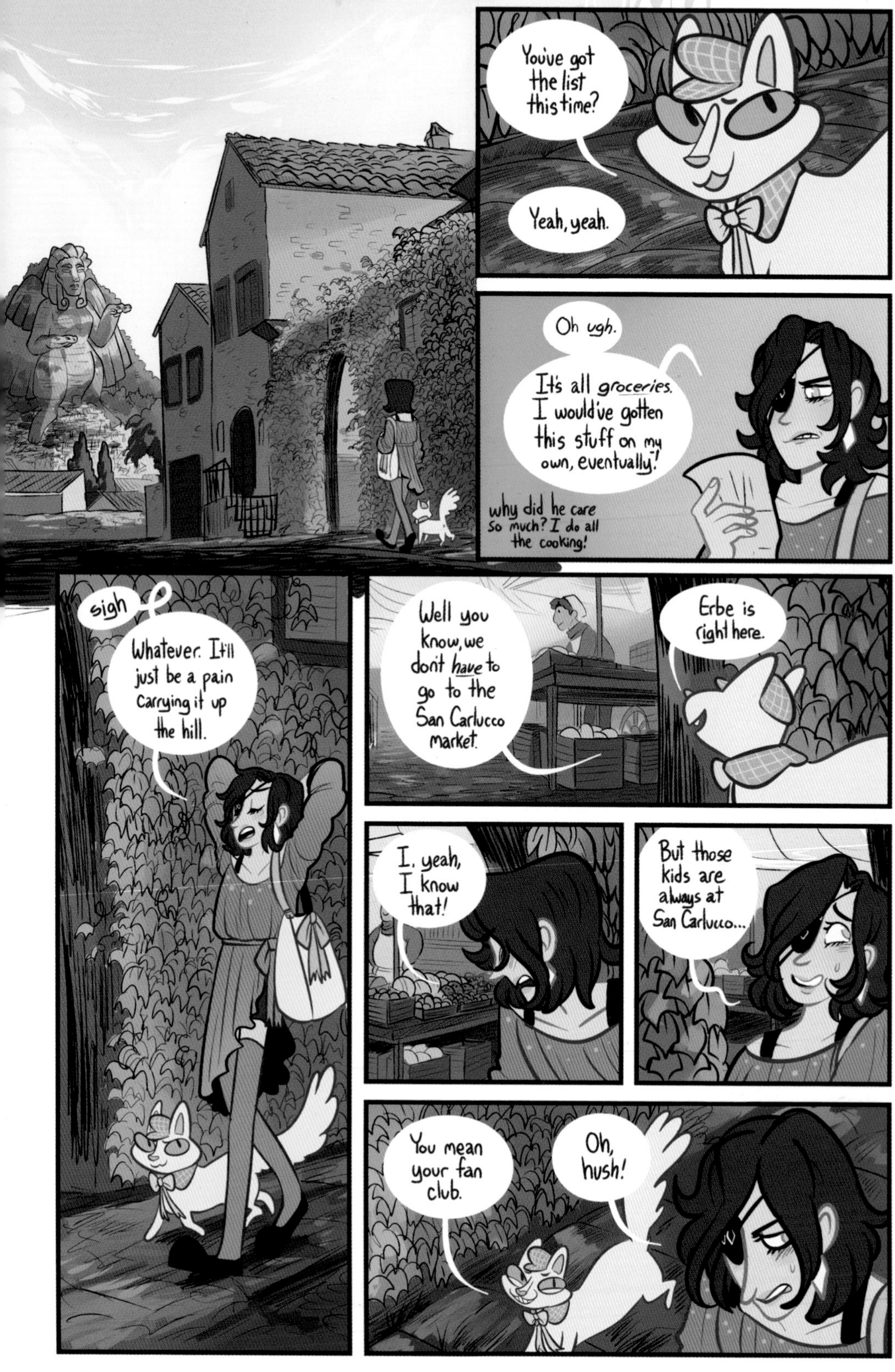

You've got the list this time?
Yeah, yeah.
Oh ugh.
It's all groceries. I would've gotten this stuff on my own, eventually!
why did he care so much? I do all the cooking!
sigh
Whatever. It'll just be a pain carrying it up the hill.
Well you know, we don't have to go to the San Carlucco market.
Erbe is right here.
I, yeah, I know that!
But those kids are always at San Carlucco...
You mean your fan club.
Oh, hush!

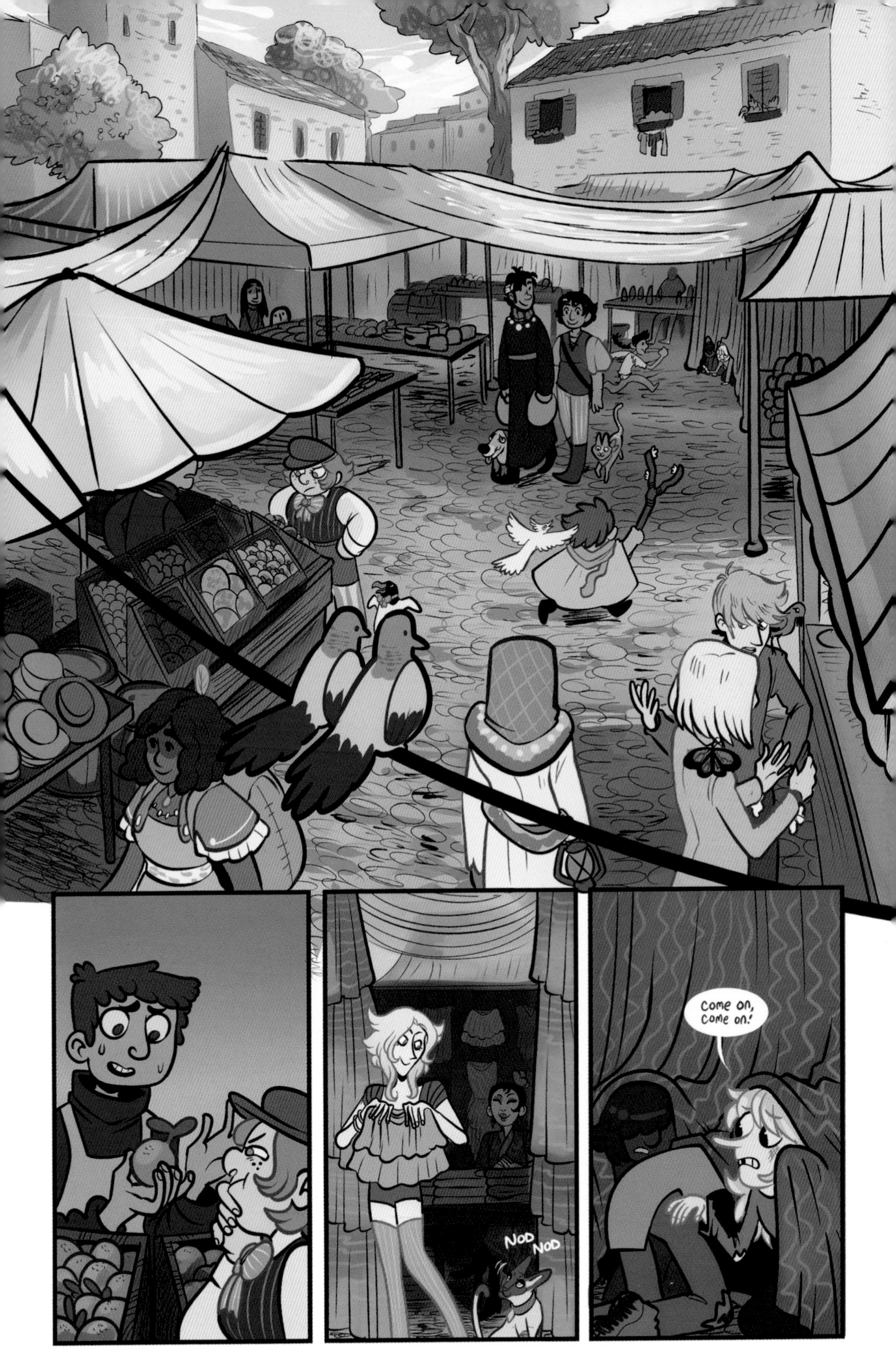
NOD
NOD
Come on,
come on!

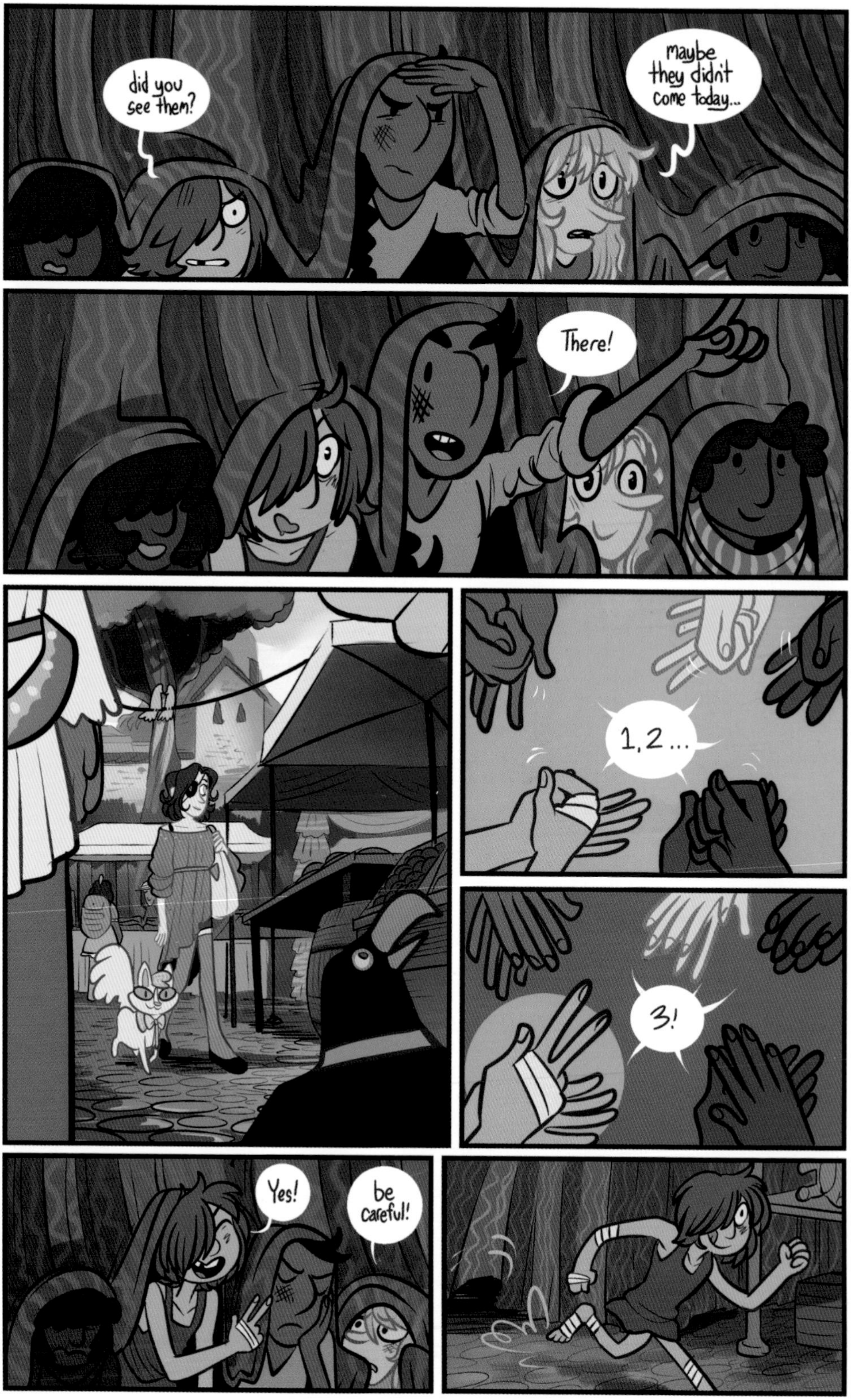
did you see them?
maybe they didn't come today...
There!
1, 2...
3!
Yes!
be careful!

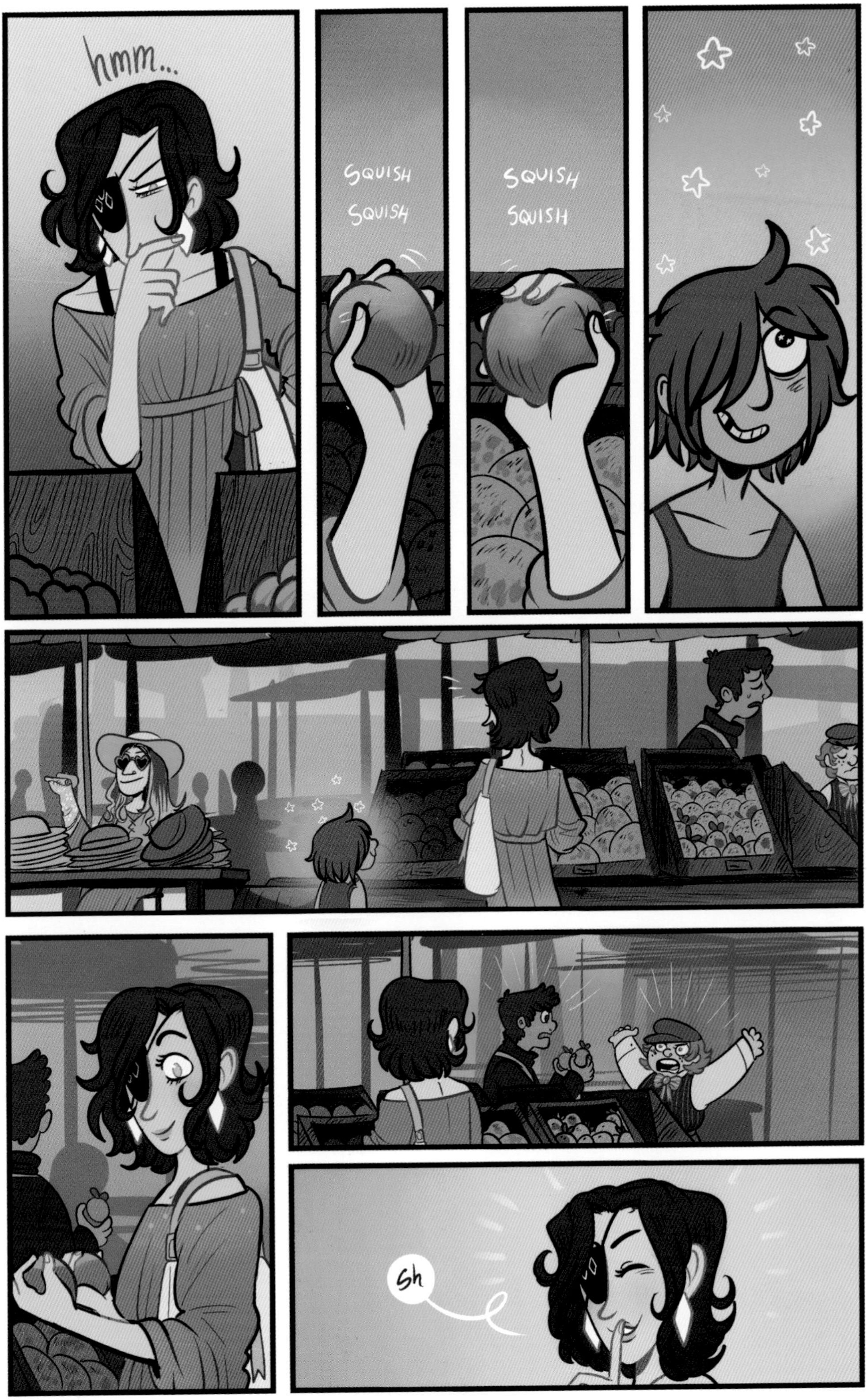
hmm...
SQUISH
SQUISH
SQUISH
SQUISH
Sh

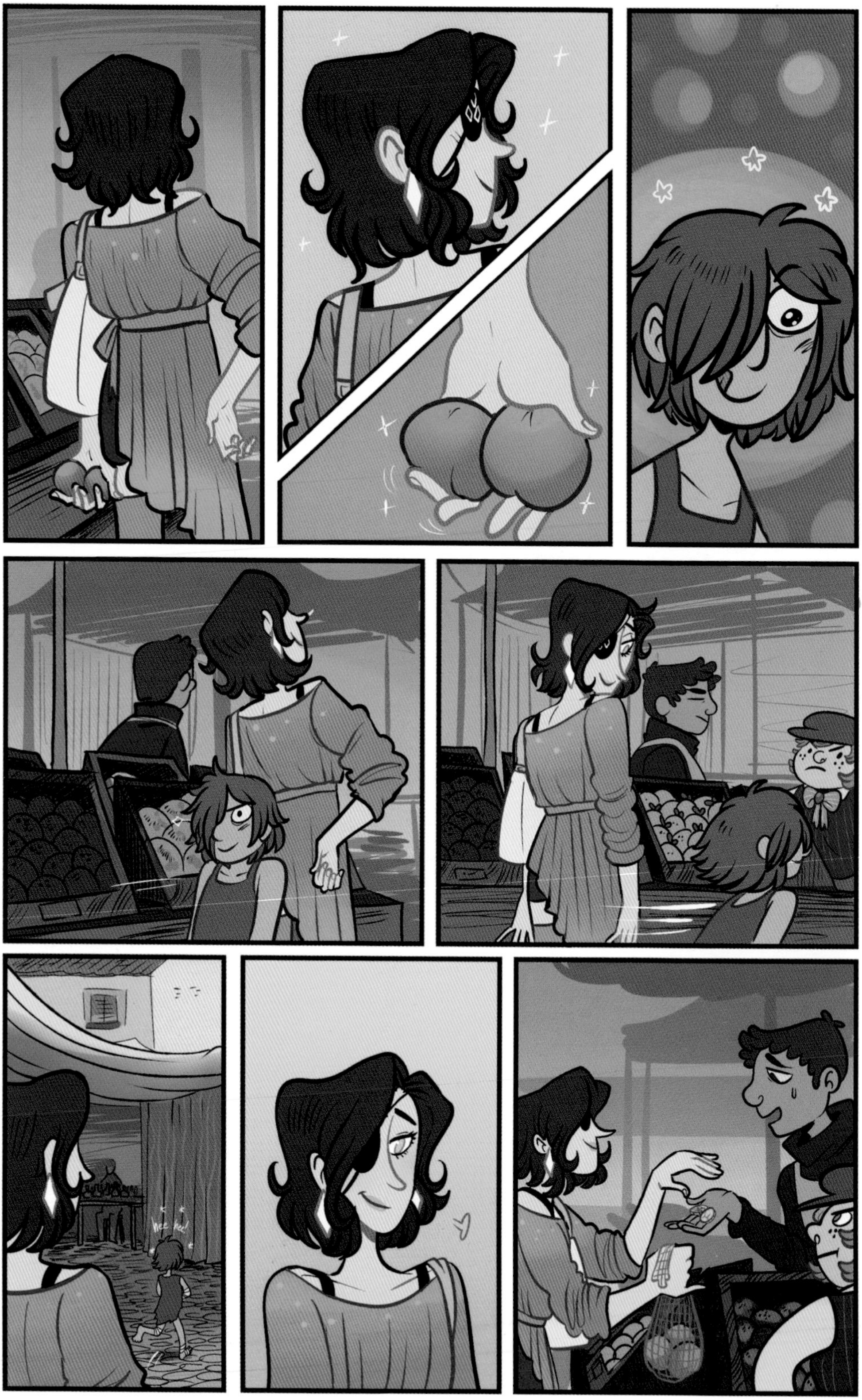
hee hee!

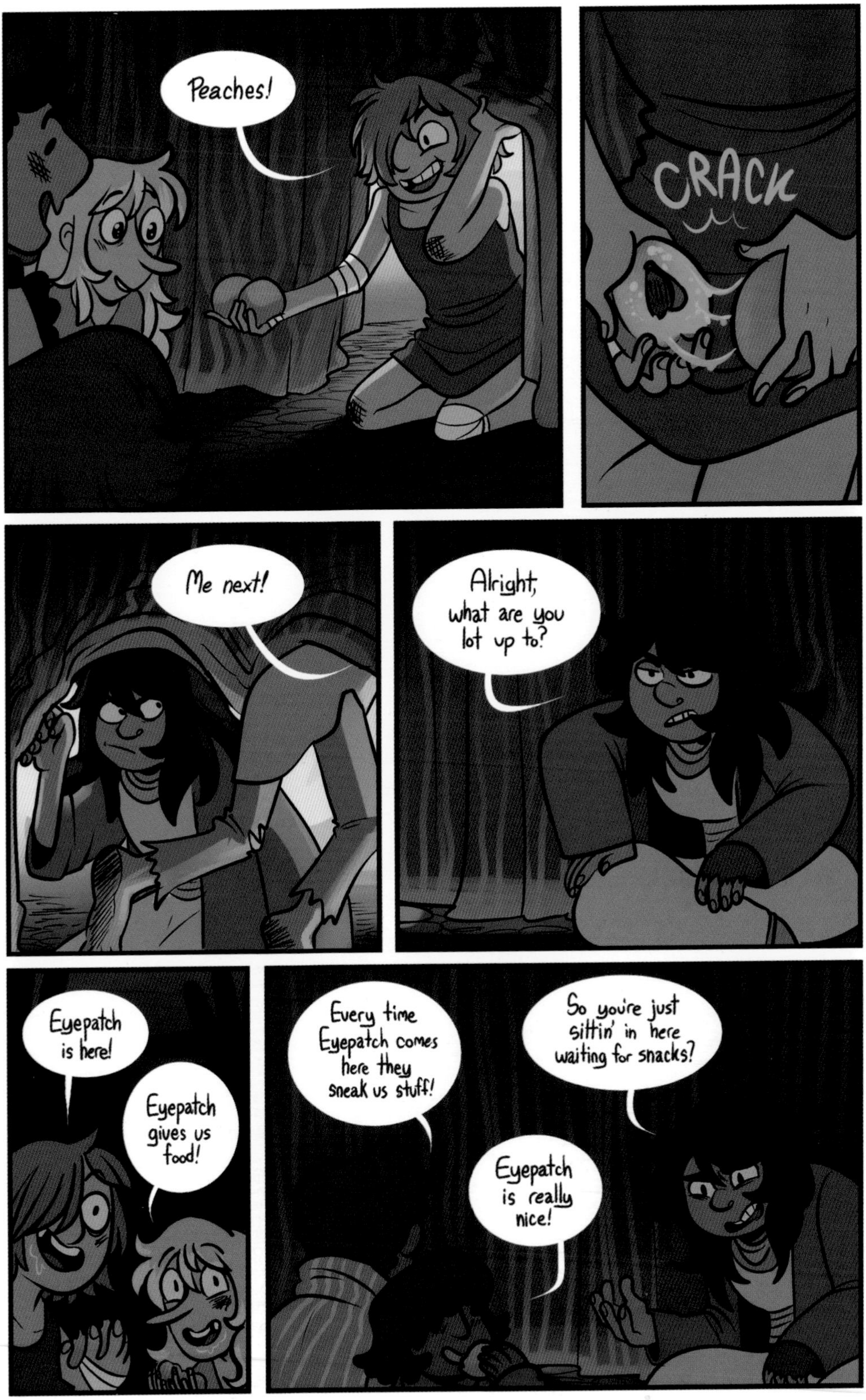
Peaches!
CRACK
Me next!
Alright, what are you lot up to?
Eyepatch is here!
Eyepatch gives us food!
Every time Eyepatch comes here they sneak us stuff!
So you're just sittin' in here waiting for snacks?
Eyepatch is really nice!

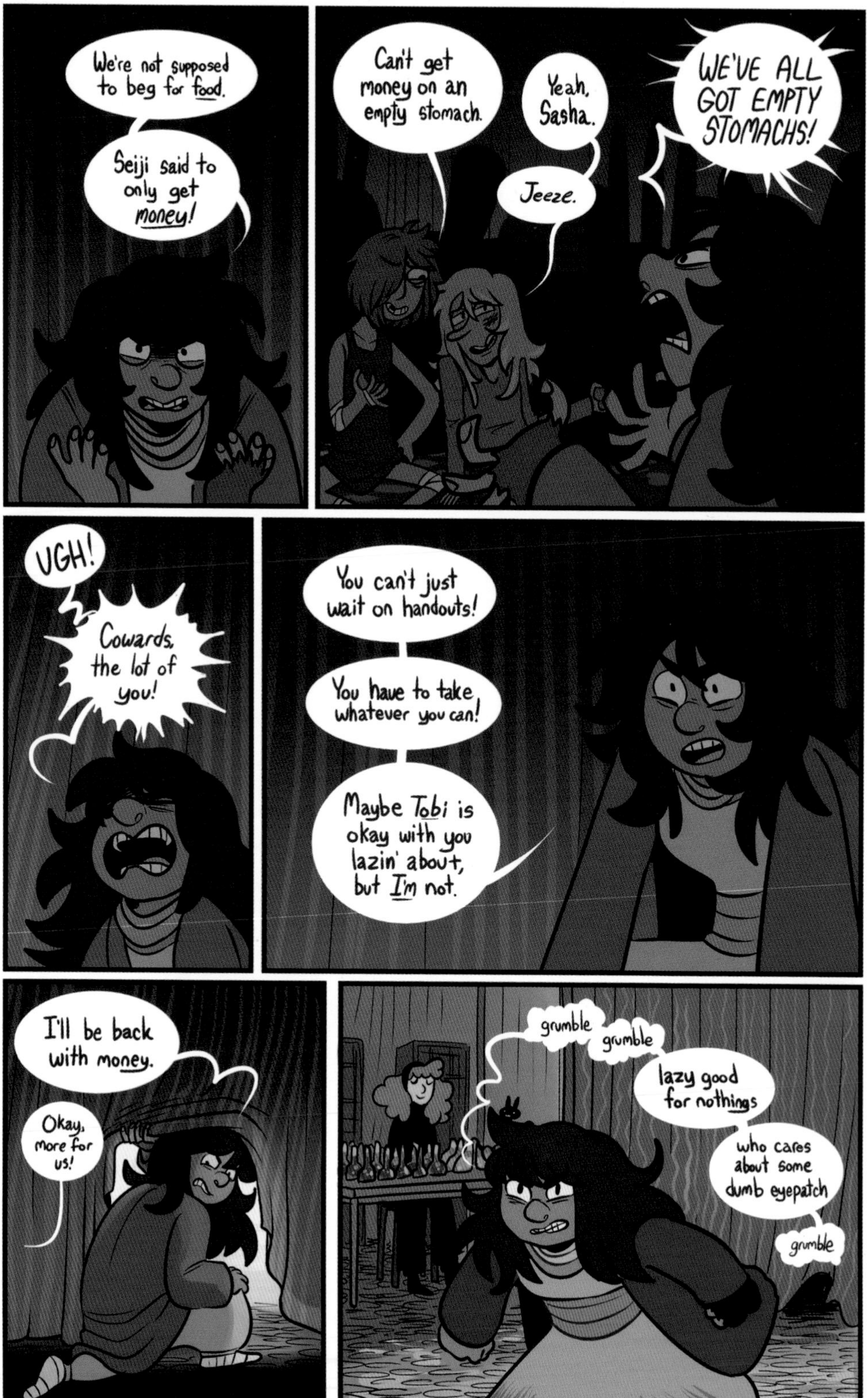
We're not supposed to beg for food.
Seiji said to only get money!
Can't get money on an empty stomach.
Yeah, Sasha.
Jeeze.
WE'VE ALL GOT EMPTY STOMACHS!
UGH!
Cowards, the lot of you!
You can't just wait on handouts!
You have to take whatever you can!
Maybe Tobi is okay with you lazin' about, but I'm not.
I'll be back with money.
Okay, more for us!
grumble
grumble
lazy good for nothings
who cares about some dumb eyepatch
grumble

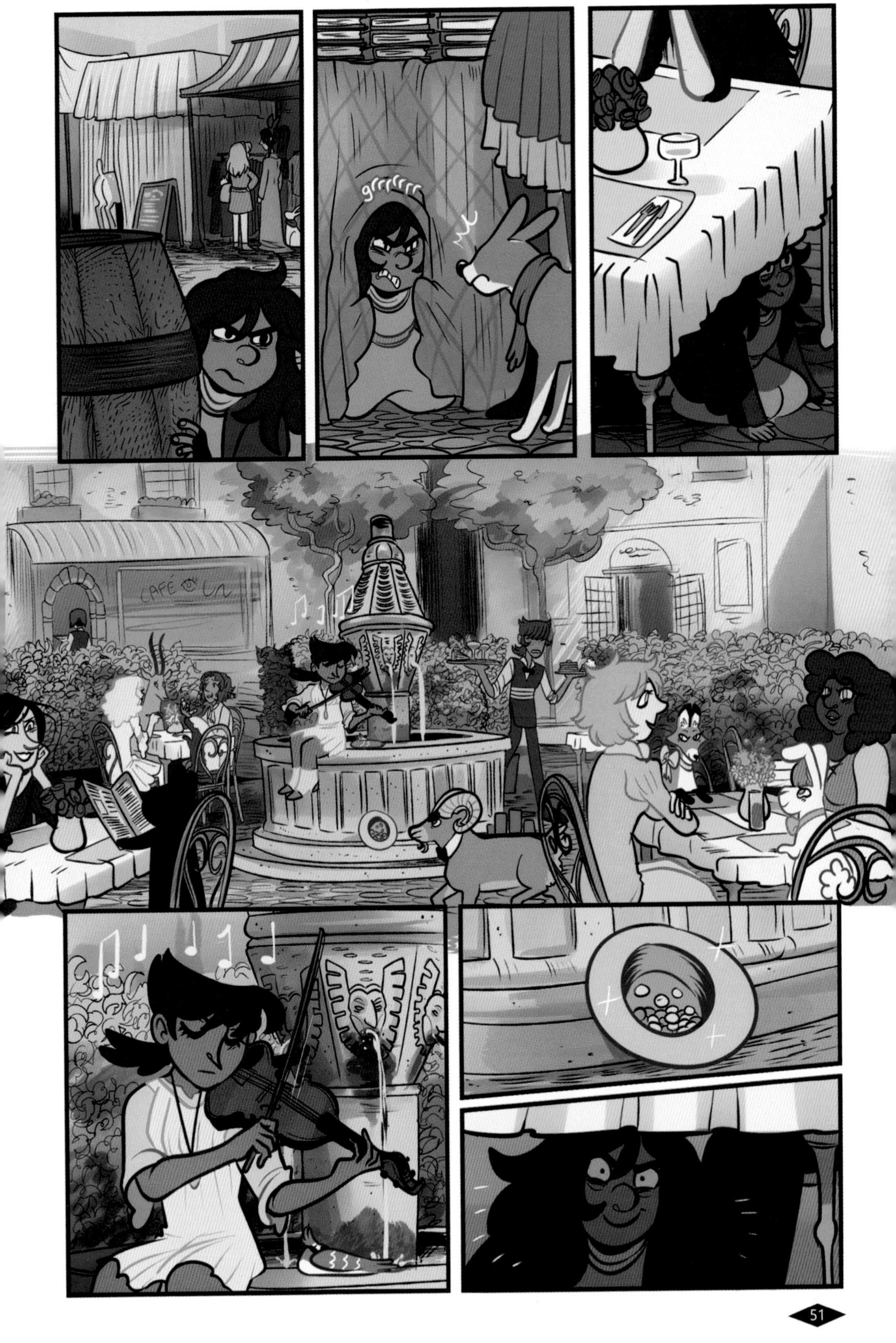
grrrrrrr
CAFÉ

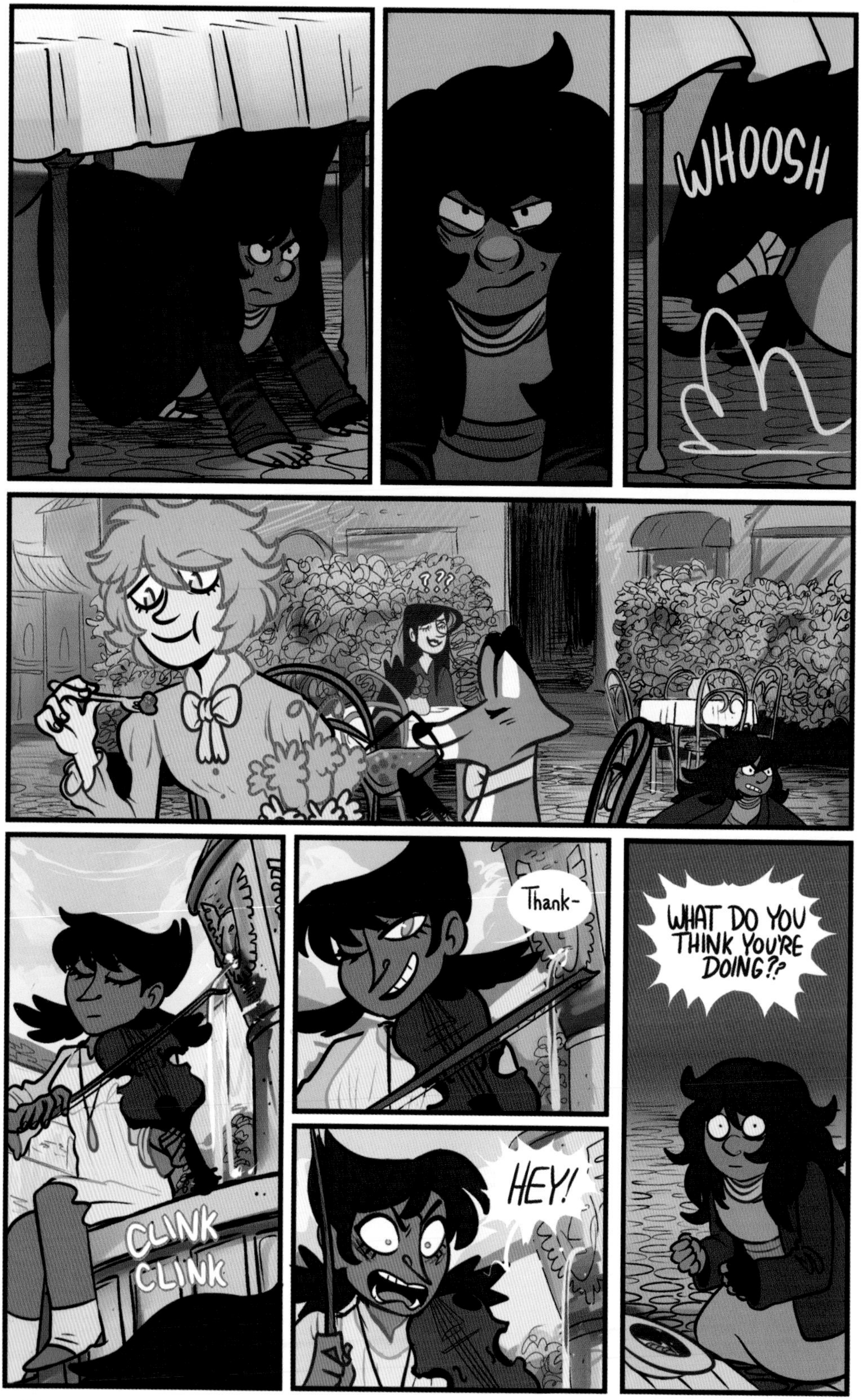
WHOOSH
???
CLINK
CLINK
Thank-
HEY!
WHAT DO YOU THINK YOU'RE DOING?!?

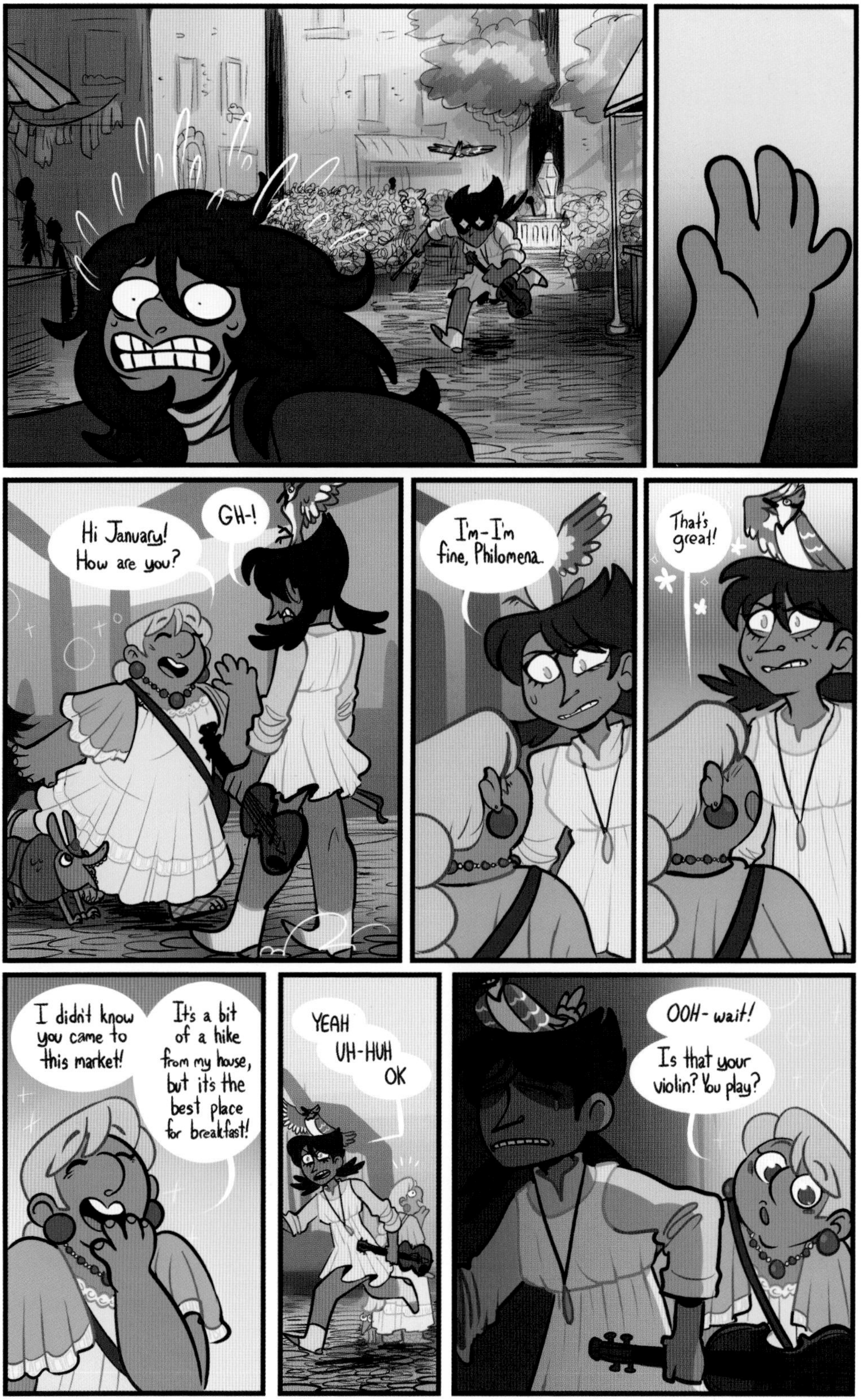

Hi January! How are you?
GH-!
I'm-I'm fine, Philomena.
That's great!
I didn't know you came to this market!
It's a bit of a hike from my house, but it's the best place for breakfast!
YEAH
UH-HUH
OK
OOH- wait!
Is that your violin? You play?

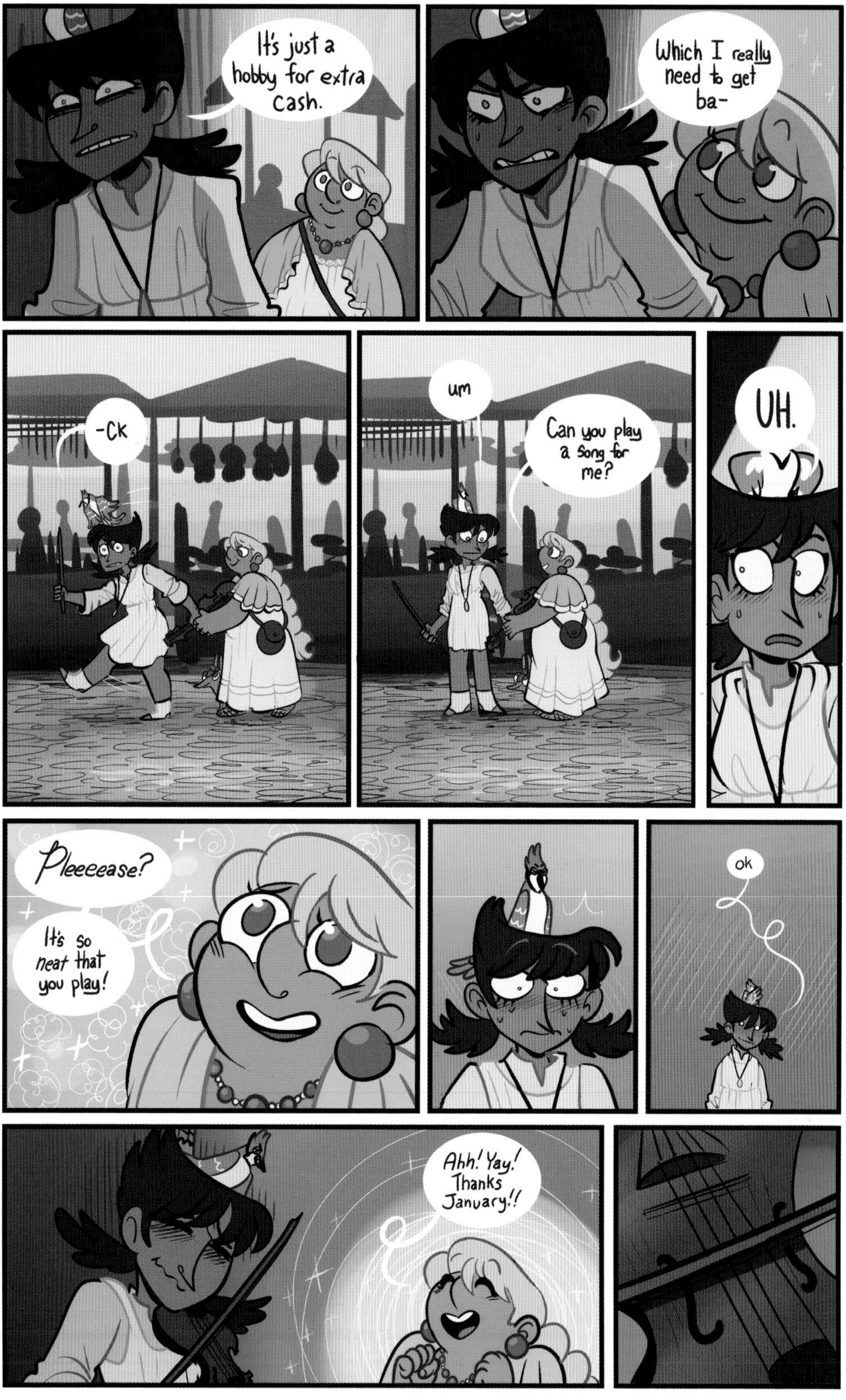
It's just a hobby for extra cash.
Which I really need to get ba-
-Ck
um
Can you play a song for me?
UH.
Pleeeease?
It's so neat that you play!
ok
Ahh! Yay! Thanks January!!

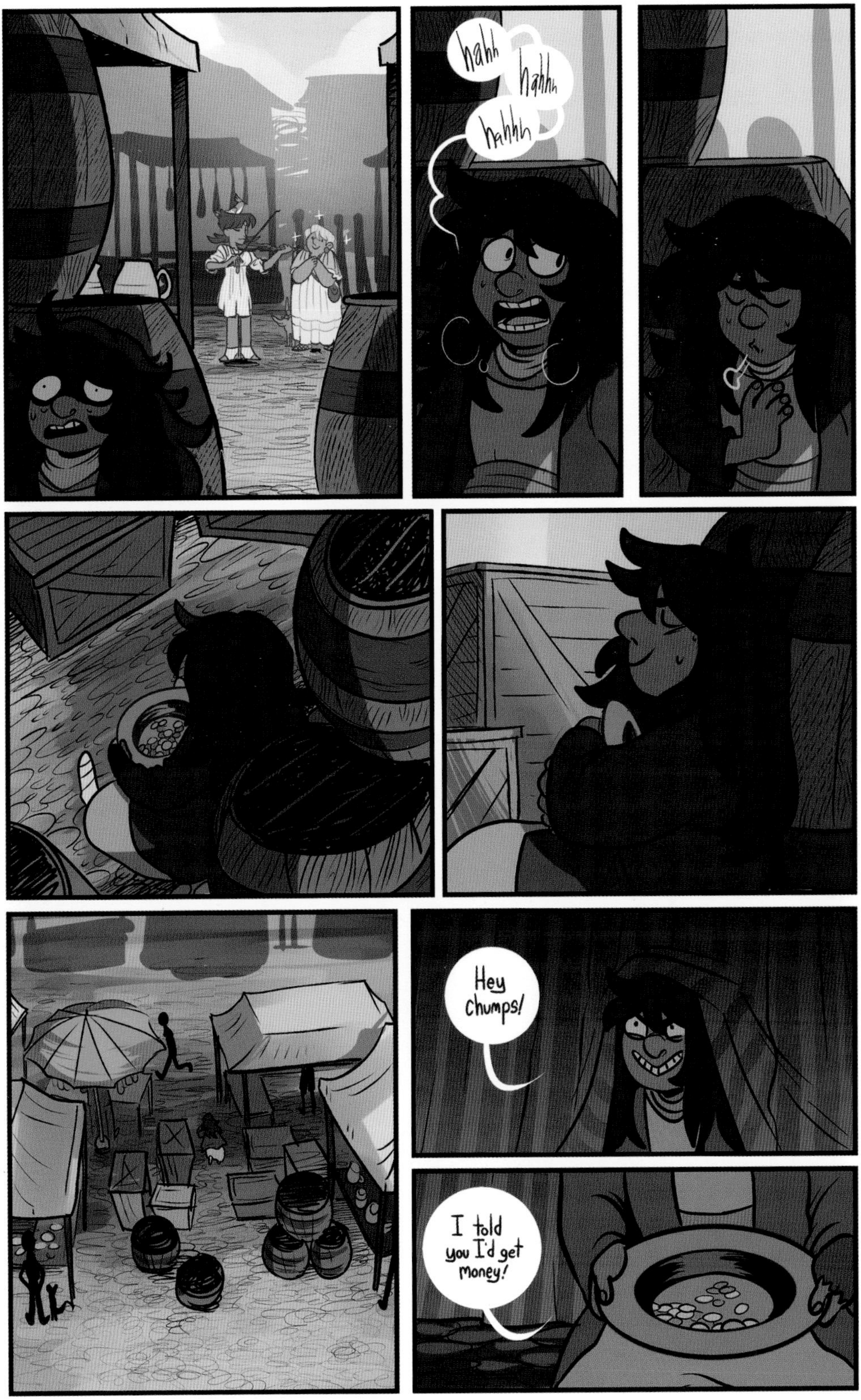
hahh
hahhh
hahhh
Hey chumps!
I told you I'd get money!

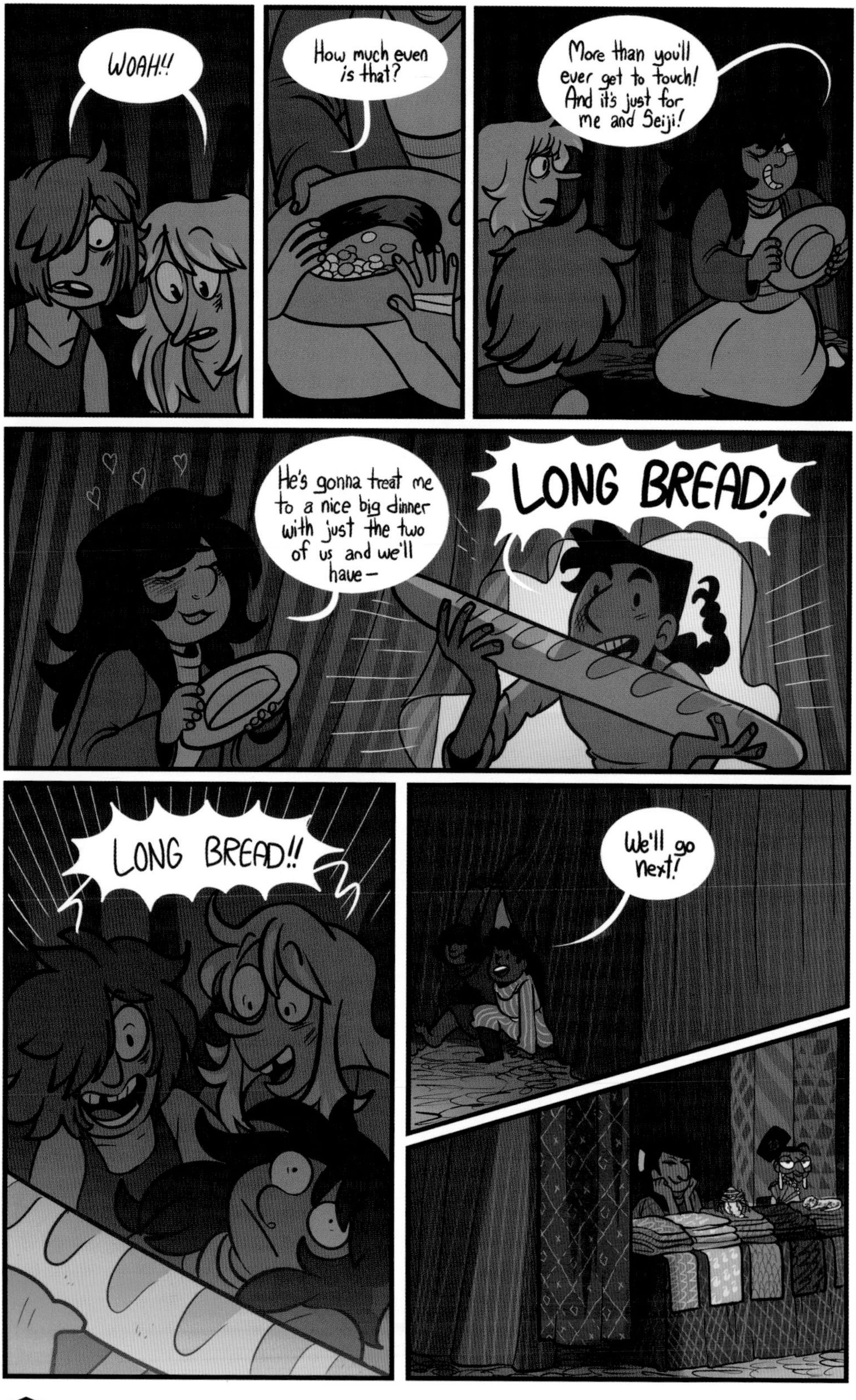
WOAH!!
How much even is that?
More than you'll ever get to touch! And it's just for me and Seiji!
He's gonna treat me to a nice big dinner with just the two of us and we'll have—
LONG BREAD!
LONG BREAD!!
We'll go next!

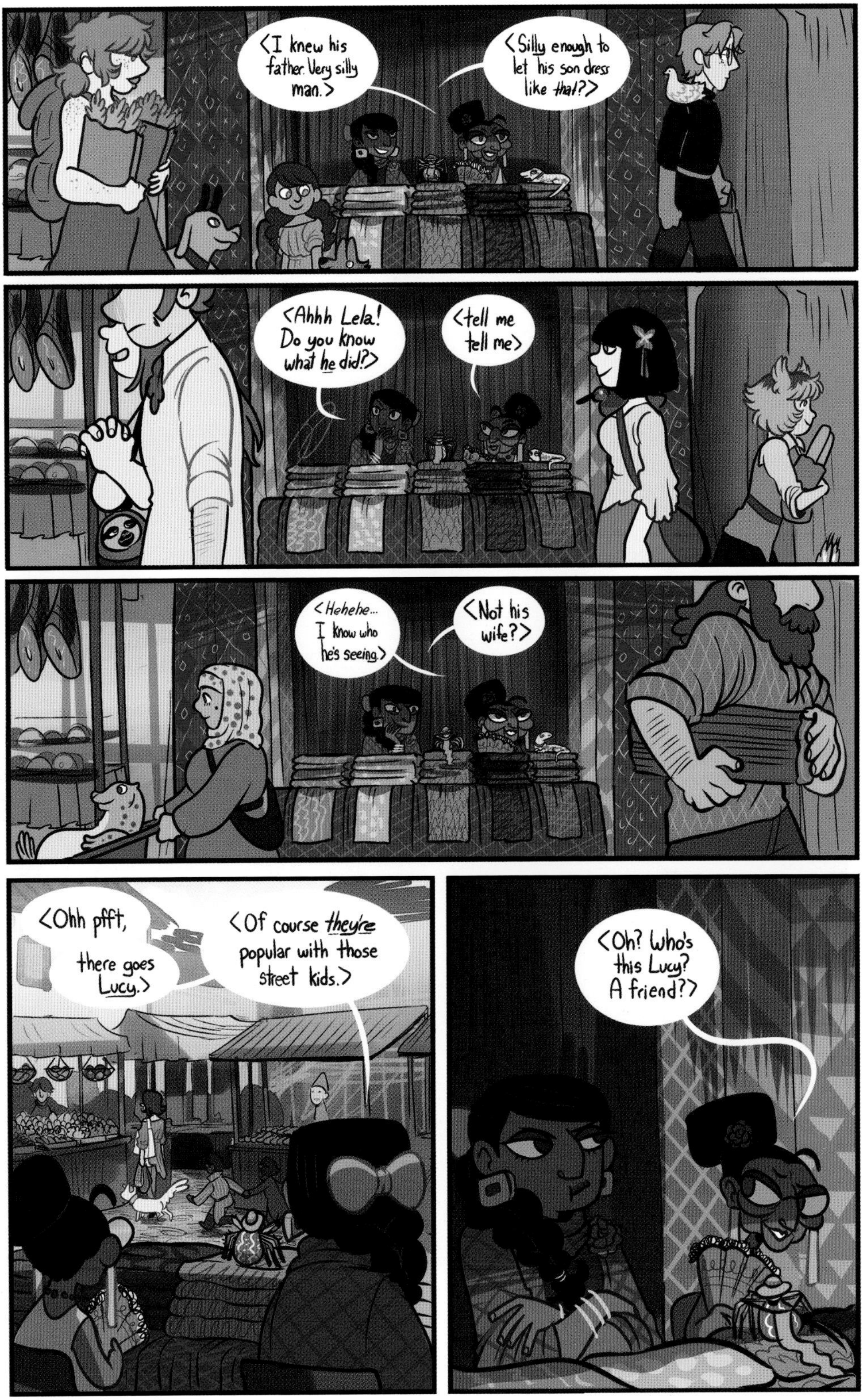

<I knew his father. Very silly man.>
<Silly enough to let his son dress like that?>
<Ahhh Lela! Do you know what he did?>
<tell me tell me>
<Hehehe... I know who he's seeing.>
<Not his wife?>
<Ohh pfft, there goes Lucy.>
<Of course they're popular with those street kids.>
<Oh? Who's this Lucy? A friend?>

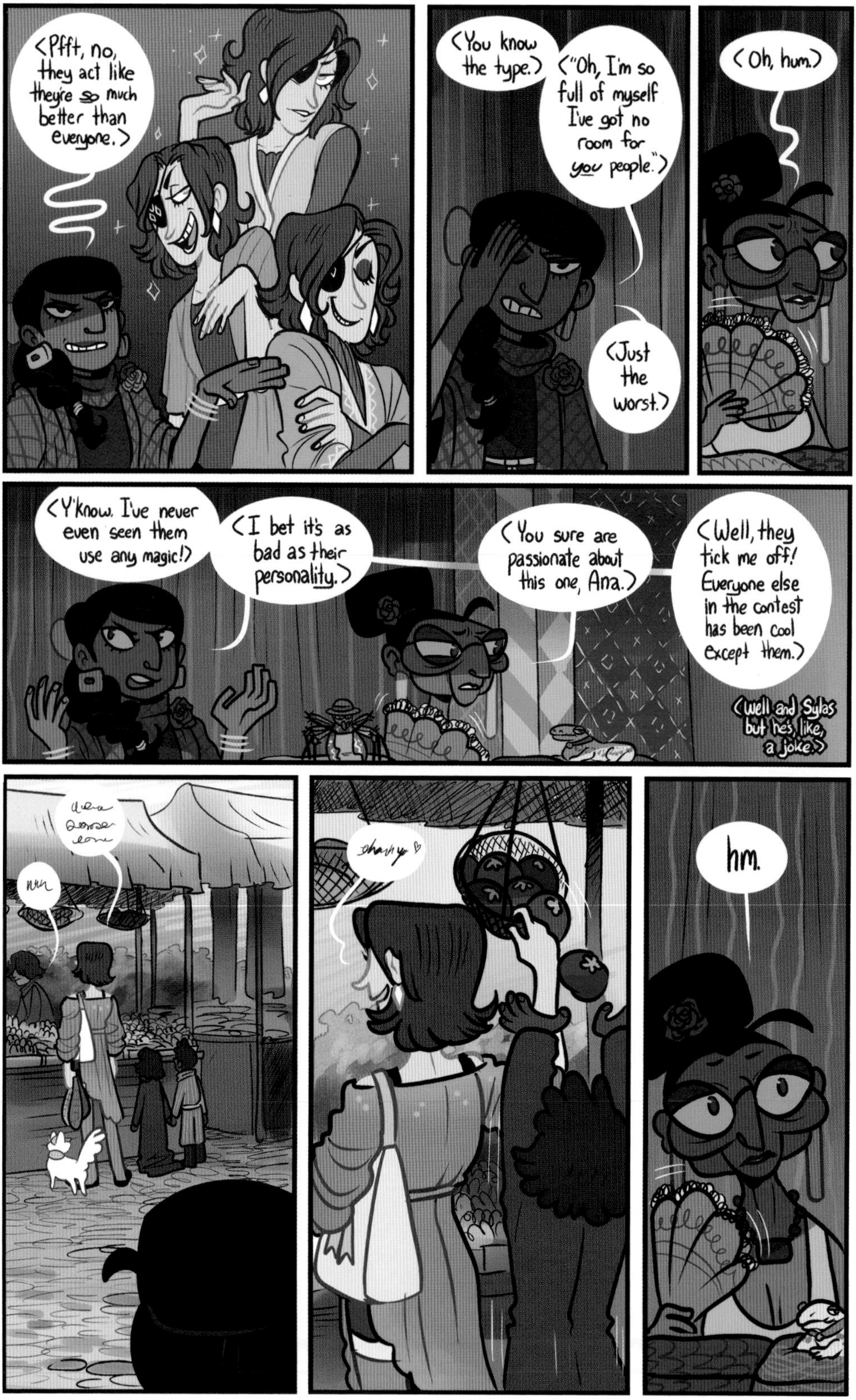
<Pfft, no, they act like they're so much better than everyone.>
<You know the type.>
<"Oh, I'm so full of myself I've got no room for you people.">
<Just the worst.>
<Oh, hum.>
<Y'know. I've never even seen them use any magic!>
<I bet it's as bad as their personality.>
<You sure are passionate about this one, Ana.>
<Well, they tick me off! Everyone else in the contest has been cool except them.>
<Well and Sylas but he's, like, a joke.>
hm.

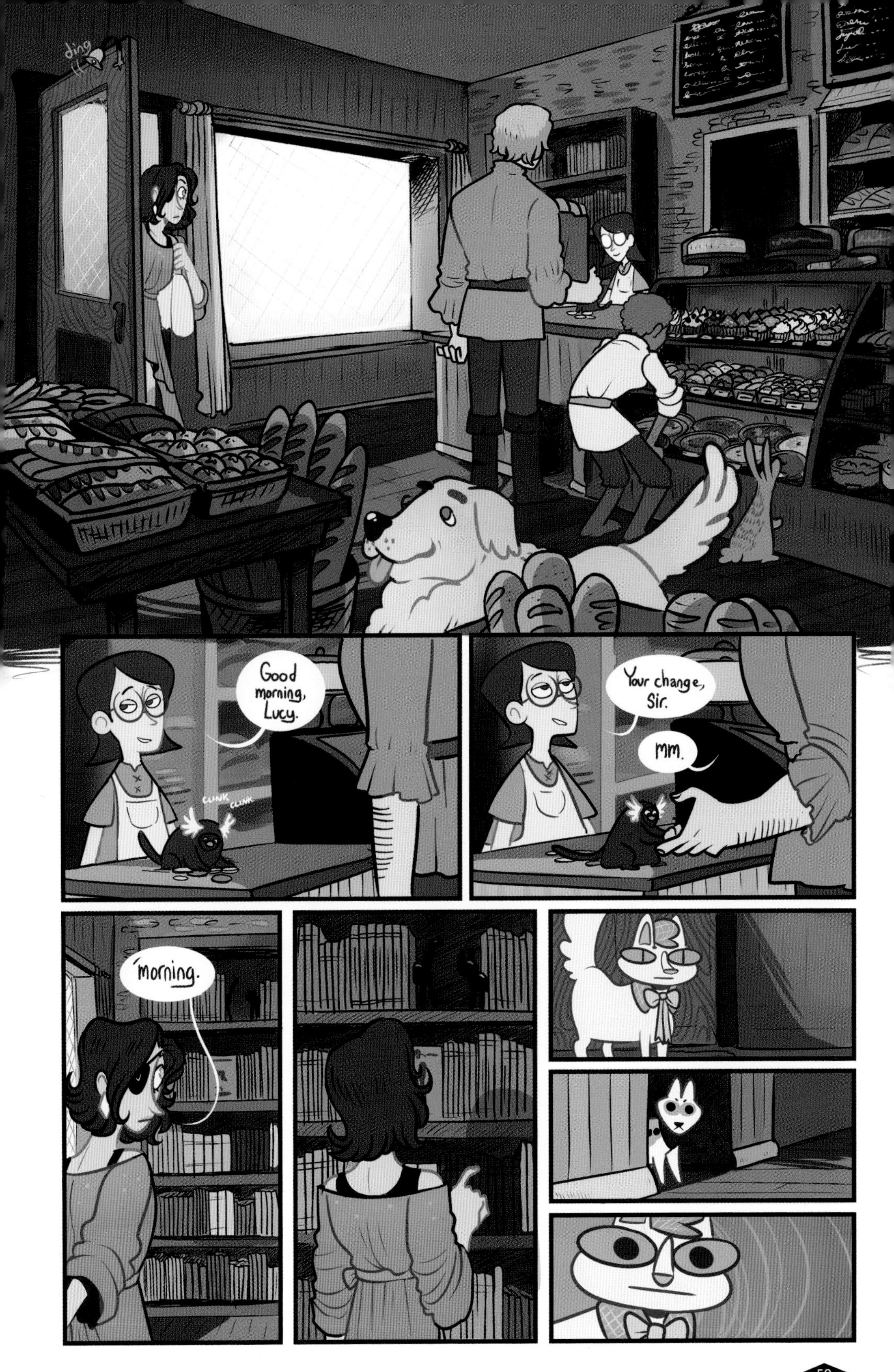
ding
Good morning, Lucy.
CLINK CLINK
Your change, sir.
mm.
'morning.

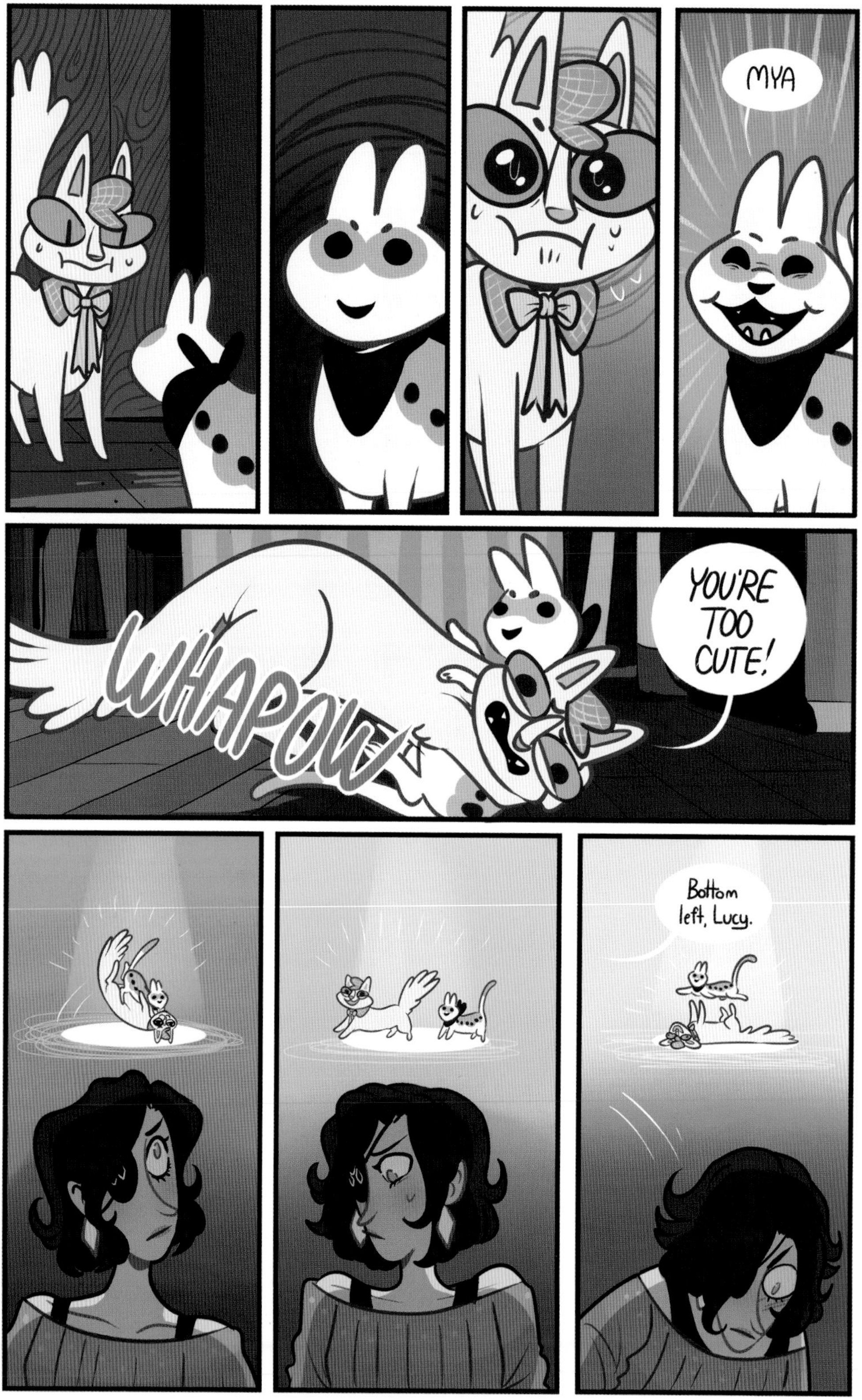
MYA
WHAPOW
YOU'RE TOO CUTE!
Bottom left, Lucy.

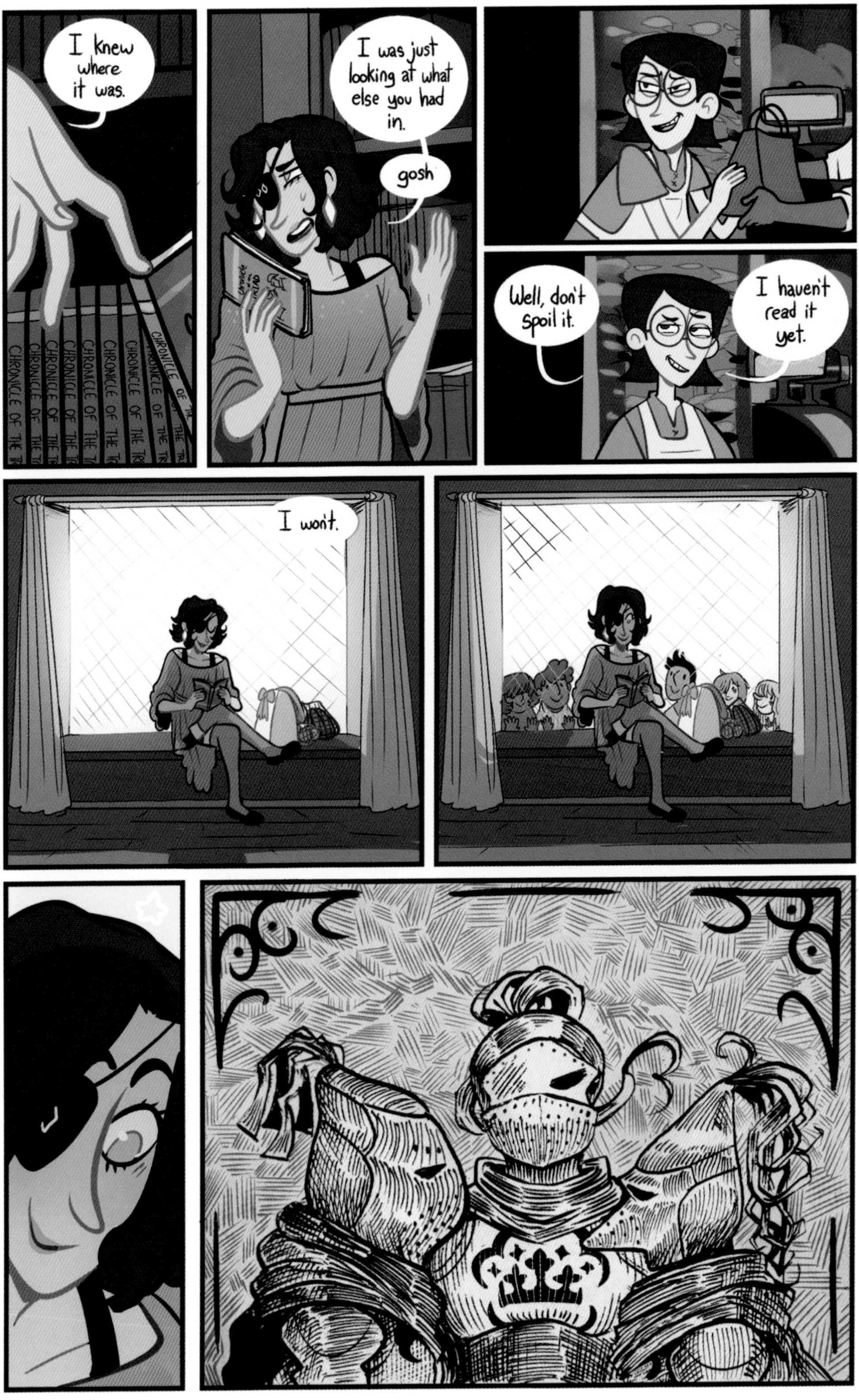
I knew where it was.
CHRONICLE OF THE TR
I was just looking at what else you had in.
gosh
Well, don't spoil it.
I haven't read it yet.
I won't.

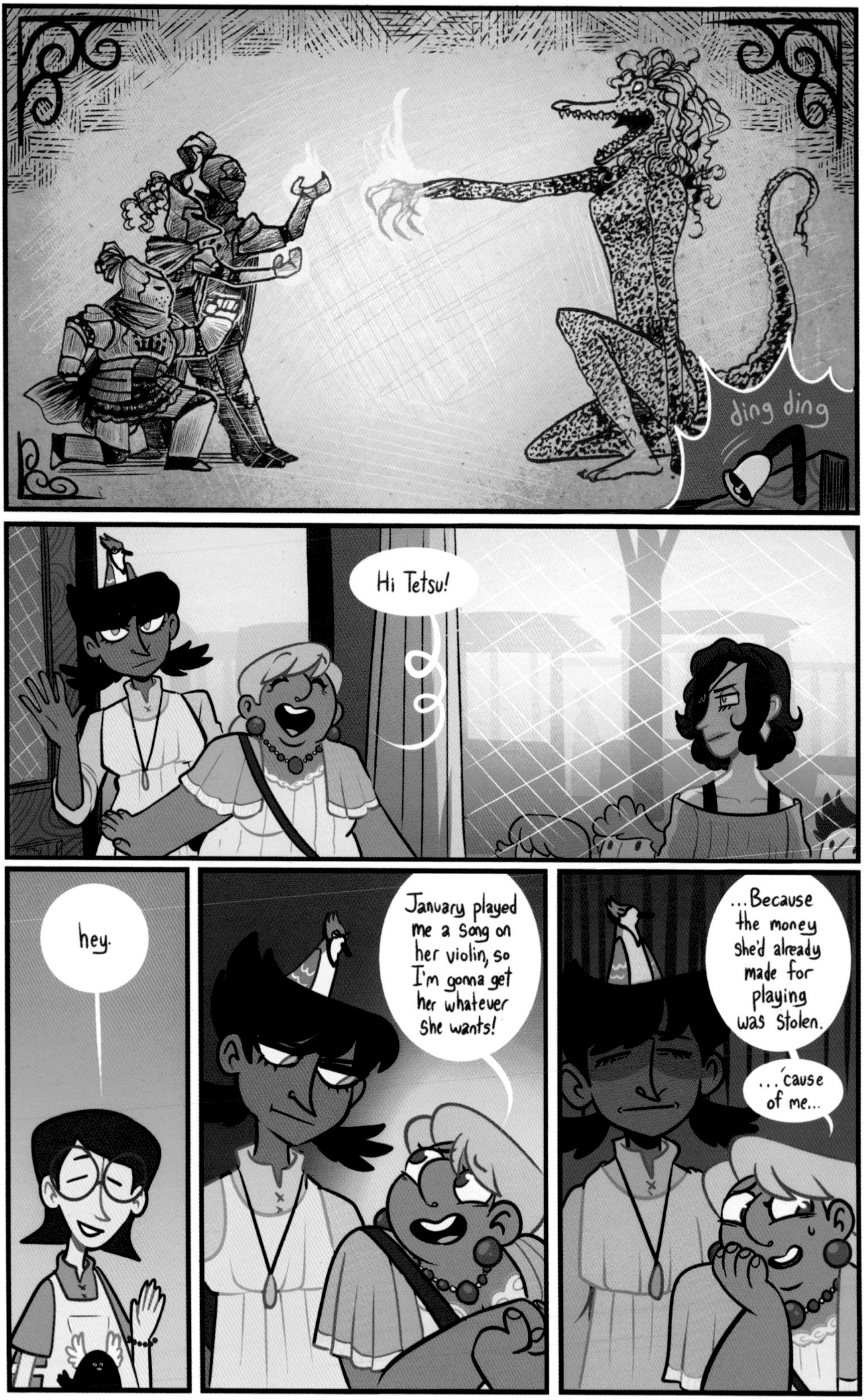
ding ding
Hi Tetsu!
hey.
January played me a Song on her violin, so I'm gonna get her whatever she wants!
...Because the money she'd already made for playing was stolen.
...'cause of me...

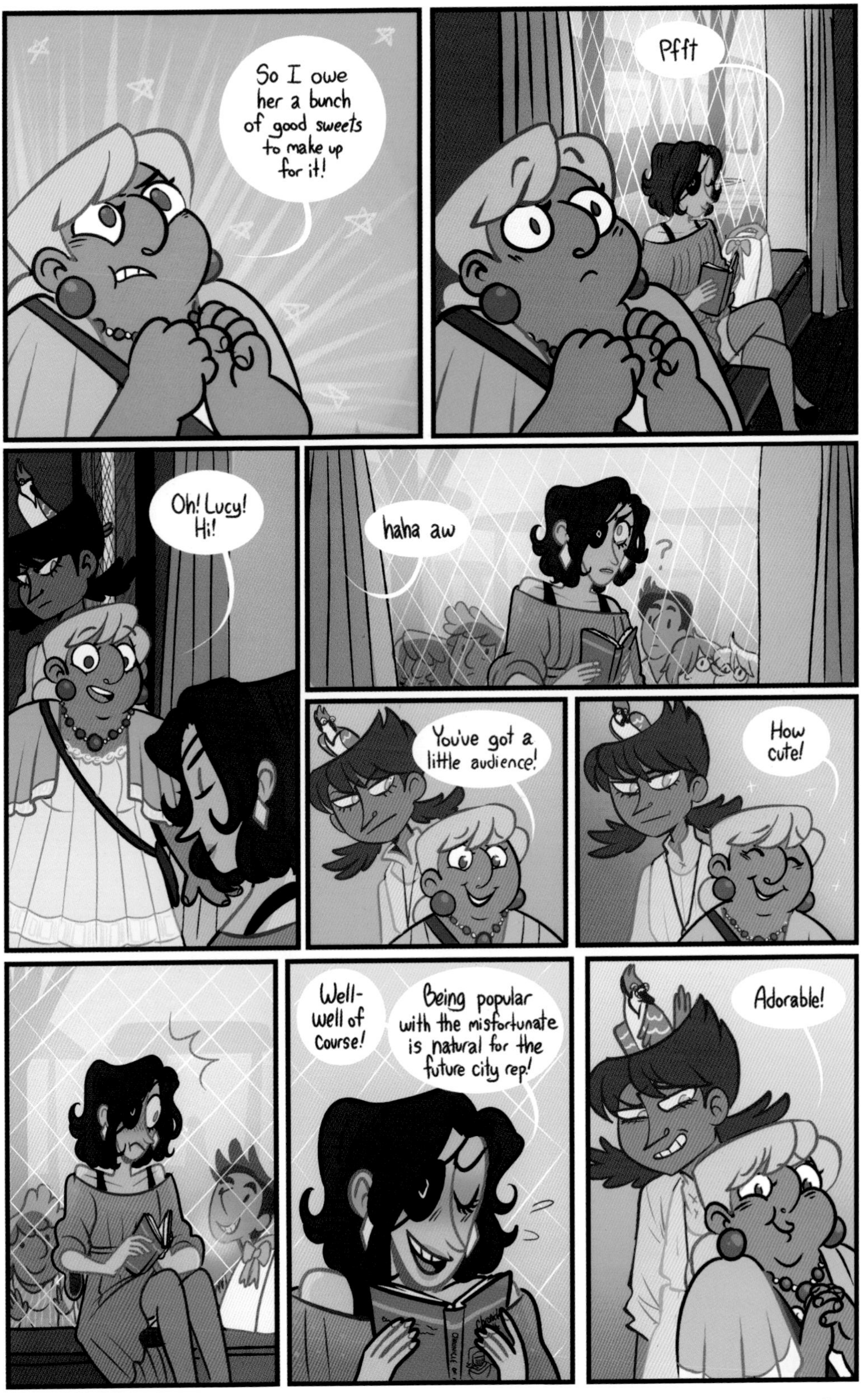
So I owe her a bunch of good sweets to make up for it!
Pfft
Oh! Lucy! Hi!
haha aw
?
You've got a little audience!
How cute!
Well- well of course!
Being popular with the misfortunate is natural for the future city rep!
Adorable!

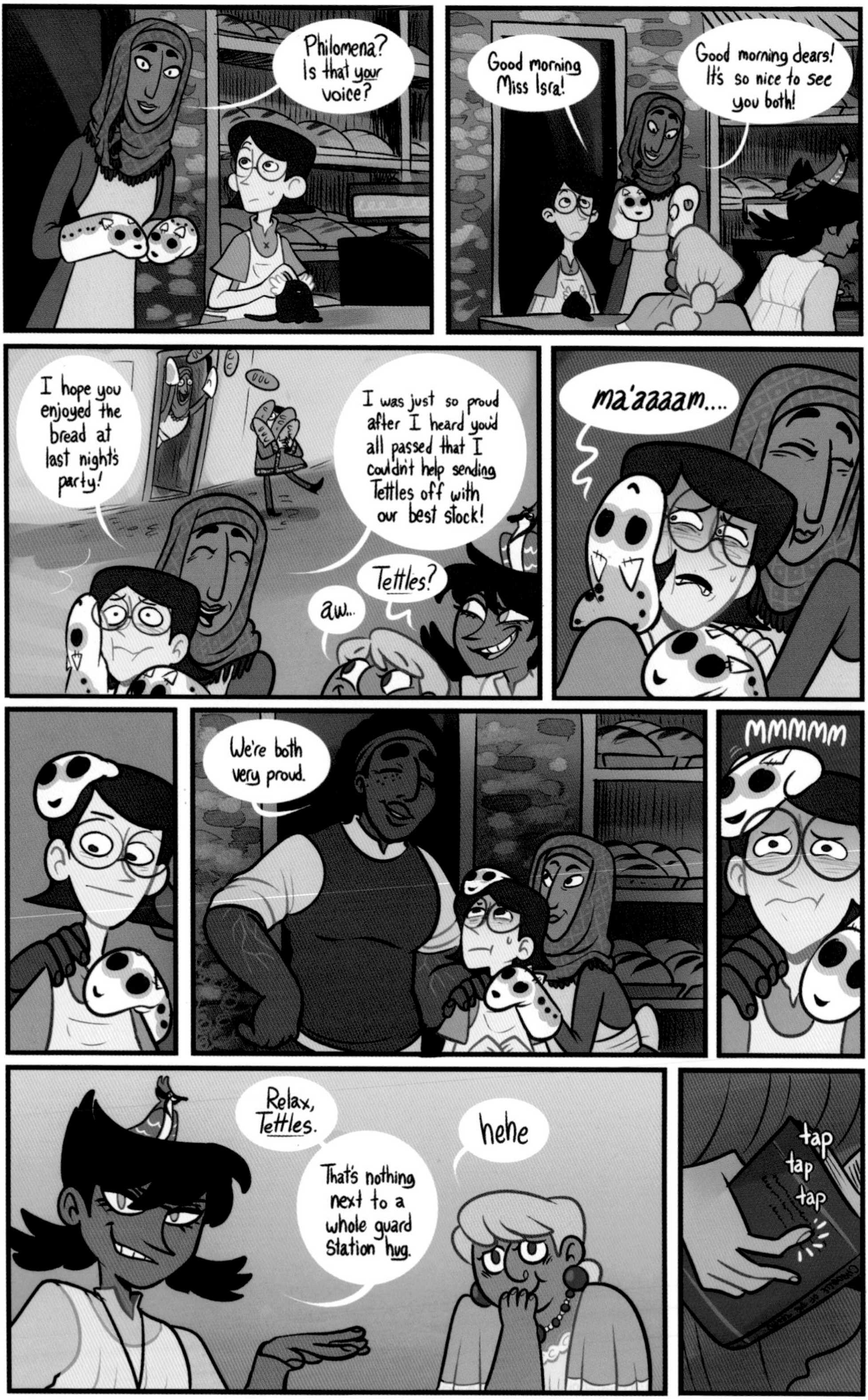

Philomena? Is that your voice?
Good morning Miss Isra!
Good morning dears! It's so nice to see you both!
I hope you enjoyed the bread at last night's party!
I was just so proud after I heard you'd all passed that I couldn't help sending Tettles off with our best stock!
Tettles?
aw...
ma'aaaam....
We're both very proud.
MMMMM
Relax, Tettles.
That's nothing next to a whole guard station hug.
hehe
tap
tap
tap

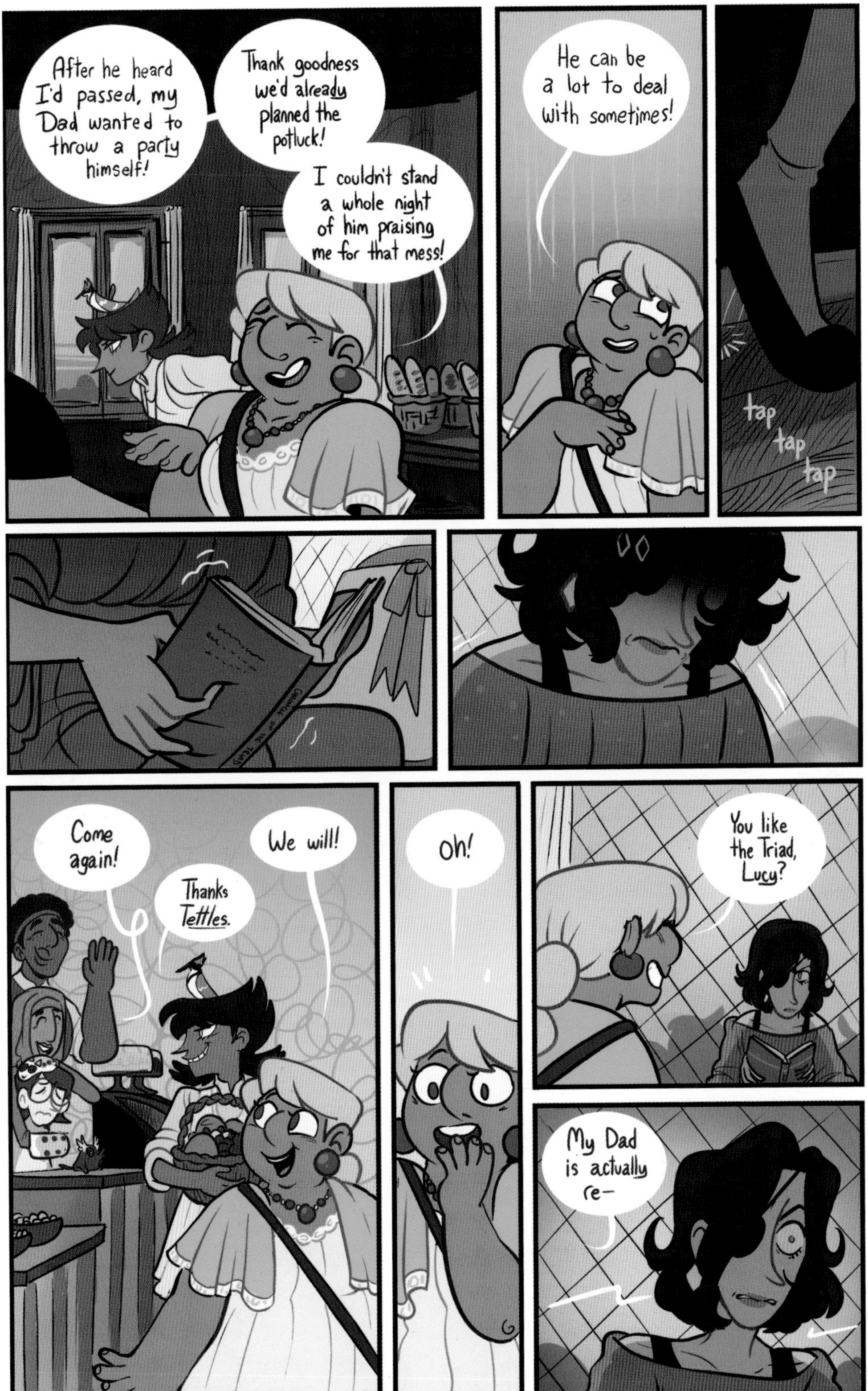
After he heard I'd passed, my Dad wanted to throw a party himself!
Thank goodness we'd already planned the potluck!
I couldn't stand a whole night of him praising me for that mess!
He can be a lot to deal with sometimes!
tap
tap
tap
Come again!
Thanks Tettles.
We will!
Oh!
You like the Triad, Lucy?
My Dad is actually re-

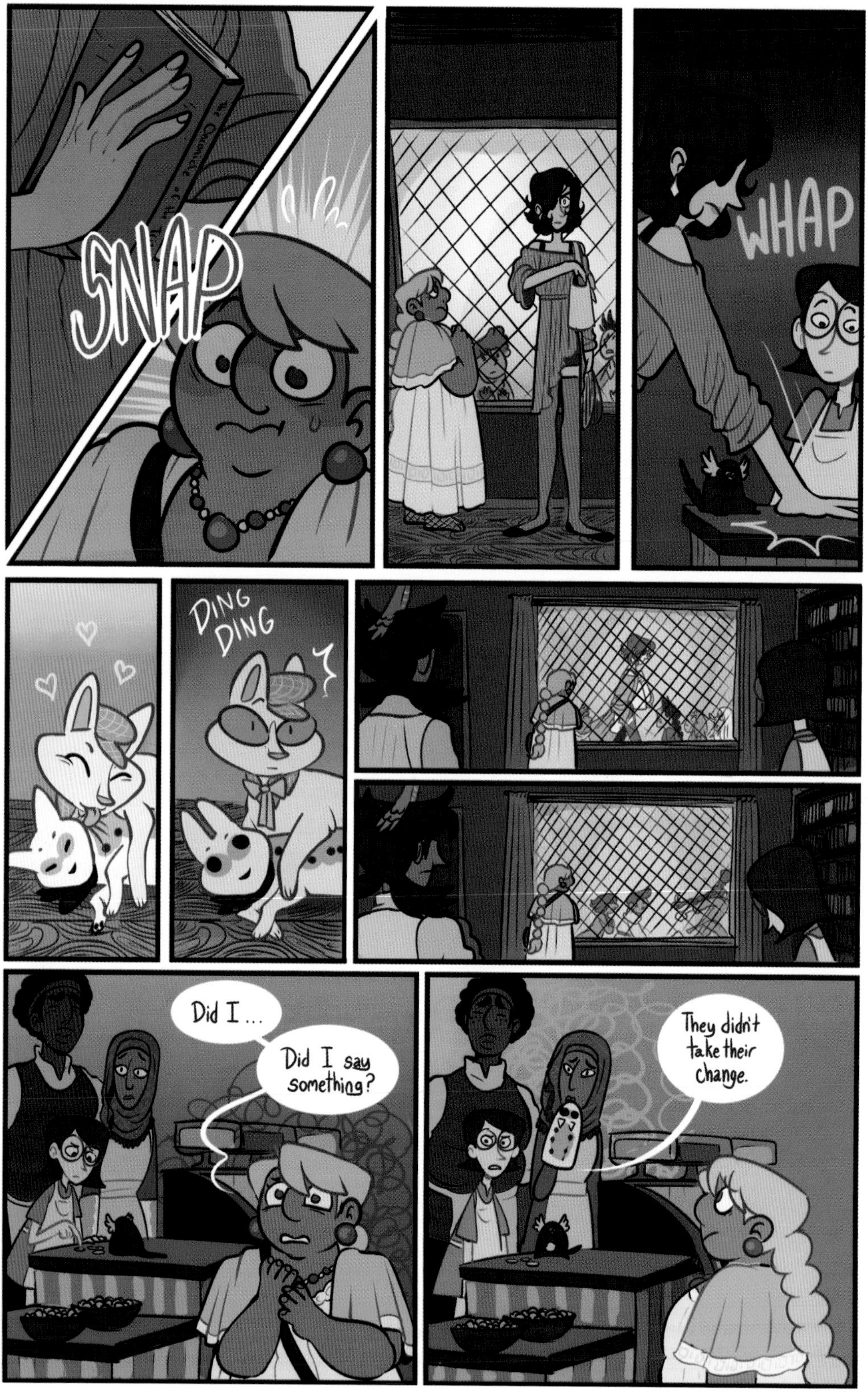
SNAP
WHAP
DING
DING
Did I...
Did I say something?
They didn't take their change.

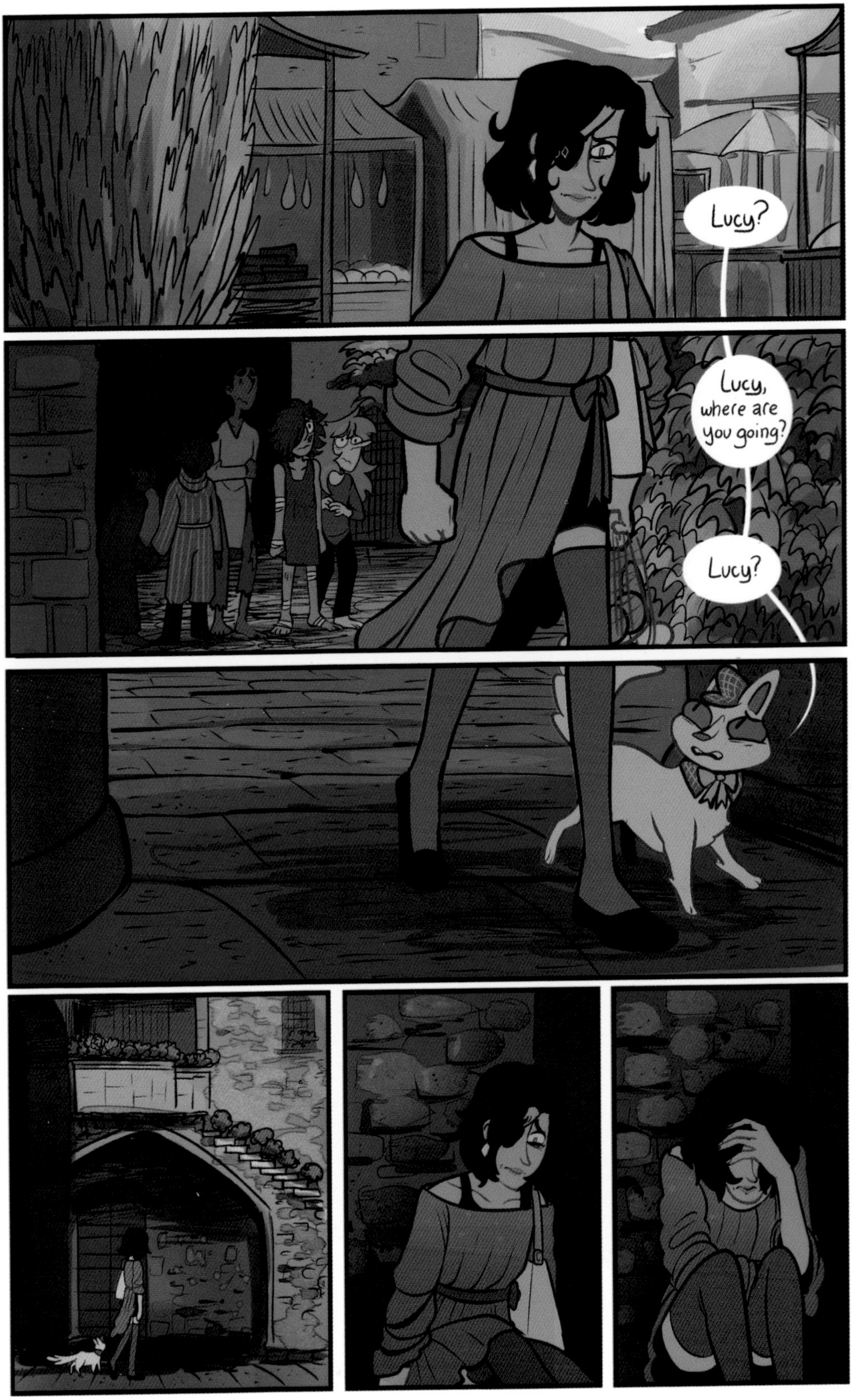
Lucy?
Lucy, where are you going?
Lucy?

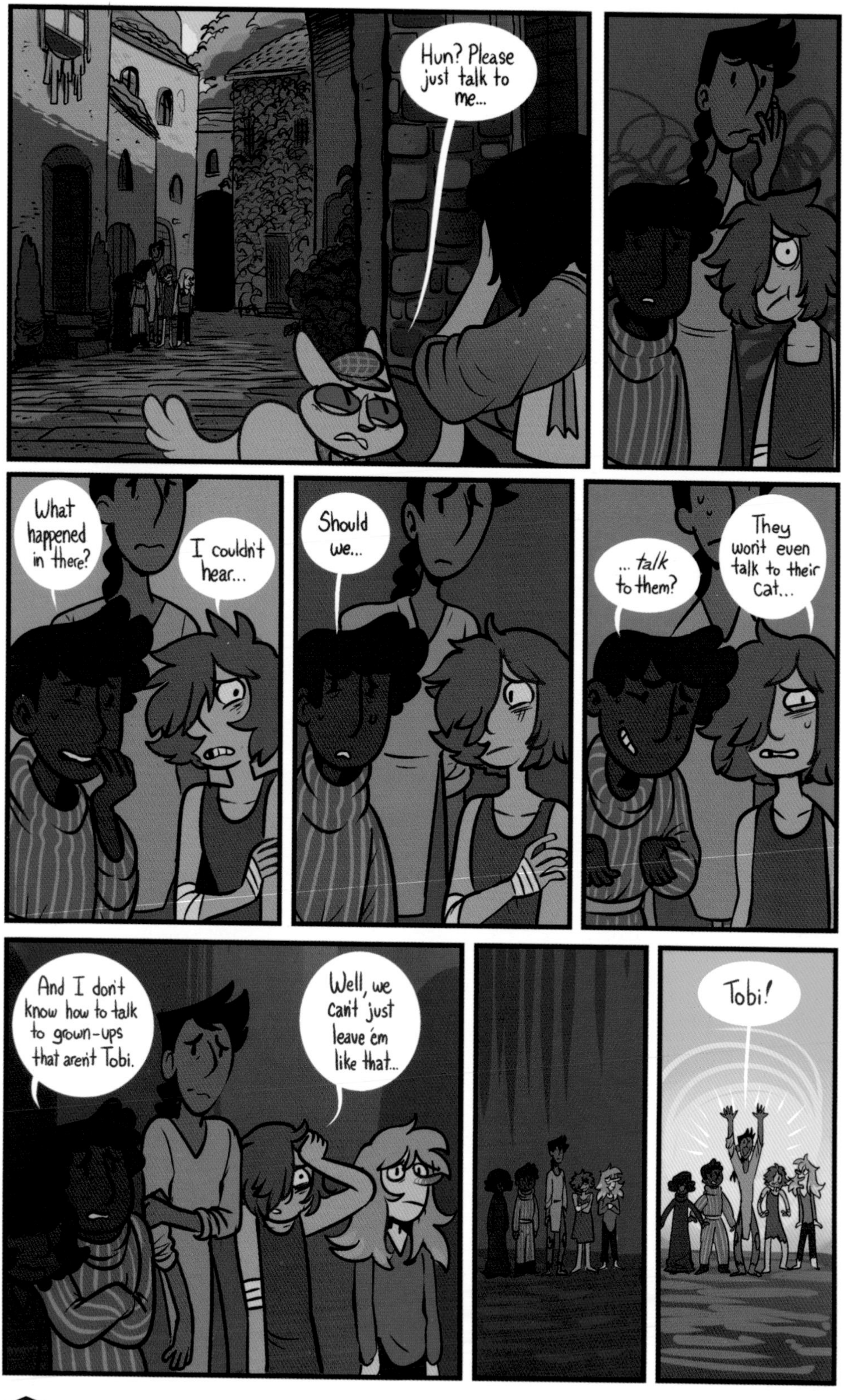

Hun? Please just talk to me...
What happened in there?
I couldn't hear...
Should we...
... *talk* to them?
They won't even talk to their cat...
And I don't know how to talk to grown-ups that aren't Tobi.
Well, we can't just leave 'em like that...
Tobi!

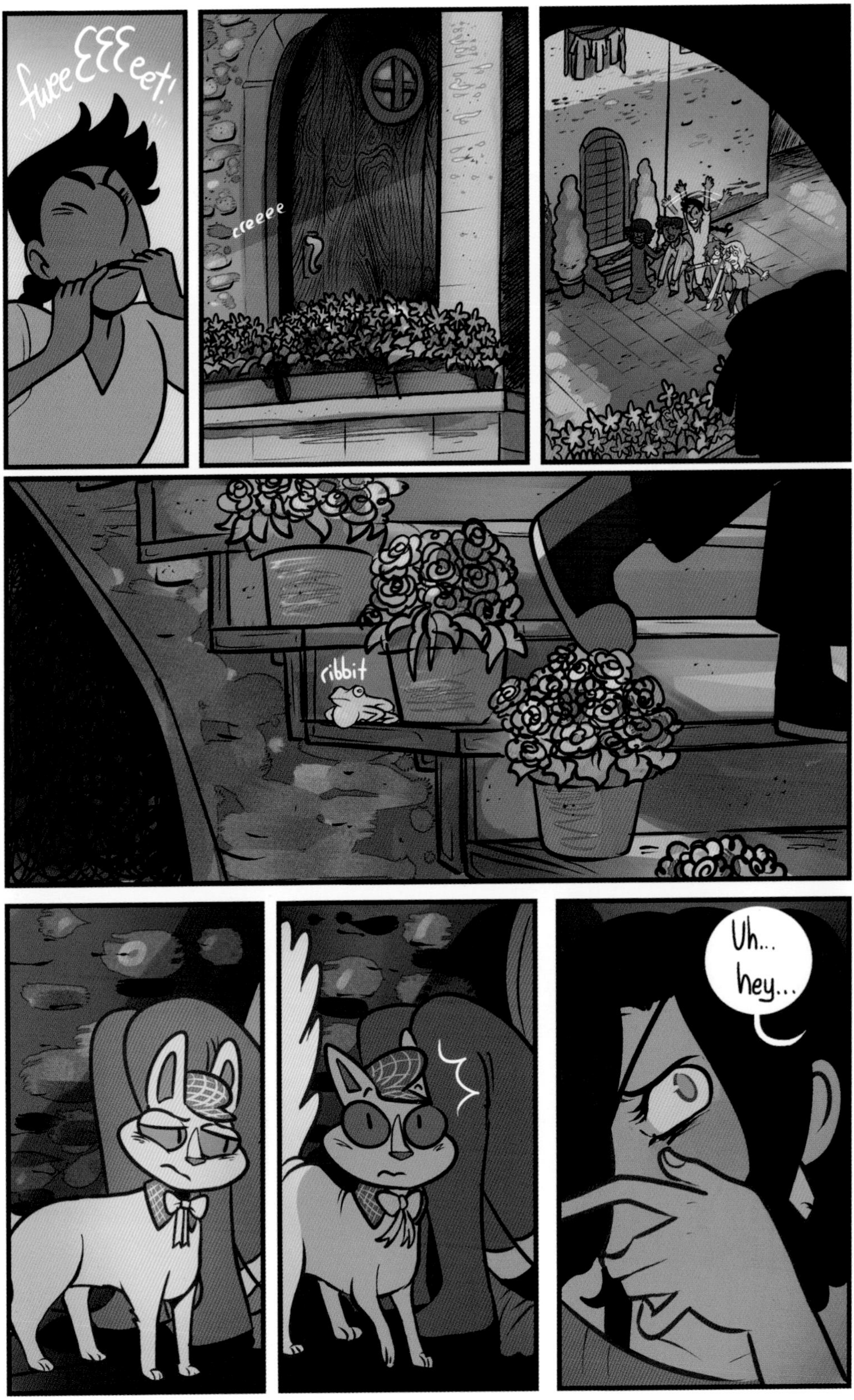
fweeEEEeet!
creeee
ribbit
Uh... hey...

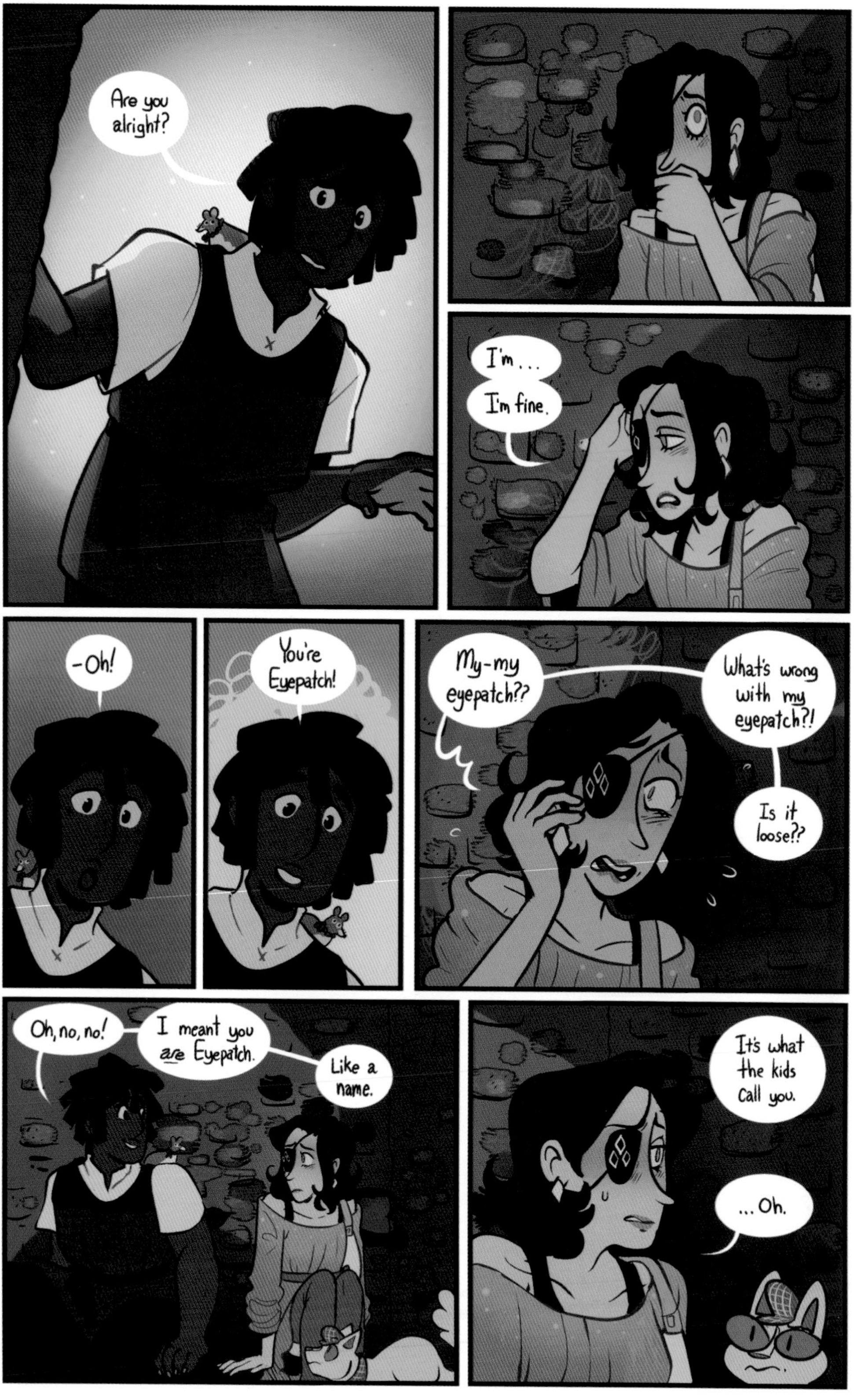

Are you alright?
I'm...
I'm fine.
-Oh!
You're Eyepatch!
My-my eyepatch??
What's wrong with my eyepatch?!
Is it loose??
Oh, no, no!
I meant you are Eyepatch.
Like a name.
It's what the kids call you.
...Oh.

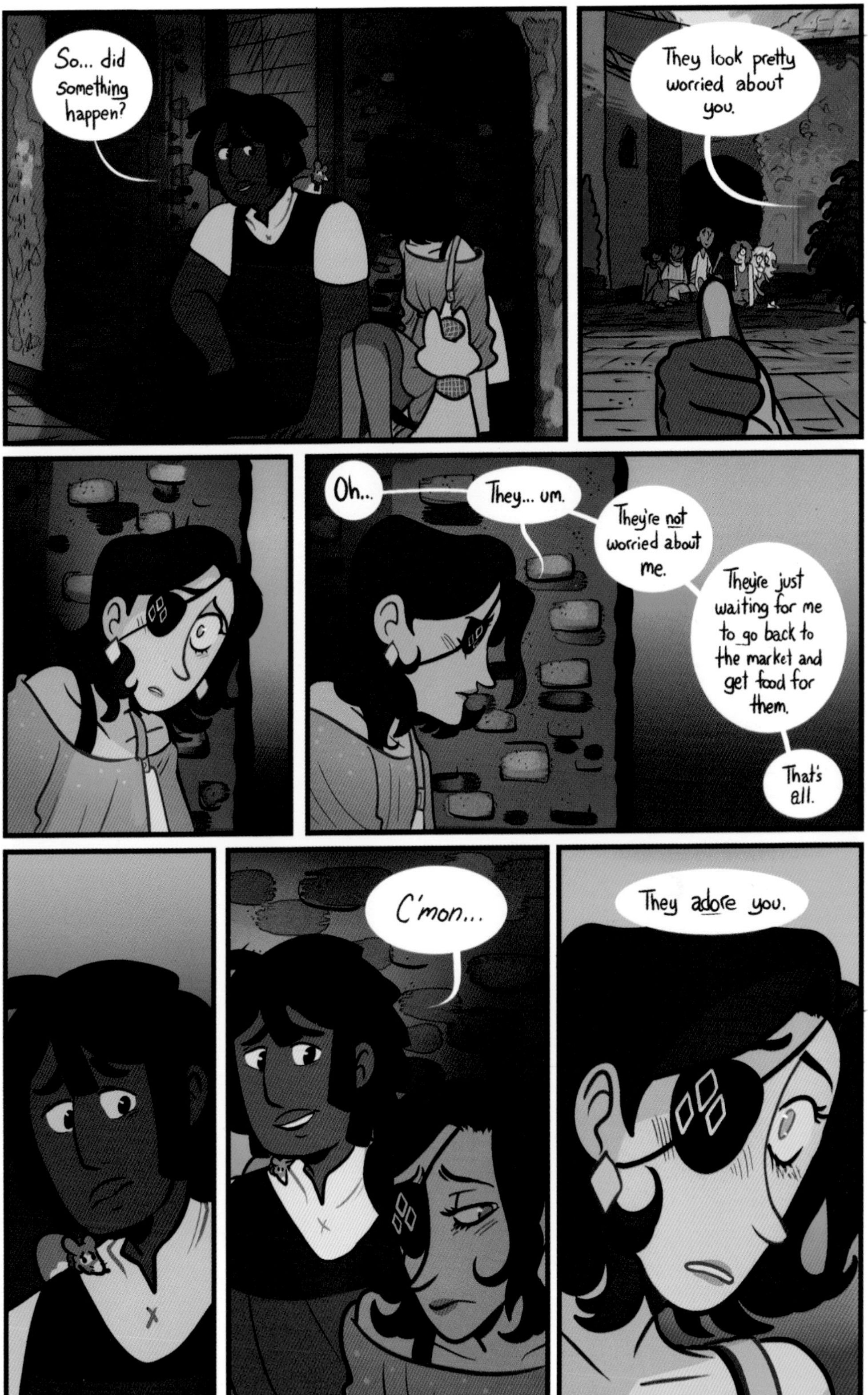
So... did something happen?
They look pretty worried about you.
Oh...
They... um.
They're not worried about me.
They're just waiting for me to go back to the market and get food for them.
That's all.
C'mon...
They adore you.

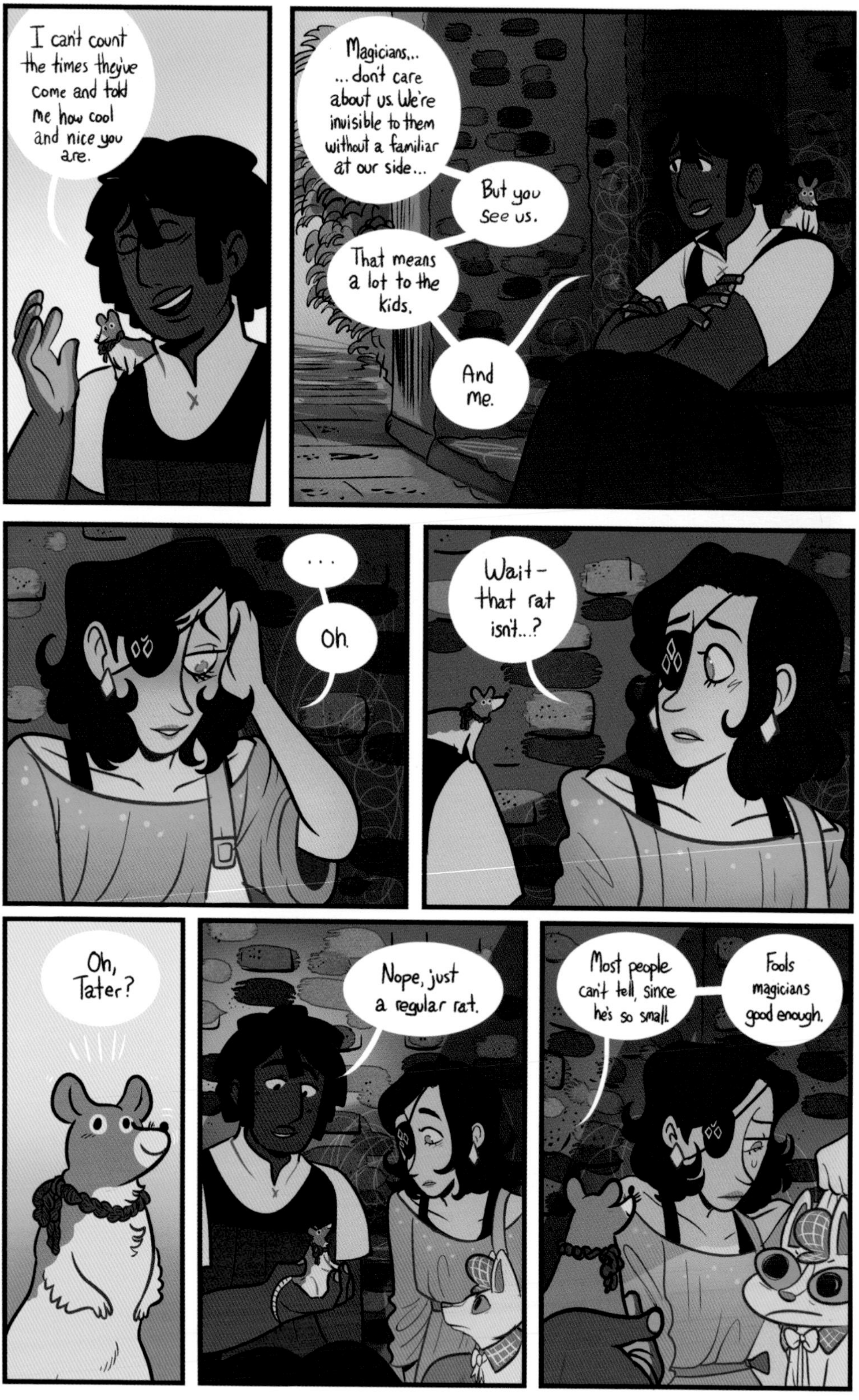
I can't count the times they've come and told me how cool and nice you are.
Magicians... ...don't care about us. We're invisible to them without a familiar at our side...
But you see us.
That means a lot to the kids.
And me.
...
Oh.
Wait- that rat isn't...?
Oh, Tater?
Nope, just a regular rat.
Most people can't tell, since he's so small.
Fools magicians good enough.

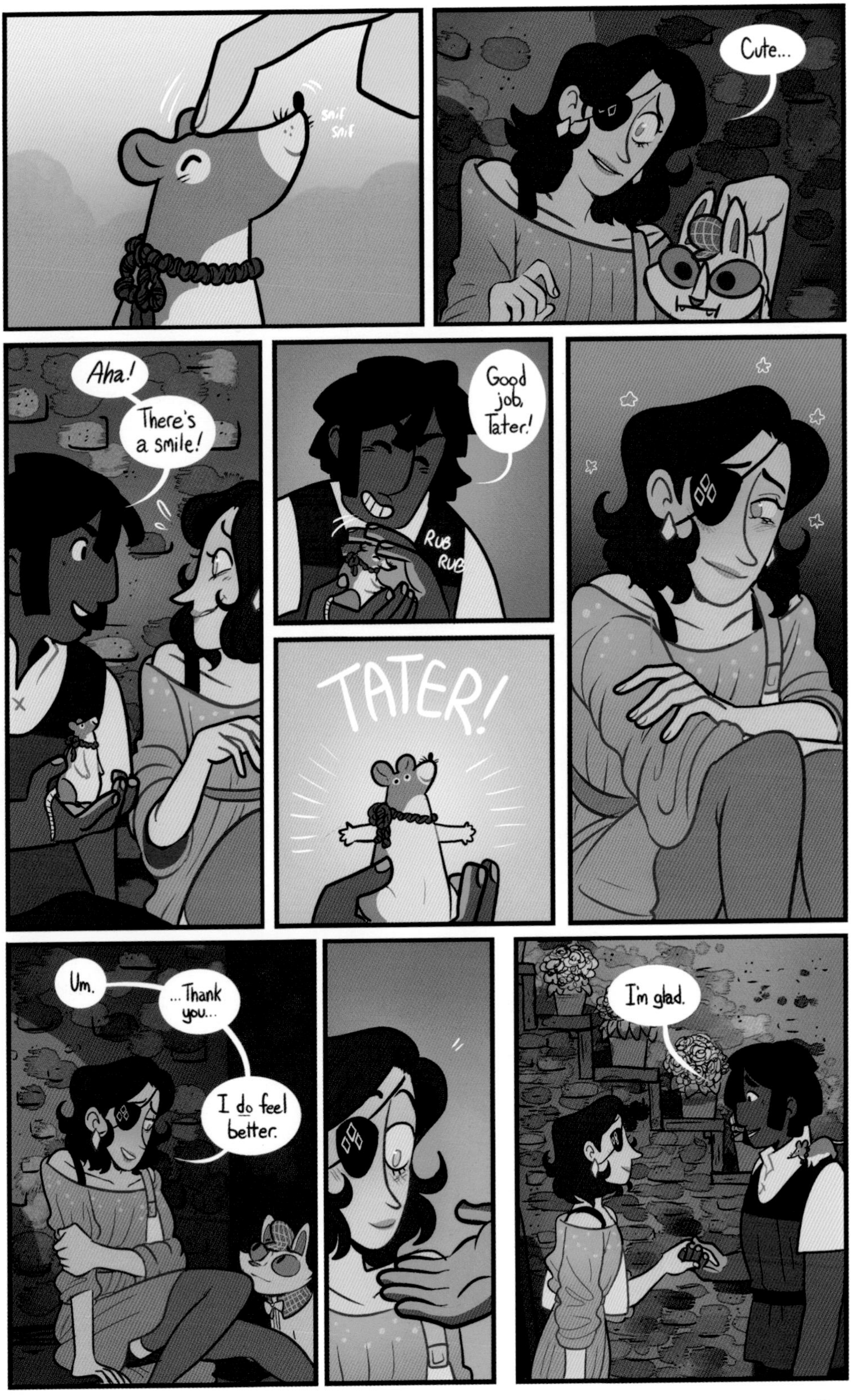
snif
snif
Cute...
Aha!
There's a smile!
Good job, Tater!
RUB
RUB
TATER!
Um.
...Thank you...
I do feel better.
I'm glad.

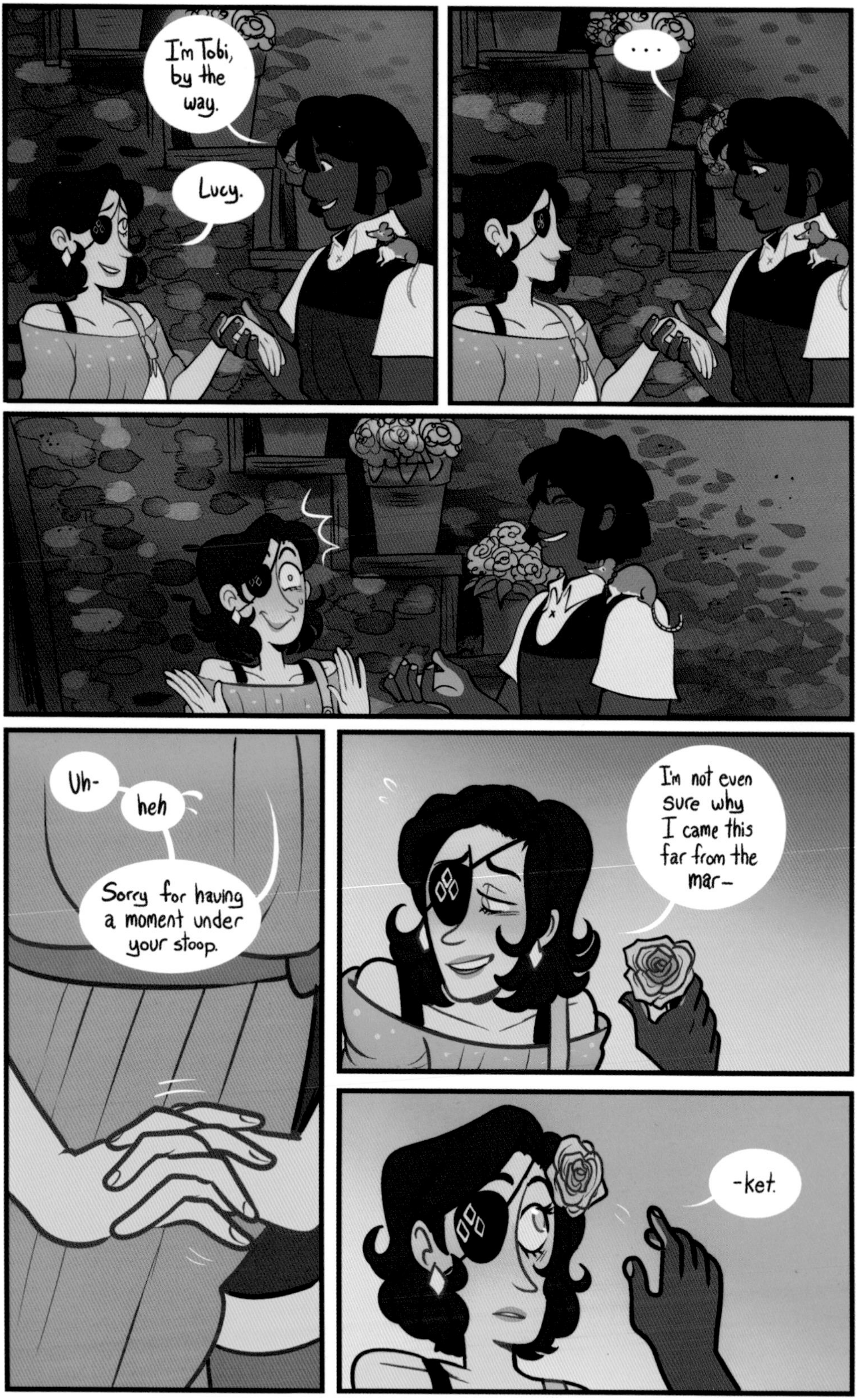

I'm Tobi, by the way.
Lucy.
...
Uh-
heh
Sorry for having a moment under your stoop.
I'm not even sure why I came this far from the mar-
-ket.

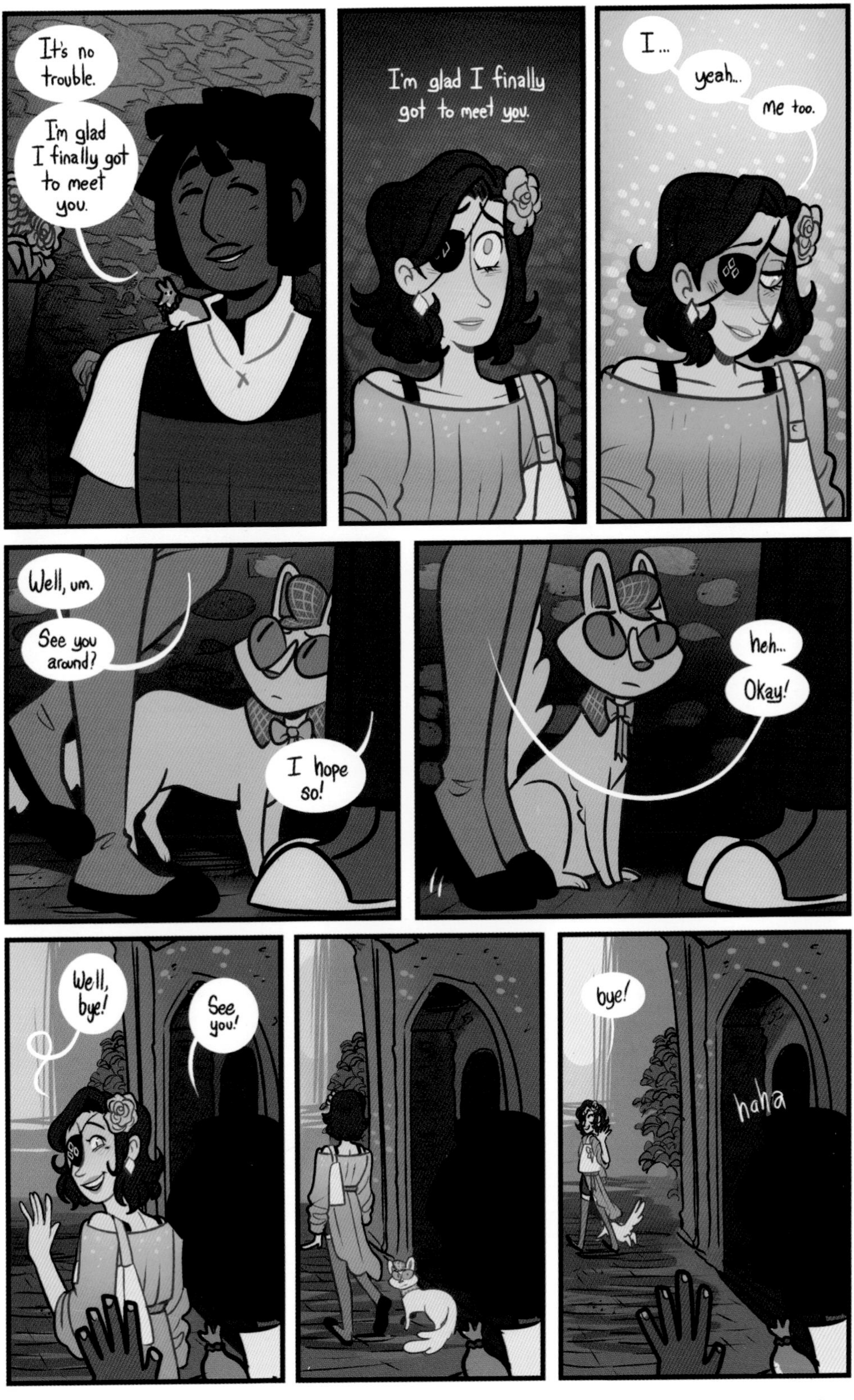
It's no trouble.
I'm glad I finally got to meet you.
I'm glad I finally got to meet you.
I...
yeah...
me too.
Well, um.
See you around?
I hope so!
heh...
Okay!
Well, bye!
See you!
bye!
haha

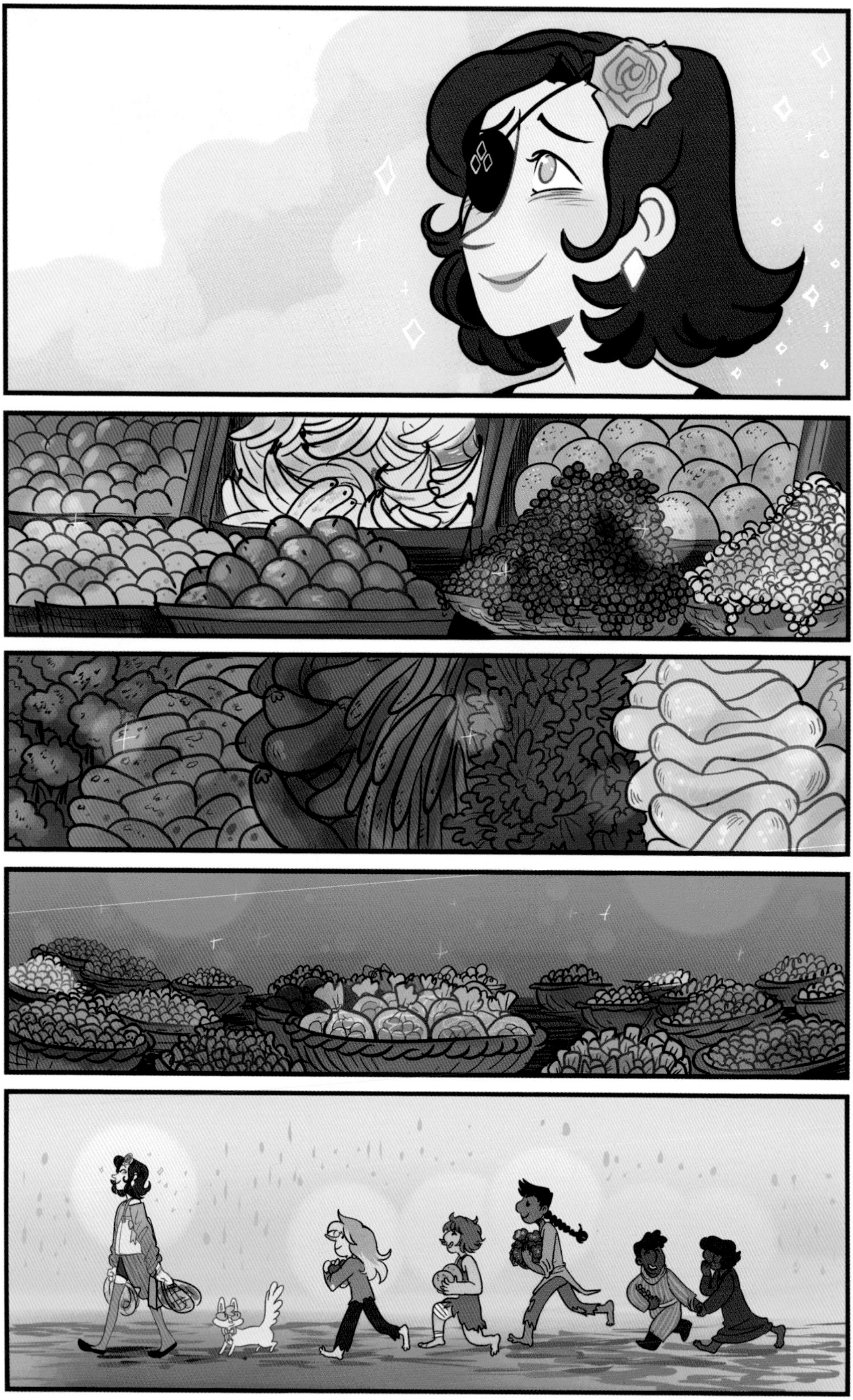

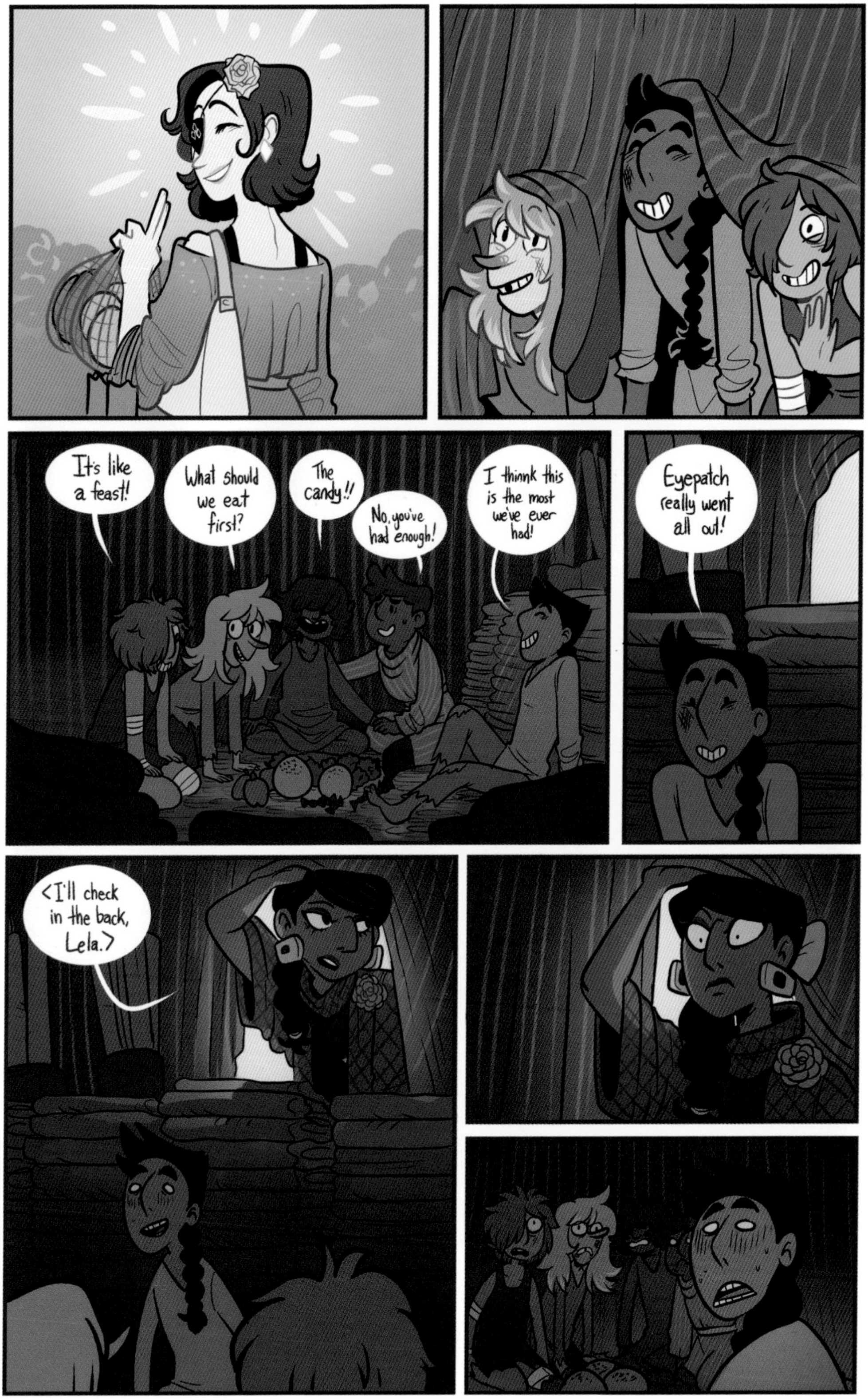
It's like a feast!
What should we eat first?
The candy!!
No, you've had enough!
I thinnk this is the most we've ever had!
Eyepatch really went all out!
<I'll check in the back, Lela.>

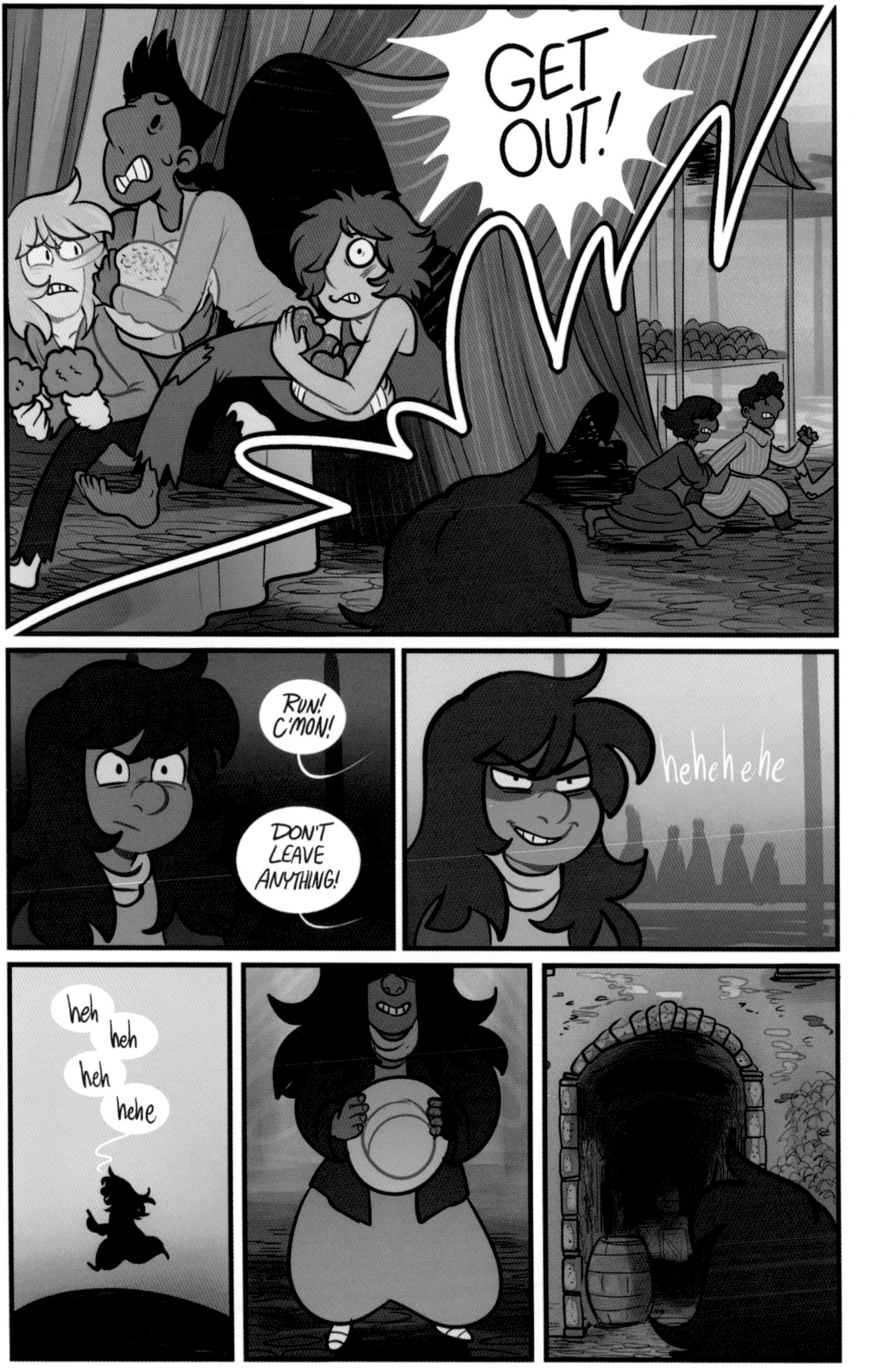
GET OUT!
RUN! C'MON!
DON'T LEAVE ANYTHING!
hehehehe
heh
heh
heh
hehe

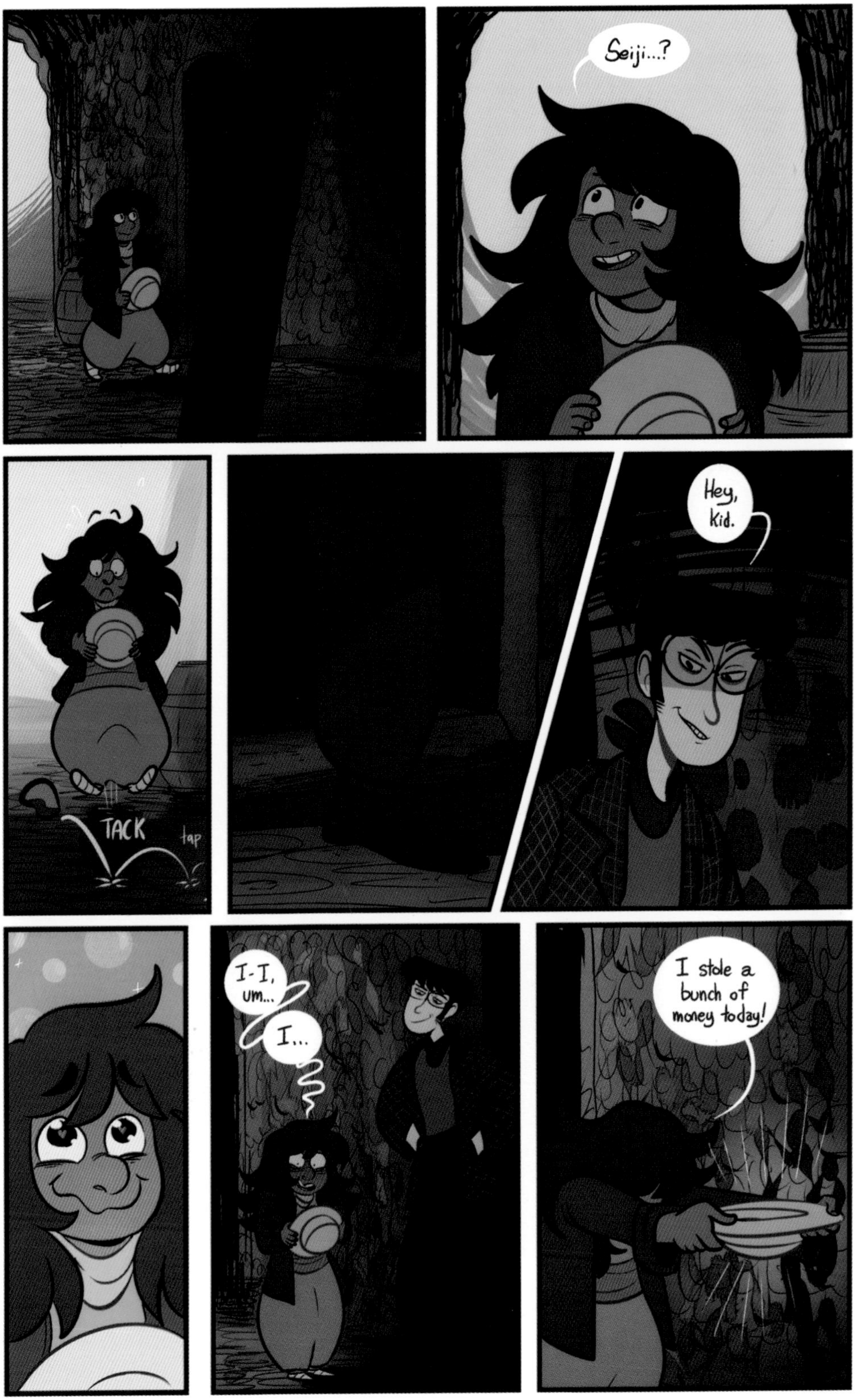

Seiji...?
TACK
tap
Hey, kid.
I-I, um...
I...
I stole a bunch of money today!

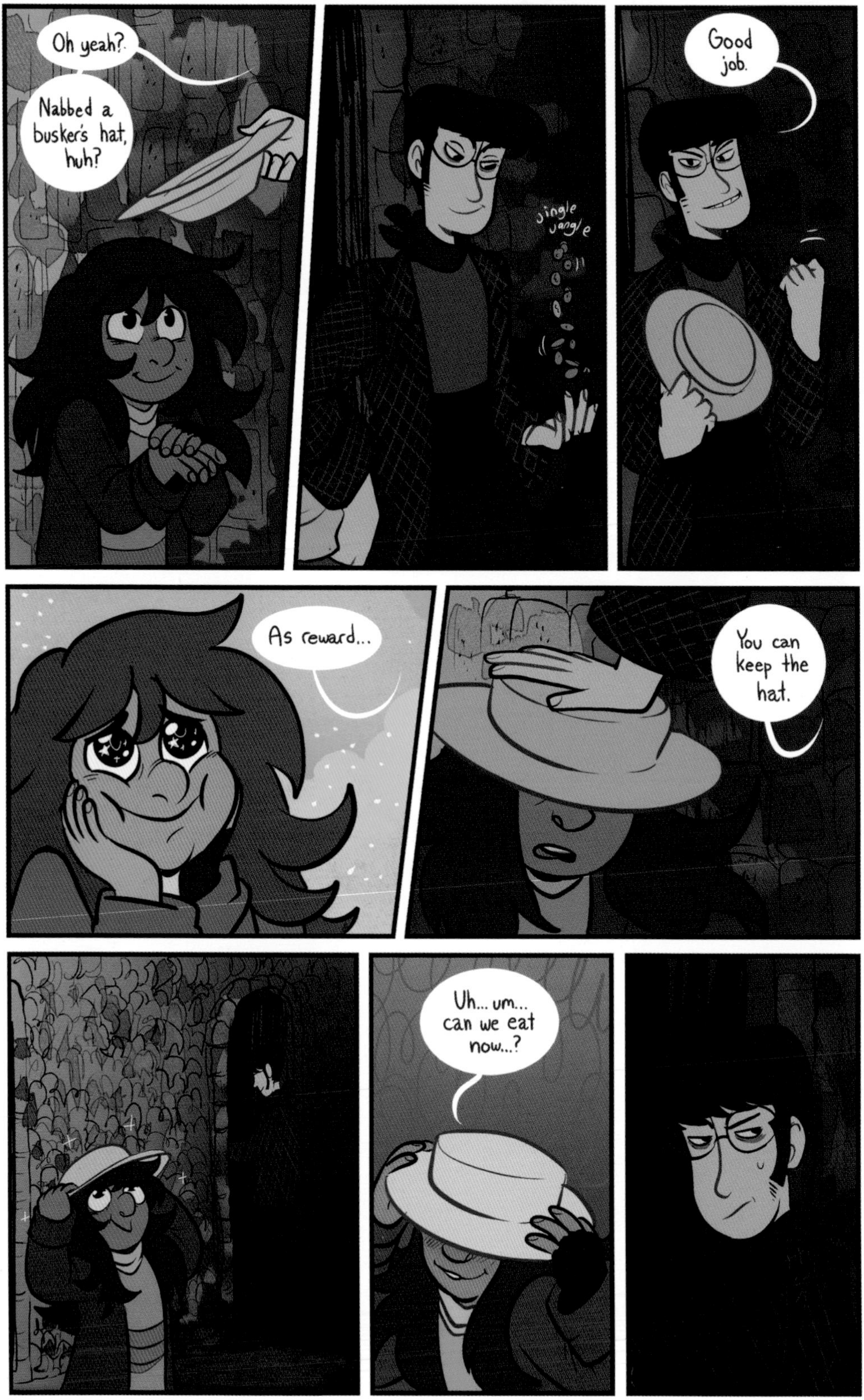
Oh yeah?
Nabbed a busker's hat, huh?
jingle jangle
Good job.
As reward...
You can keep the hat.
Uh... um... can we eat now...?

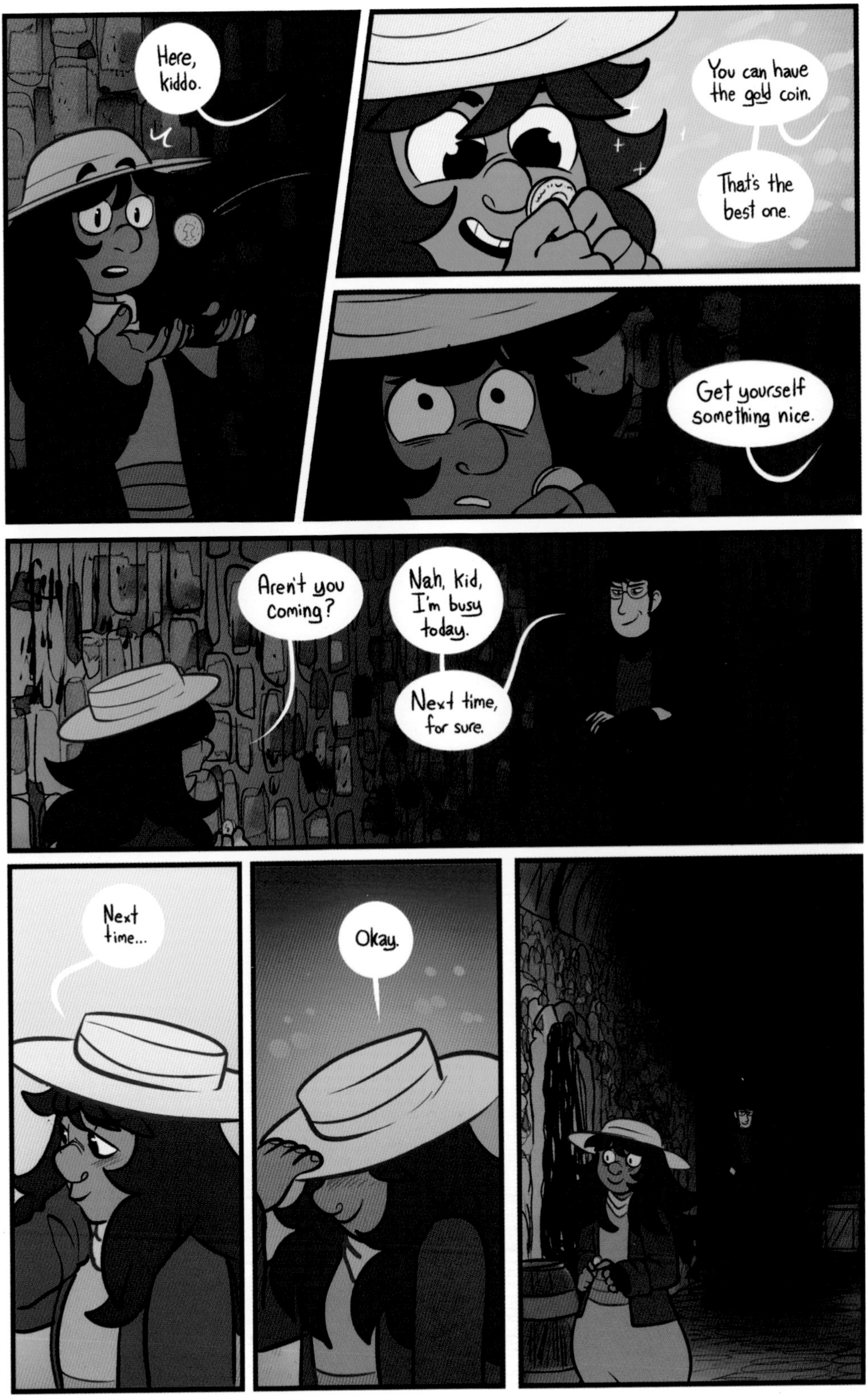
Here, kiddo.
You can have the gold coin.
That's the best one.
Get yourself something nice.
Aren't you coming?
Nah, kid, I'm busy today.
Next time, for sure.
Next time...
Okay.

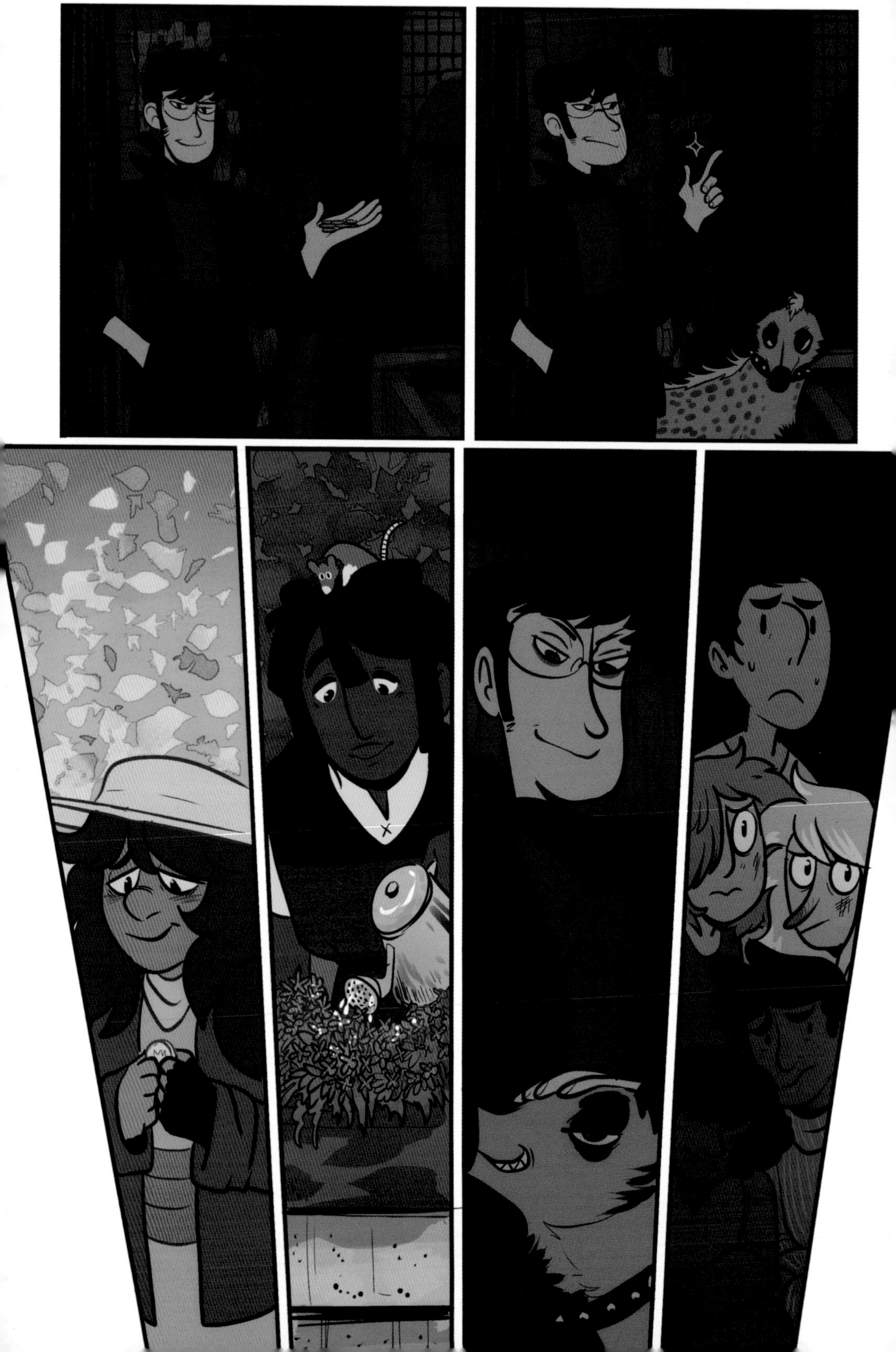
SNAP

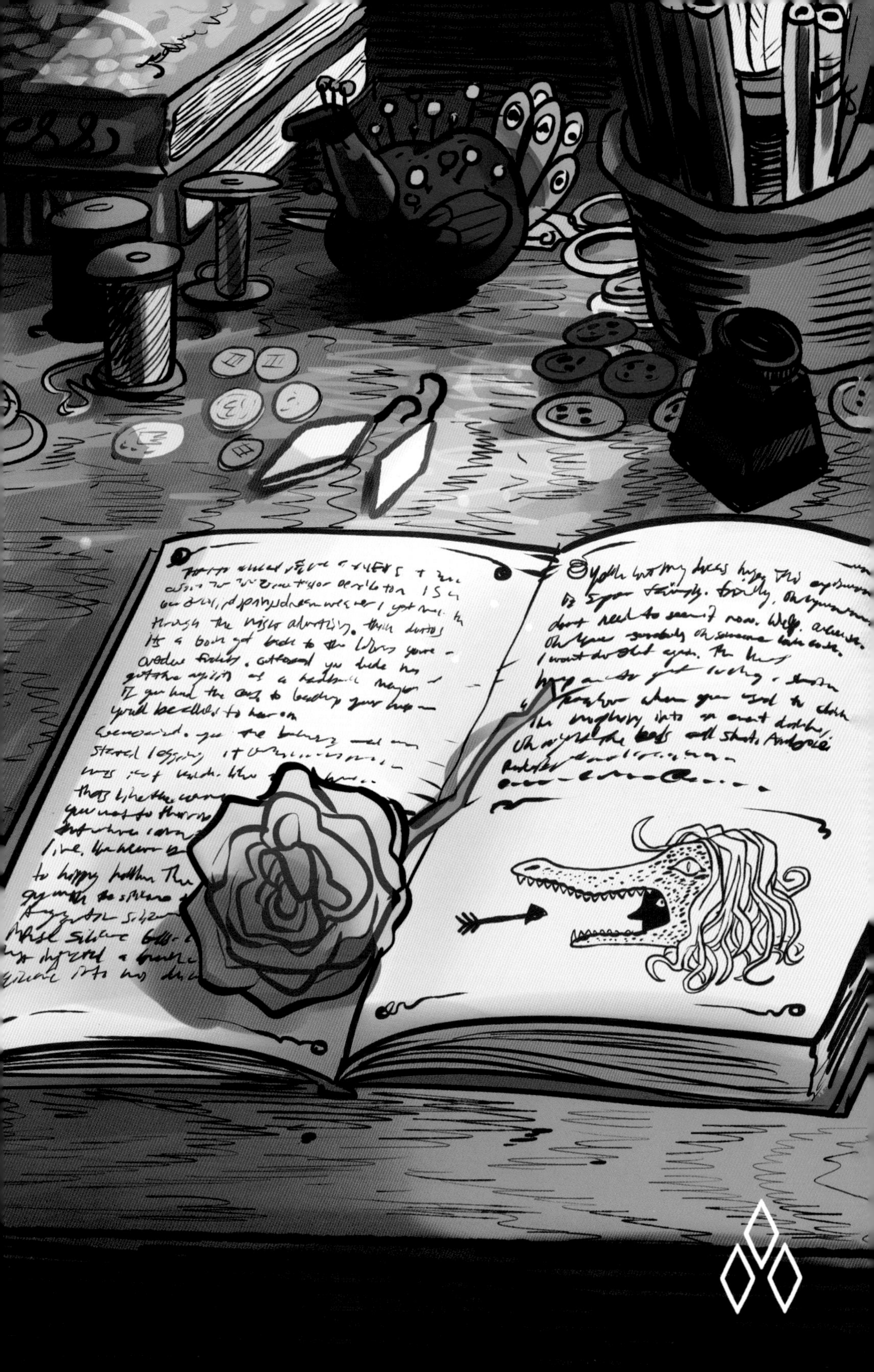

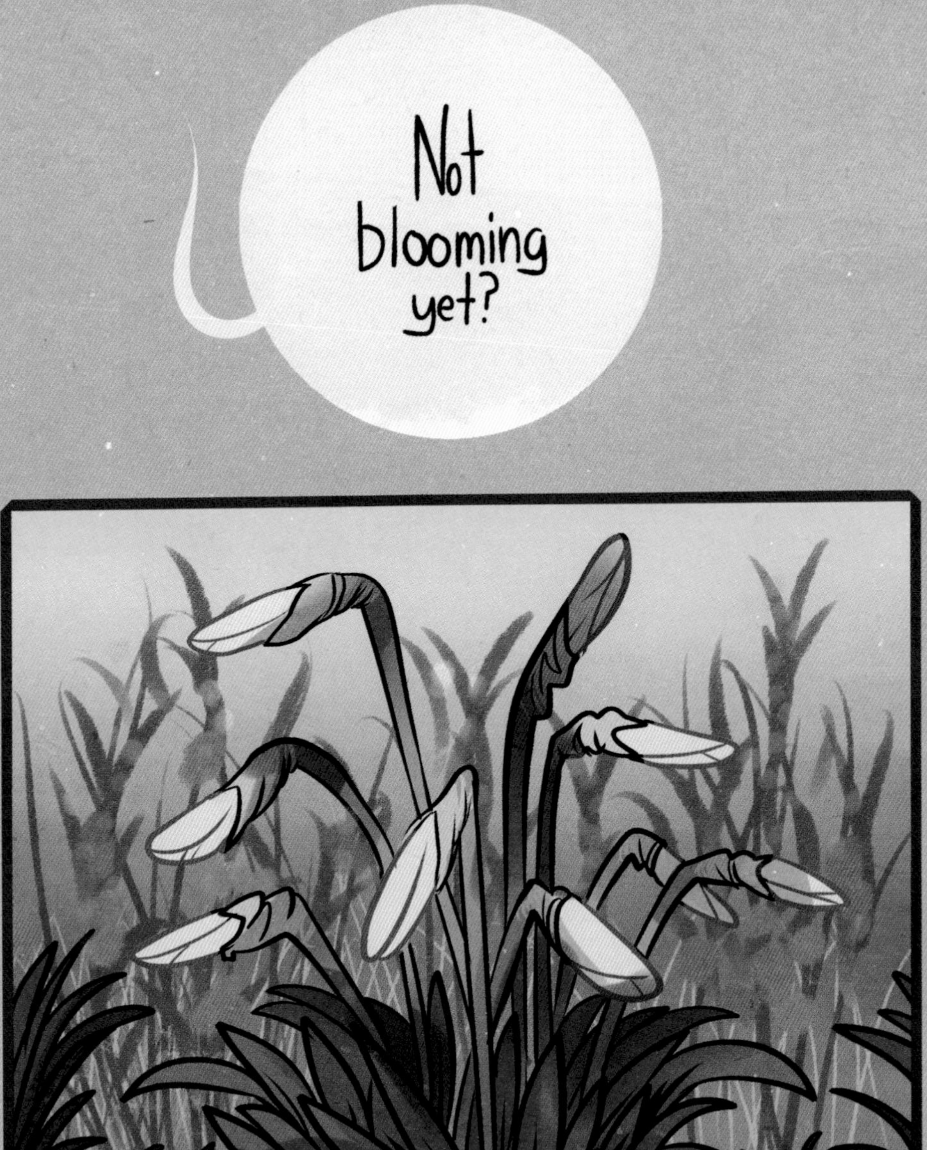
Not blooming yet?

III

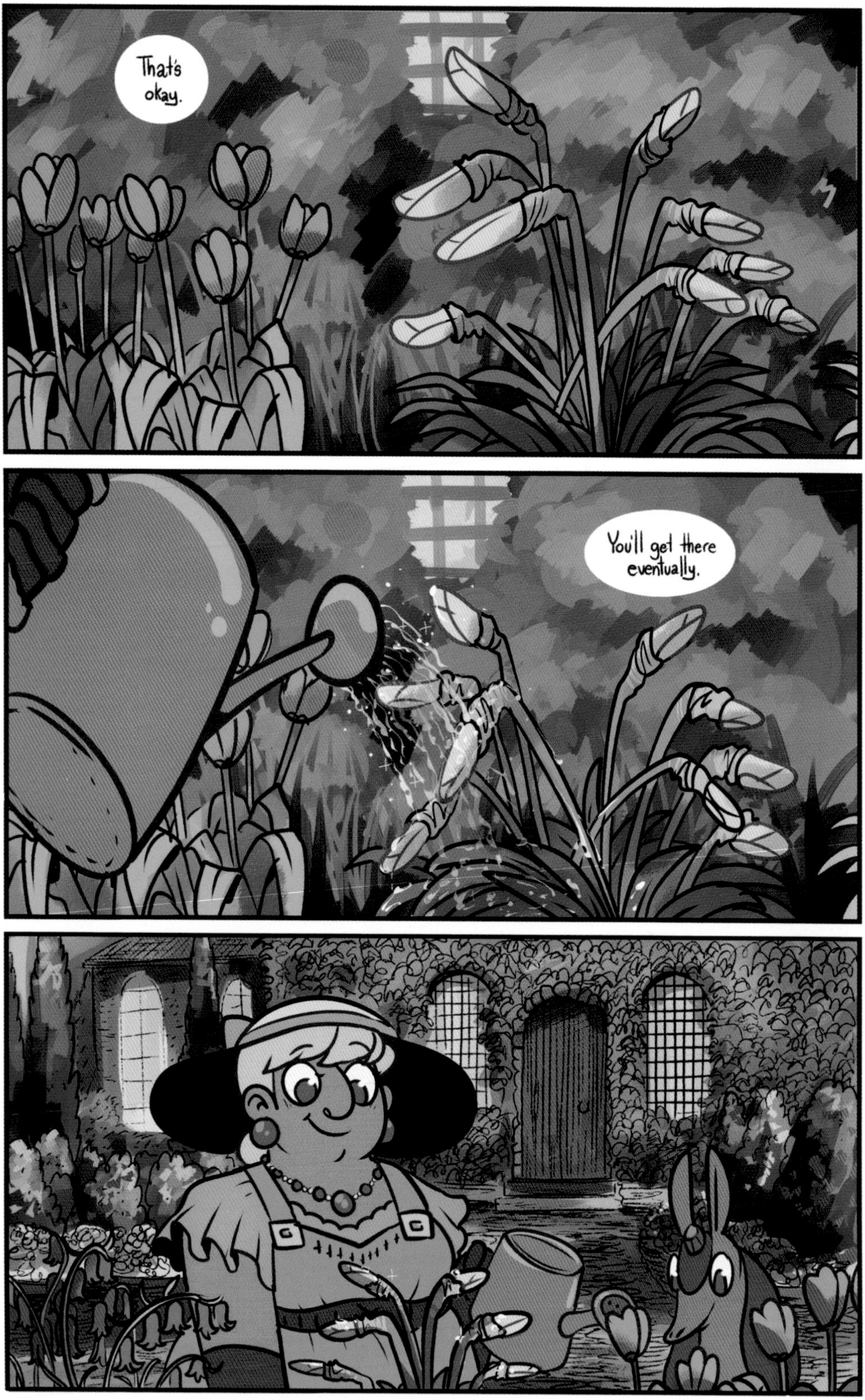
That's okay.
You'll get there eventually.

They've all come in so nicely this year!

Don't you think so, Tully?

mm

sniff

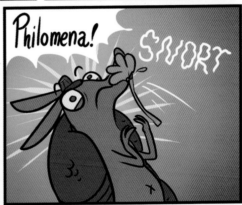

Philomena!

SNORT

Yeah Dad?

ACHOO!

It's time for your lessons, dear.

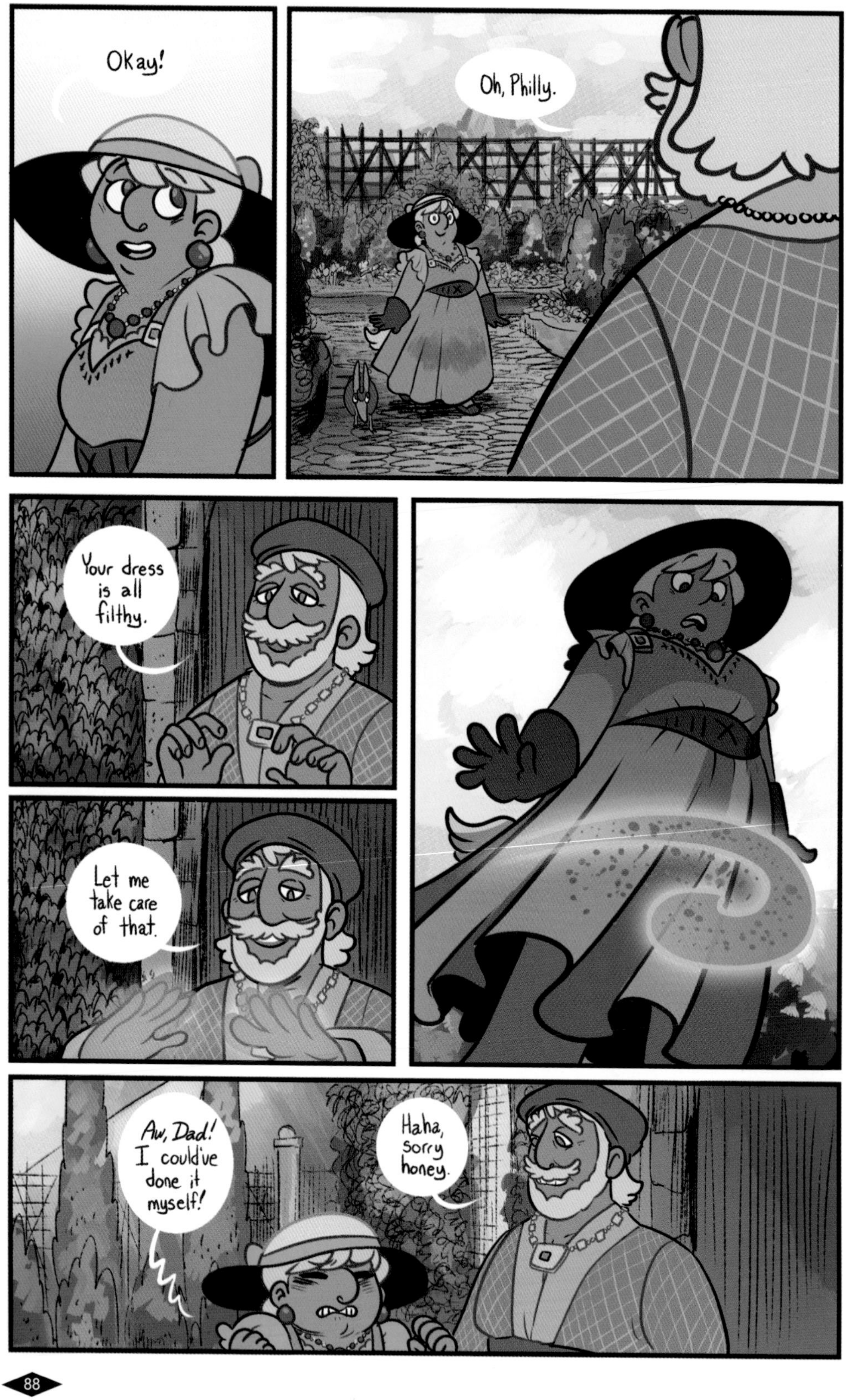
Okay!
Oh, Philly.
Your dress is all filthy.
Let me take care of that.
Aw, Dad! I could've done it myself!
Haha, sorry honey.

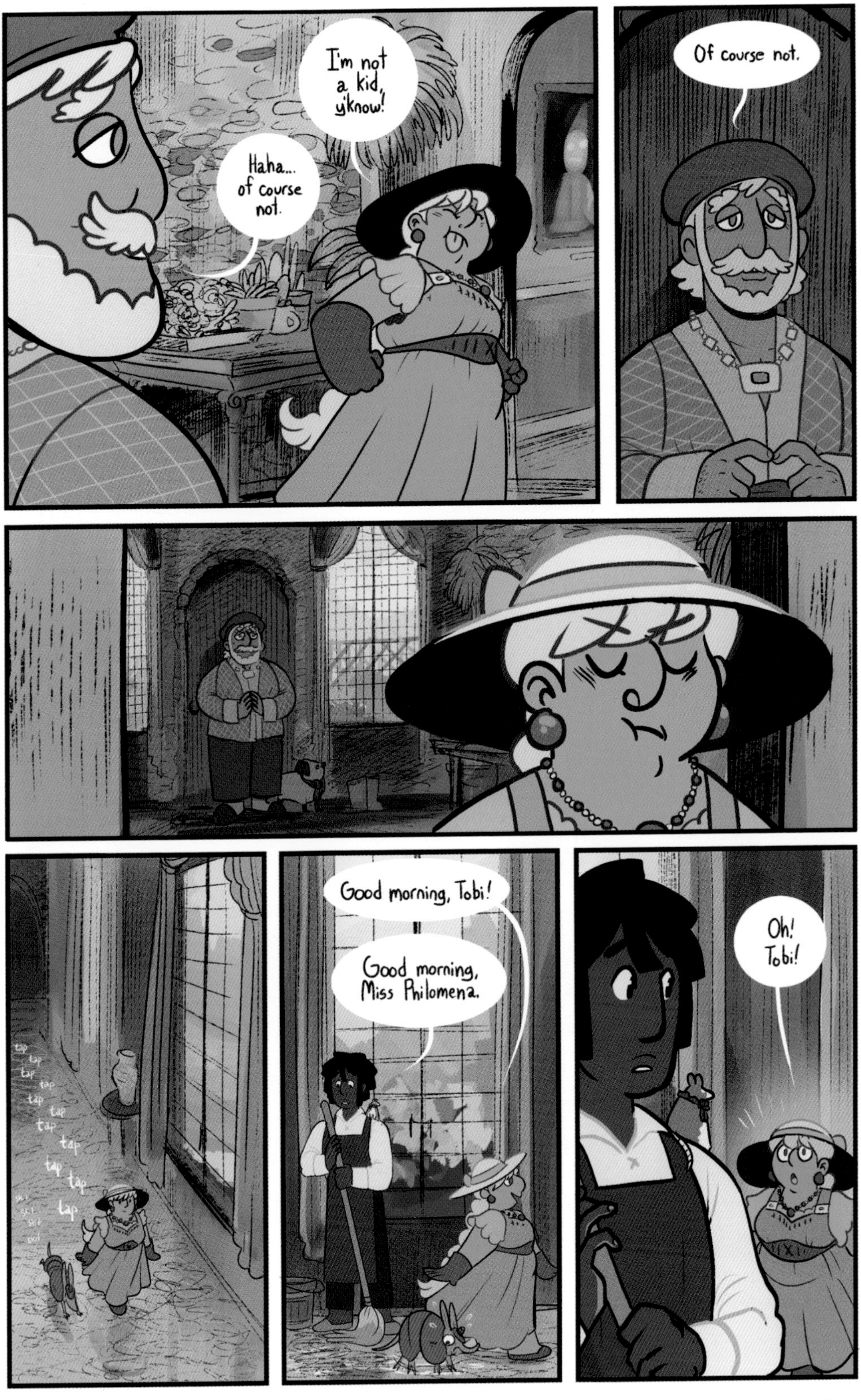
I'm not a kid, y'know!
Haha... of course not.
Of course not.
tap tap tap tap tap tap tap tap tap tap tap
Good morning, Tobi!
Good morning, Miss Philomena.
Oh! Tobi!

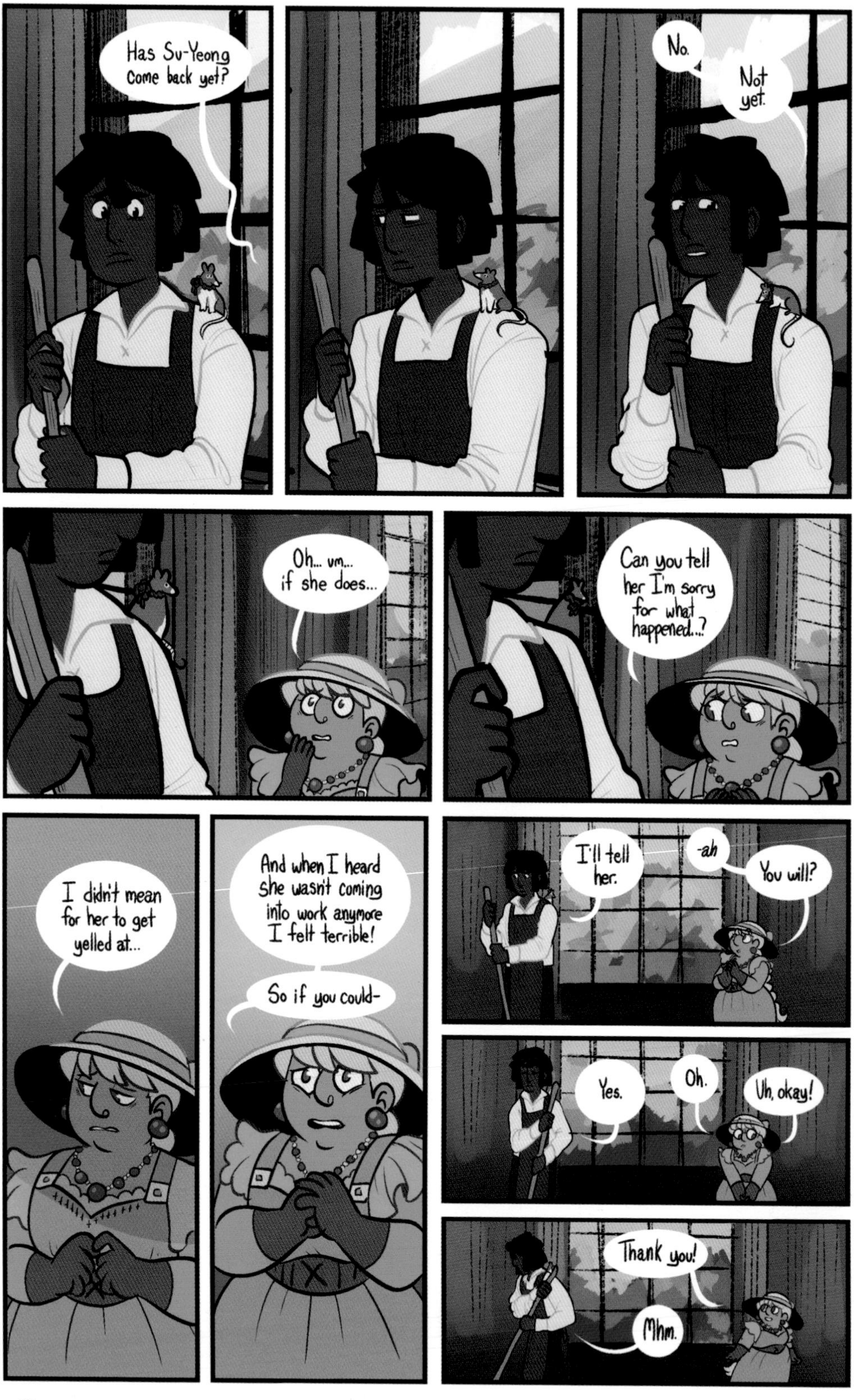
Has Su-Yeong come back yet?
No.
Not yet.
Oh... um... if she does...
Can you tell her I'm sorry for what happened...?
I didn't mean for her to get yelled at...
And when I heard she wasn't coming into work anymore I felt terrible!
So if you could-
I'll tell her.
-ah
You will?
Yes.
Oh.
Uh, okay!
Thank you!
Mhm.

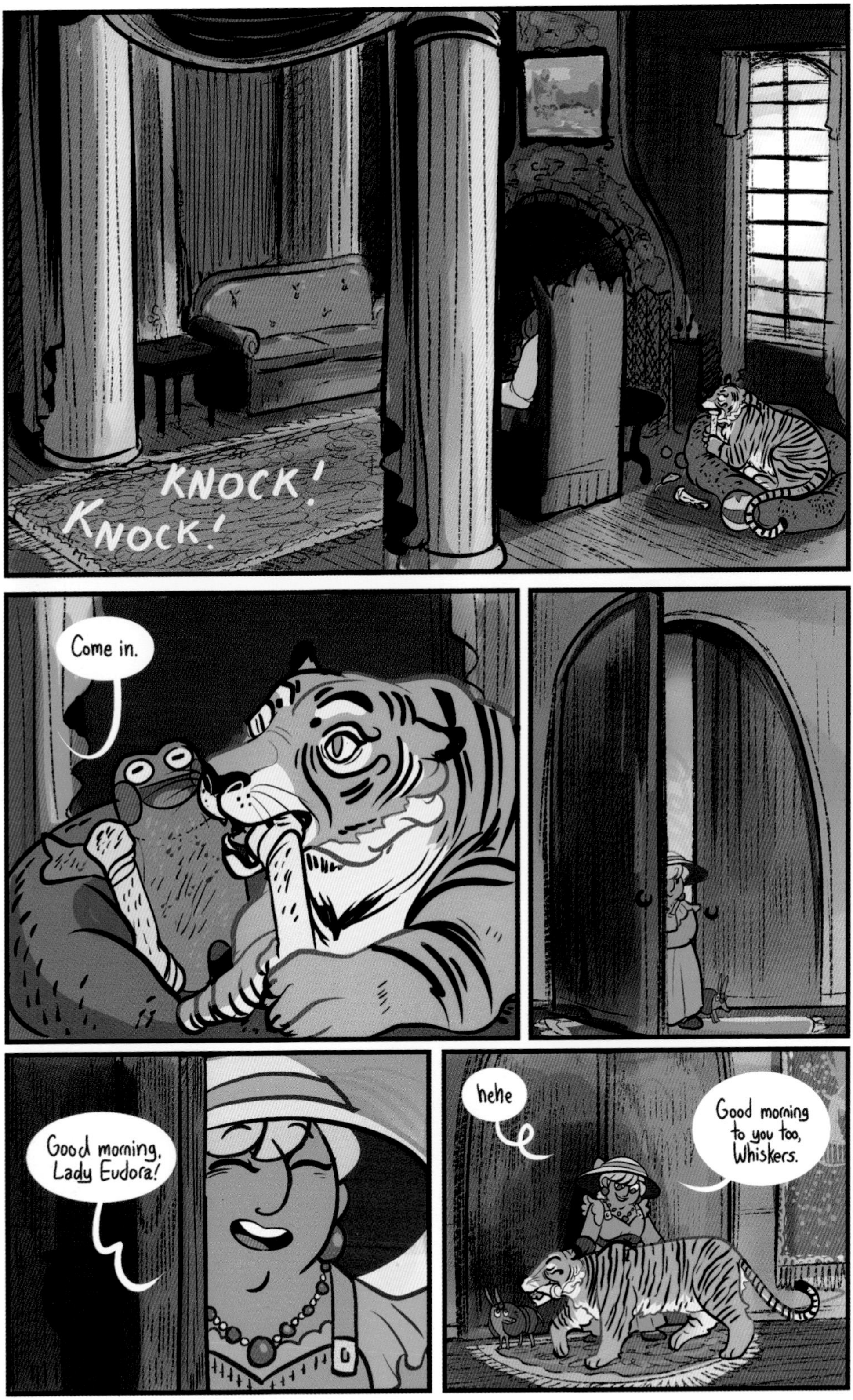
KNOCK!
KNOCK!
Come in.
Good morning, Lady Eudora!
hehe
Good morning to you too, Whiskers.

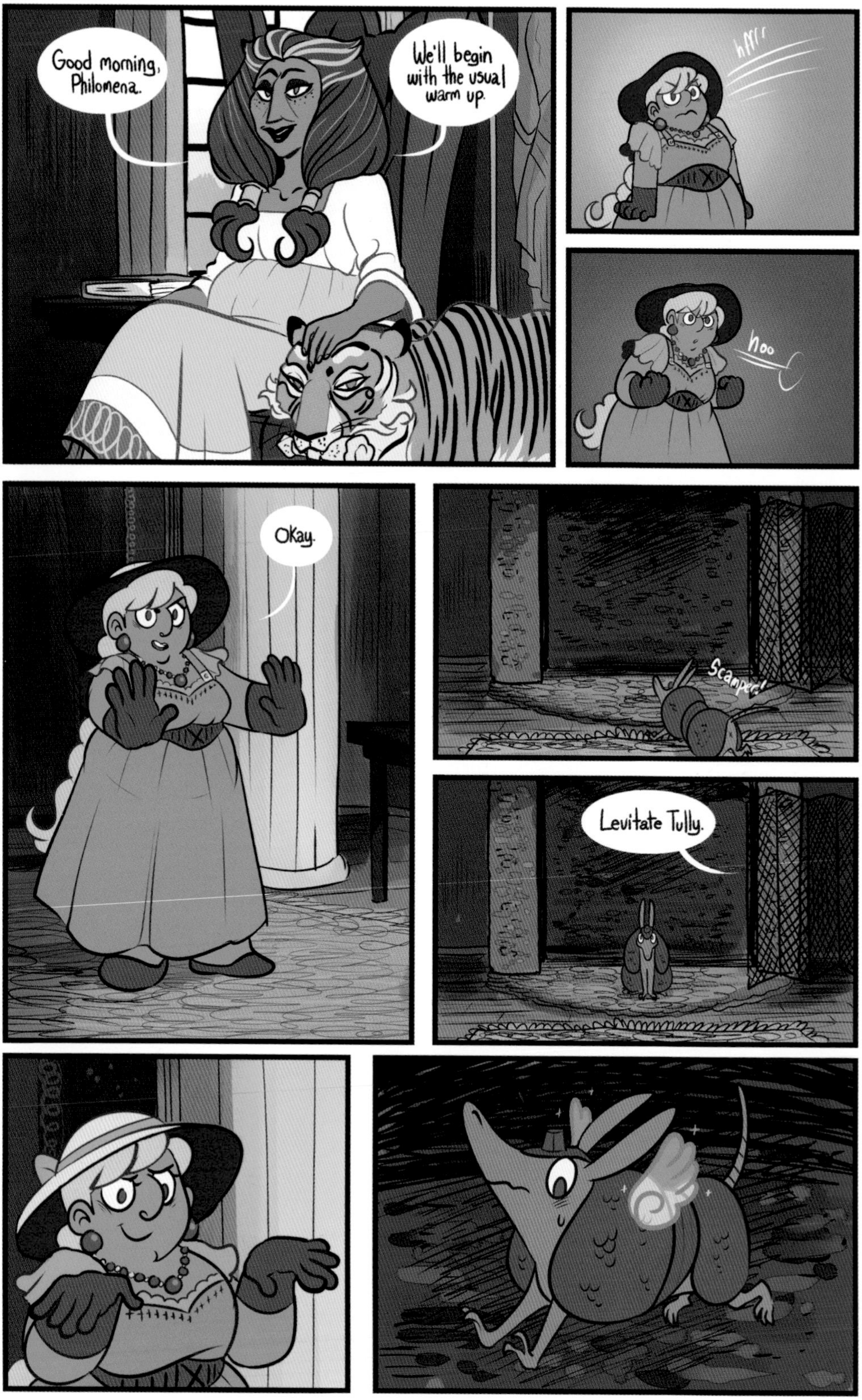
Good morning, Philomena.
We'll begin with the usual warm up.
hMrr
hoo
Okay.
Scamper!
Levitate Tully.

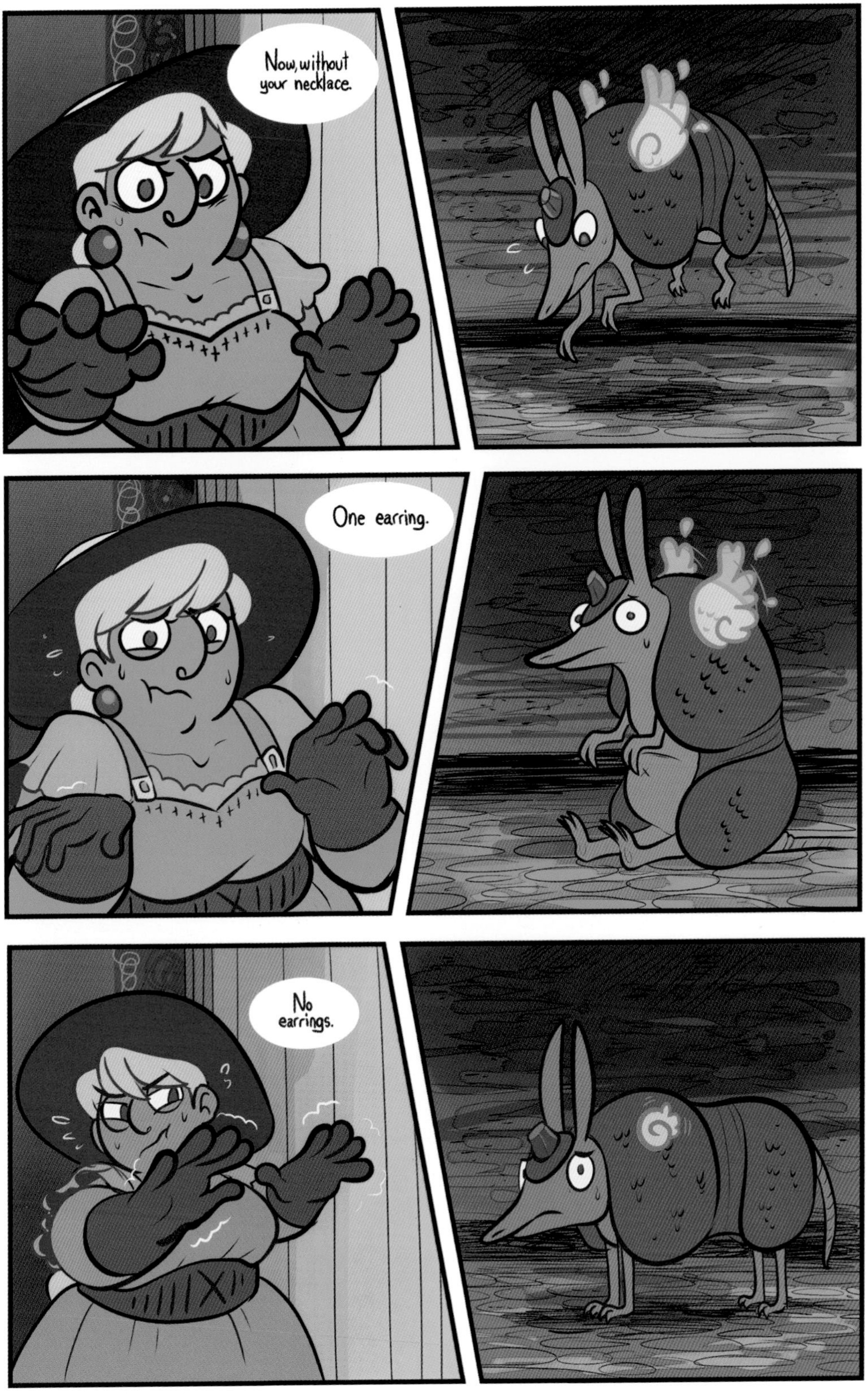
Now, without your necklace.
One earring.
No earrings.

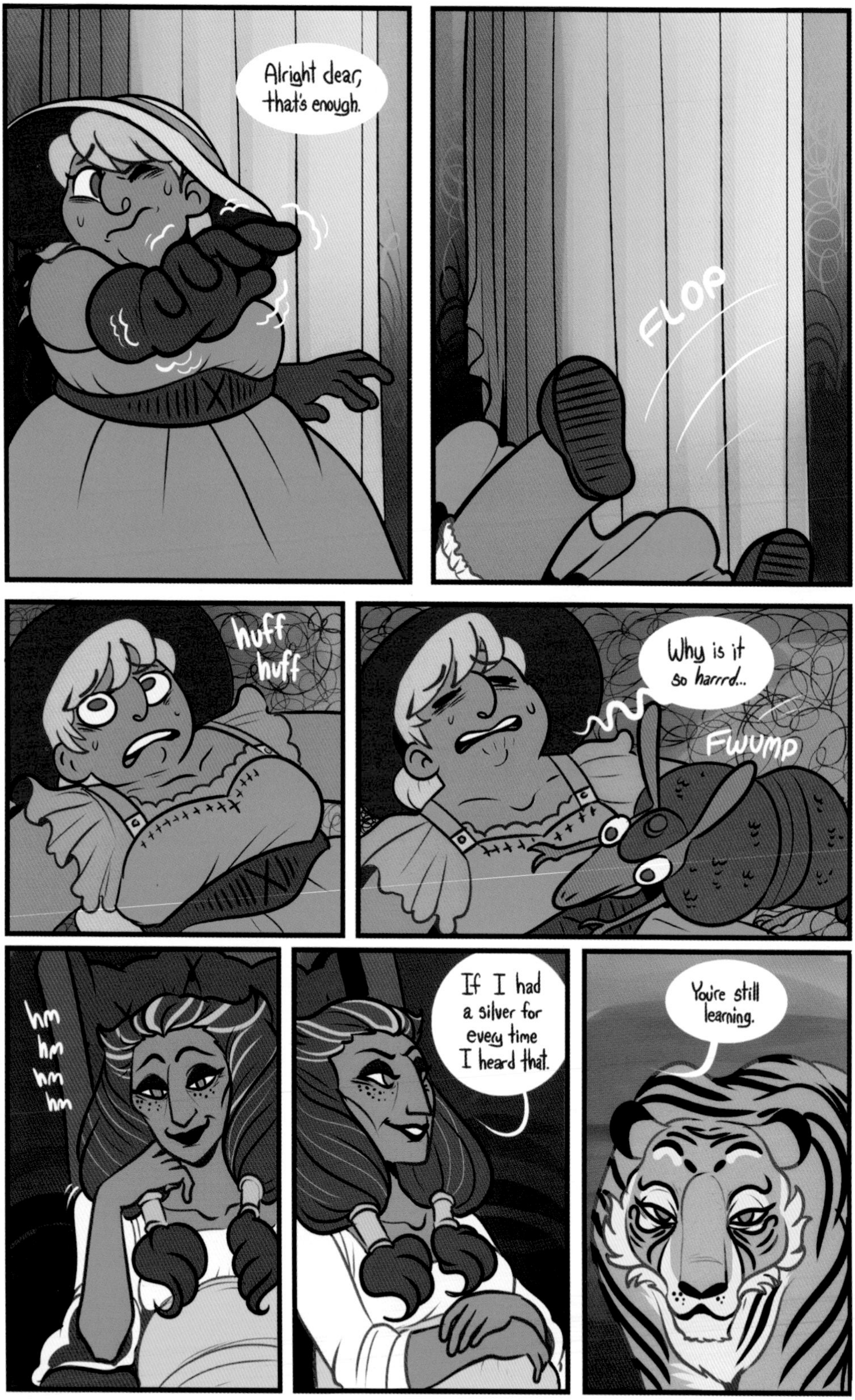
Alright dear, that's enough.
FLOP
huff huff
Why is it so harrrd...
FWUMP
hm hm hm hm
If I had a silver for every time I heard that.
You're still learning.

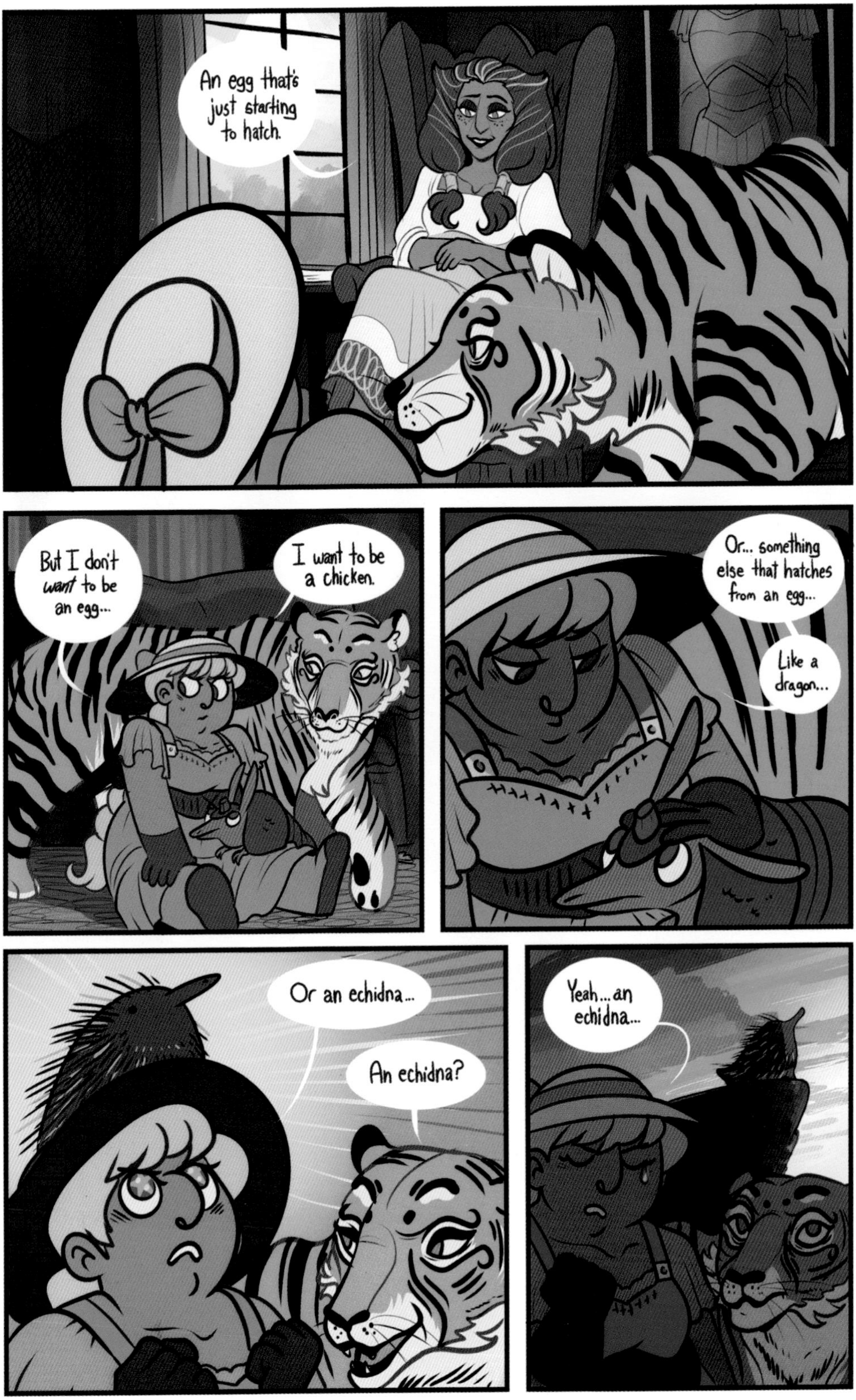
An egg that's just starting to hatch.
But I don't *want* to be an egg...
I want to be a chicken.
Or... something else that hatches from an egg...
Like a dragon...
Or an echidna...
An echidna?
Yeah... an echidna...

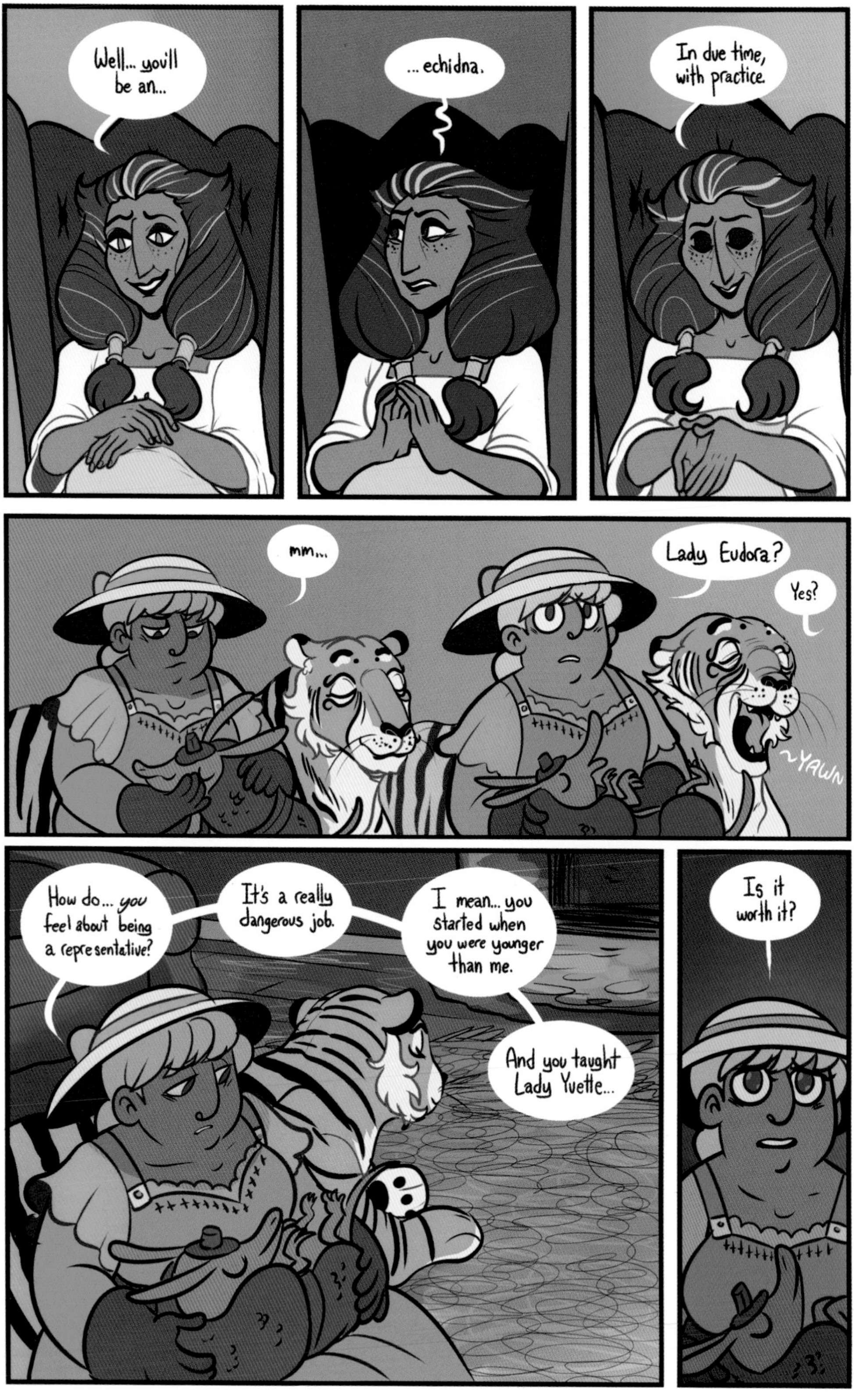
Well... you'll be an...
... echidna.
In due time, with practice.
mm...
Lady Eudora?
Yes?
~YAWN
How do... you feel about being a representative?
It's a really dangerous job.
I mean... you started when you were younger than me.
And you taught Lady Yvette...
Is it worth it?

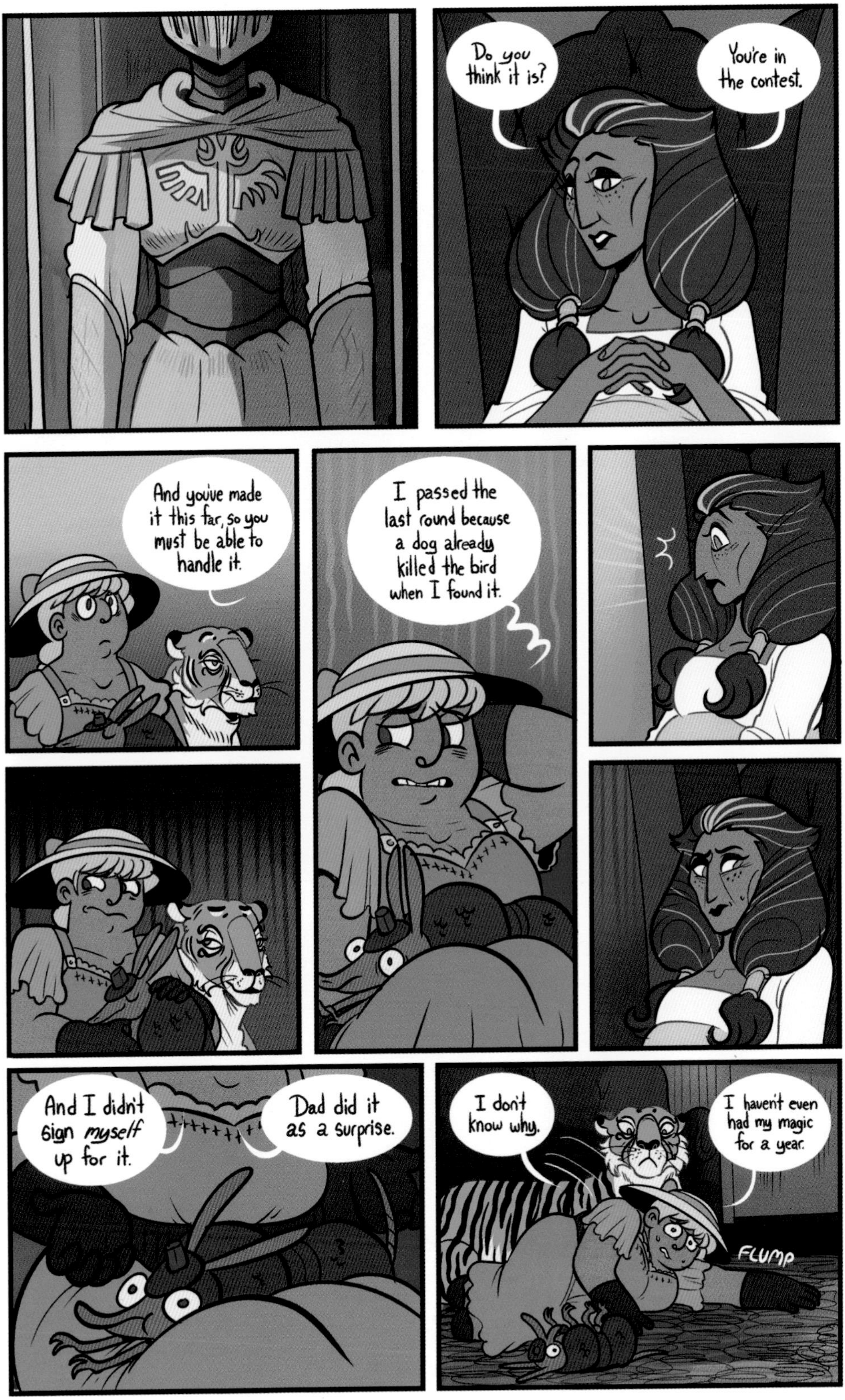
Do you think it is?
You're in the contest.
And you've made it this far, so you must be able to handle it.
I passed the last round because a dog already killed the bird when I found it.
And I didn't sign *myself* up for it.
Dad did it as a surprise.
I don't know why.
I haven't even had my magic for a year.
FLUMP

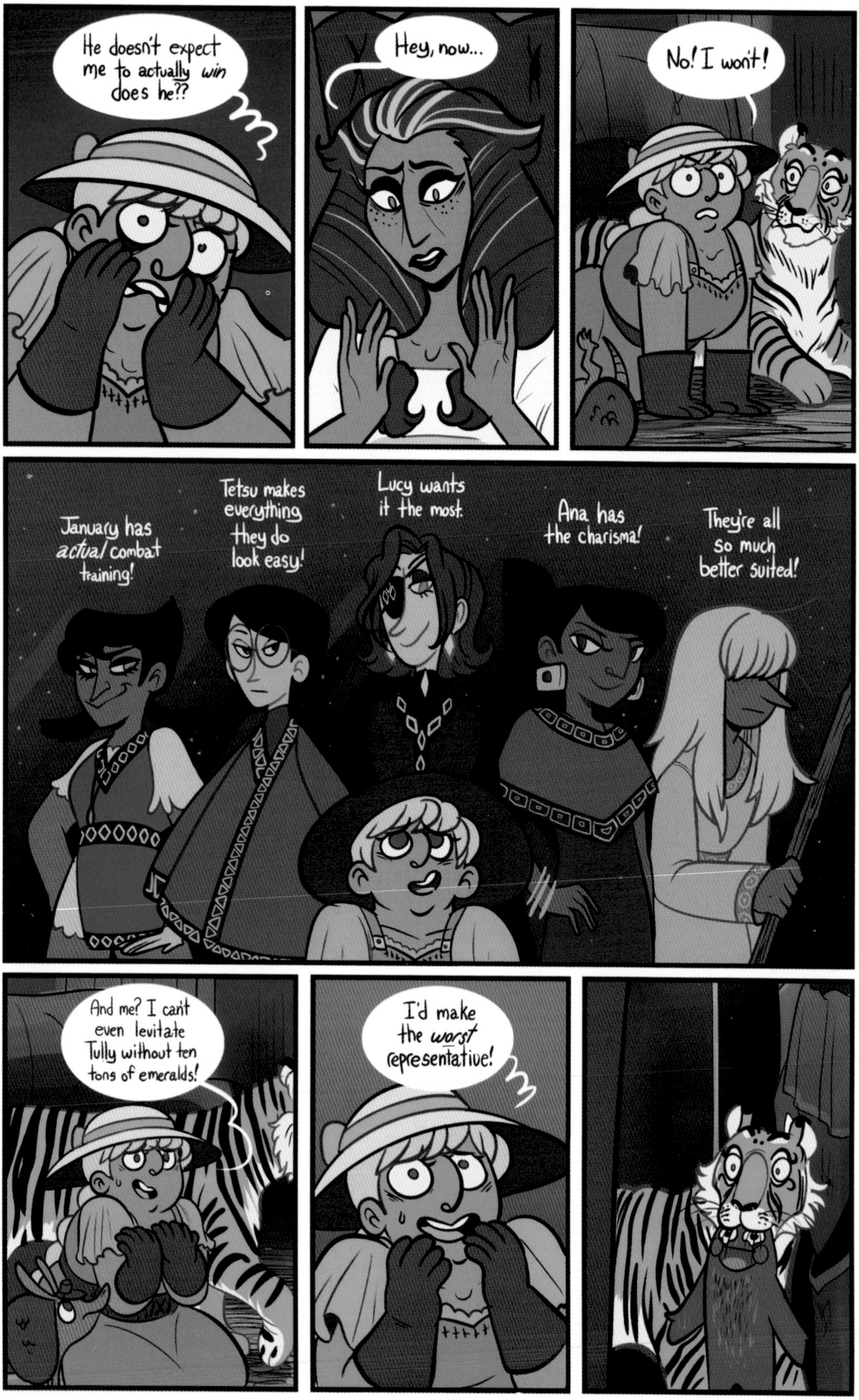
He doesn't expect me to actually *win* does he??
Hey, now...
No! I won't!
January has *actual* combat training!
Tetsu makes everything they do look easy!
Lucy wants it the most.
Ana has the charisma!
They're all so much better suited!
And me? I can't even levitate Tully without ten tons of emeralds!
I'd make the *worst* representative!

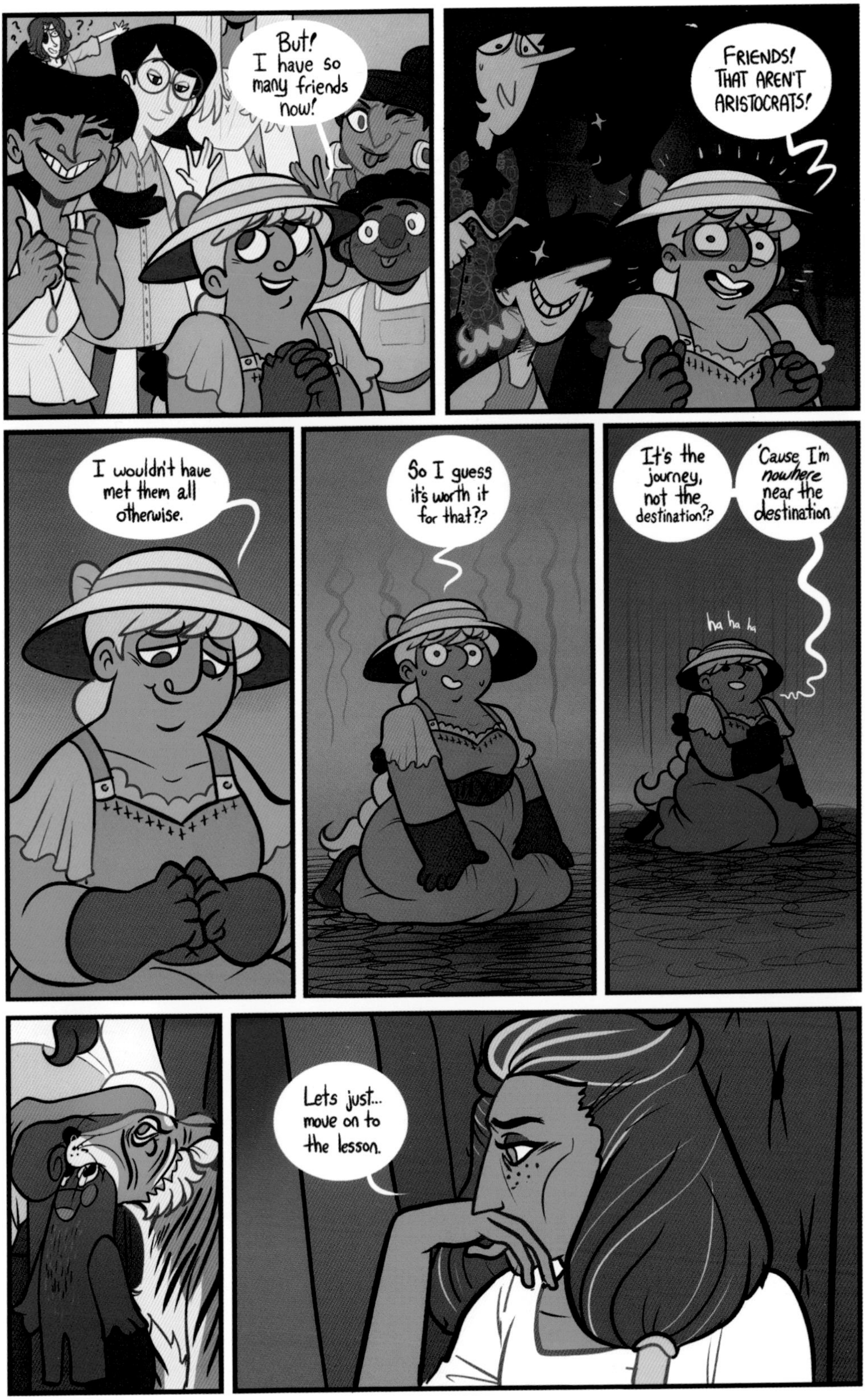
But! I have so many friends now!
FRIENDS! THAT AREN'T ARISTOCRATS!
I wouldn't have met them all otherwise.
So I guess it's worth it for that??
It's the journey, not the destination??
'Cause I'm *nowhere* near the destination
ha ha ha
Lets just... move on to the lesson.

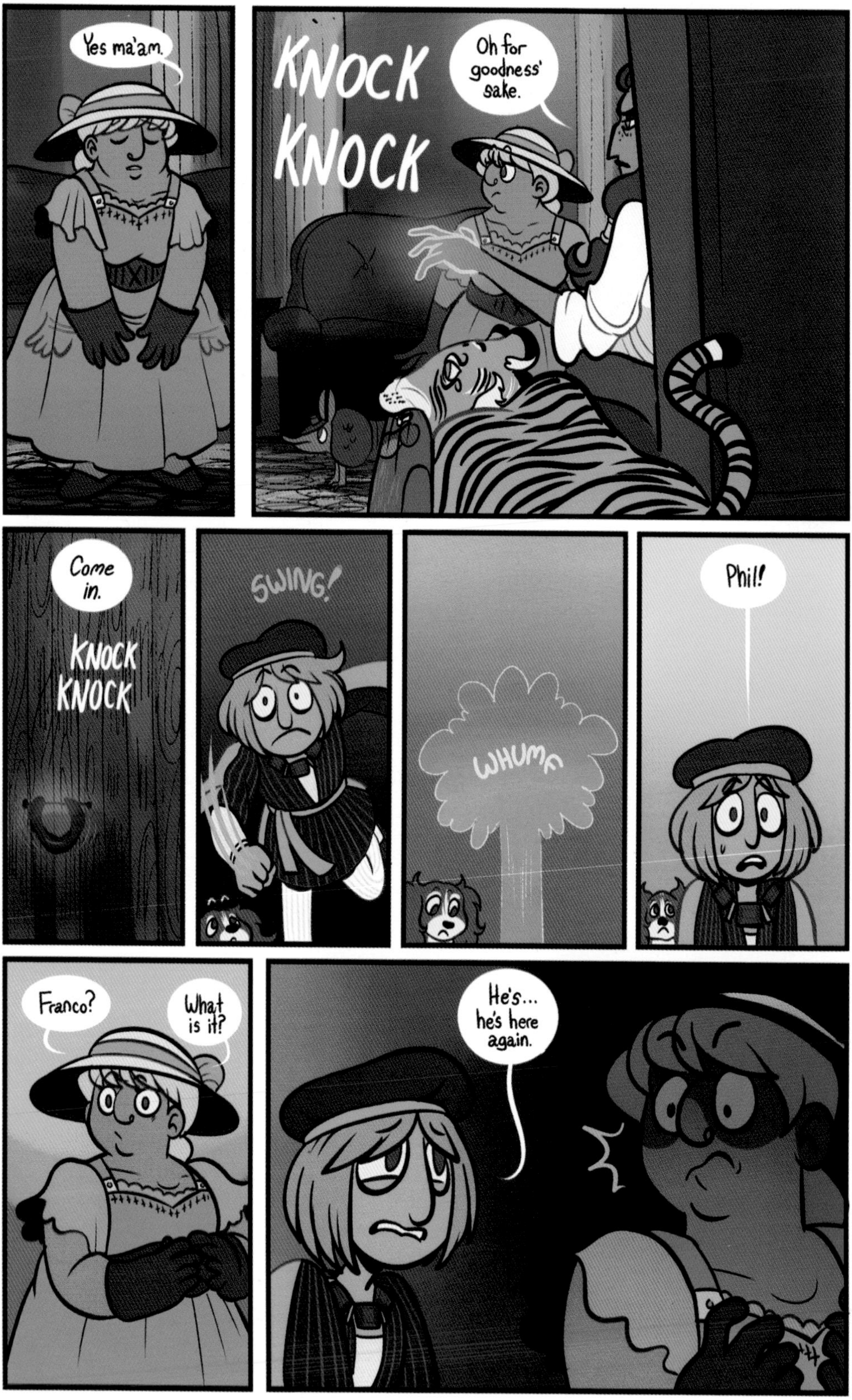
Yes ma'am.
KNOCK KNOCK
Oh for goodness' sake.
Come in.
KNOCK KNOCK
SWING!
WHUMF
Phil!
Franco?
What is it?
He's... he's here again.

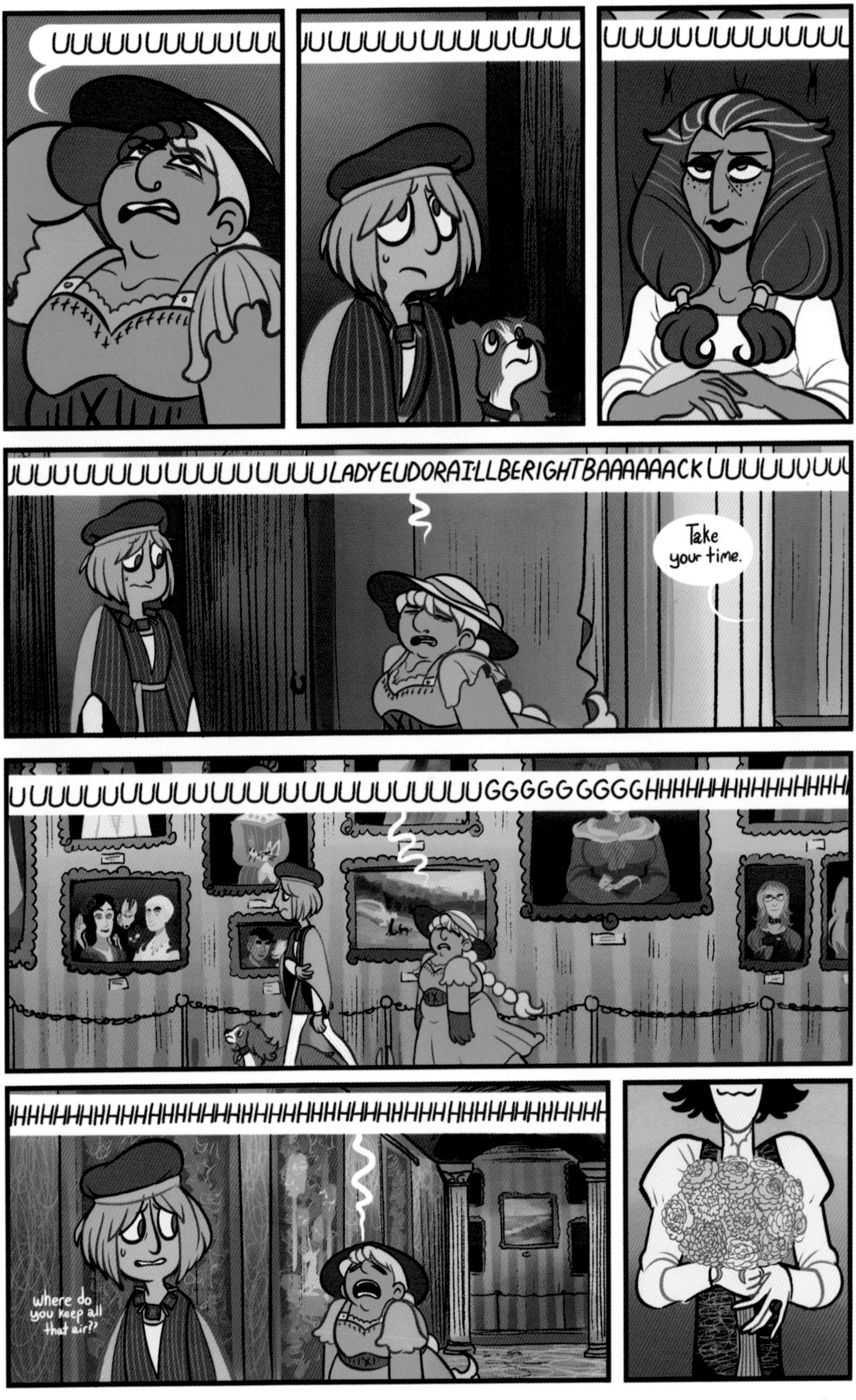
UUUUUUUUUUUUU
UUUUUUUUUUUUUUU
UUUUUUUUUUUUUUU
UUUUUUUUUUUUUUUUUUULADYEUDORAI'LLBERIGHTBAAAAAACKUUUUUUUU
Take your time.
UUUUUUUUUUUUUUUUUUUUUUUUUUUGGGGGGGGHHHHHHHHHHHHHH
HHHHHHHHHHHHHHHHHHHHHHHHHHHHHHHHHHHHHHHHHHHH
where do you keep all that air??

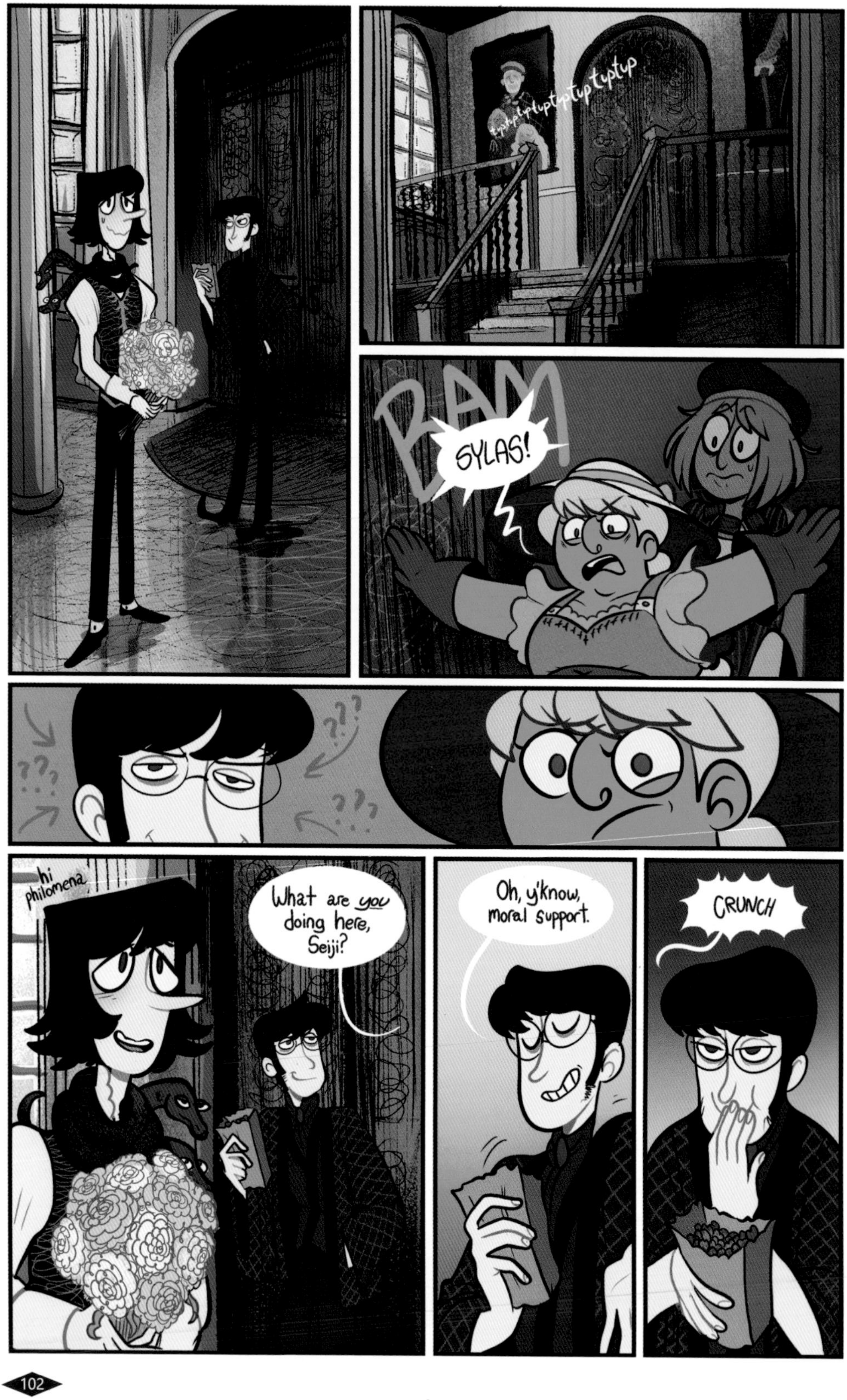

typtyptyptyptyptyptyptyptyp
BAM
SYLAS!
??
??
??
hi philomena
What are you doing here, Seiji?
Oh, y'know, moral support.
CRUNCH

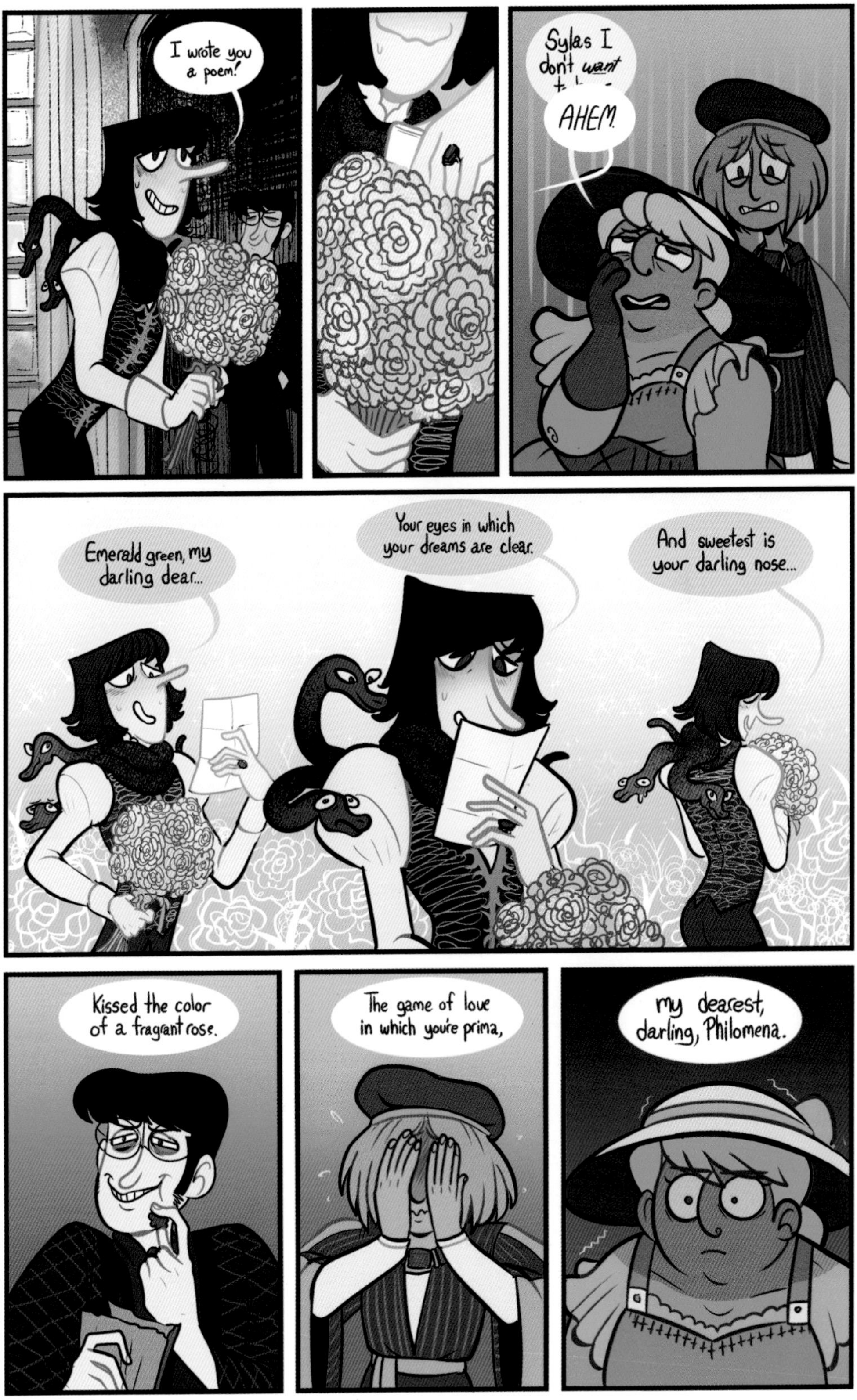
I wrote you a poem!
Sylas I don't want
AHEM.
Emerald green, my darling dear...
Your eyes in which your dreams are clear.
And sweetest is your darling nose...
Kissed the color of a fragrant rose.
The game of love in which you're prima,
my dearest, darling, Philomena.

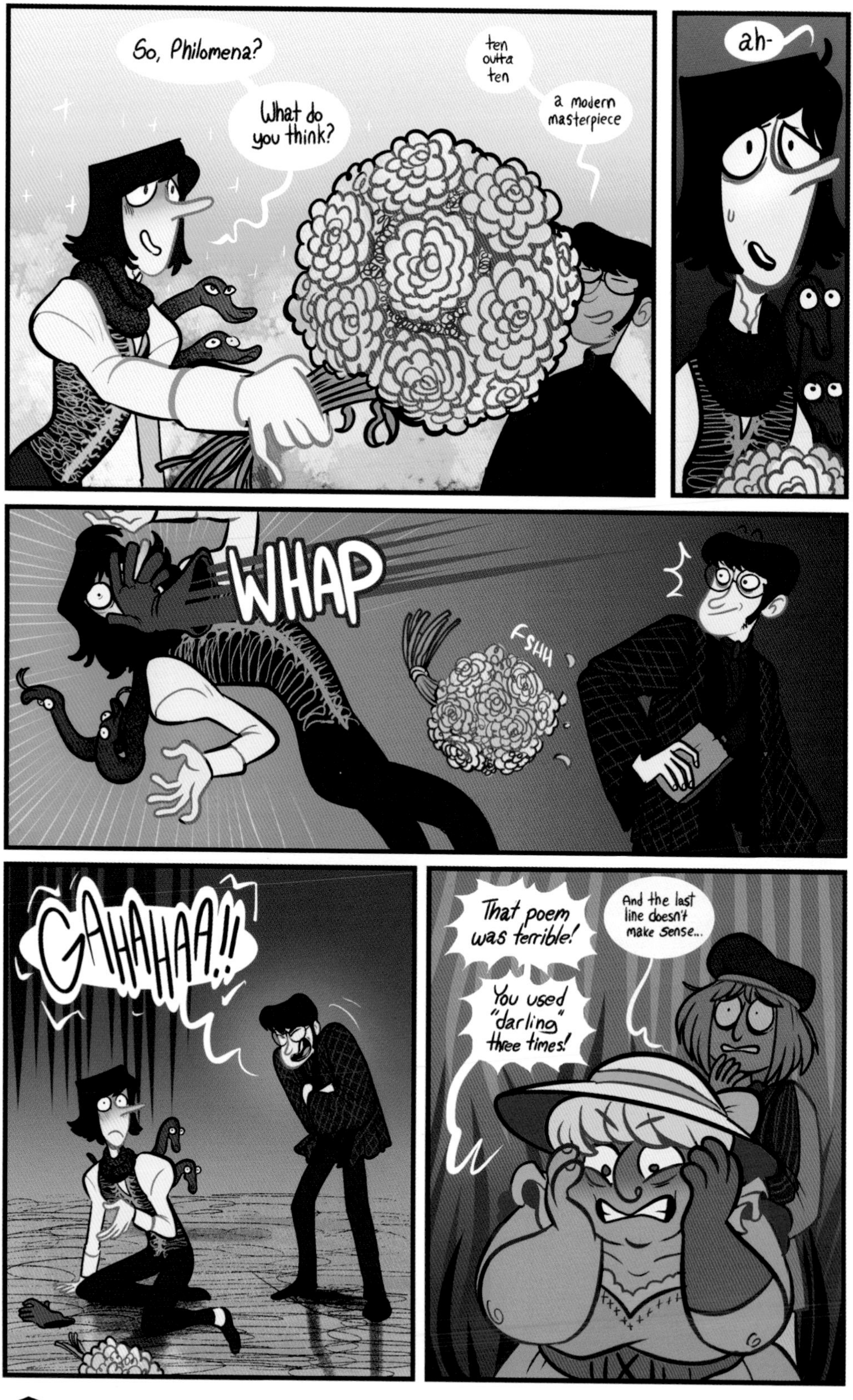
So, Philomena?
What do you think?
ten outta ten
a modern masterpiece
ah-
WHAP
FSHH
GAHAHAA!!
That poem was terrible!
You used "darling" three times!
And the last line doesn't make sense...

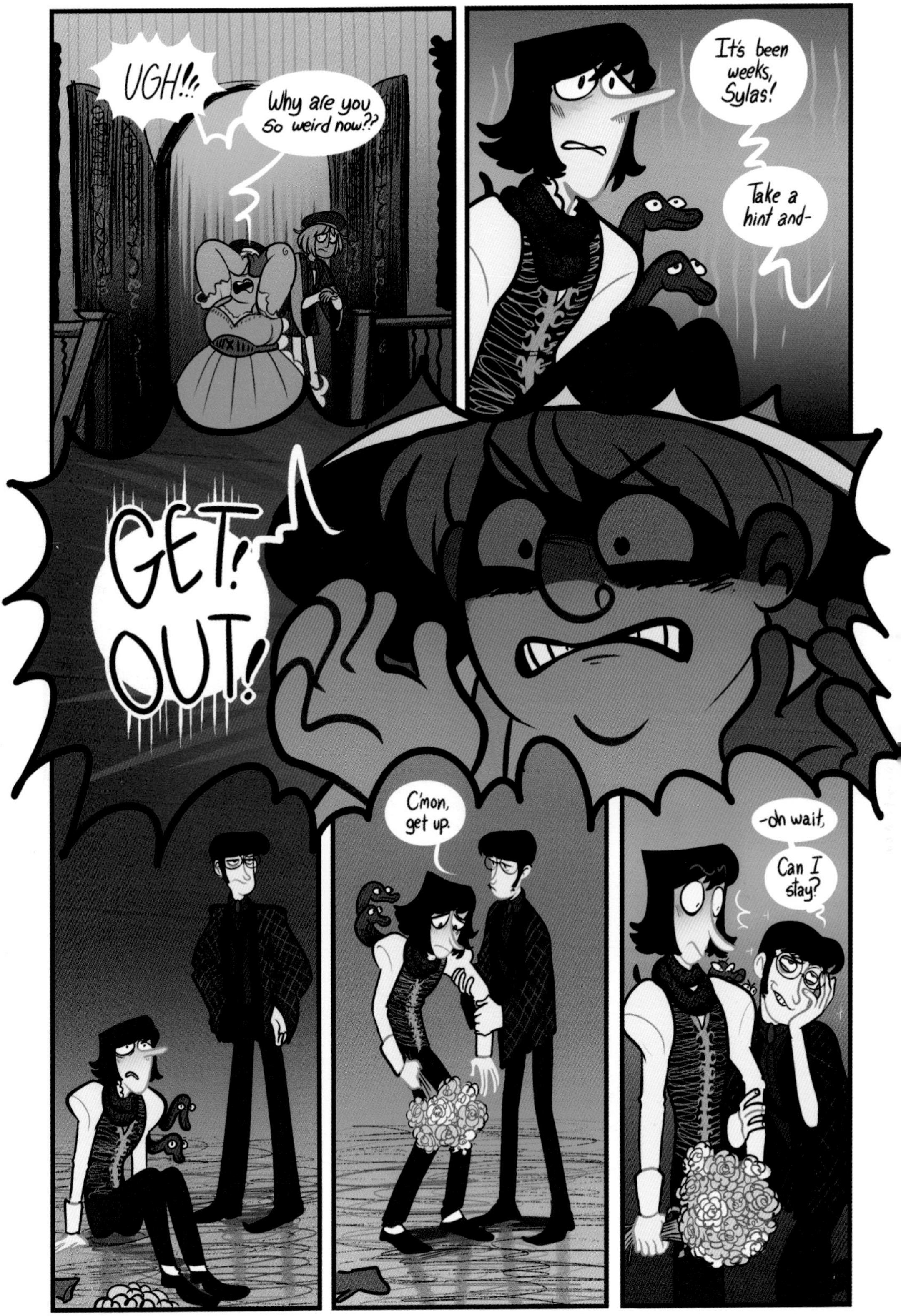
UGH!!
Why are you so weird now??
It's been weeks, Sylas!
Take a hint and-
GET OUT!
C'mon, get up.
-oh wait,
Can I stay?

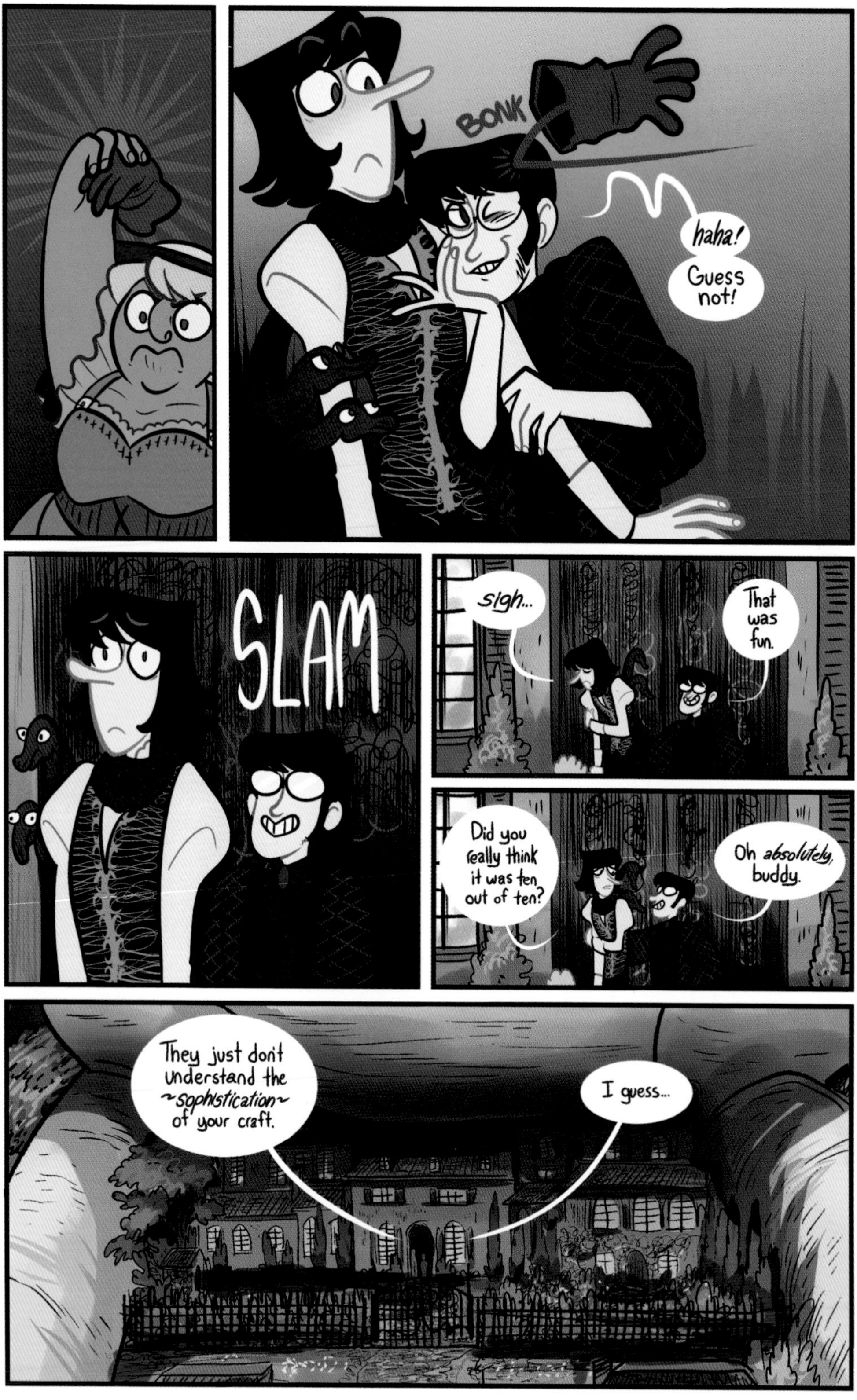
BONK
haha! Guess not!
SLAM
sigh...
That was fun.
Did you really think it was ten out of ten?
Oh absolutely, buddy.
They just don't understand the ~sophistication~ of your craft.
I guess...

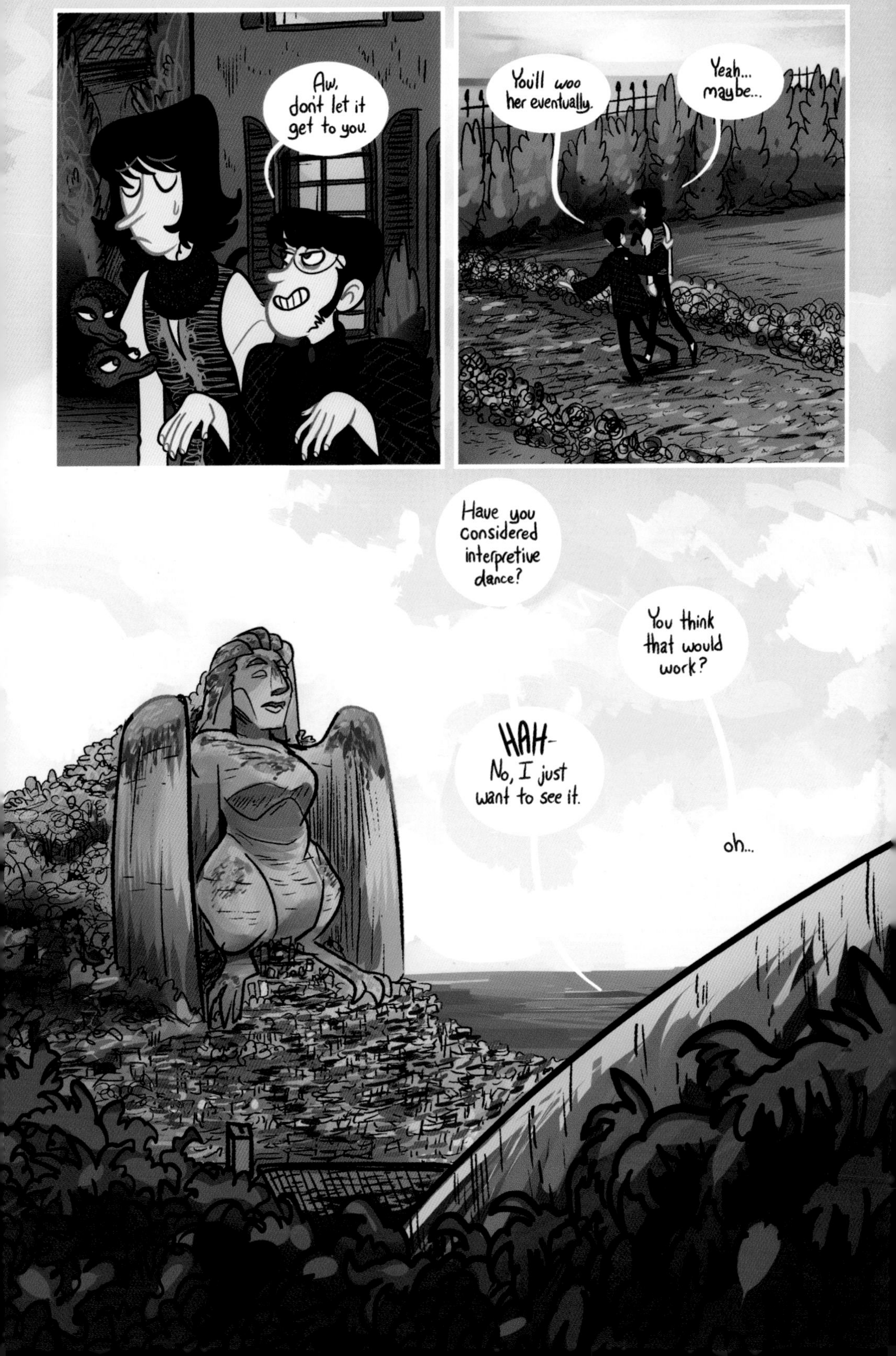
Aw, don't let it get to you.
You'll woo her eventually.
Yeah... maybe...
Have you considered interpretive dance?
You think that would work?
HAH- No, I just want to see it.
oh...

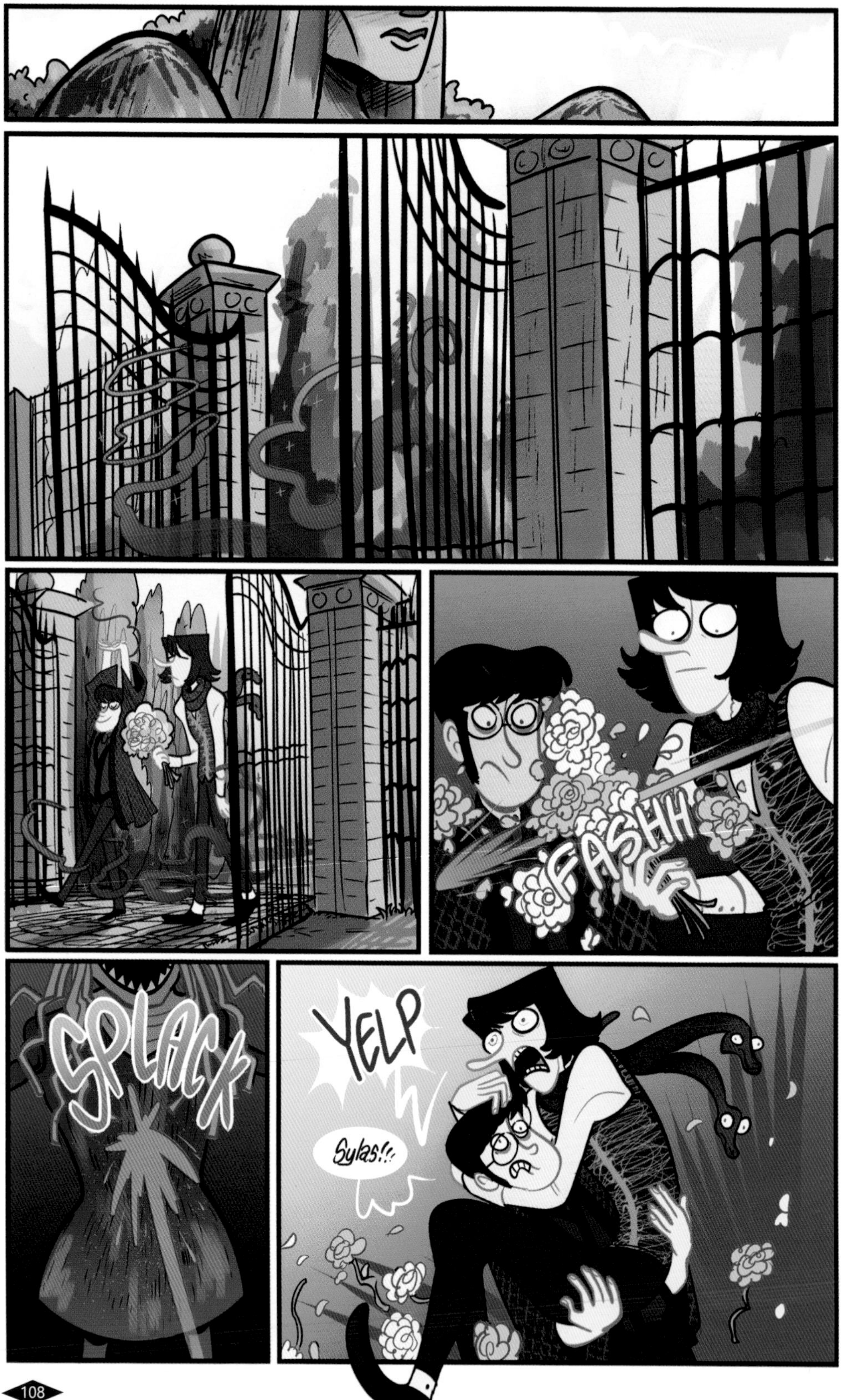
FASHH
SPLACK
YELP
Sylas!!!

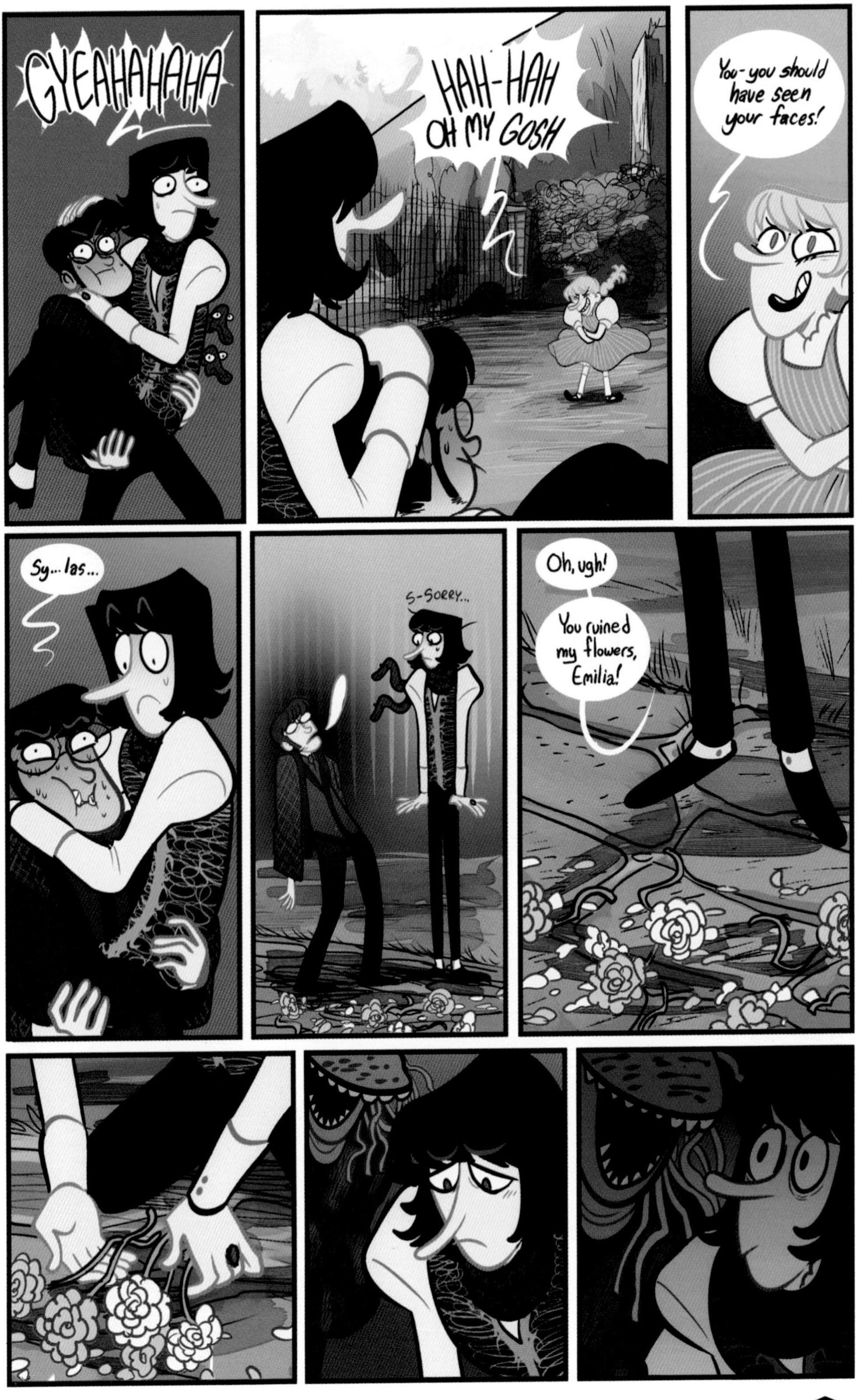
GYEAHAHAHA
HAH-HAH OH MY GOSH
You-you should have seen your faces!
Sy...las...
S-SORRY...
Oh, ugh!
You ruined my flowers, Emilia!

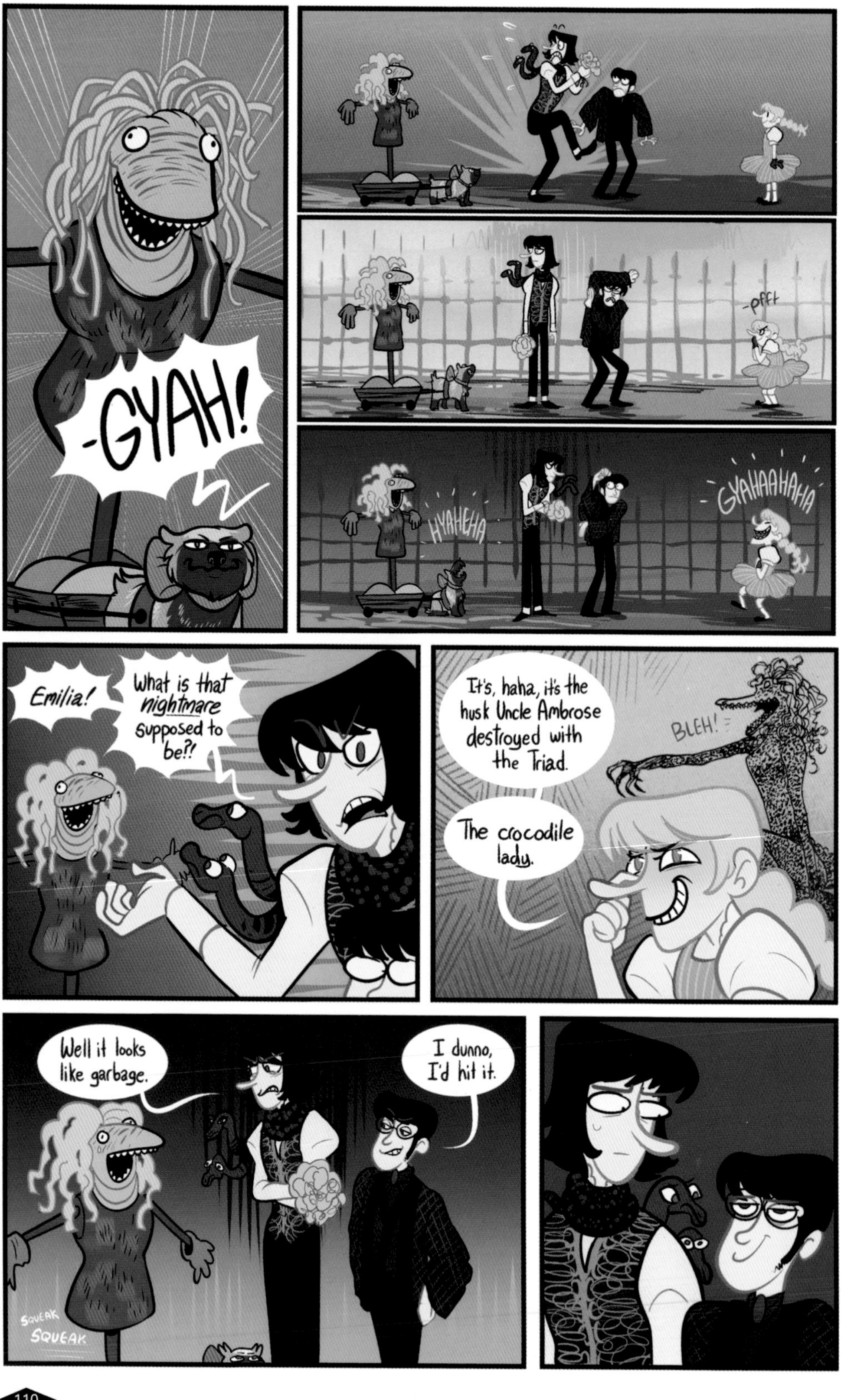
-GYAH!
-pfft
HYAHEHA
GYAHAAHAHA
Emilia!
What is that nightmare supposed to be?!
It's, haha, it's the husk Uncle Ambrose destroyed with the Triad.
The crocodile lady.
BLEH!
Well it looks like garbage.
I dunno, I'd hit it.
SQUEAK
SQUEAK

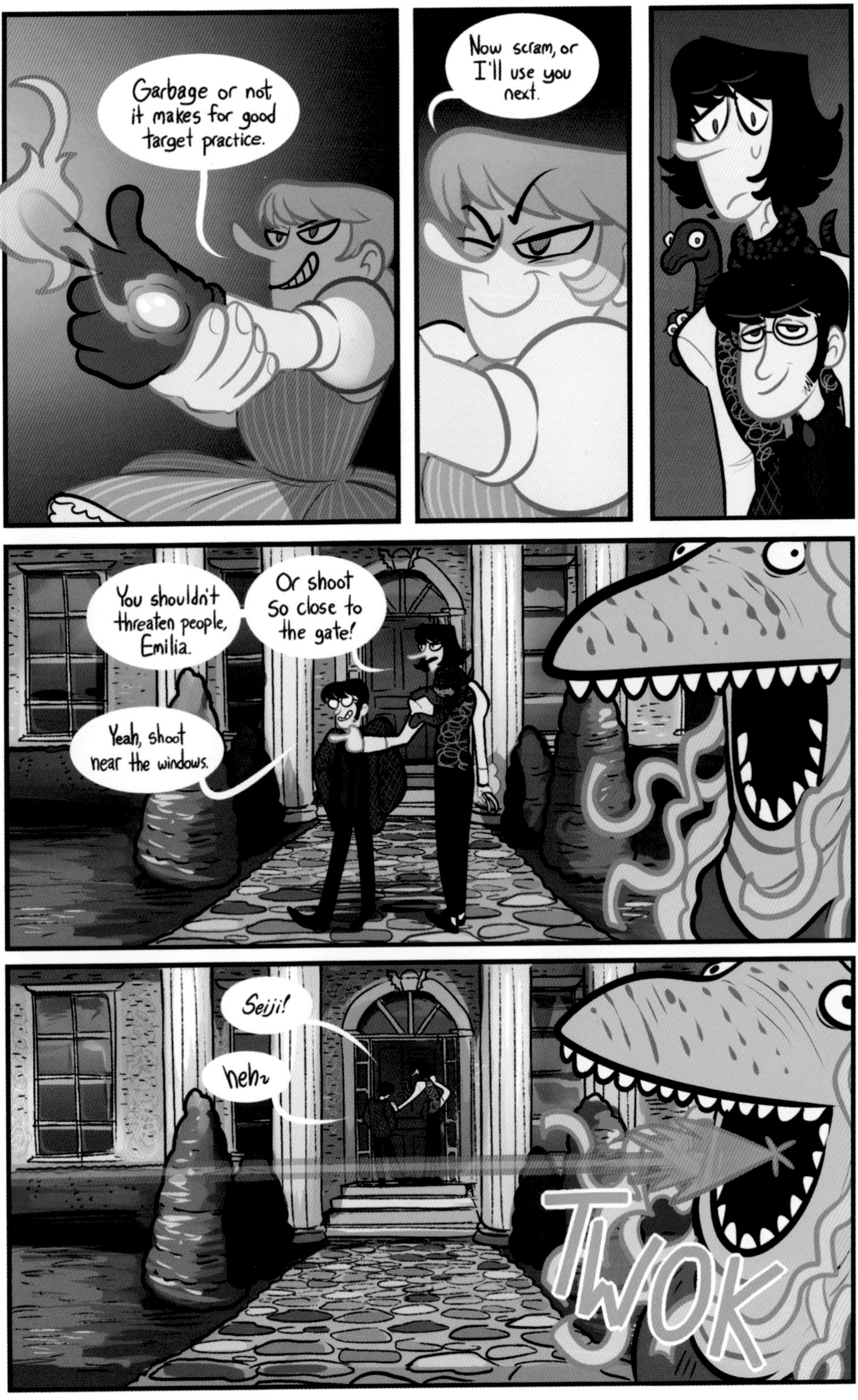

Garbage or not it makes for good target practice.
Now scram, or I'll use you next.
You shouldn't threaten people, Emilia.
Or shoot so close to the gate!
Yeah, shoot near the windows.
Seiji!
heh~
TWOK

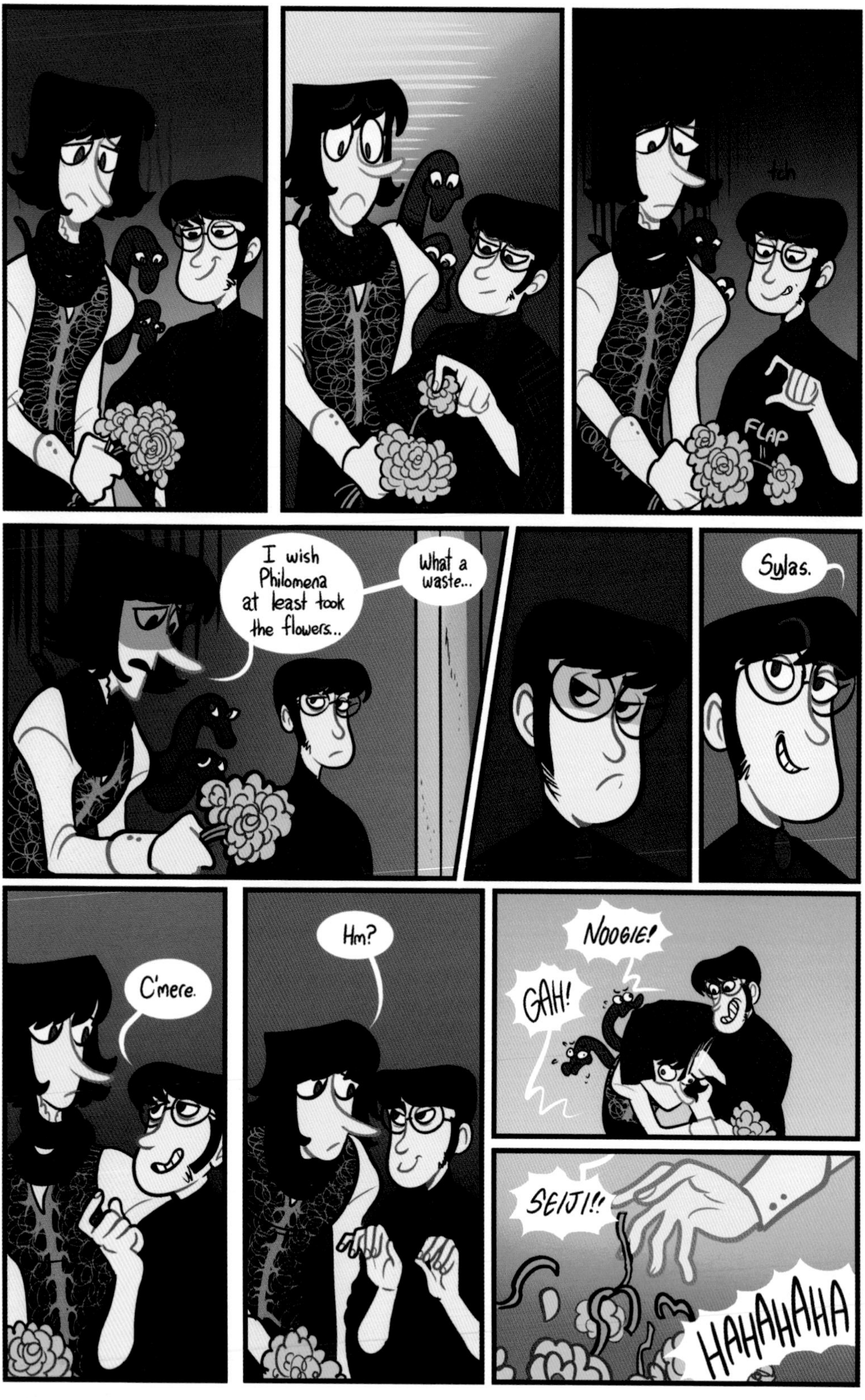
tch
FLAP
I wish Philomena at least took the flowers...
What a waste...
Sylas.
C'mere.
Hm?
NOOGIE!
GAH!
SEIJI!!
HAHAHAHA

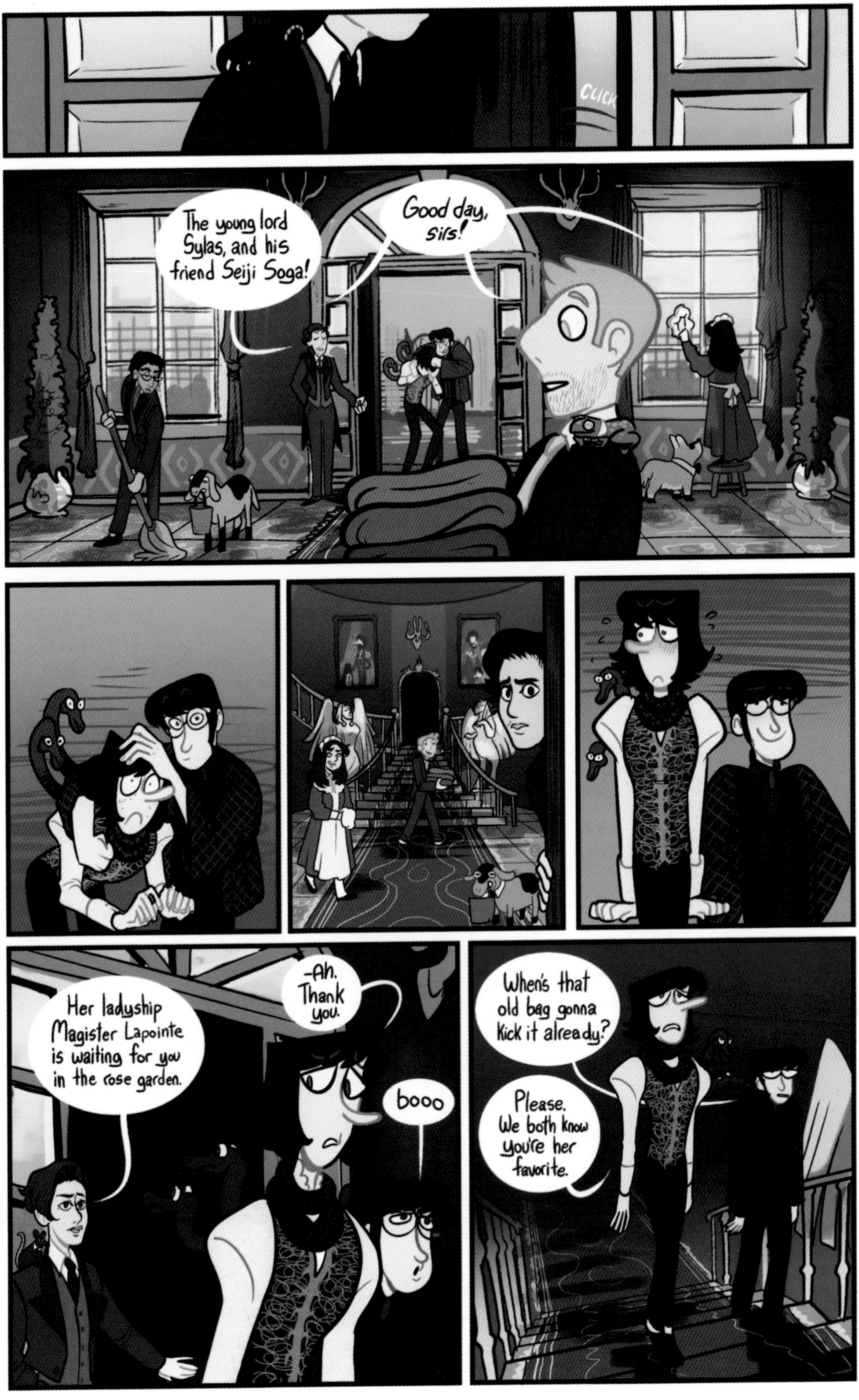
CLICK
The young lord Sylas, and his friend Seiji Soga!
Good day, sirs!
Her ladyship Magister Lapointe is waiting for you in the rose garden.
-Ah. Thank you.
booo
When's that old bag gonna kick it already?
Please. We both know you're her favorite.

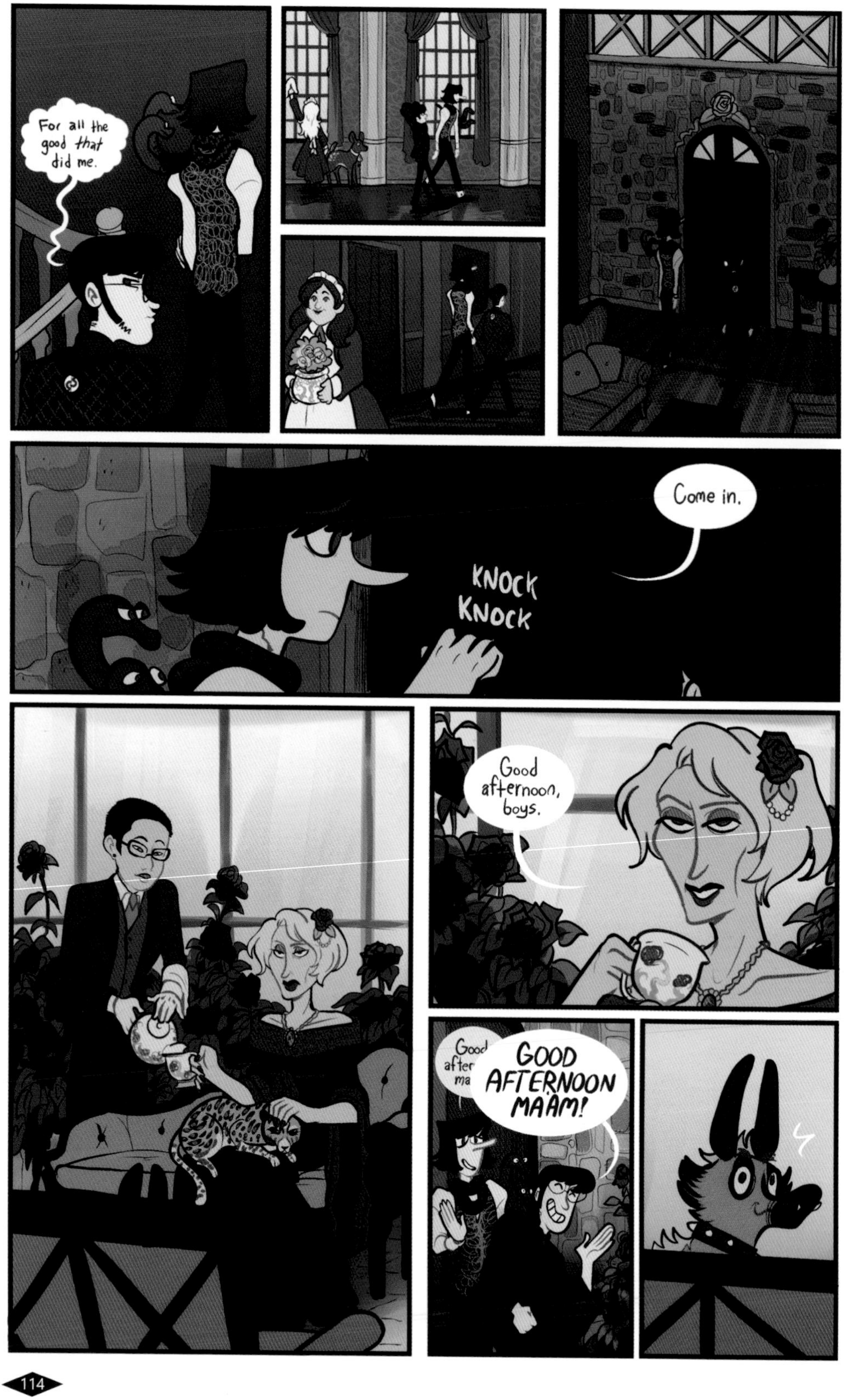
For all the good *that* did me.
Come in.
KNOCK KNOCK
Good afternoon, boys.
GOOD AFTERNOON MA'AM!

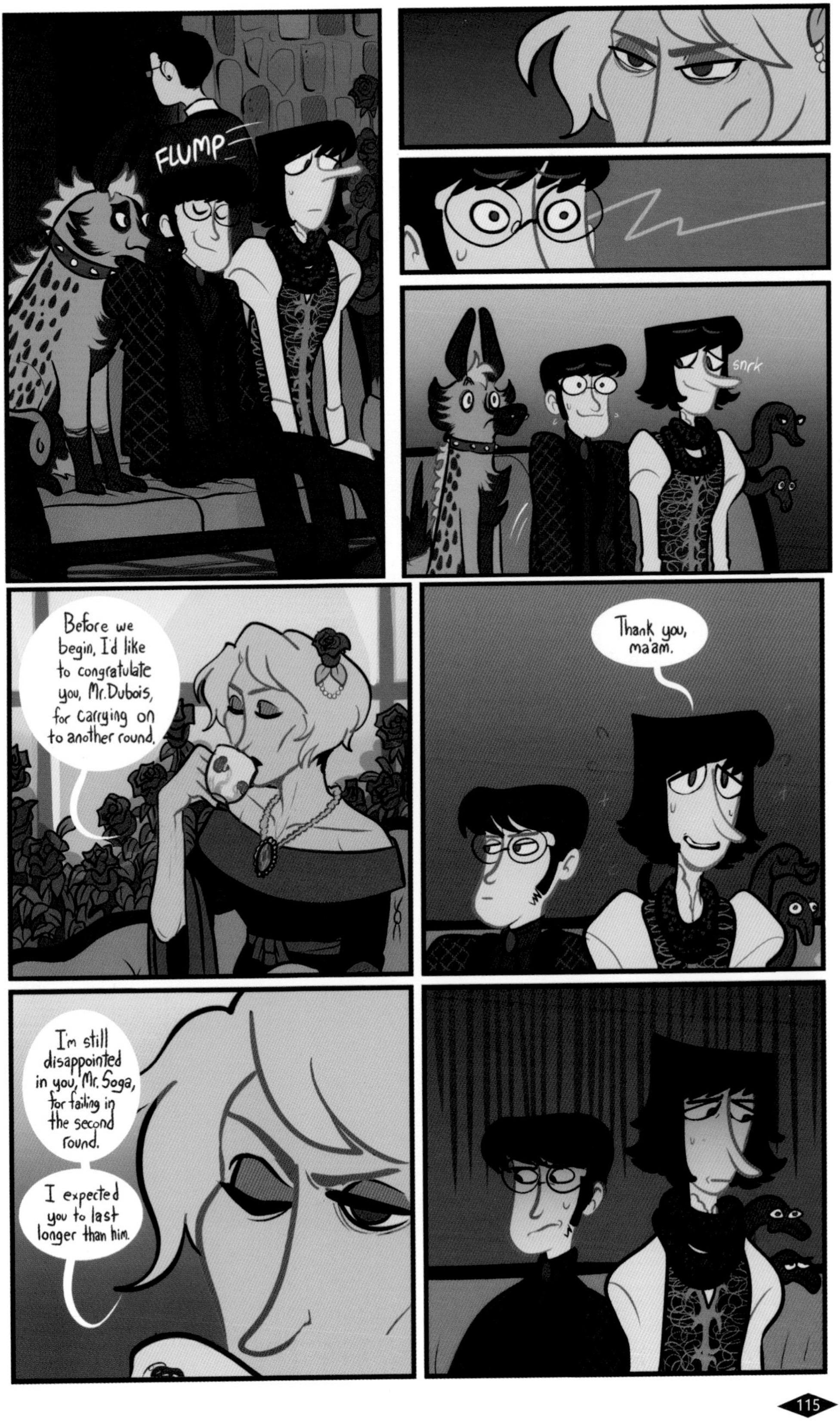
FLUMP
snrk
Before we begin, I'd like to congratulate you, Mr. Dubois, for carrying on to another round.
Thank you, ma'am.
I'm still disappointed in you, Mr. Soga, for failing in the second round.
I expected you to last longer than him.

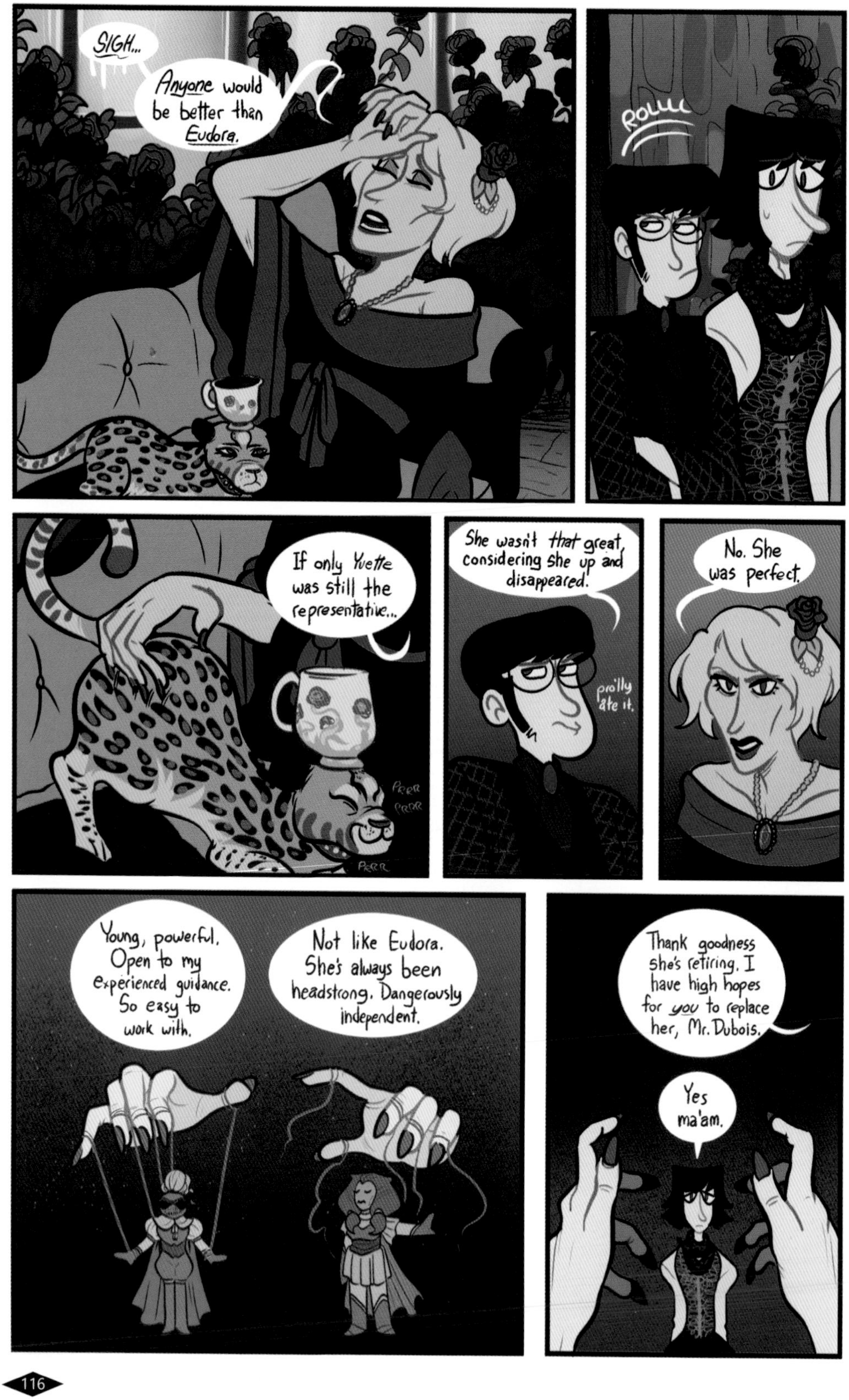
SIGH...
Anyone would be better than Eudora.
ROLLLL
If only Yvette was still the representative...
PRRR
PRRR
PRRR
She wasn't that great, considering she up and disappeared.
pro'lly ate it.
No. She was perfect.
Young, powerful. Open to my experienced guidance. So easy to work with.
Not like Eudora. She's always been headstrong. Dangerously independent.
Thank goodness she's retiring. I have high hopes for you to replace her, Mr. Dubois.
Yes ma'am.

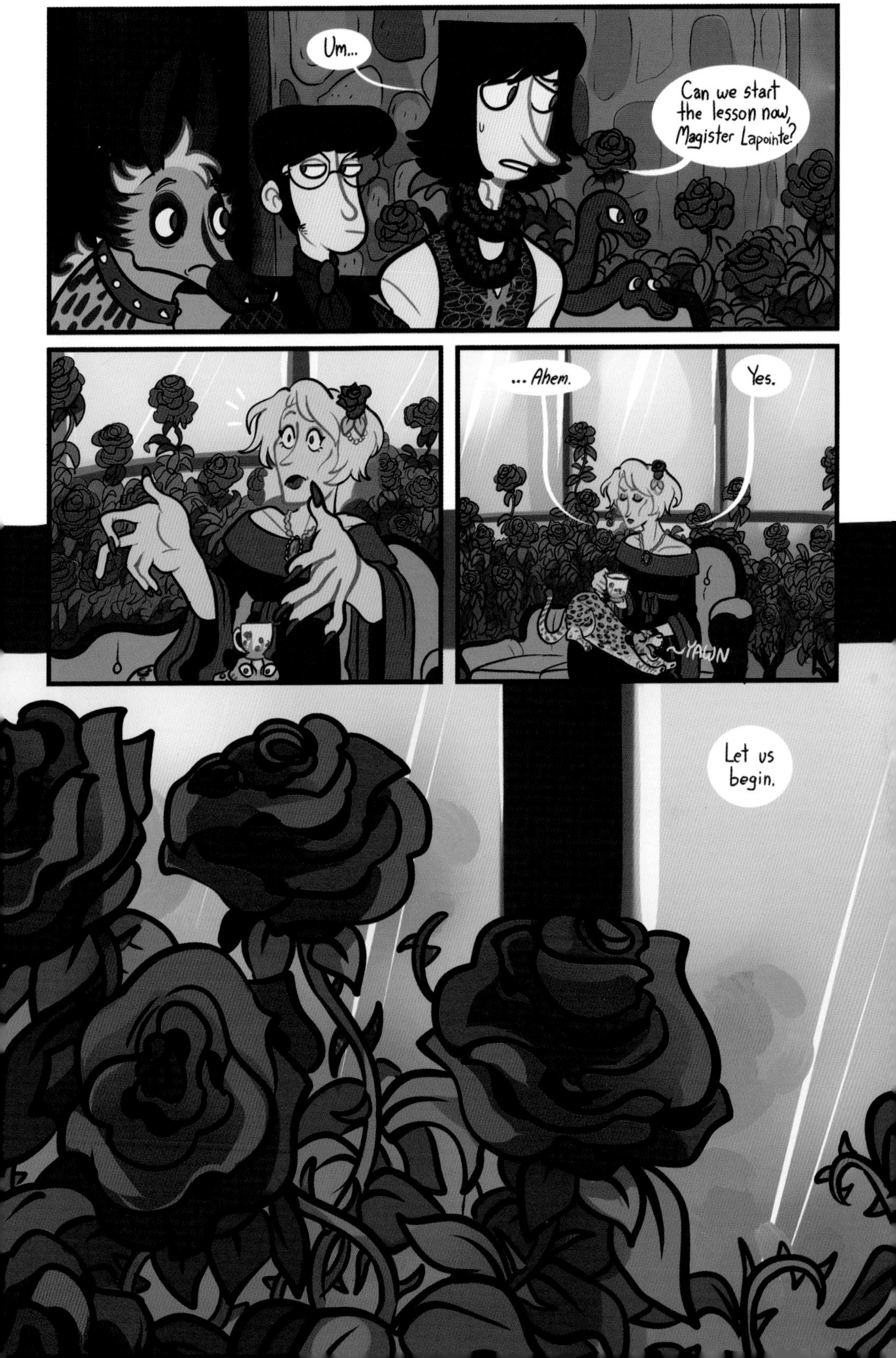
Um...
Can we start the lesson now, Magister Lapointe?
... Ahem.
Yes.
~YAWN
Let us begin.

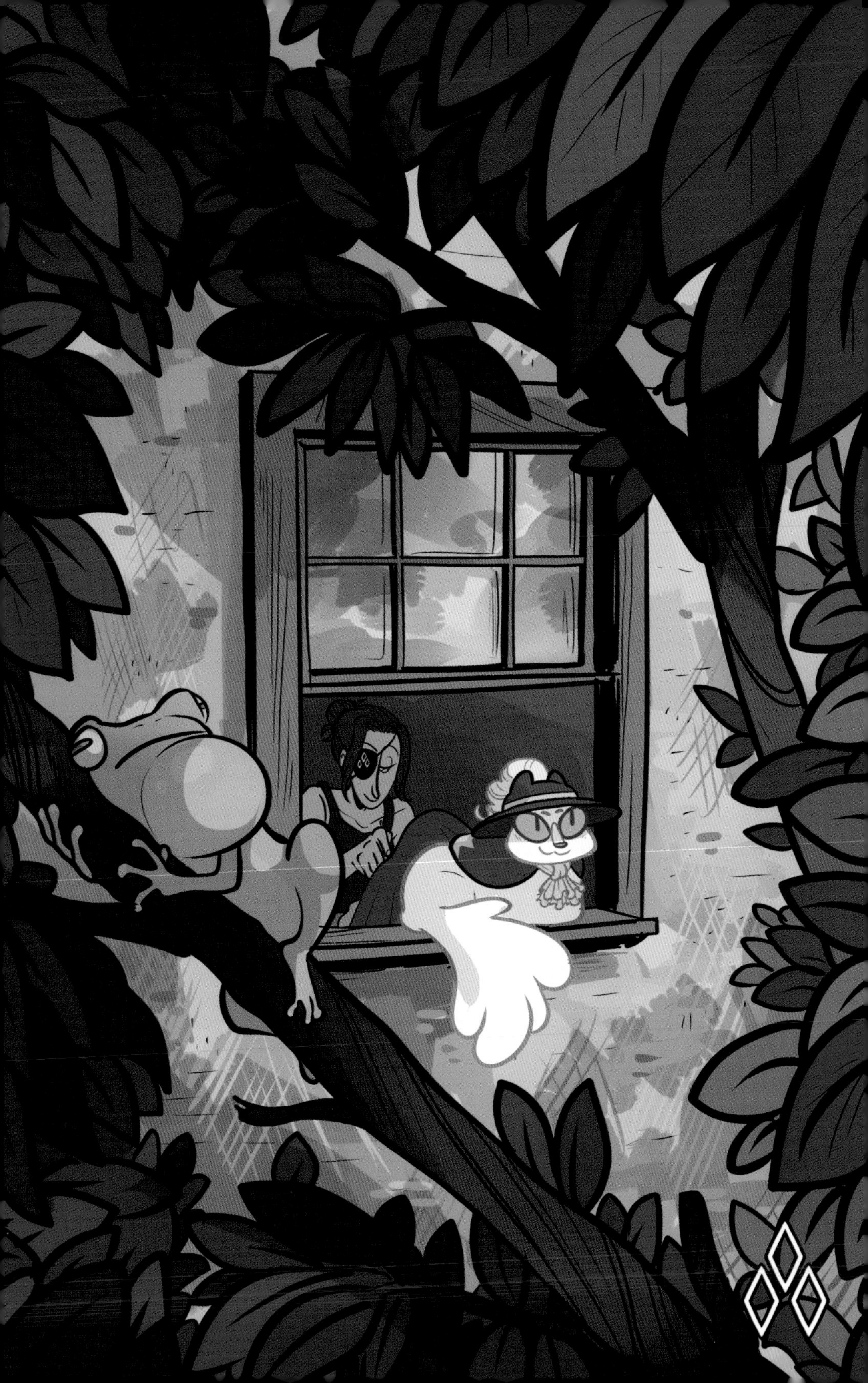

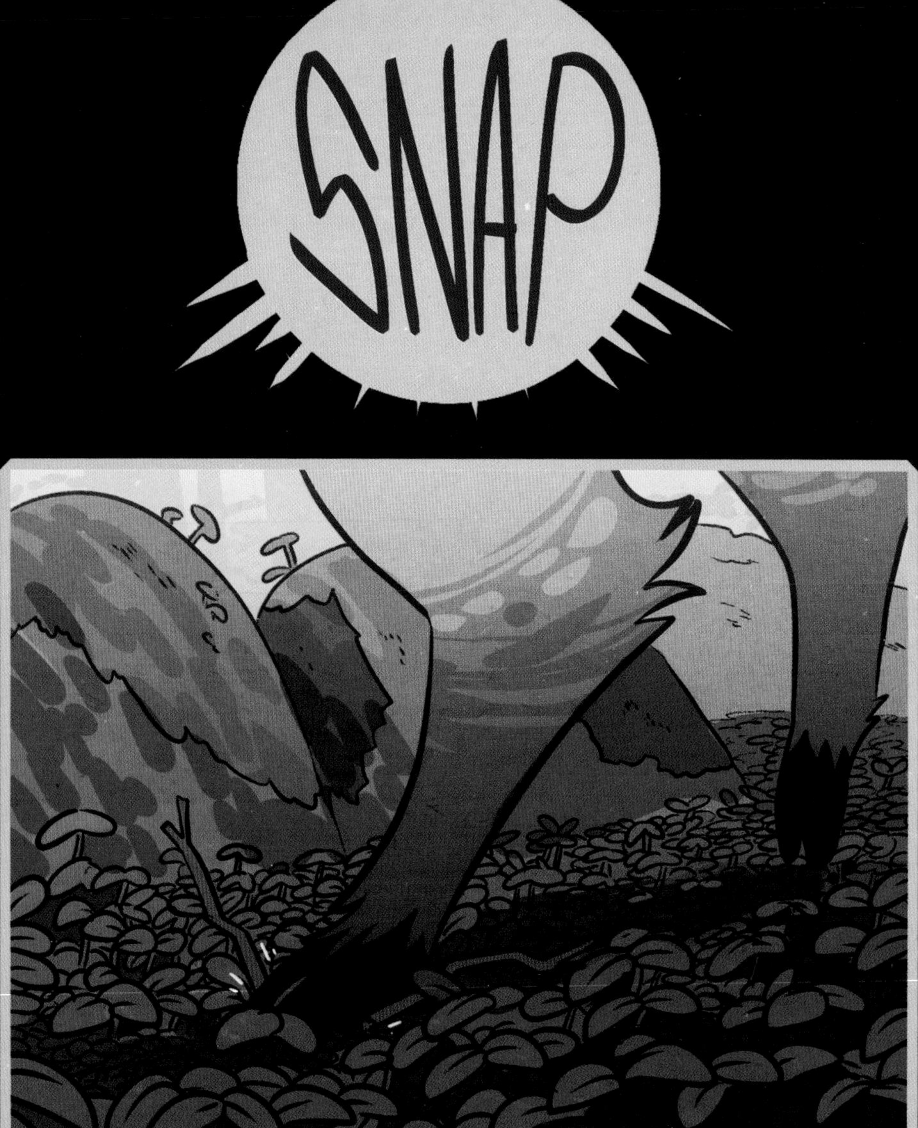
SNAP

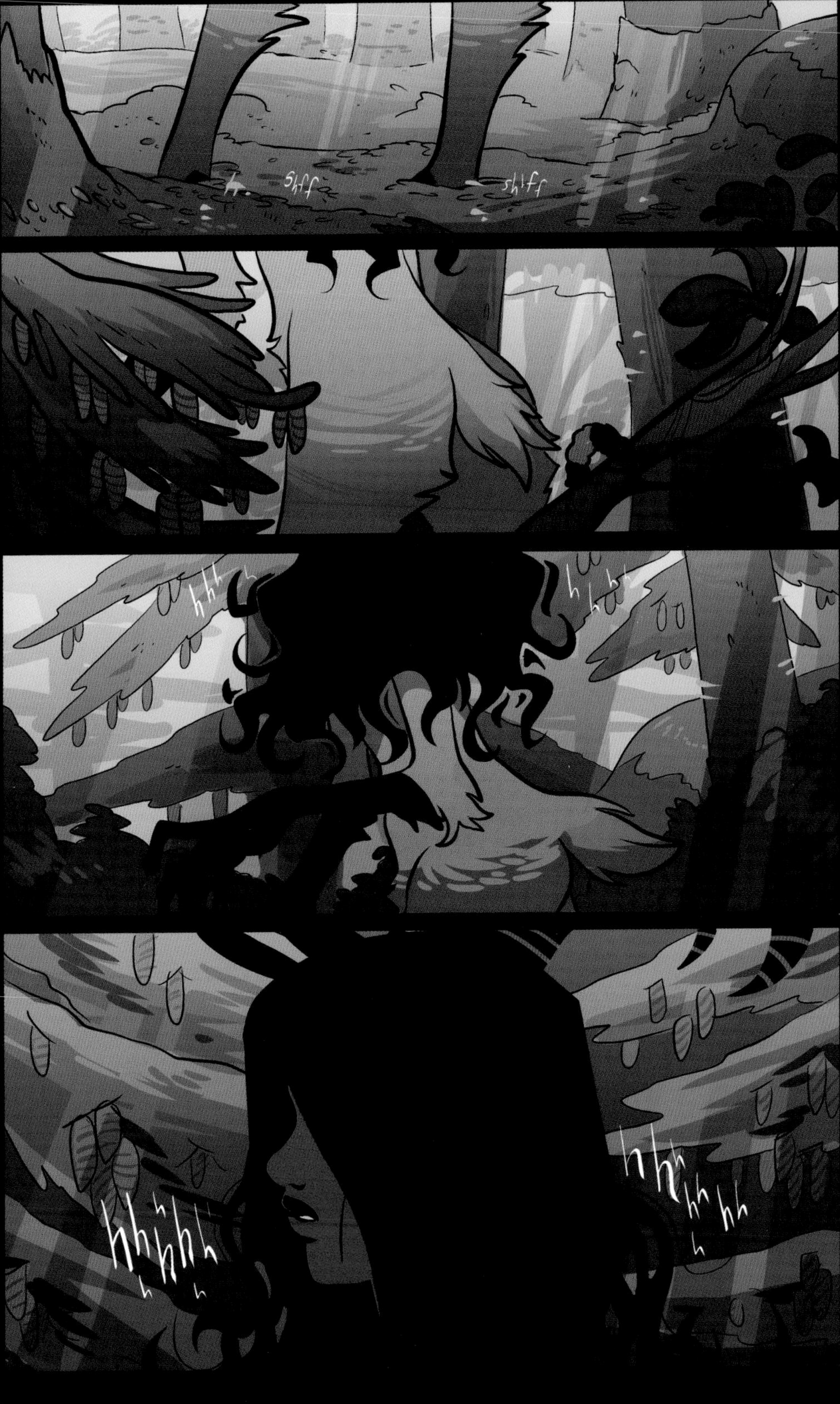
shff
shiff

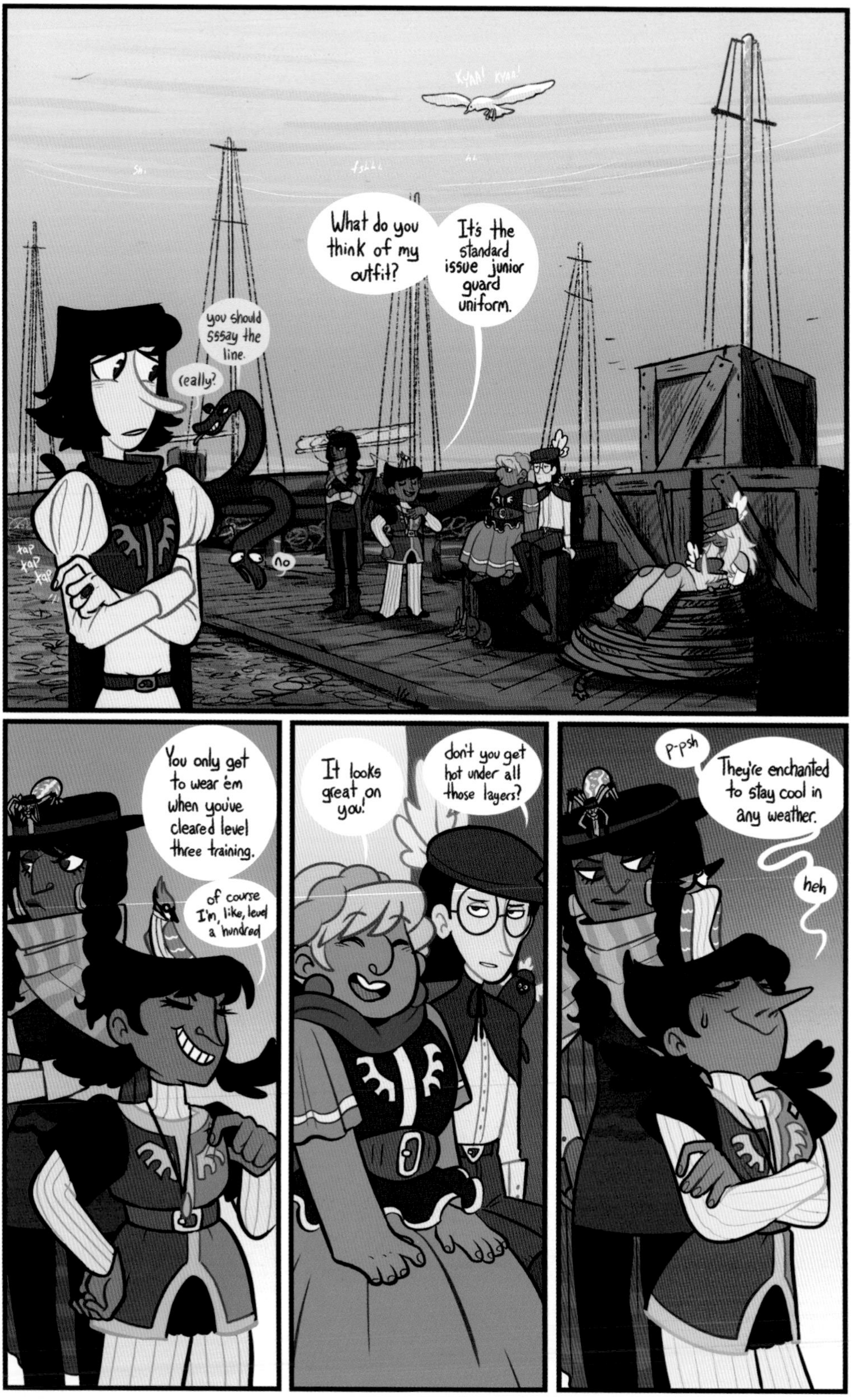
KYAA! KYAA!
What do you think of my outfit?
It's the standard issue junior guard uniform.
you should sssay the line.
really?
no
tap tap tap
You only get to wear 'em when you've cleared level three training.
of course I'm, like, level a hundred
It looks great on you!
don't you get hot under all those layers?
p-psh
They're enchanted to stay cool in any weather.
heh

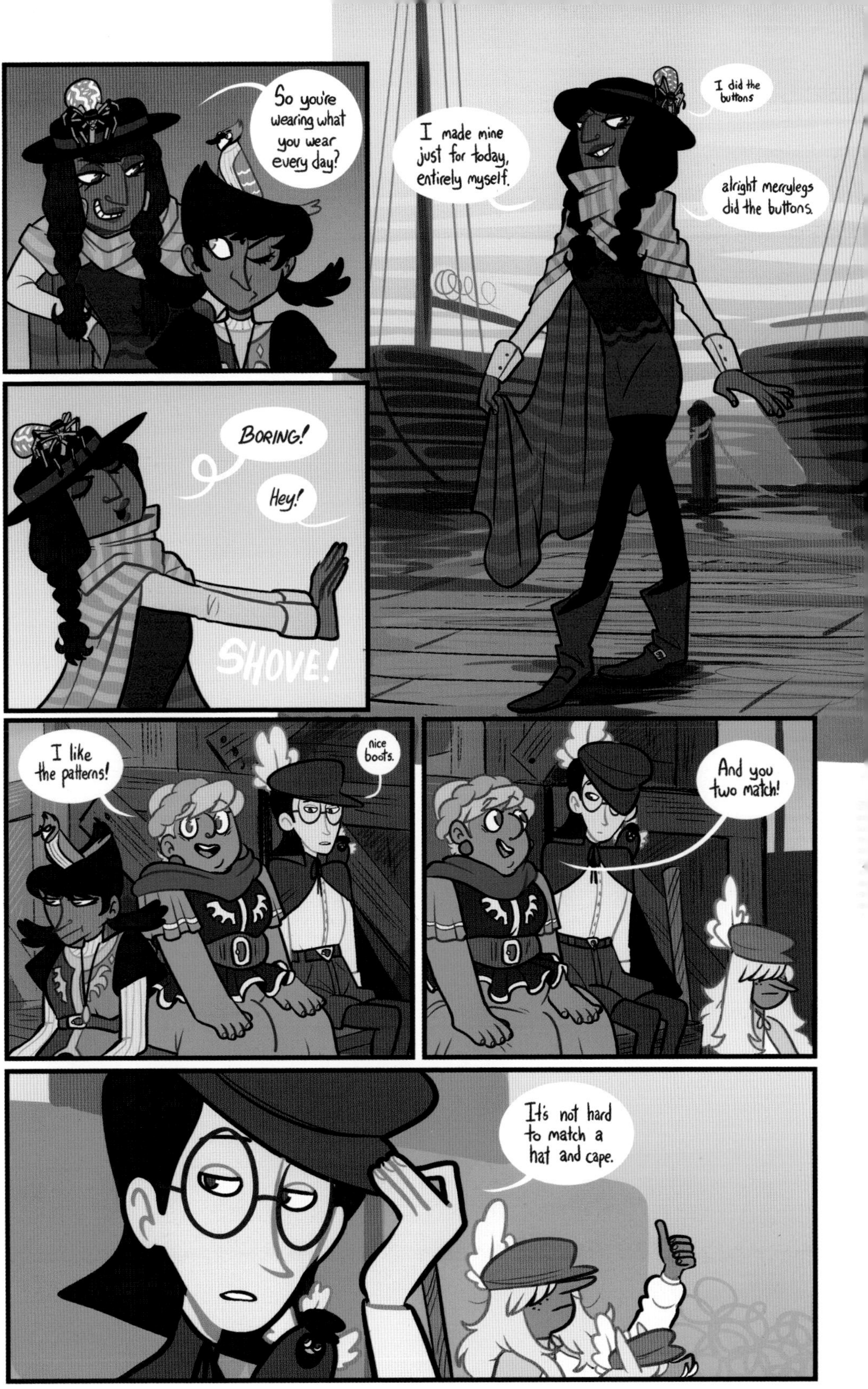
So you're wearing what you wear every day?
BORING!
Hey!
SHOVE!
I made mine just for today, entirely myself.
I did the buttons
alright merrylegs did the buttons.
I like the patterns!
nice boots.
And you two match!
It's not hard to match a hat and cape.

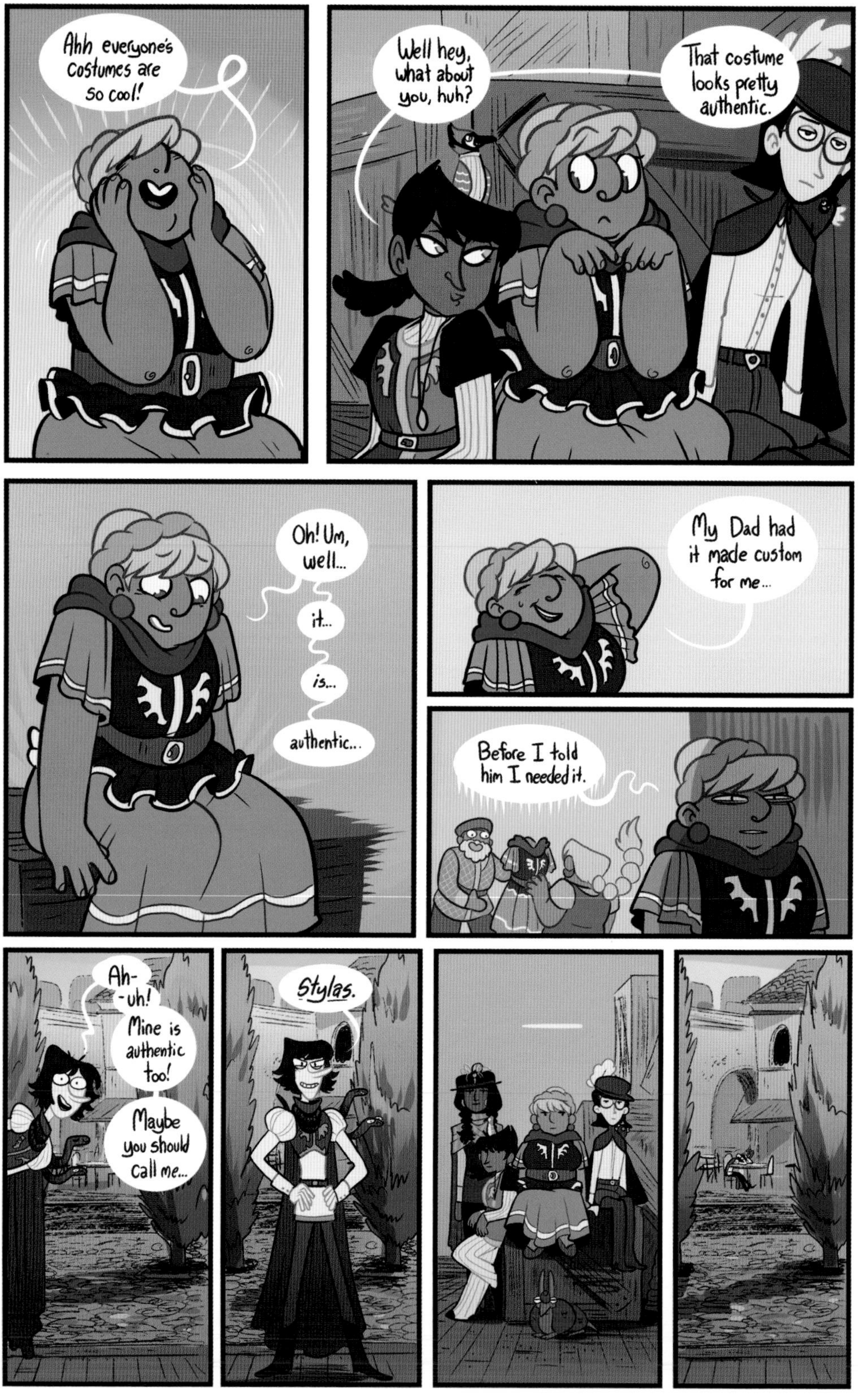

Ahh everyone's costumes are so cool!
Well hey, what about you, huh?
That costume looks pretty authentic.
Oh! Um, well...
it...
is...
authentic...
My Dad had it made custom for me...
Before I told him I needed it.
Ah- -uh!
Mine is authentic too!
Maybe you should call me...
Stylas.

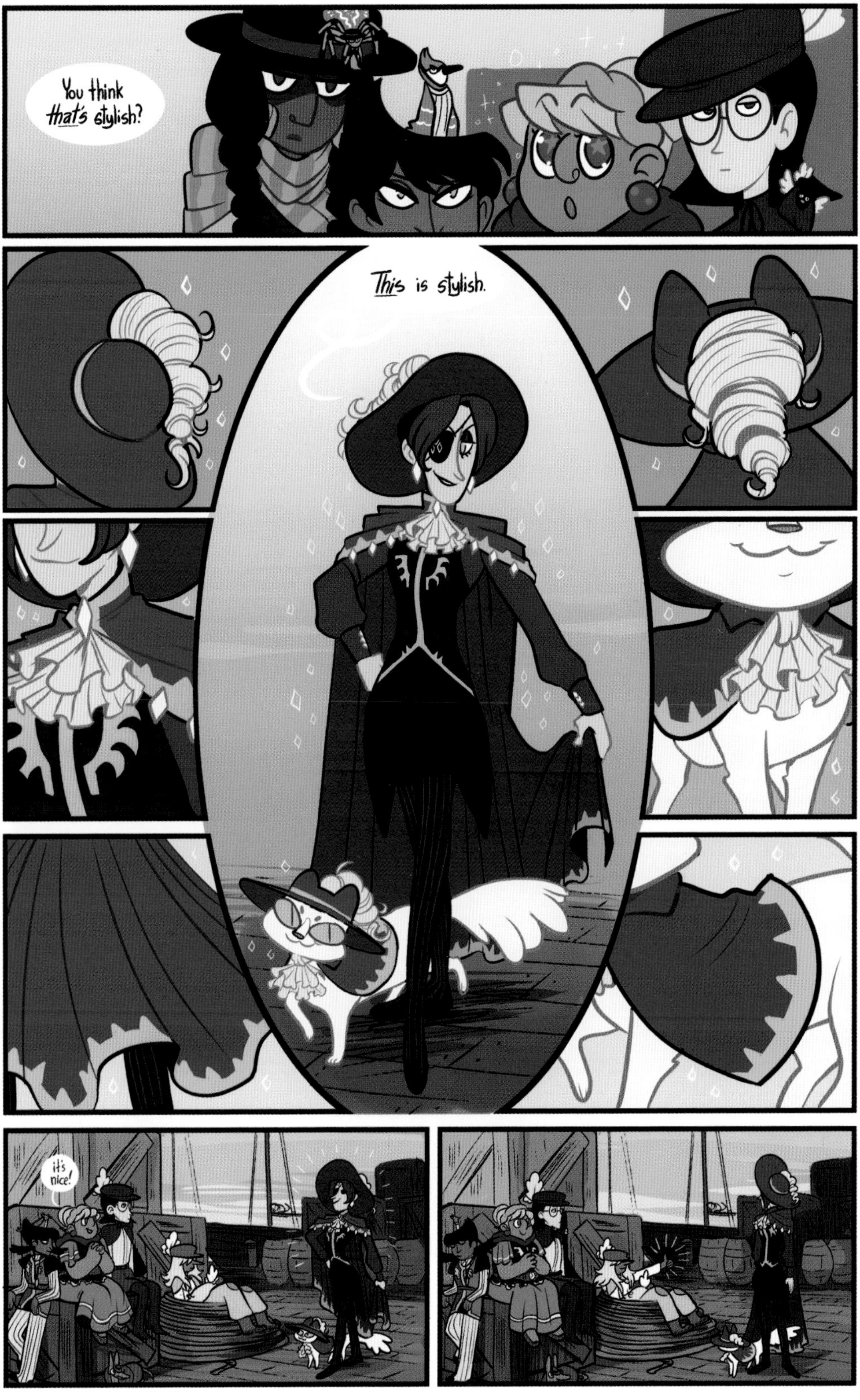
You think
that's stylish?
This is stylish.
it's
nice!

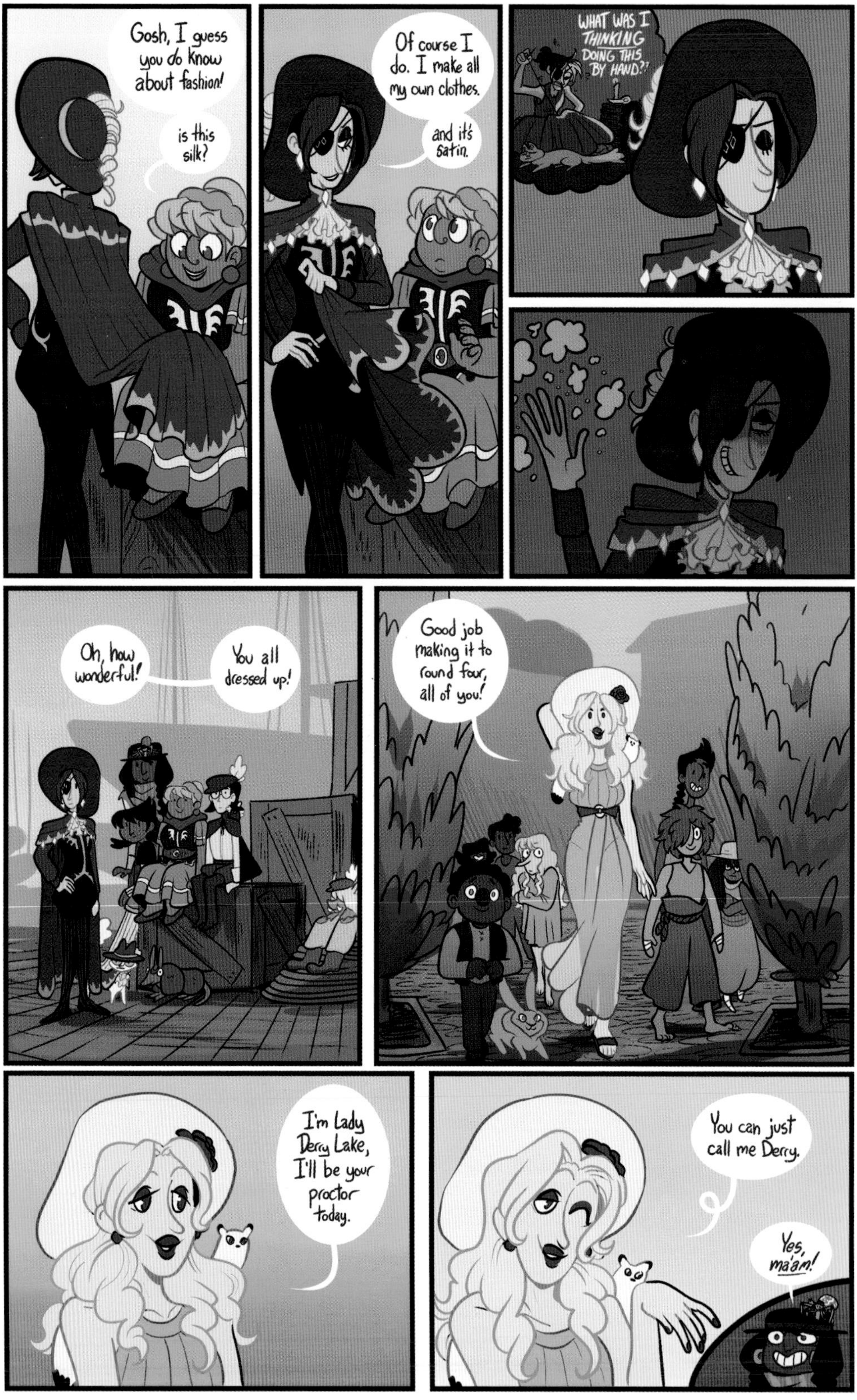
Gosh, I guess you do know about fashion!
is this silk?
Of course I do. I make all my own clothes.
and it's satin.
WHAT WAS I THINKING DOING THIS BY HAND?!
Oh, how wonderful!
You all dressed up!
Good job making it to round four, all of you!
I'm Lady Derry Lake, I'll be your proctor today.
You can just call me Derry.
Yes, ma'am!

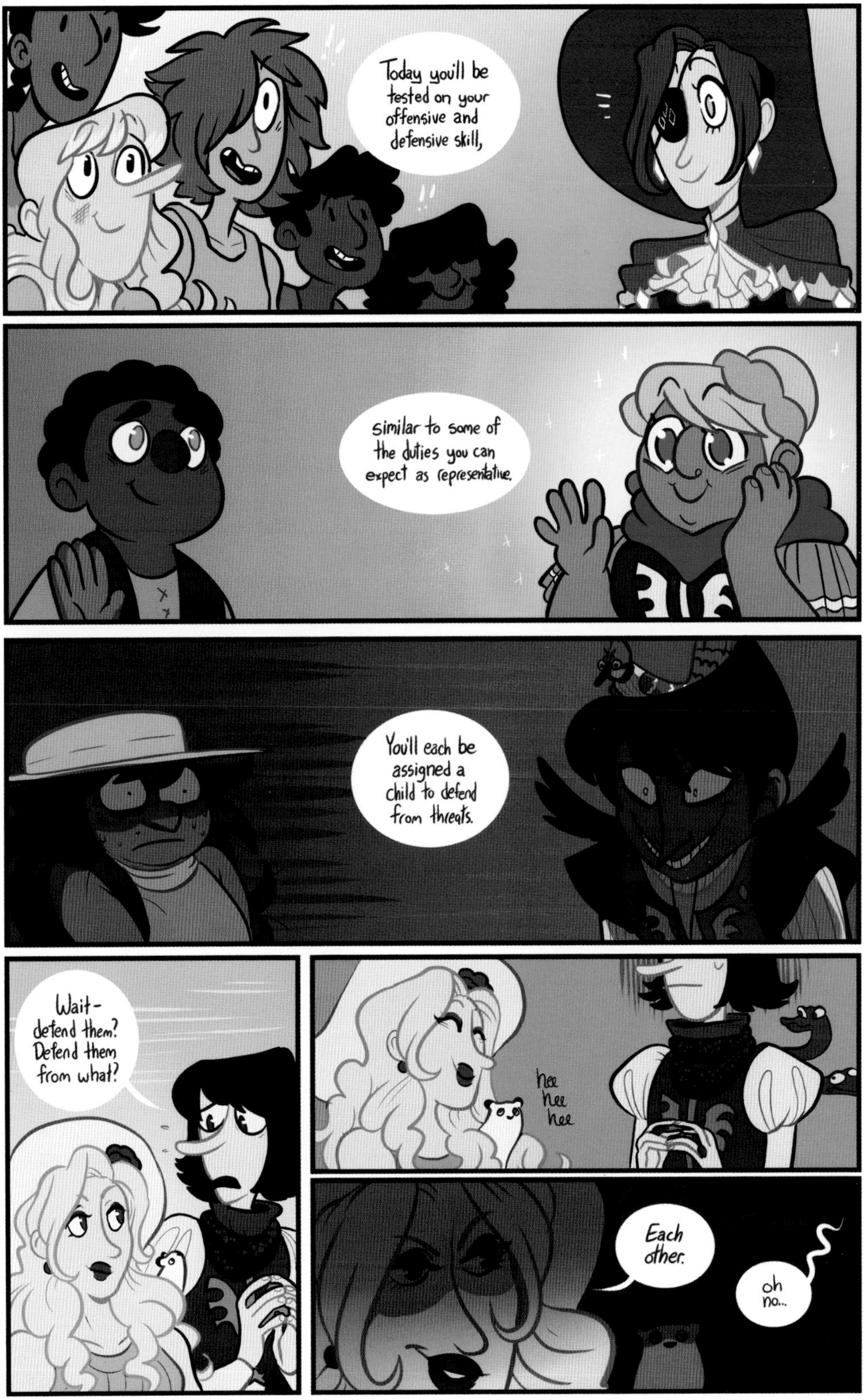
Today you'll be tested on your offensive and defensive skill,
similar to some of the duties you can expect as representative.
You'll each be assigned a child to defend from threats.
Wait- defend them? Defend them from what?
hee hee hee
Each other.
oh no...

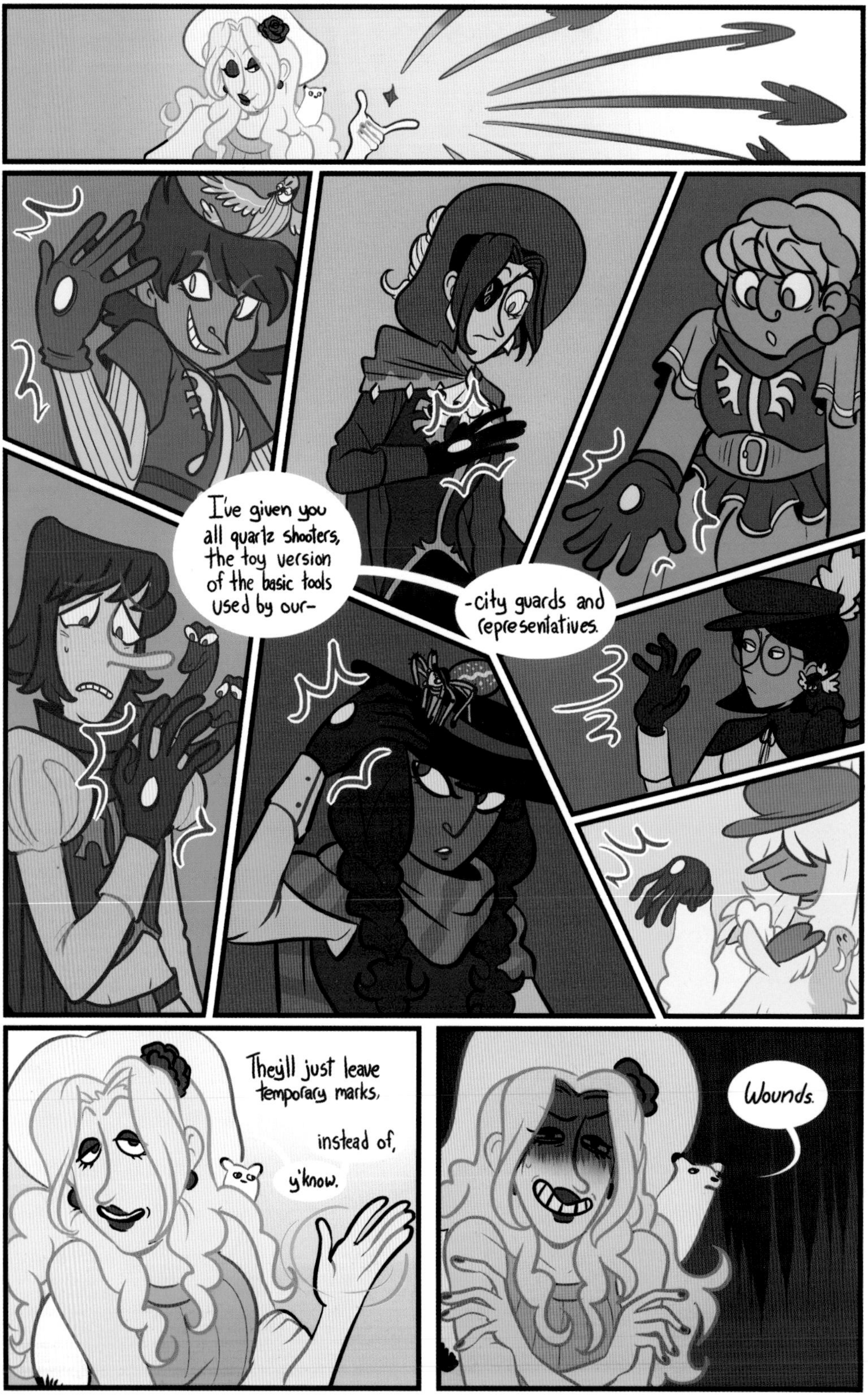
I've given you all quartz shooters, the toy version of the basic tools used by our-
-city guards and representatives.
They'll just leave temporary marks,
instead of,
y'know.
Wounds.

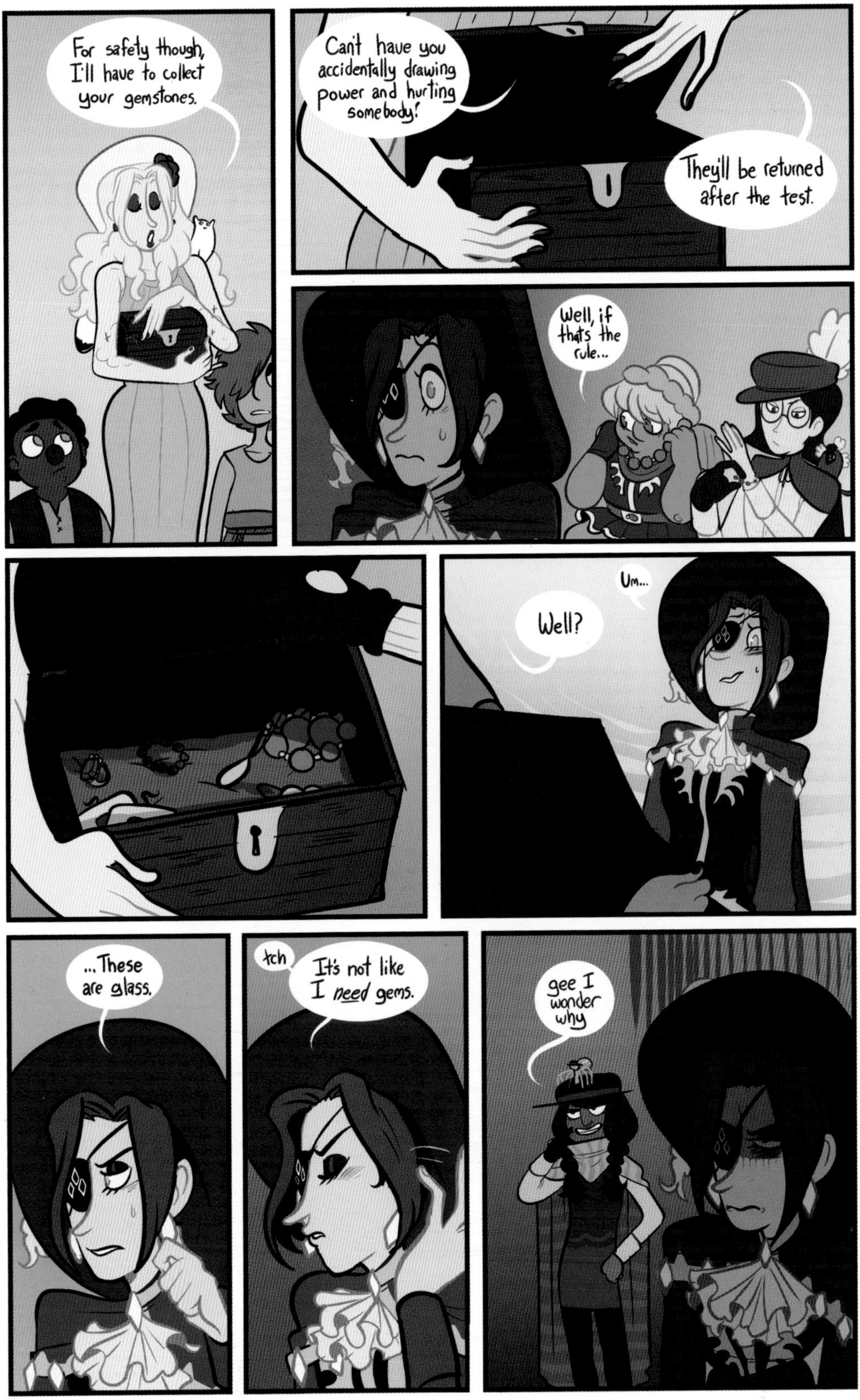
For safety though, I'll have to collect your gemstones.
Can't have you accidentally drawing power and hurting somebody!
They'll be returned after the test.
Well, if that's the rule...
Um...
Well?
...These are glass.
tch
It's not like I need gems.
gee I wonder why

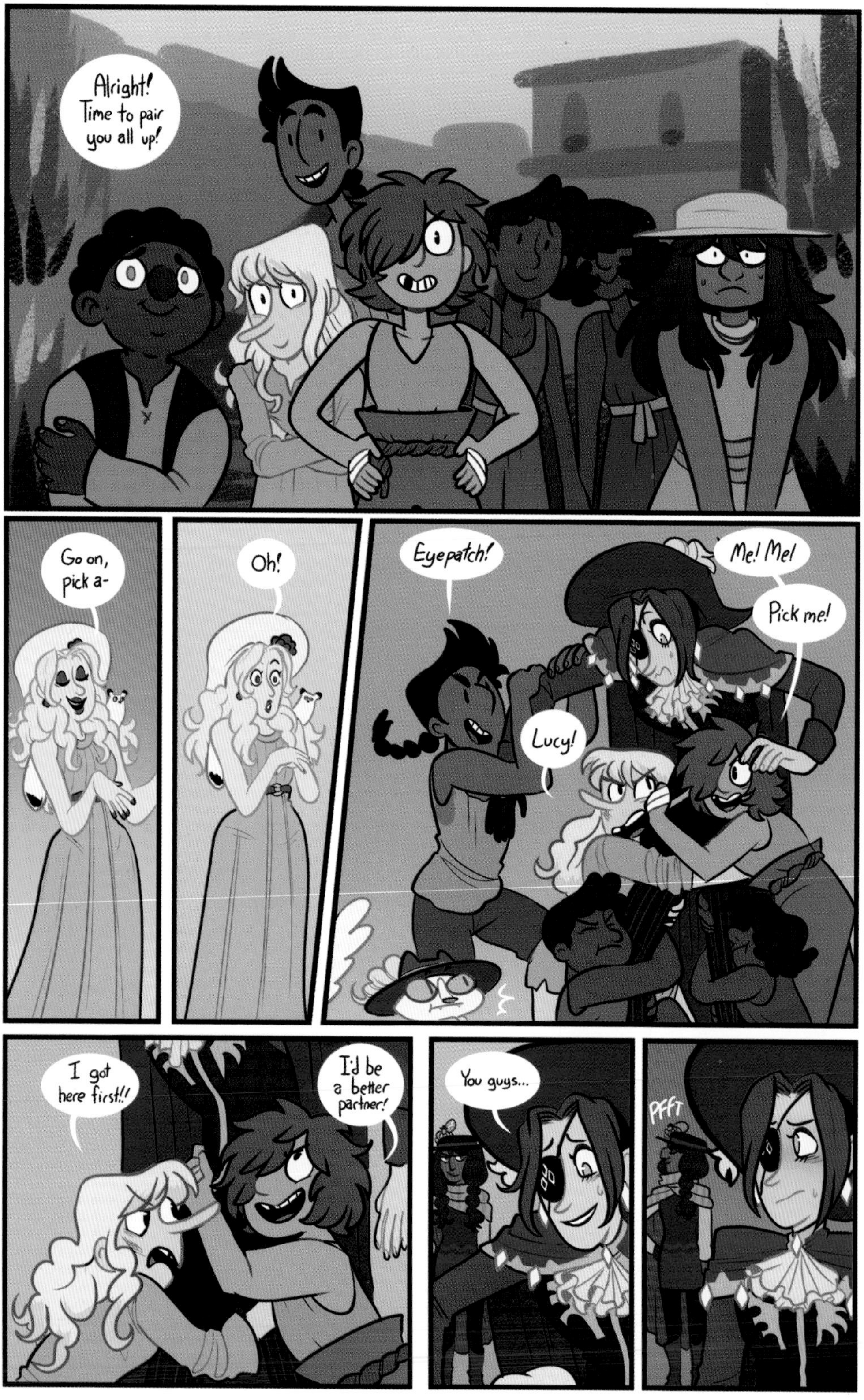

Alright! Time to pair you all up!
Go on, pick a-
Oh!
Eyepatch!
Me! Me!
Pick me!
Lucy!
I got here first!!
I'd be a better partner!
You guys...
PFFT

GAHAHAHA

Ohhh isn't that just the *cutest*?

Uh

Yeah.

Super adorable.

!!!!

Come on, you can't *all* be partnered up with them...

1

2

3!

Yes!

Peony wins!

HEY
HI MY NA
PEONY I LI
YOUR COSTUM
A WHOLE LOT AN
UR HAIR IS RE
VICE AND YOUR
EYEPATCH IS RI
OOL AND I A
LL BE A GO
PARTNER A
E'LL B

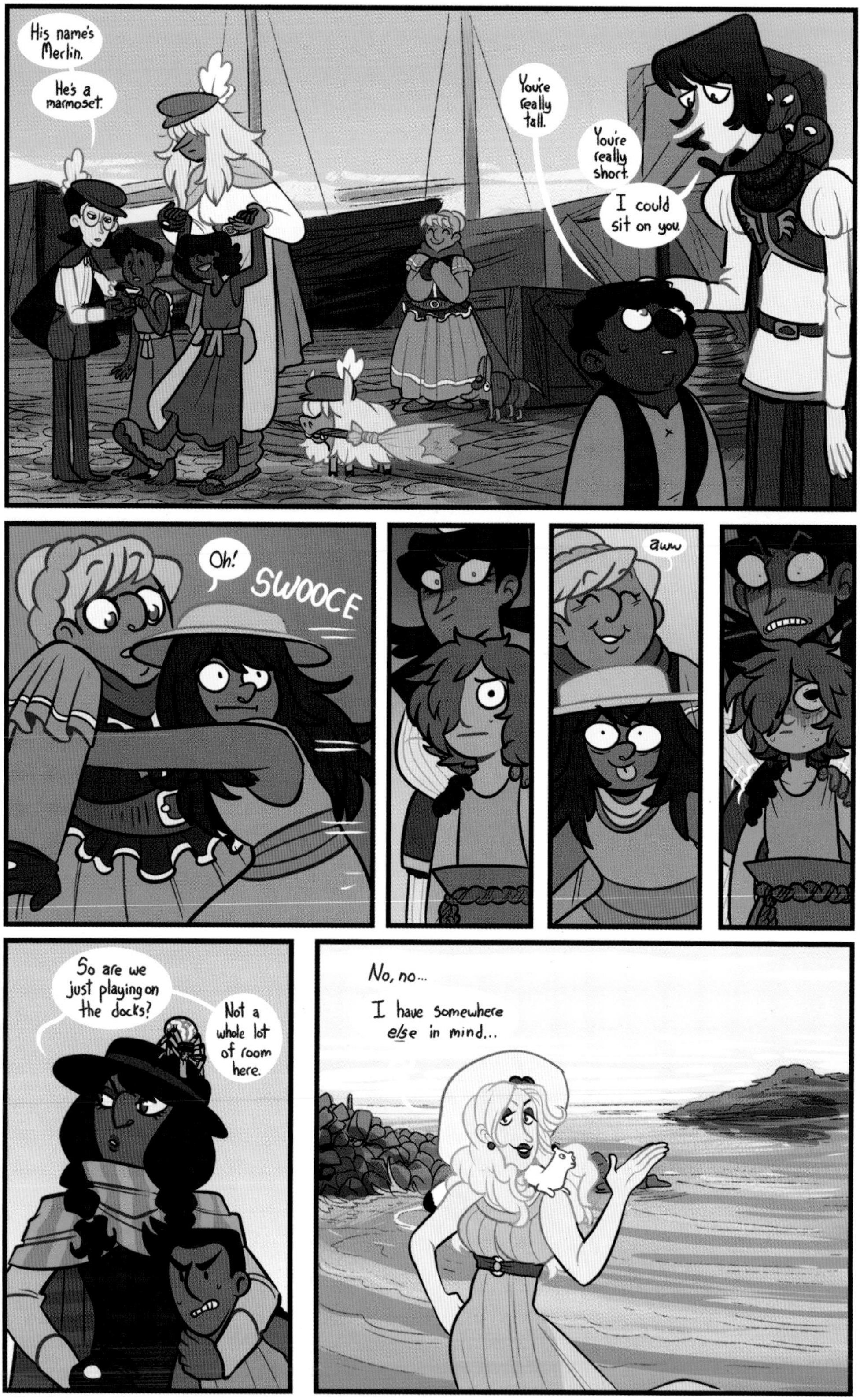
His name's Merlin.
He's a marmoset.
You're really tall.
You're really short.
I could sit on you.
Oh!
SWOOCE
aww
So are we just playing on the docks?
Not a whole lot of room here.
No, no...
I have somewhere else in mind...

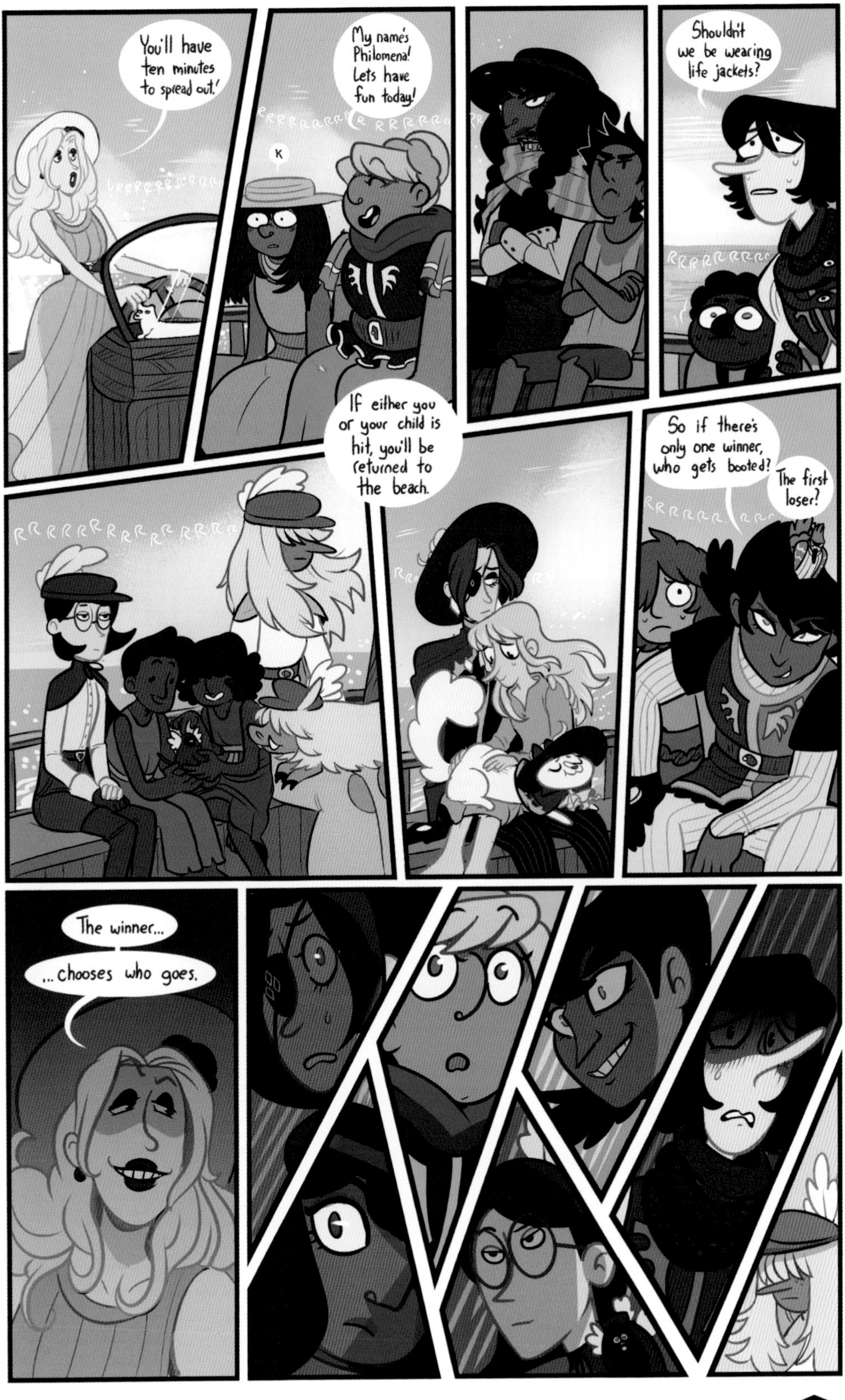
You'll have ten minutes to spread out.'
My name's Philomena! Lets have fun today!
K
Shouldn't we be wearing life jackets?
If either you or your child is hit, you'll be returned to the beach.
So if there's only one winner, who gets booted?
The first loser?
The winner...
...chooses who goes.

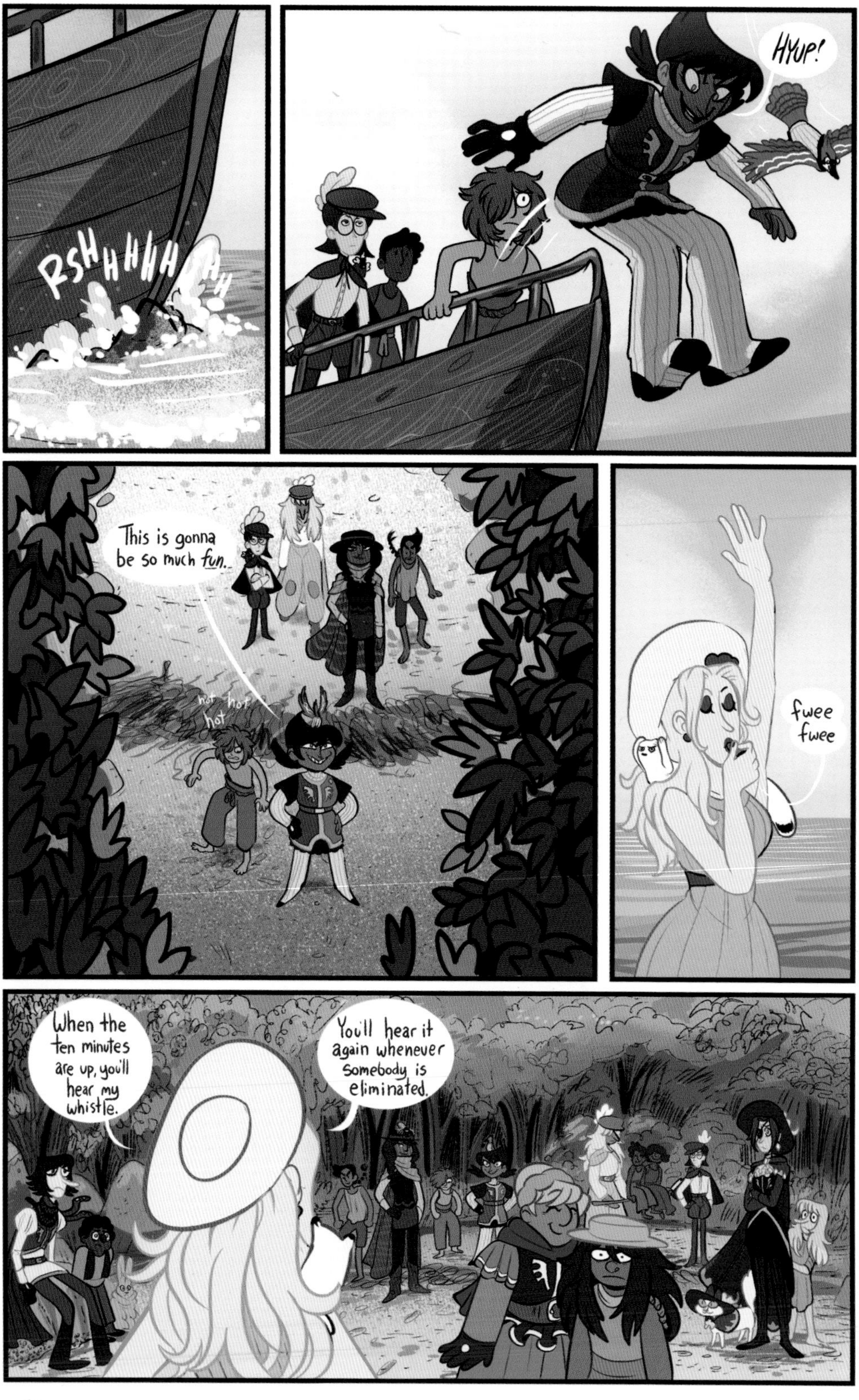
RSHHHHHHHH
HYUP!
This is gonna be so much fun.
hot hot hot
fwee fwee
When the ten minutes are up, you'll hear my whistle.
You'll hear it again whenever somebody is eliminated.

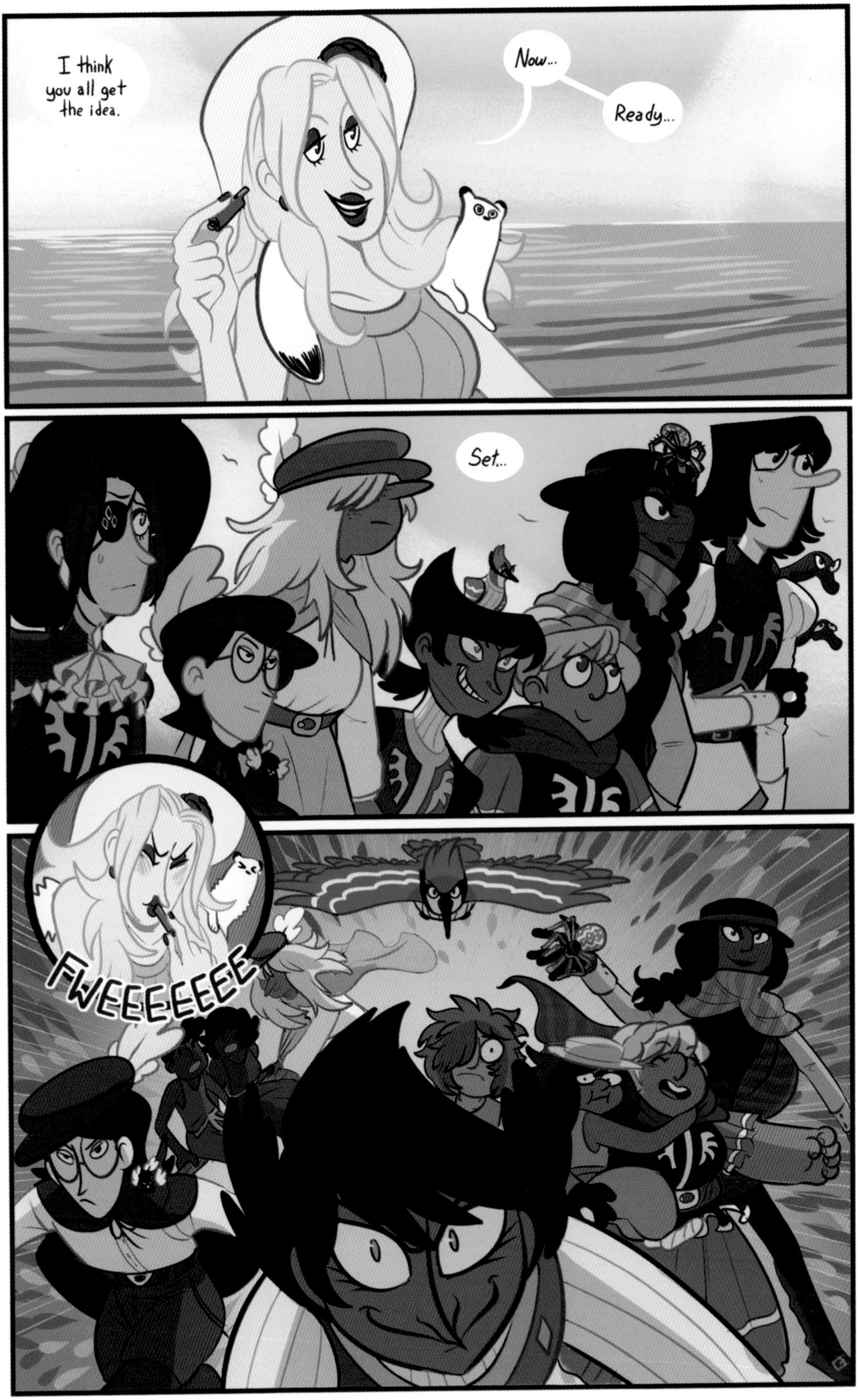
I think you all get the idea.
Now...
Ready...
Set...
FWEEEEEEE

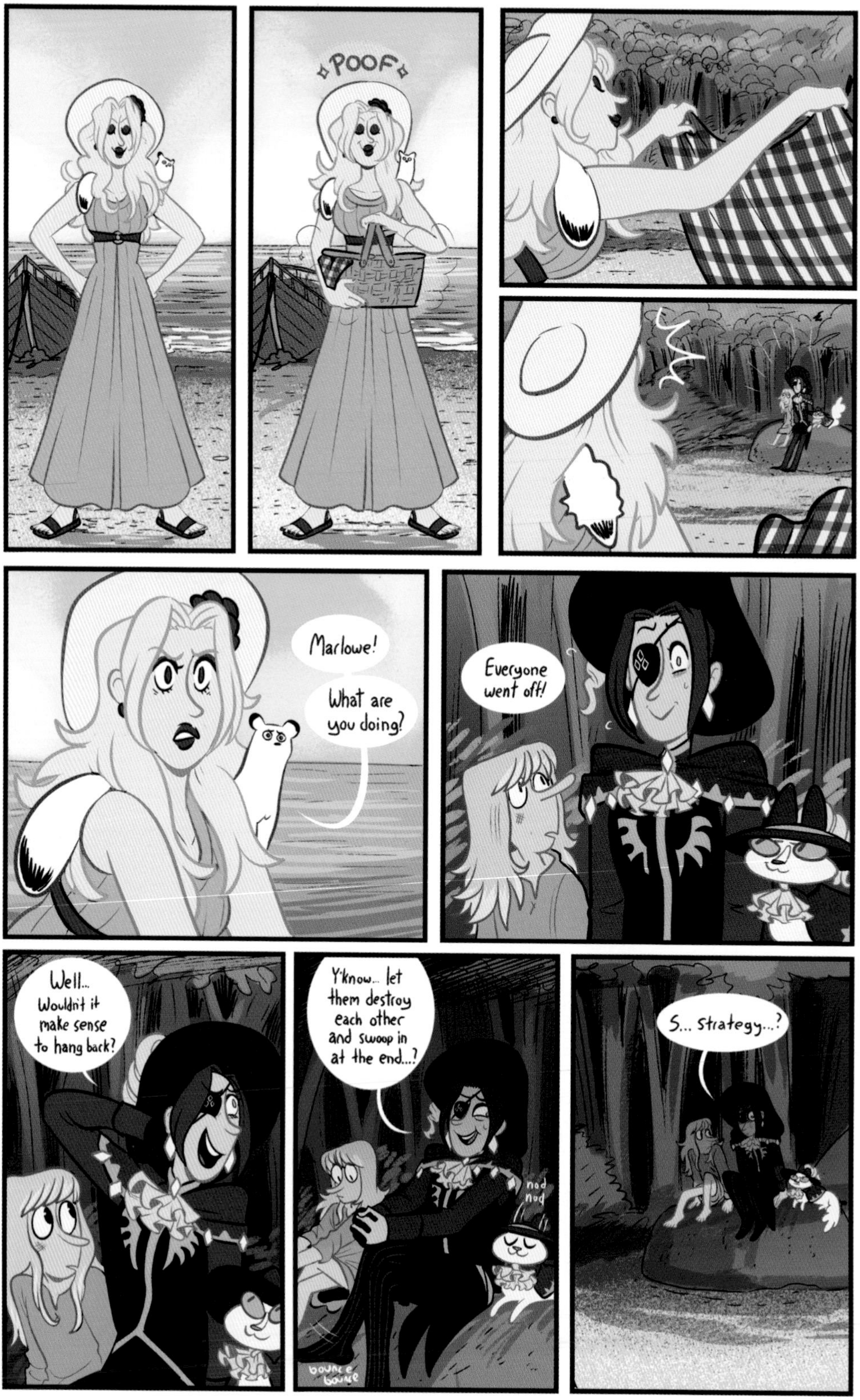
POOF
Marlowe!
What are you doing?
Everyone went off!
Well... Wouldn't it make sense to hang back?
Y'know... let them destroy each other and swoop in at the end...?
nod nod
bounce bounce
S... strategy...?

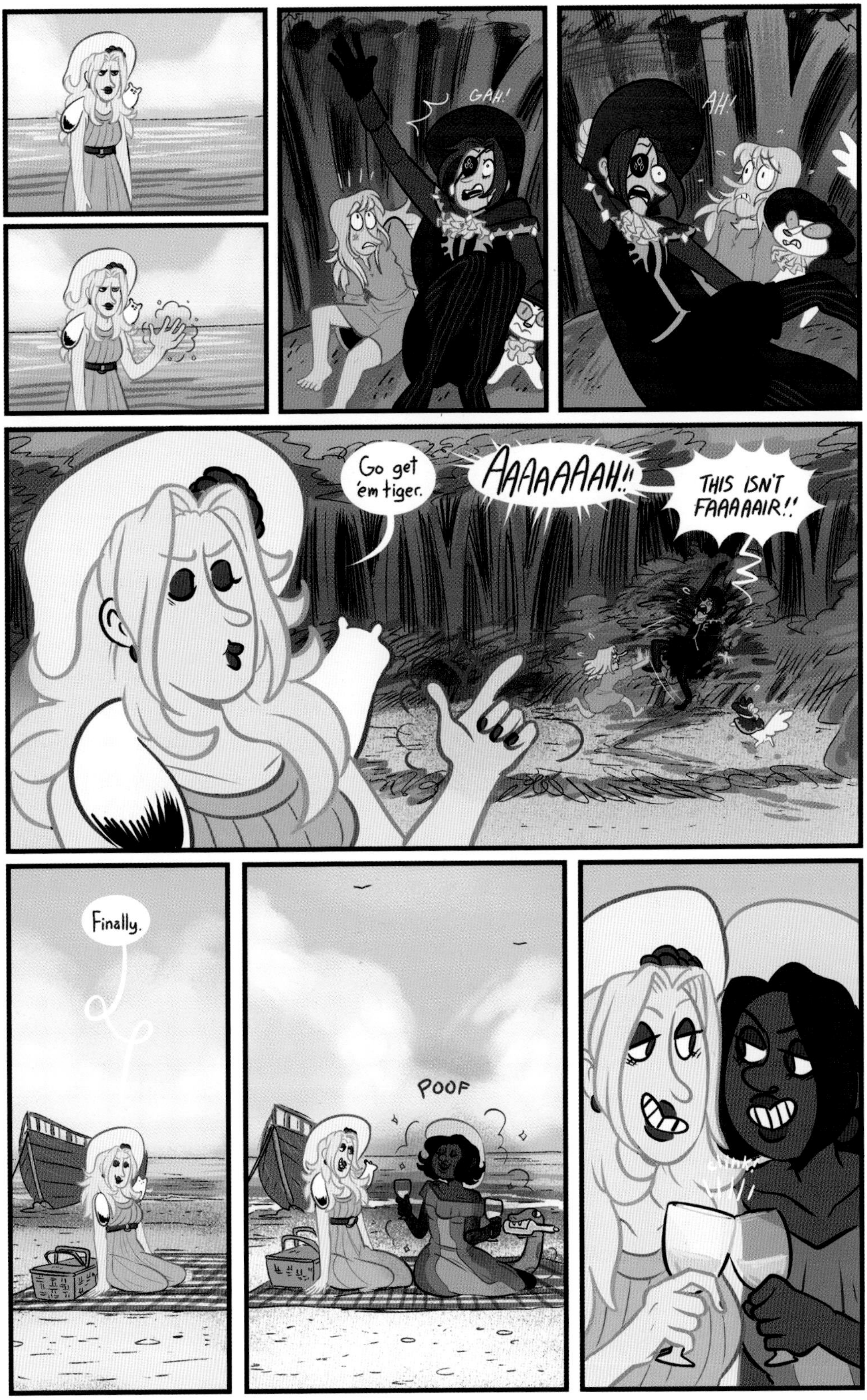
GAH!
AH!
Go get 'em tiger.
AAAAAAAH!!
THIS ISN'T FAAAAAIR!!
Finally.
POOF

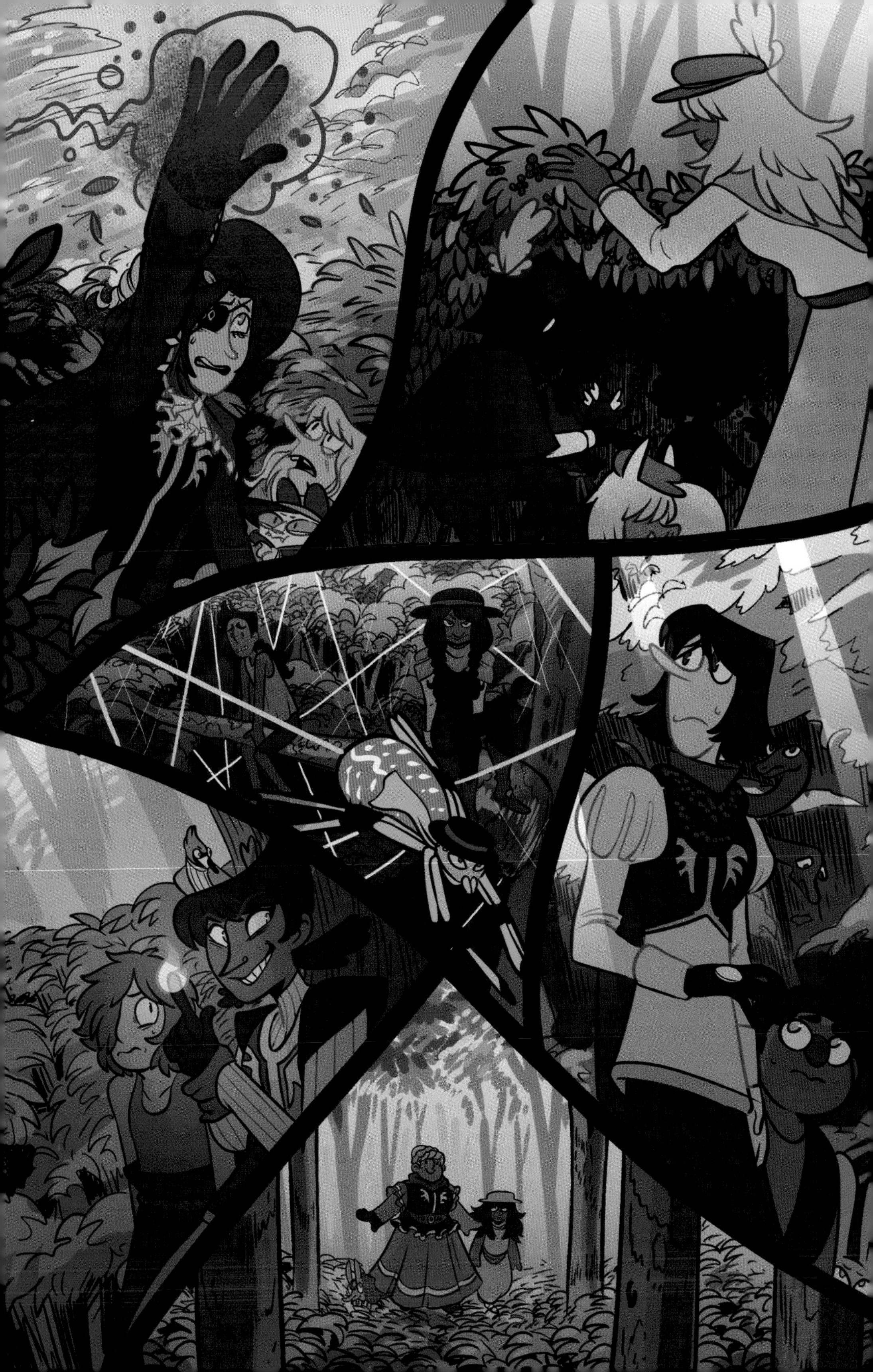

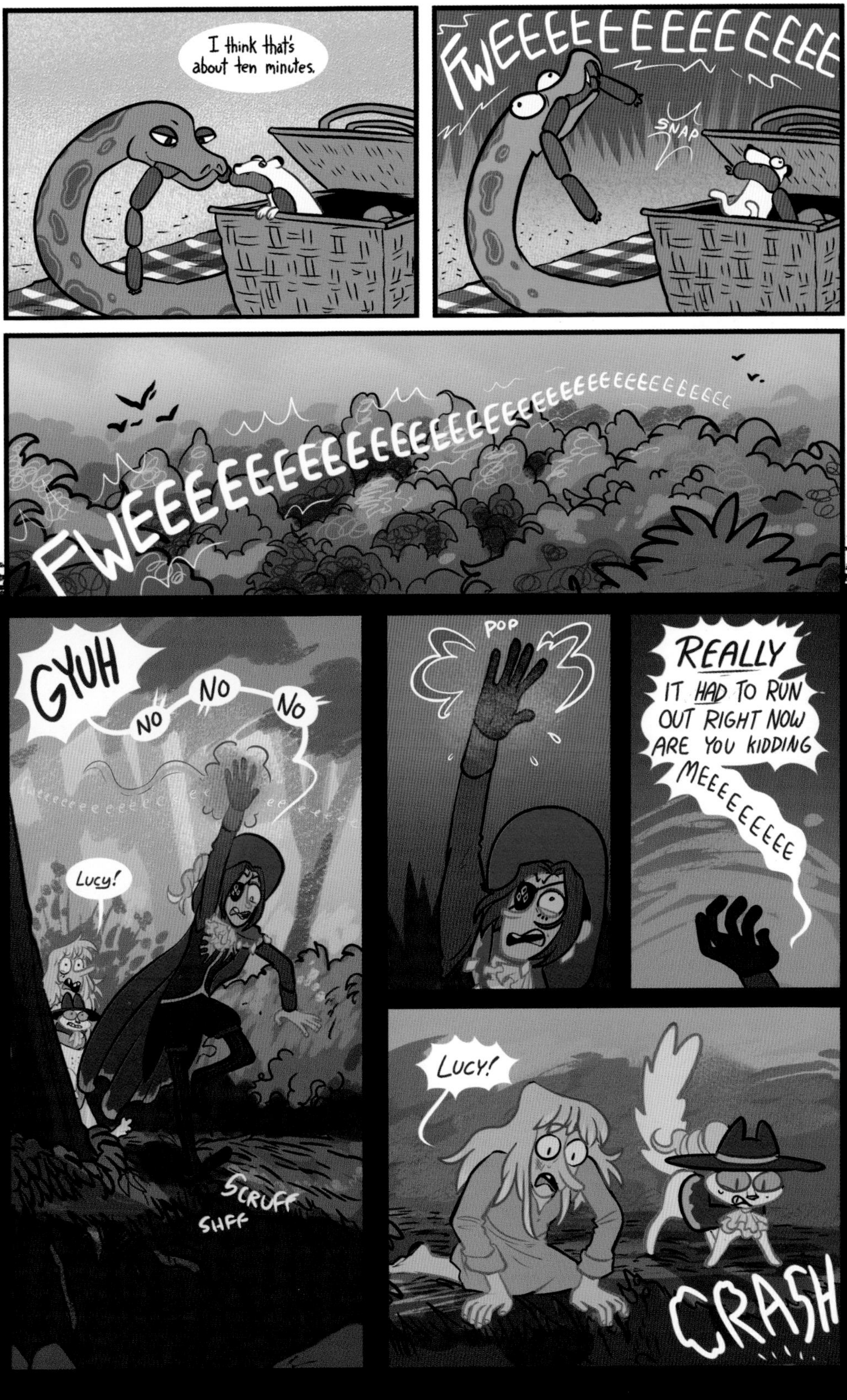
I think that's about ten minutes.
FWEEEEEEEEEEEEEE
SNAP
FWEEEEEEEEEEEEEEEEEEEEEEEEEEEEEEEEEEE
GYUH
NO
NO
NO
Lucy!
SCRUFF
SHFF
POP
REALLY
IT HAD TO RUN OUT RIGHT NOW ARE YOU KIDDING
MEEEEEEEEE
LUCY!
CRASH

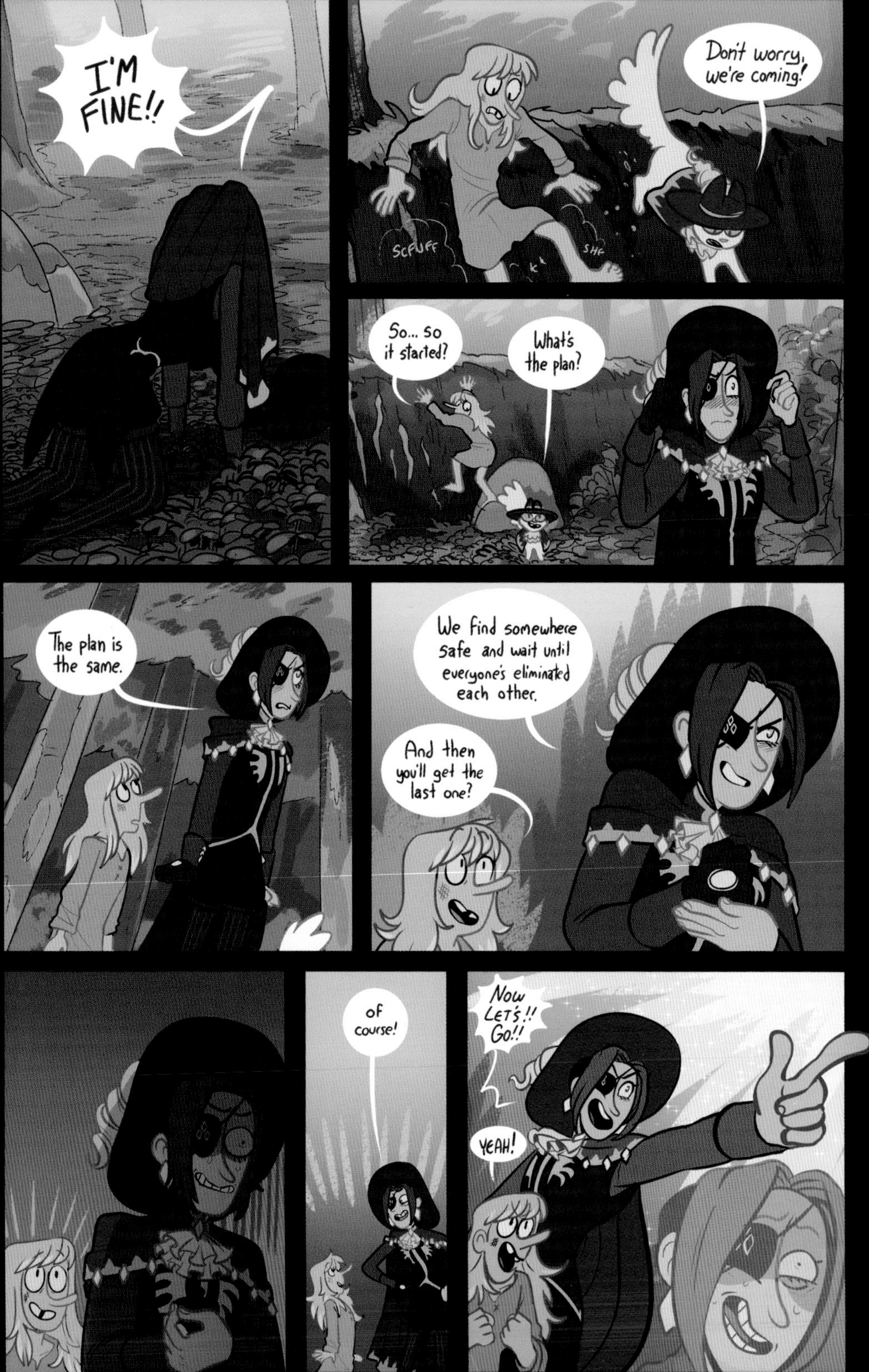

I'M FINE!!
Don't worry, we're coming!
SCFUFF
SHF
So... so it started?
What's the plan?
The plan is the same.
We find somewhere safe and wait until everyone's eliminated each other.
And then you'll get the last one?
of course!
Now LET'S!! GO!!
YEAH!

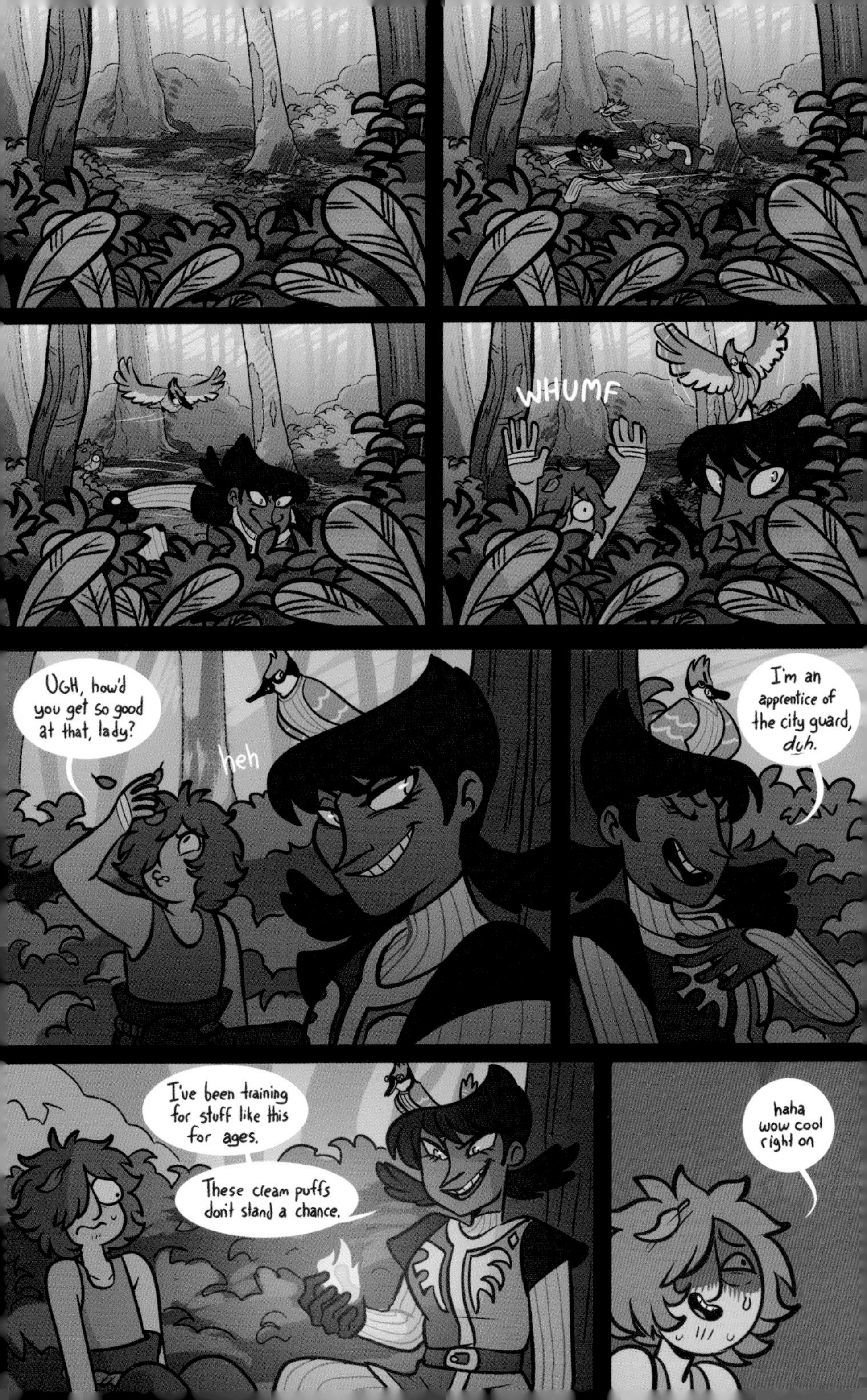
WHUMF
UGH, how'd you get so good at that, lady?
heh
I'm an apprentice of the city guard, duh.
I've been training for stuff like this for ages.
These cream puffs don't stand a chance.
haha wow cool right on

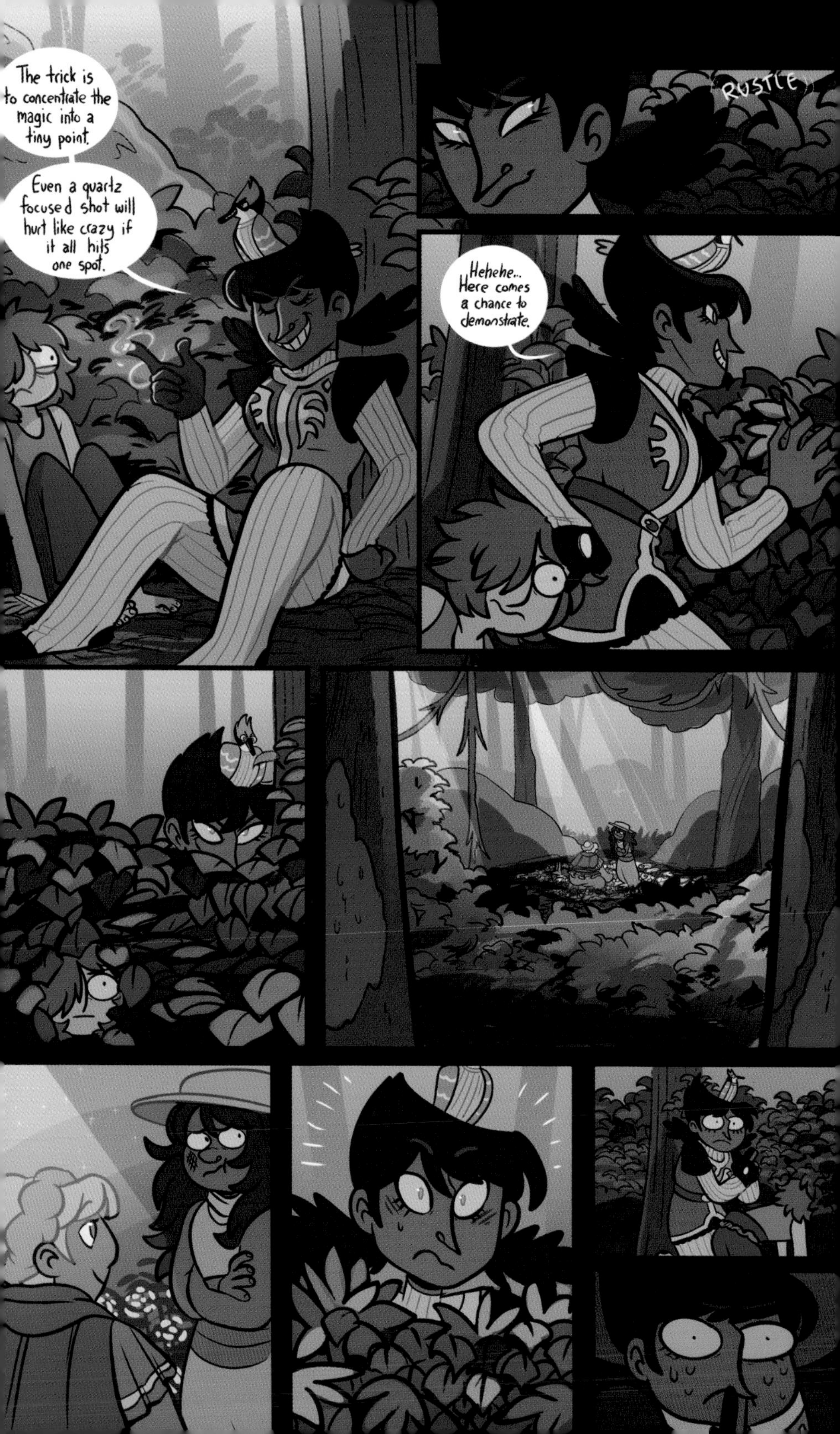
The trick is to concentrate the magic into a tiny point.
Even a quartz focused shot will hurt like crazy if it all hits one spot.
RUSTLE
Hehehe... Here comes a chance to demonstrate.

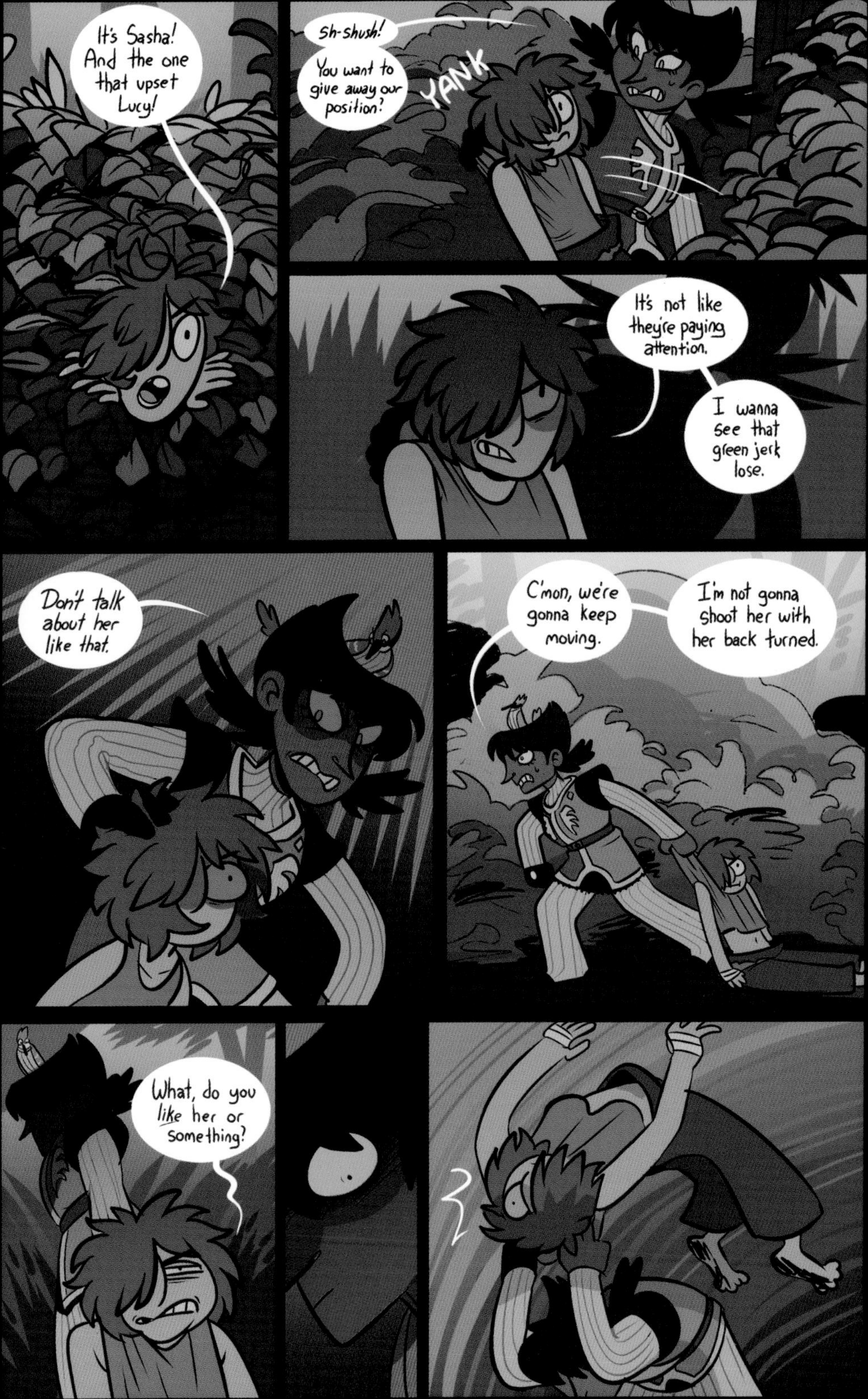

It's Sasha! And the one that upset Lucy!
Sh-shush!
You want to give away our position?
YANK
It's not like they're paying attention.
I wanna see that green jerk lose.
Don't talk about her like that.
C'mon, we're gonna keep moving.
I'm not gonna shoot her with her back turned.
What, do you like her or something?

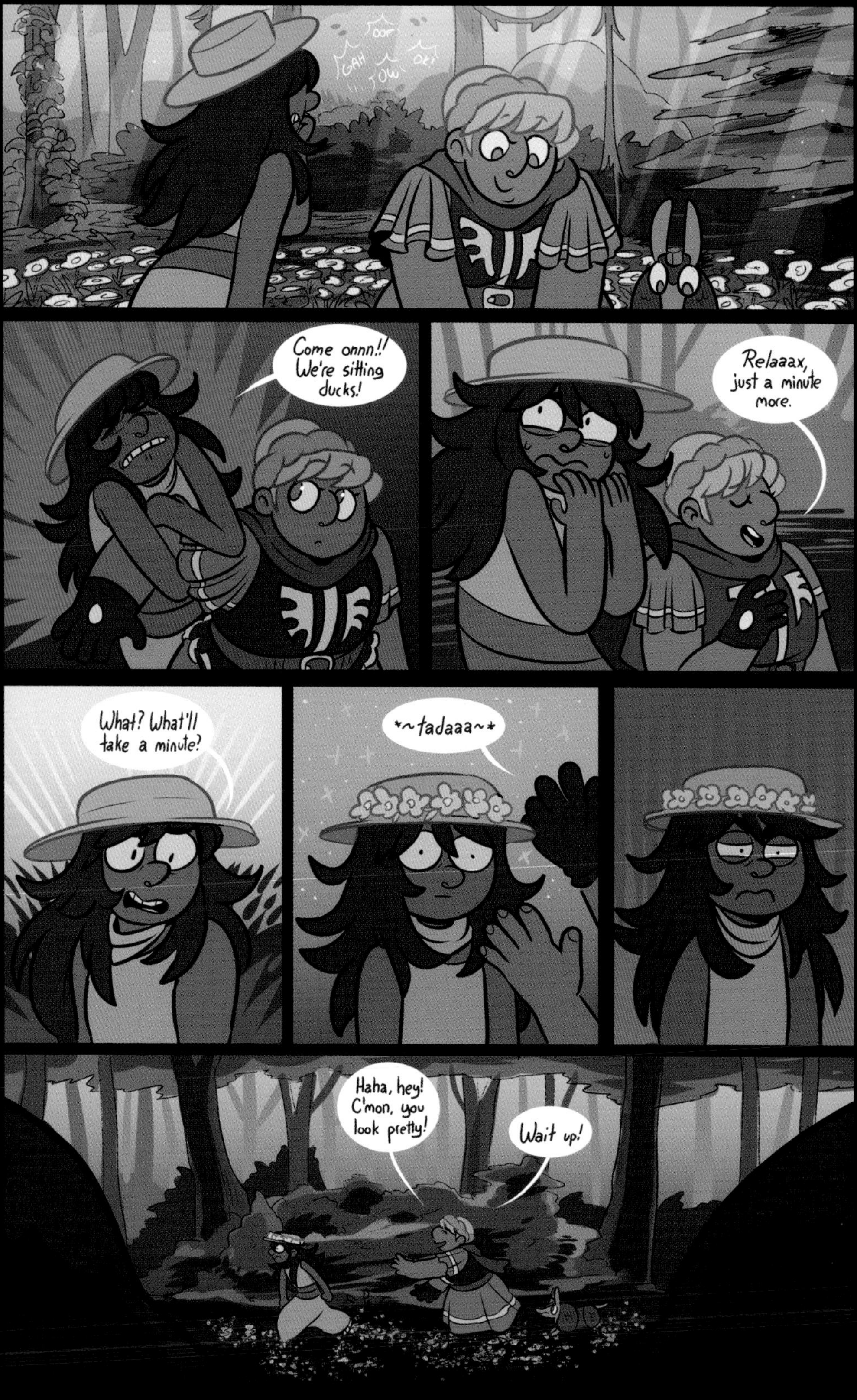
OOF
GAH
OW
OK!
Come onnn!! We're sitting ducks!
Relaaax, just a minute more.
What? What'll take a minute?
~tadaaa~
Haha, hey! C'mon, you look pretty!
Wait up!

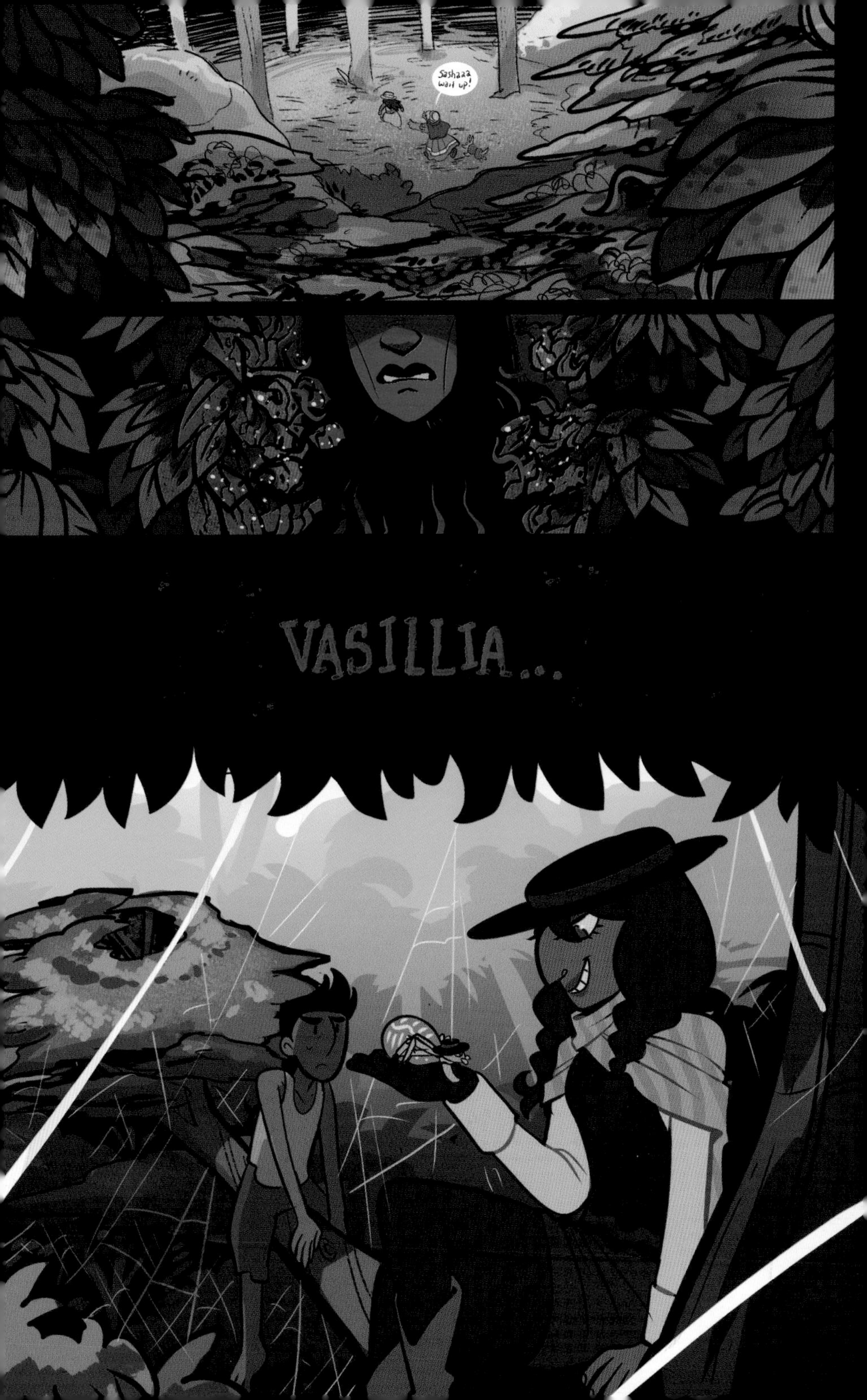
Sashaaa wait up!
VASILLIA...

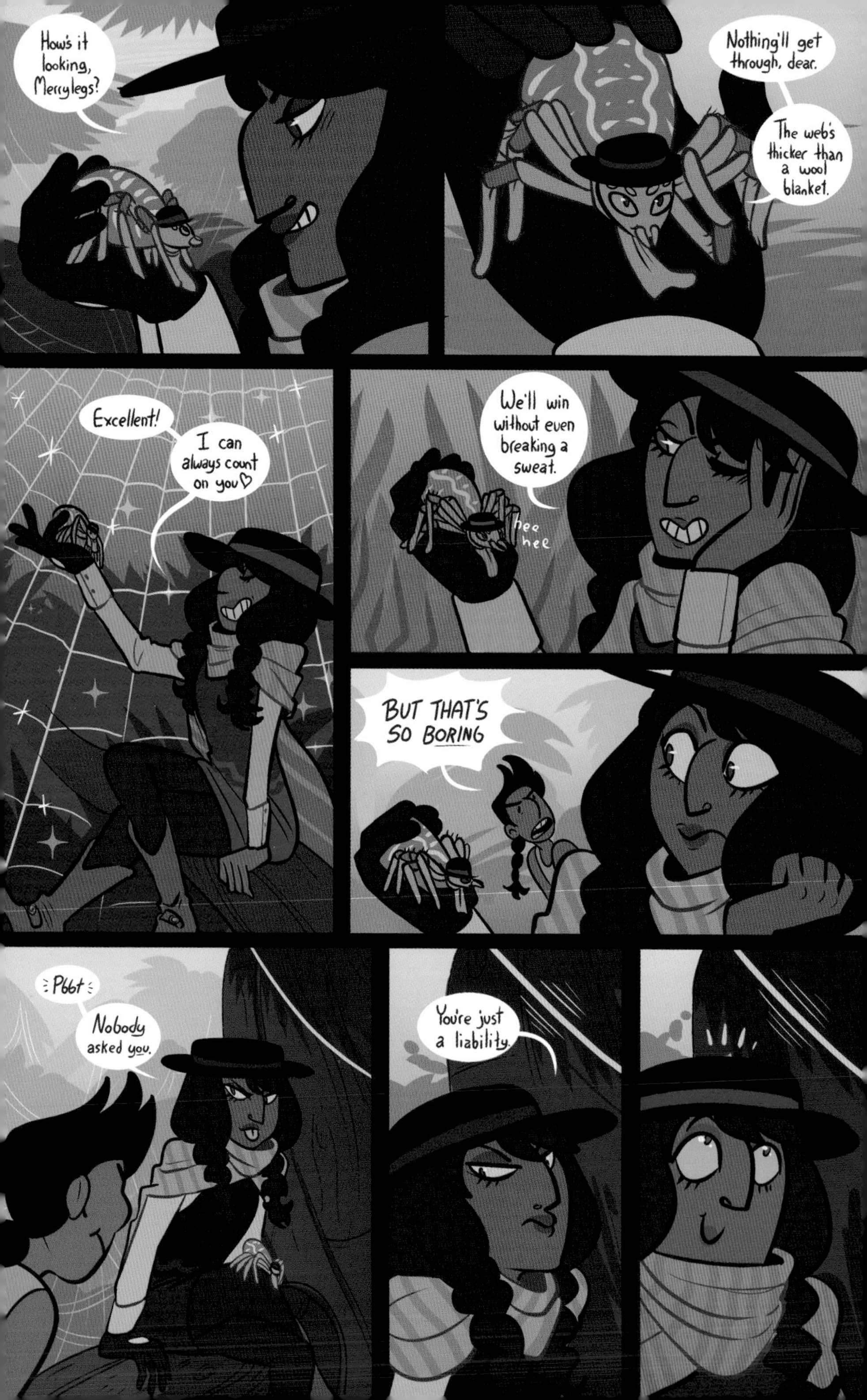
How's it looking, Merrylegs?
Nothing'll get through, dear.
The web's thicker than a wool blanket.
Excellent!
I can always count on you♡
We'll win without even breaking a sweat.
hee hee
BUT THAT'S SO BORING
Pbbt
Nobody asked you.
You're just a liability.

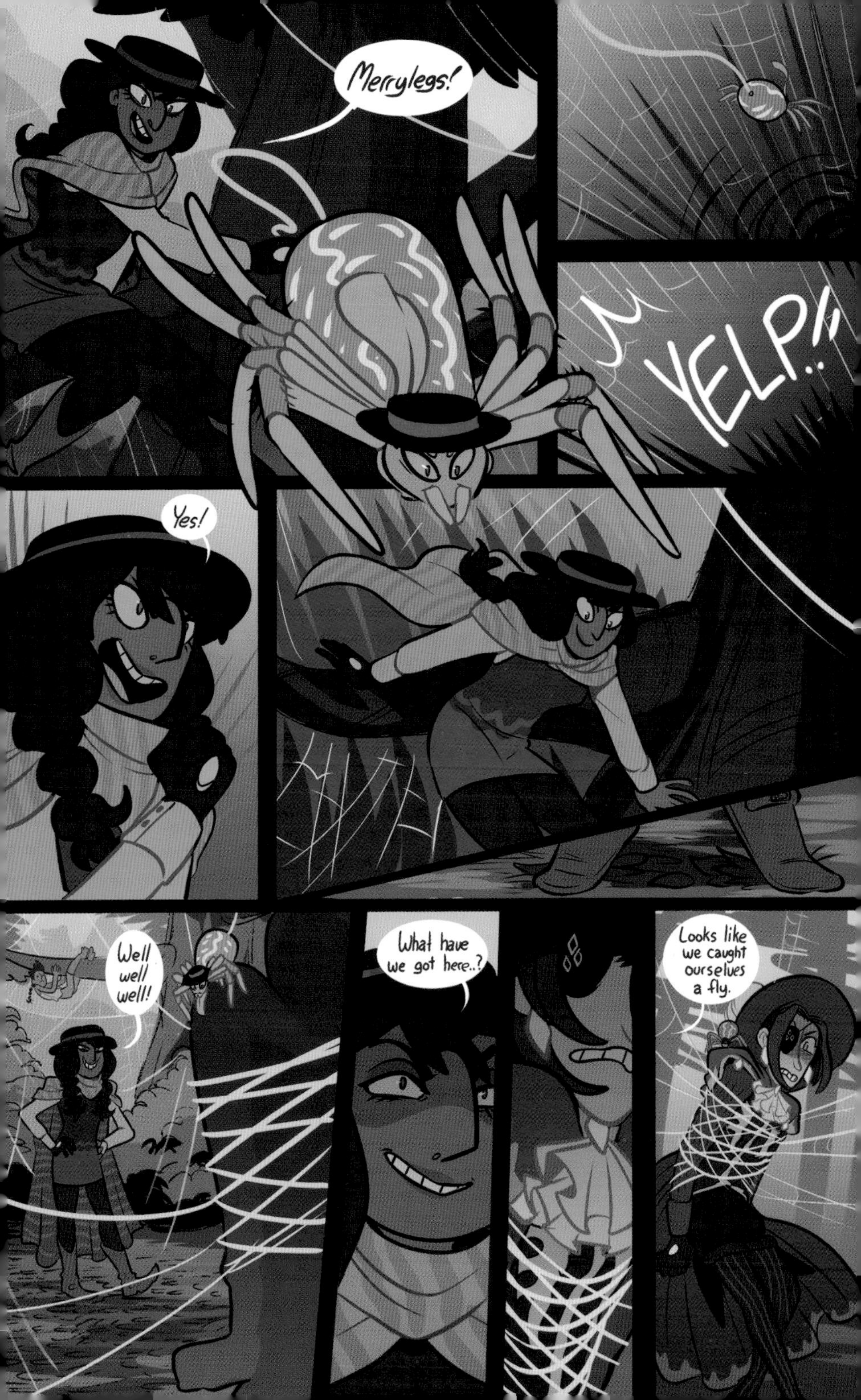

Merrylegs!
YELP!!
Yes!
Well well well!
What have we got here..?
Looks like we caught ourselves a fly.

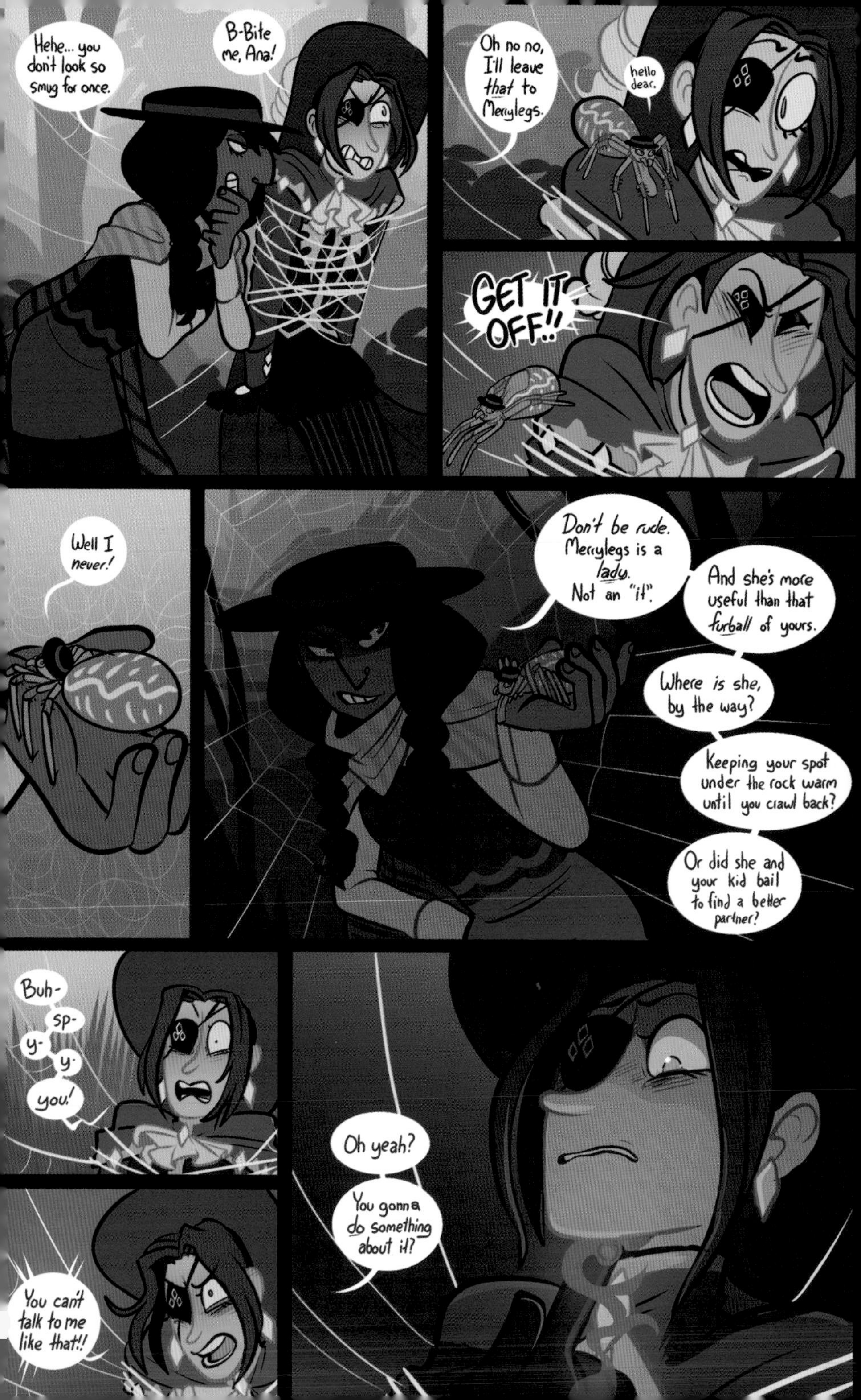
Hehe... you don't look so smug for once.
B-Bite me, Ana!
Oh no no, I'll leave that to Merrylegs.
hello dear.
GET IT OFF!!
Well I never!
Don't be rude. Merrylegs is a lady. Not an "it".
And she's more useful than that furball of yours.
Where is she, by the way?
Keeping your spot under the rock warm until you crawl back?
Or did she and your kid bail to find a better partner?
Buh- sp- y- y- you!
You can't talk to me like that!!
Oh yeah?
You gonna do something about it?

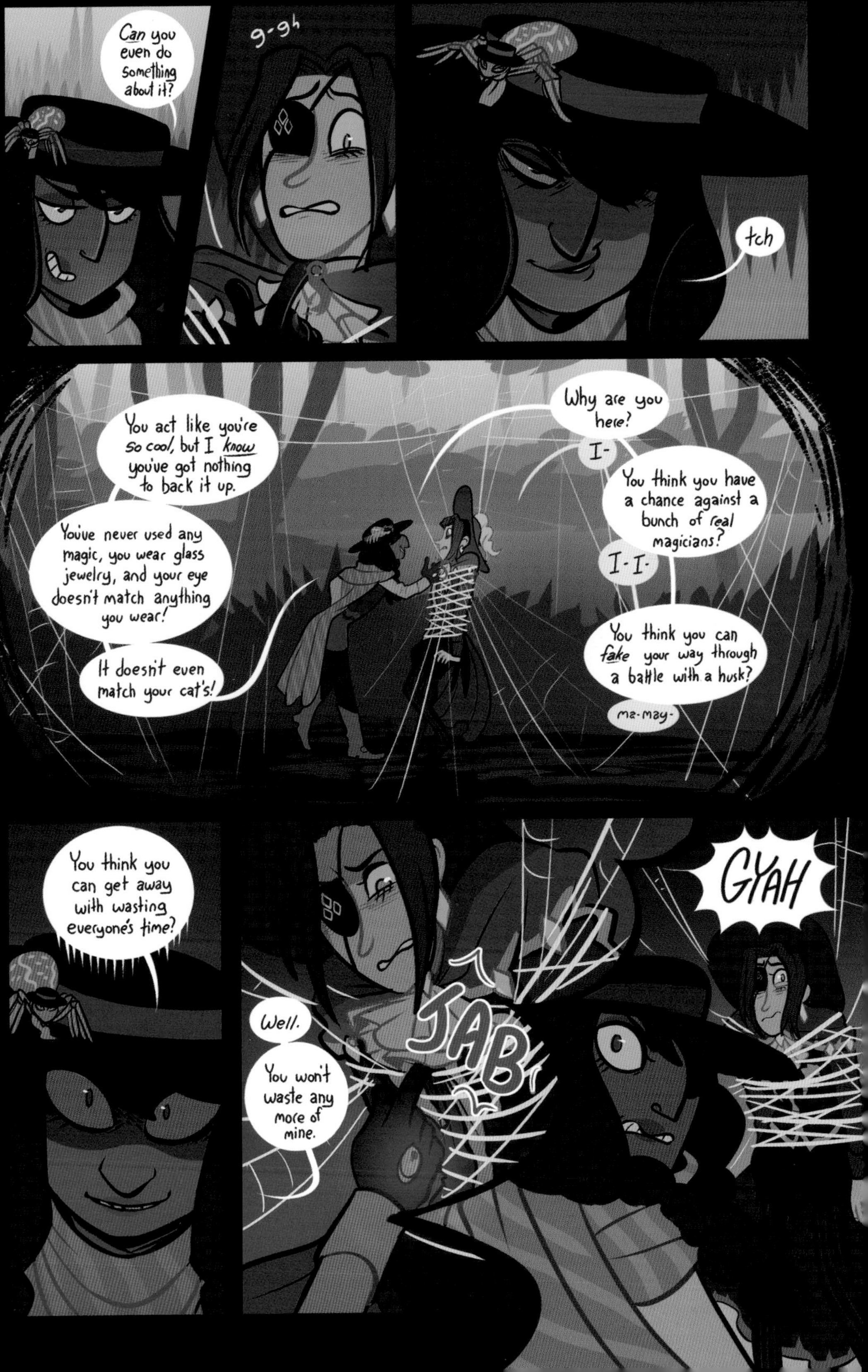
Can you even do something about it?
g-gh
tch
You act like you're so cool, but I know you've got nothing to back it up.
You've never used any magic, you wear glass jewelry, and your eye doesn't match anything you wear!
It doesn't even match your cat's!
Why are you here?
I-
You think you have a chance against a bunch of real magicians?
I-I-
You think you can fake your way through a battle with a husk?
ma-may-
You think you can get away with wasting everyone's time?
Well.
You won't waste any more of mine.
JAB
GYAH

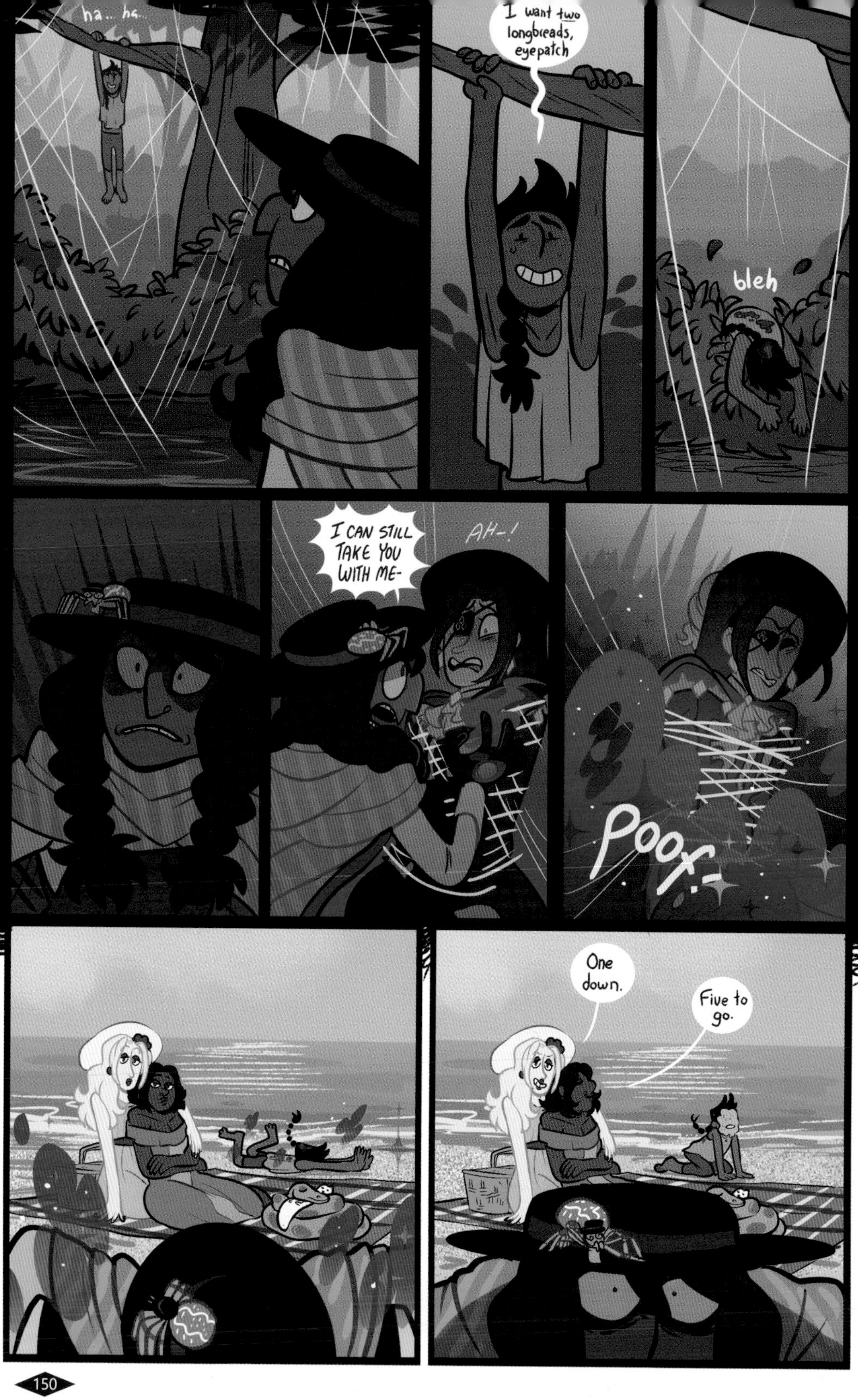
ha... ha...
I want two longbreads, eyepatch
bleh
I CAN STILL TAKE YOU WITH ME-
AH-!
POOF-
One down.
Five to go.

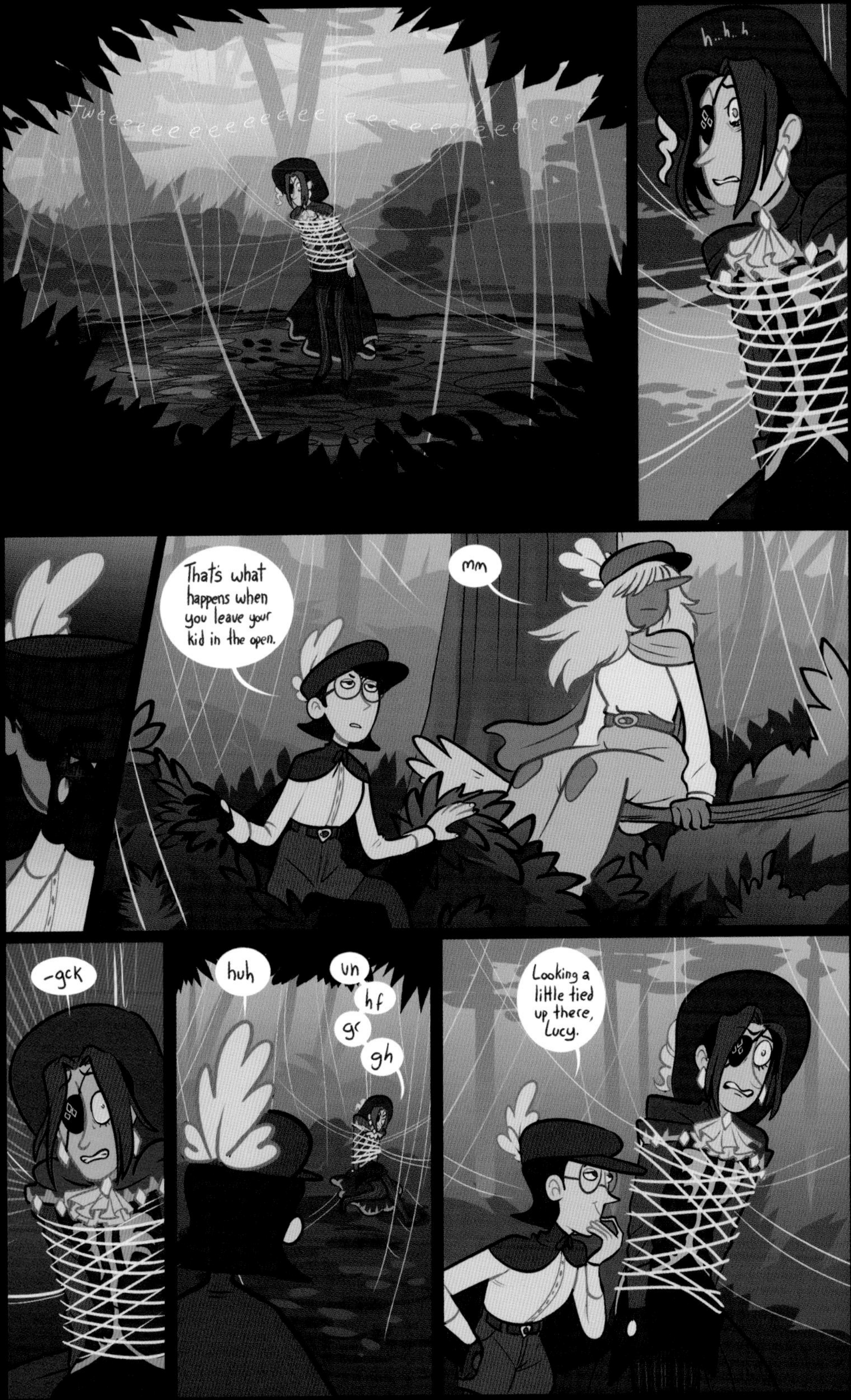
tweeeeeeeeeeeee eeeeeeeeeeeee
h.. h.. h.
That's what happens when you leave your kid in the open.
mm
-gck
huh
un
hf
gr
gh
Looking a little tied up there, Lucy.

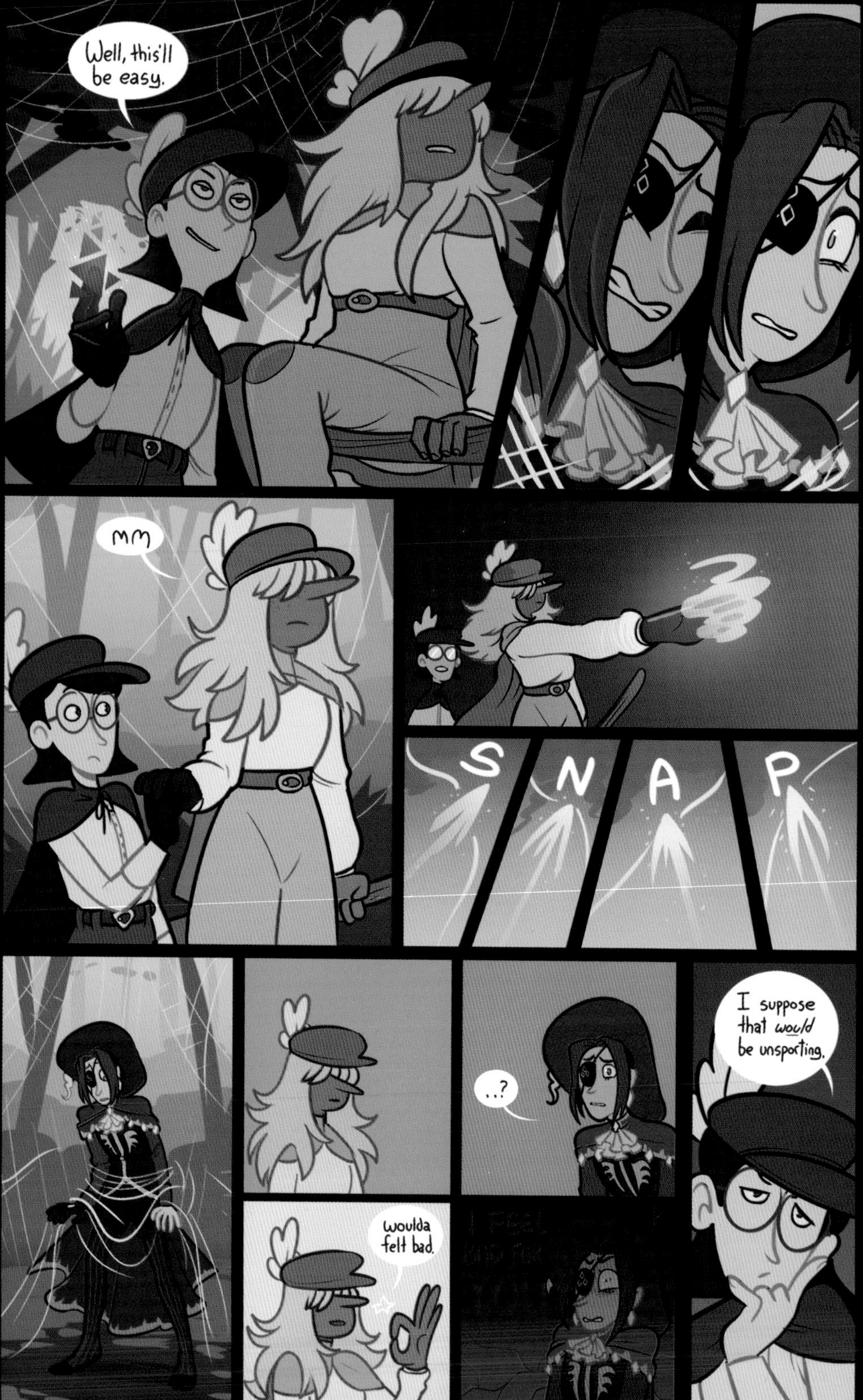
Well, this'll be easy.
MM
SNAP
..?
woulda felt bad.
I suppose that would be unsporting.

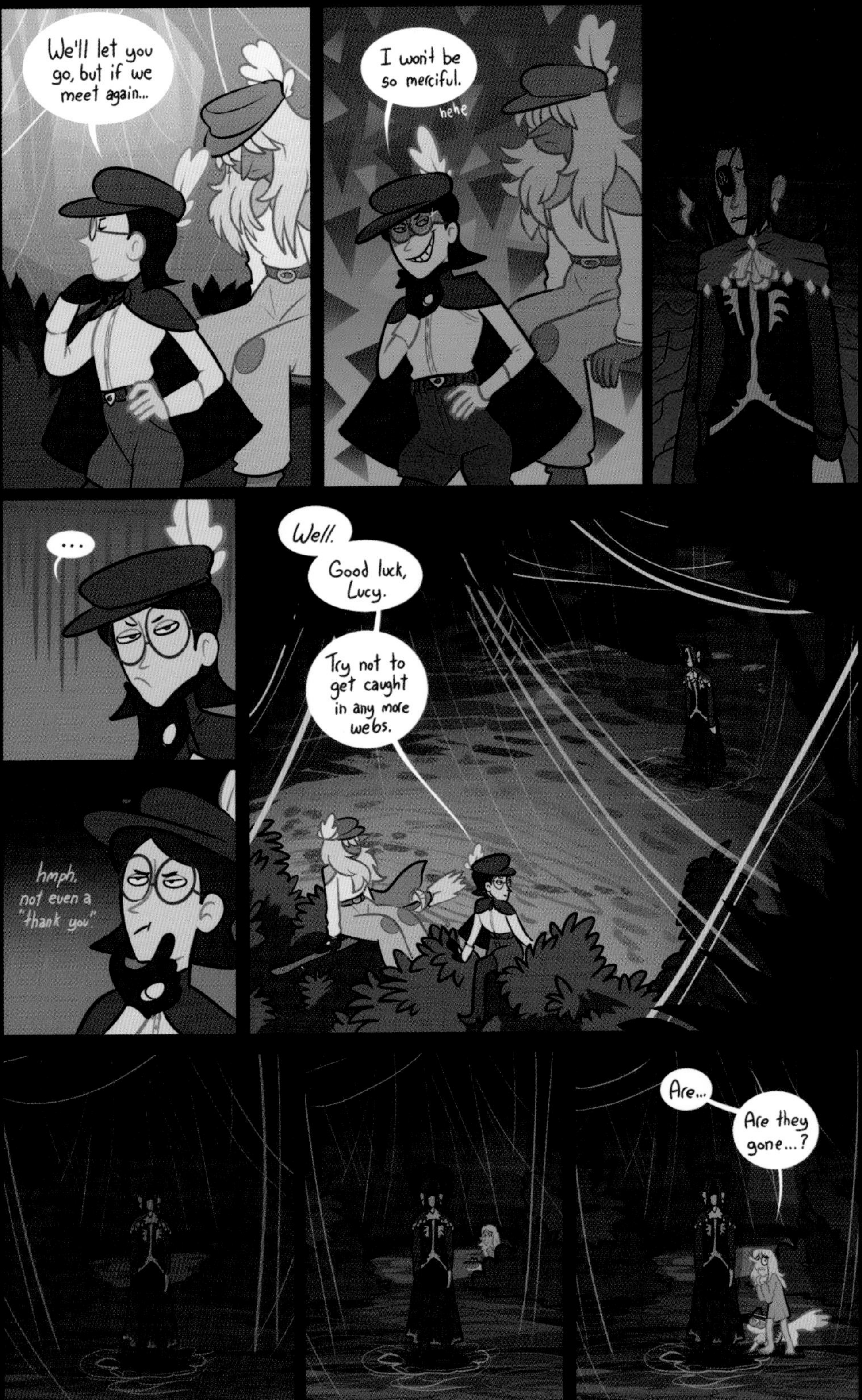
We'll let you go, but if we meet again...
I won't be so merciful.
hehe
...
hmph, not even a "thank you."
Well.
Good luck, Lucy.
Try not to get caught in any more webs.
Are...
Are they gone...?

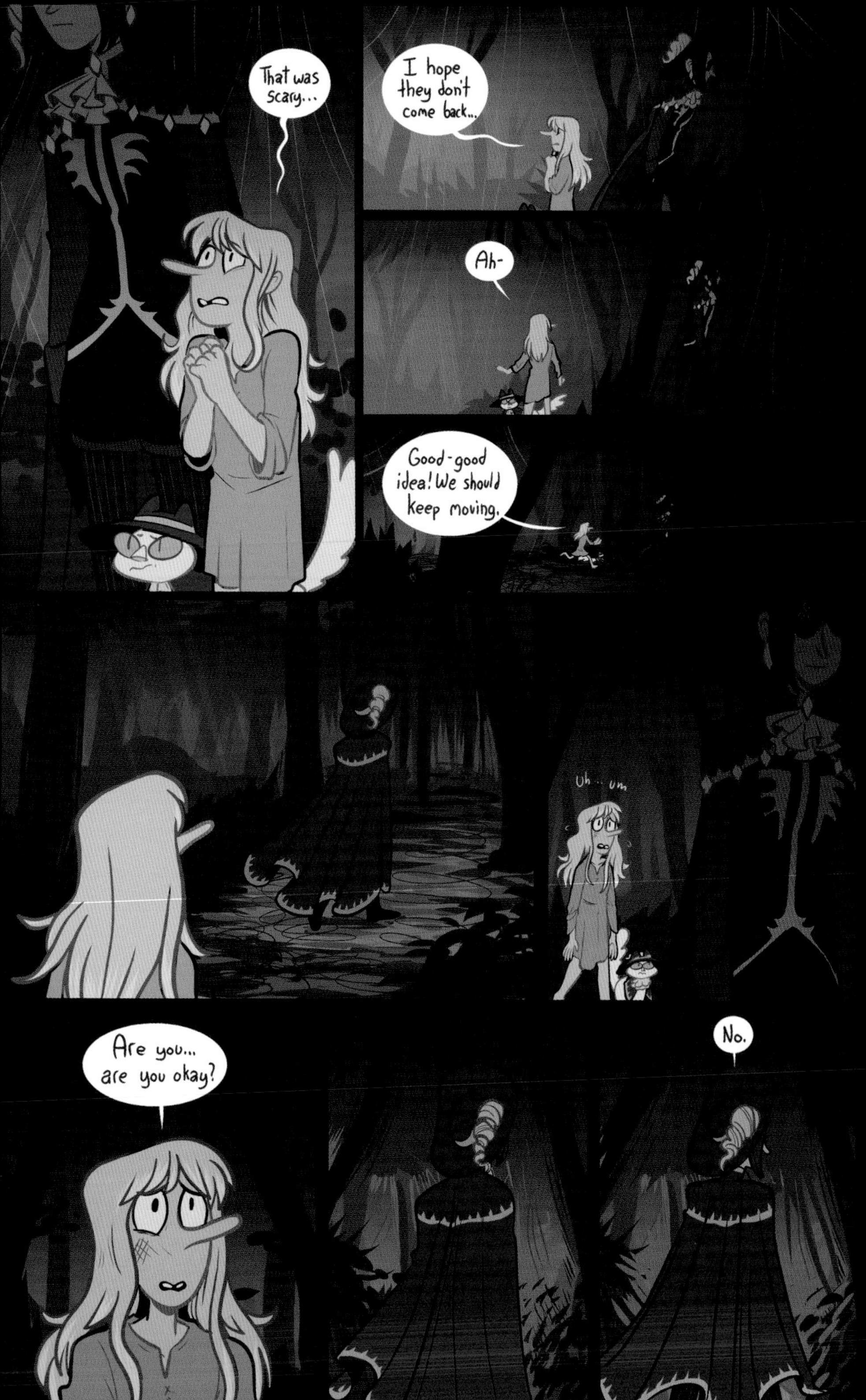
That was scary...
I hope they don't come back...
Ah-
Good-good idea! We should keep moving.
Uh... um
Are you... are you okay?
No.

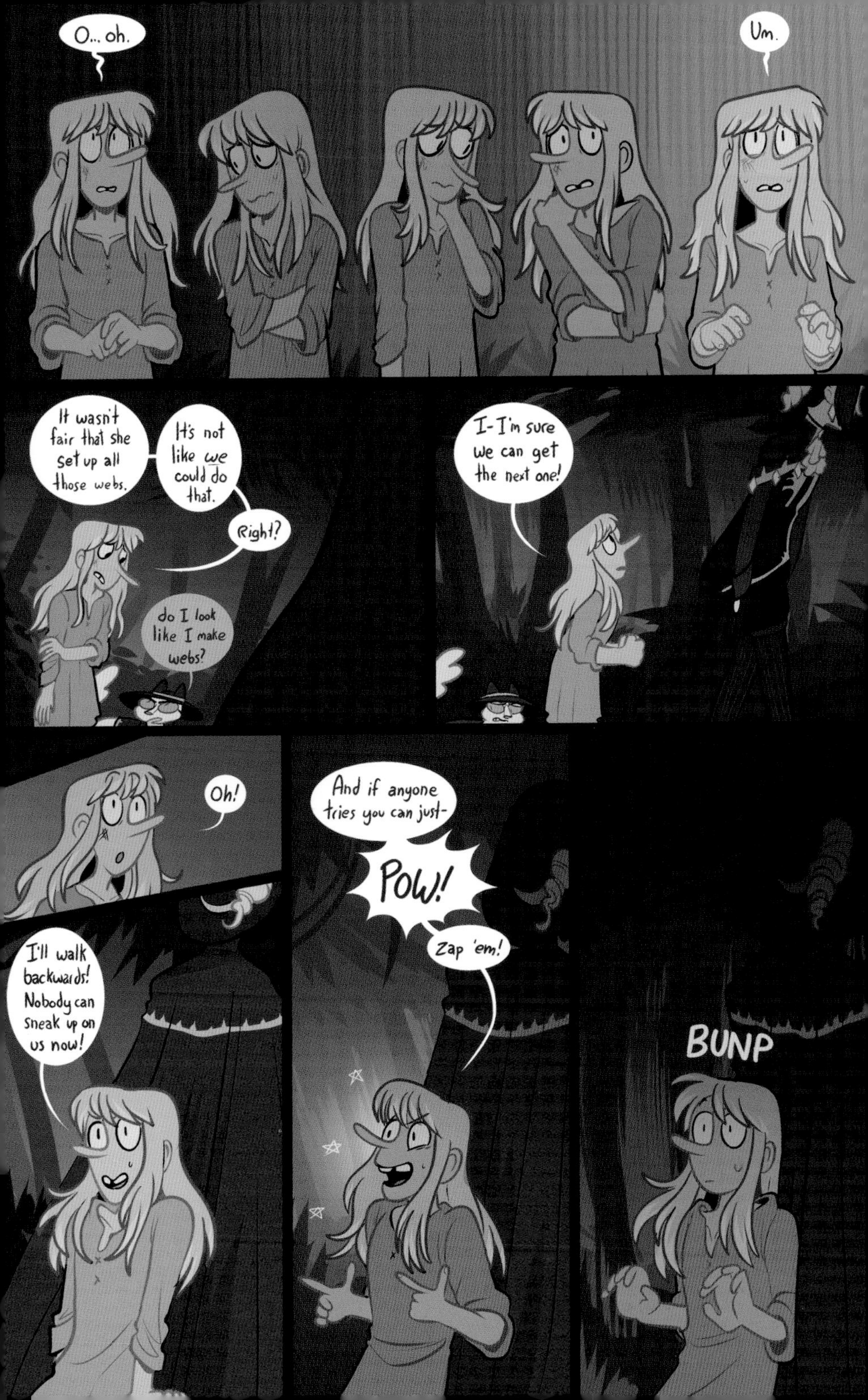
O... oh.
Um.
It wasn't fair that she set up all those webs.
It's not like we could do that.
Right?
do I look like I make webs?
I-I'm sure we can get the next one!
Oh!
I'll walk backwards! Nobody can sneak up on us now!
And if anyone tries you can just-
POW!
Zap 'em!
BUNP

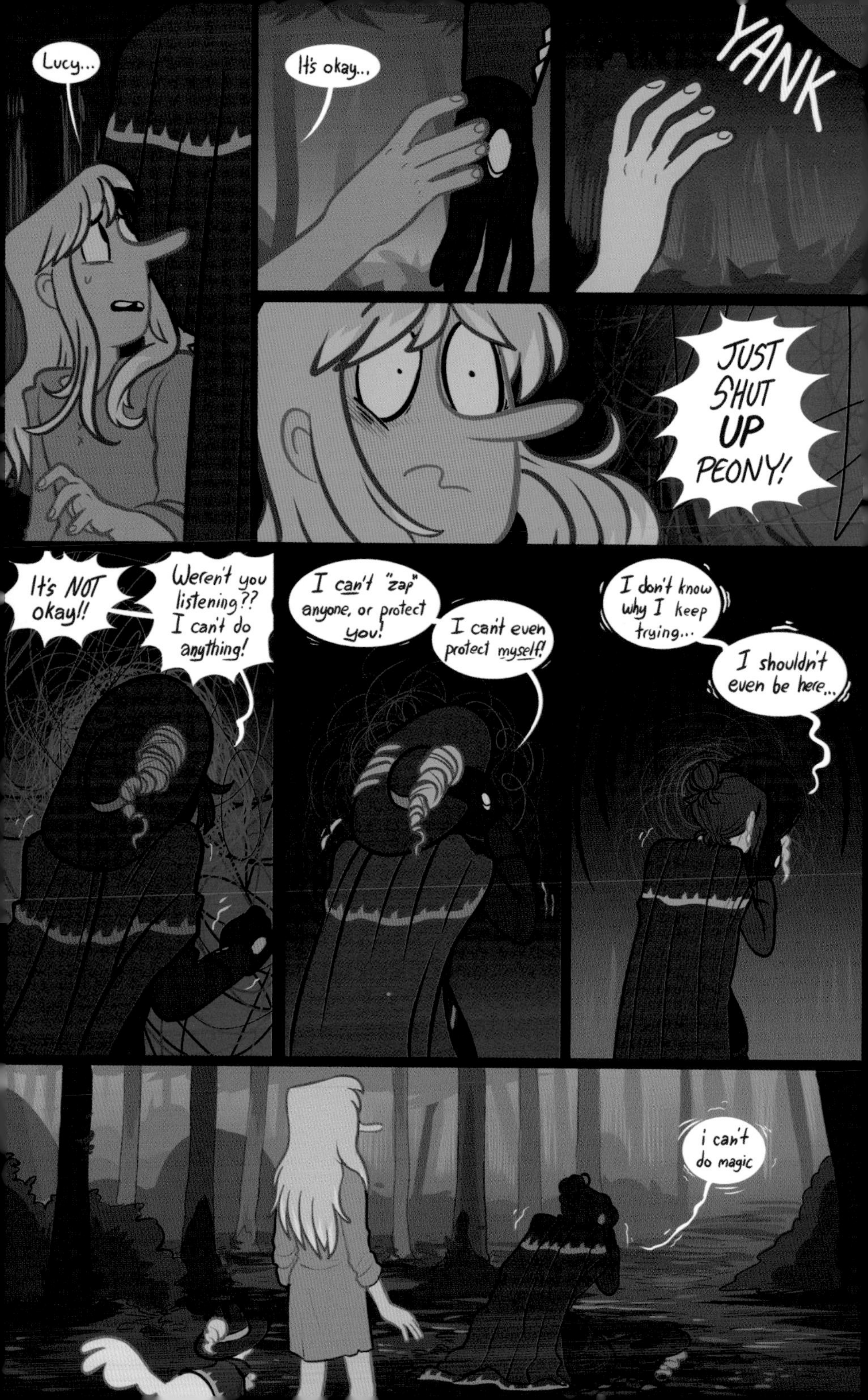
Lucy...
It's okay...
YANK
JUST SHUT UP PEONY!
It's NOT okay!!
Weren't you listening?? I can't do anything!
I can't "zap" anyone, or protect you!
I can't even protect myself!
I don't know why I keep trying...
I shouldn't even be here...
i can't do magic

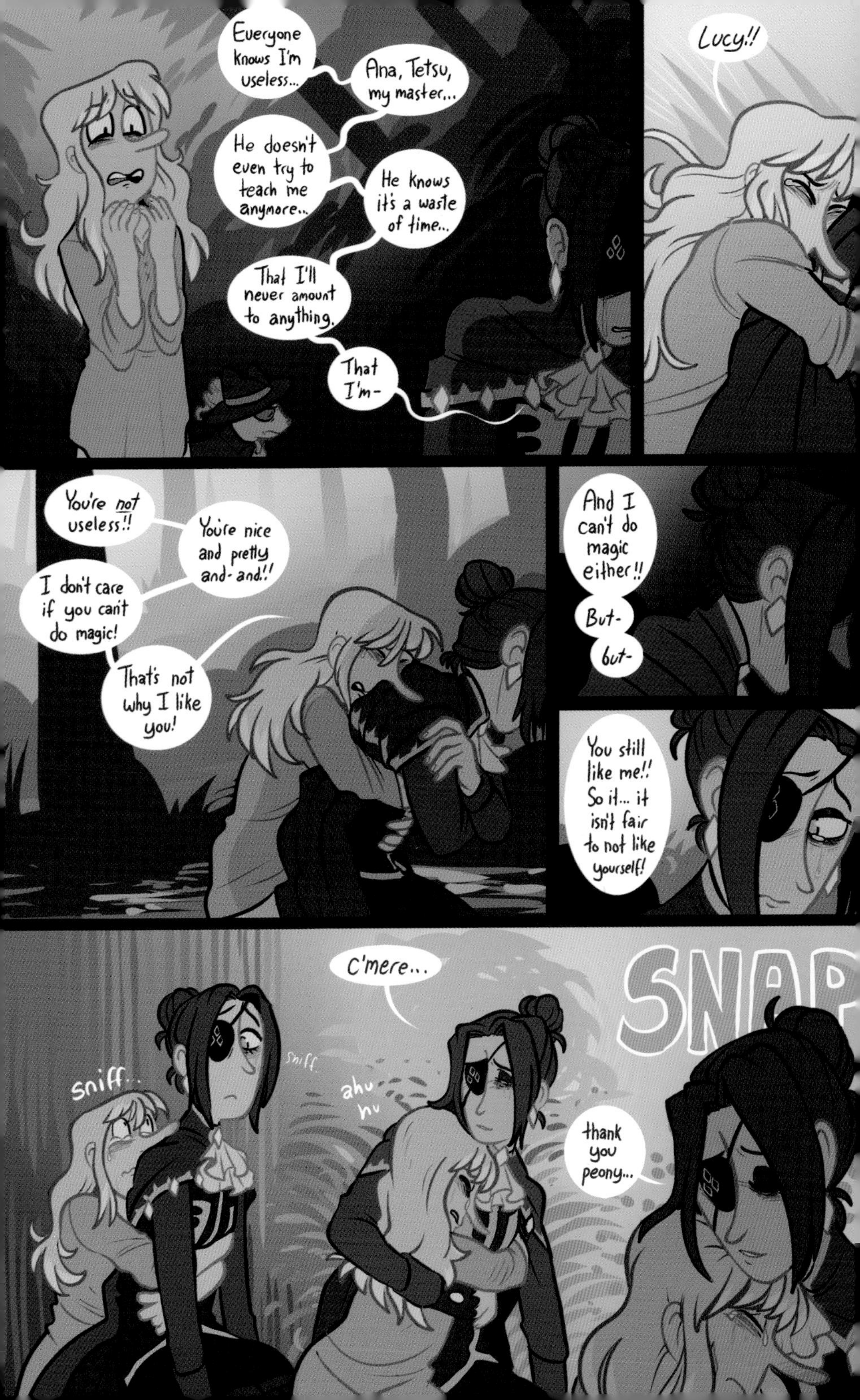

Everyone knows I'm useless...
Ana, Tetsu, my master...
He doesn't even try to teach me anymore...
He knows it's a waste of time...
That I'll never amount to anything.
That I'm-
Lucy!!
You're not useless!!
You're nice and pretty and- and!!
I don't care if you can't do magic!
That's not why I like you!
And I can't do magic either!!
But-
but-
You still like me!! So it... it isn't fair to not like yourself!
sniff...
sniff
C'mere...
ahu hu
SNAP
thank you peony...

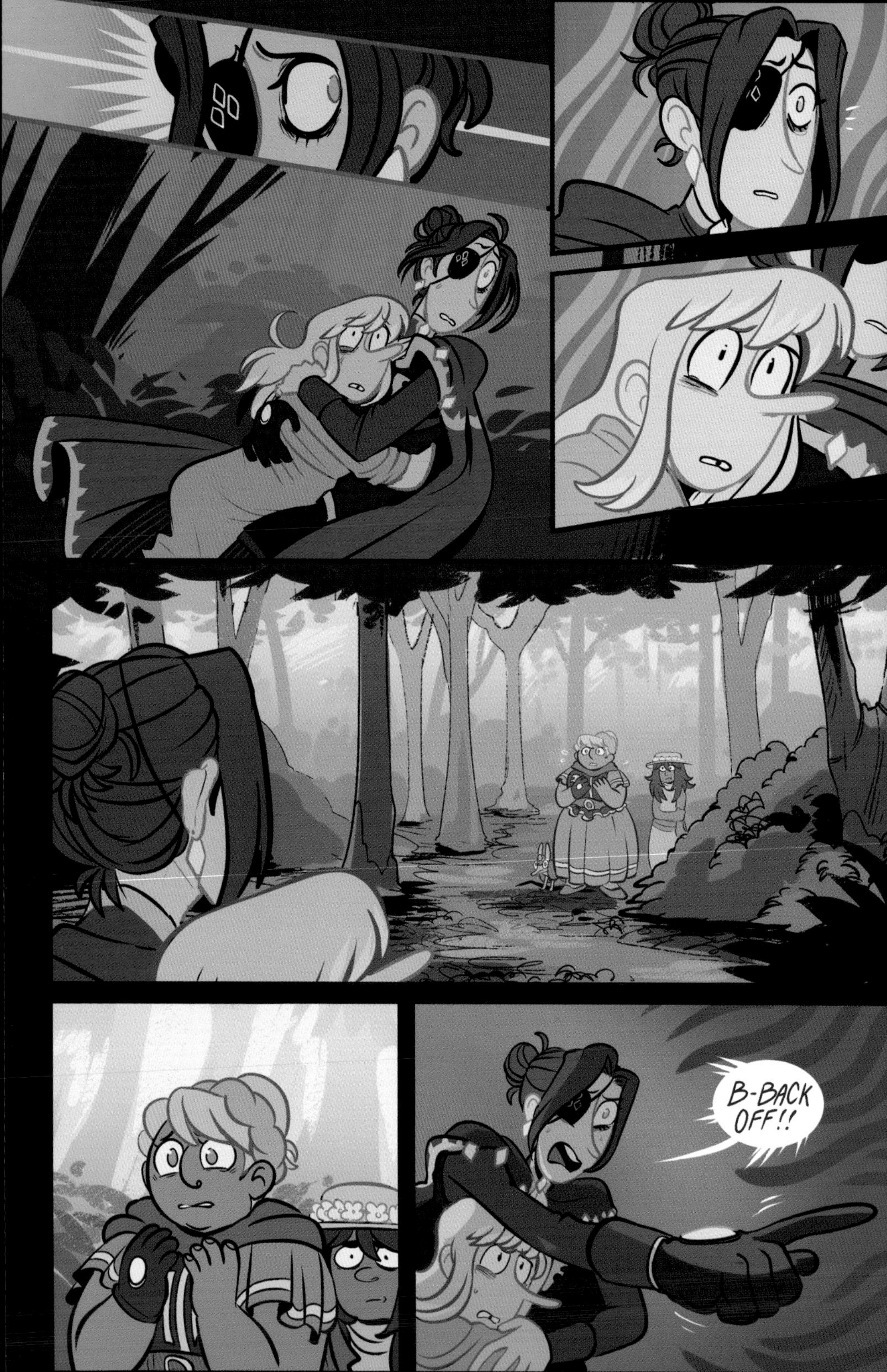
B-BACK OFF!!

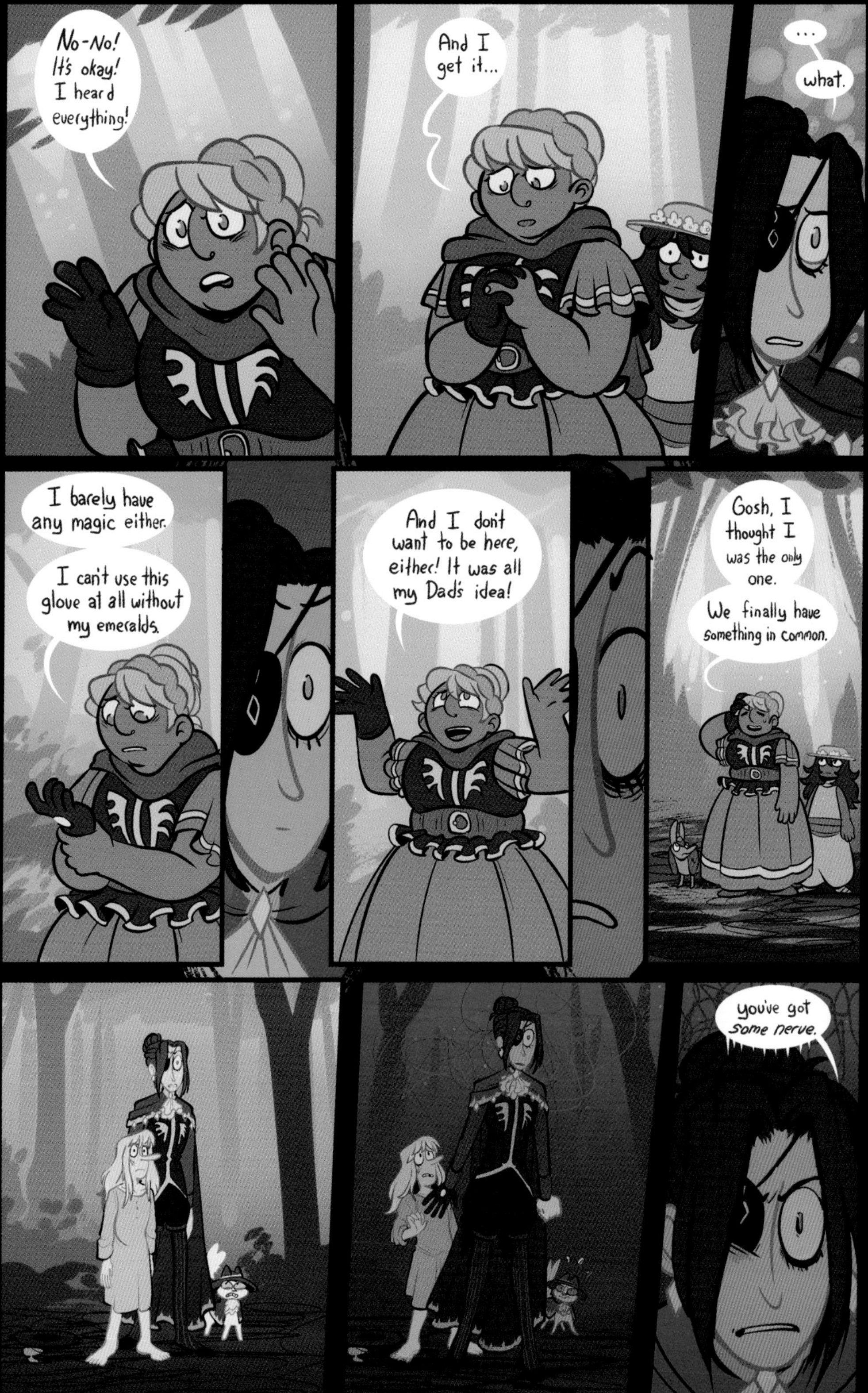
No-No! It's okay! I heard everything!
And I get it...
...
what.
I barely have any magic either.
I can't use this glove at all without my emeralds.
And I don't want to be here, either! It was all my Dad's idea!
Gosh, I thought I was the only one.
We finally have something in common.
you've got some nerve.

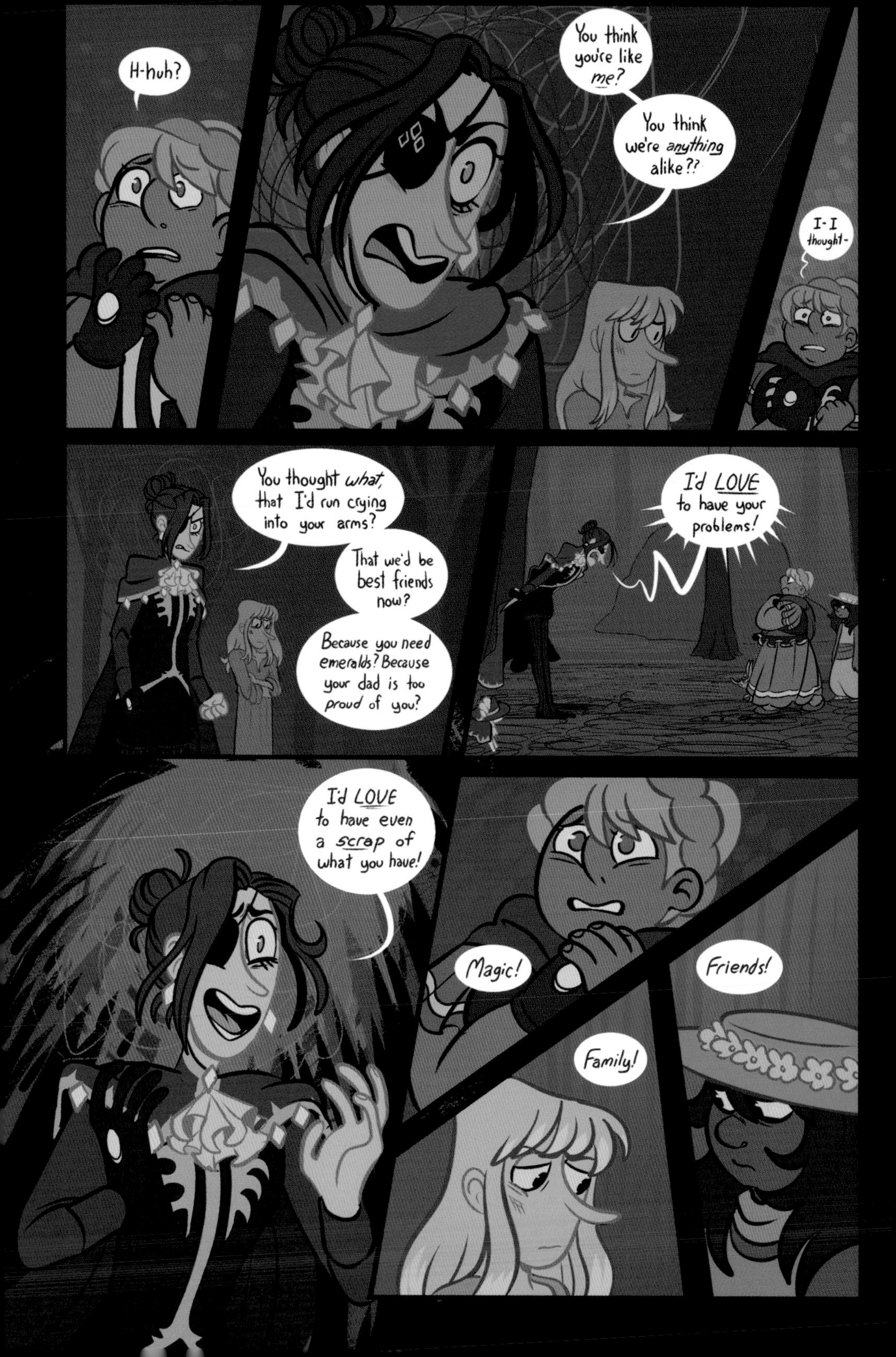
H-huh?
You think you're like me?
You think we're anything alike??
I-I thought-
You thought what, that I'd run crying into your arms?
That we'd be best friends now?
Because you need emeralds? Because your dad is too proud of you?
I'd LOVE to have your problems!
I'd LOVE to have even a scrap of what you have!
Magic!
Friends!
Family!

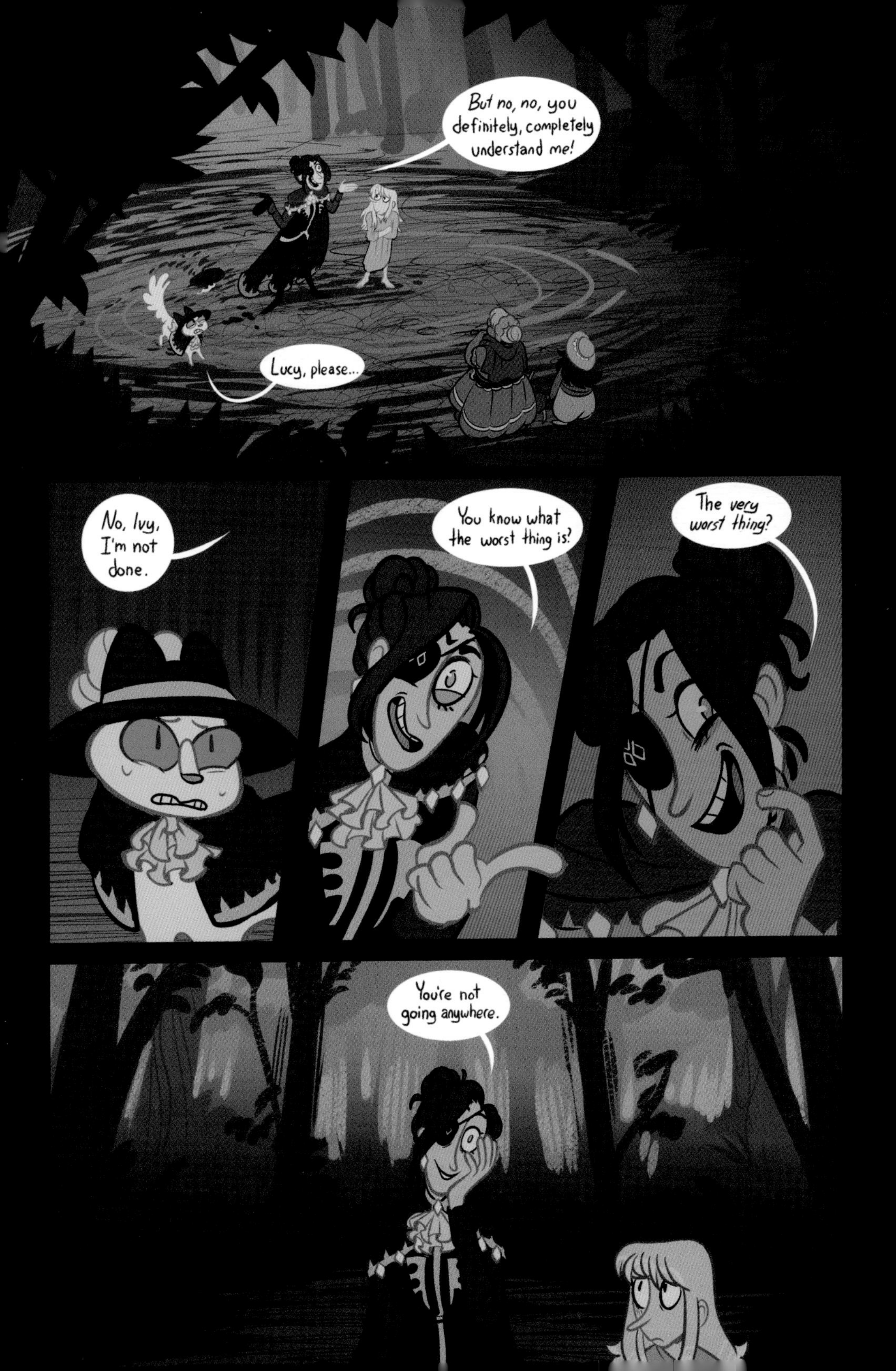

But no, no, you definitely, completely understand me!
Lucy, please...
No, Ivy, I'm not done.
You know what the worst thing is?
The very worst thing?
You're not going anywhere.

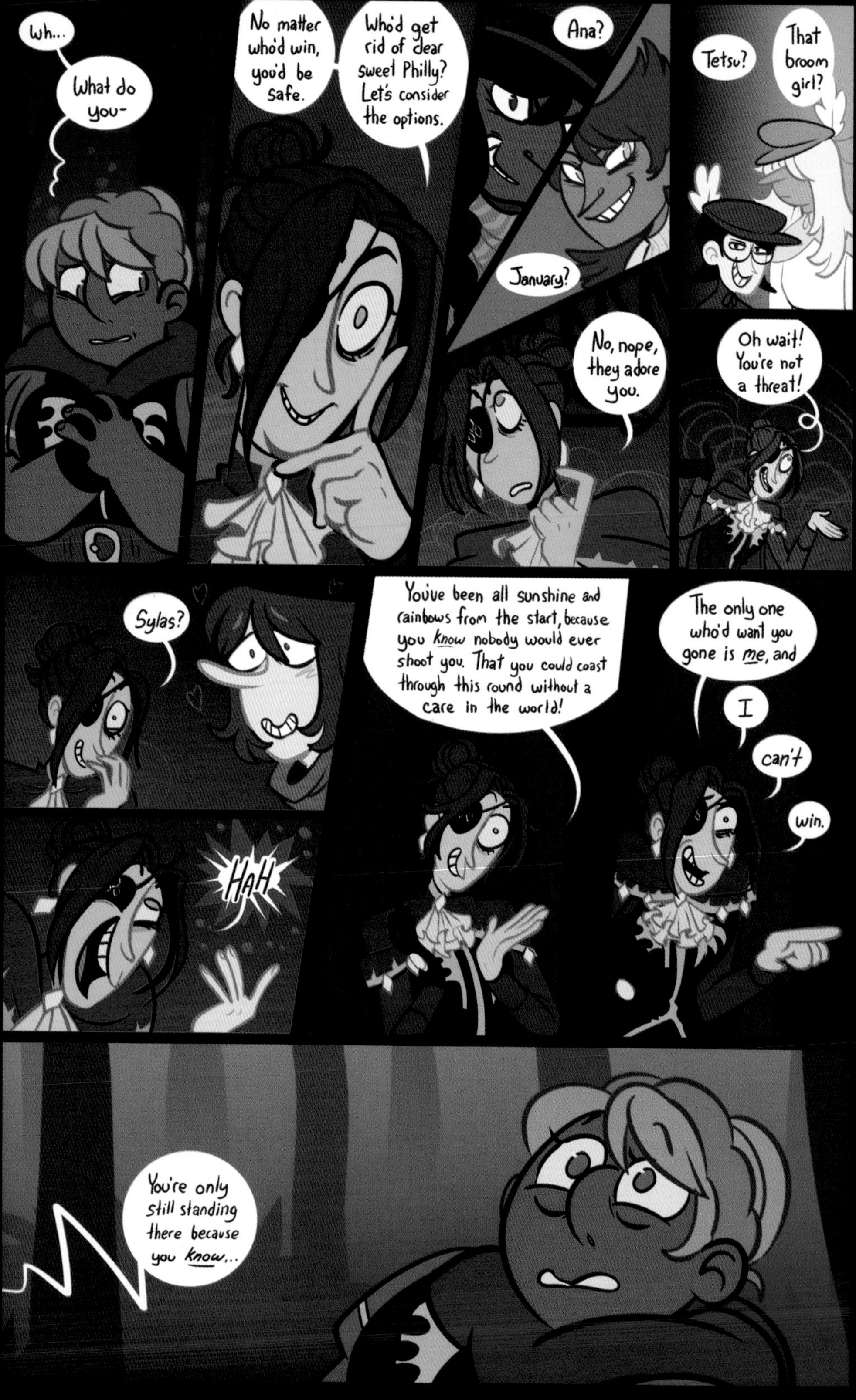
Wh...
What do you-
No matter who'd win, you'd be safe.
Who'd get rid of dear sweet Philly? Let's consider the options.
Ana?
January?
Tetsu?
That broom girl?
No, nope, they adore you.
Oh wait! You're not a threat!
Sylas?
HAH
You've been all sunshine and rainbows from the start, because you know nobody would ever shoot you. That you could coast through this round without a care in the world!
The only one who'd want you gone is me, and
I
can't
win.
You're only still standing there because you know...

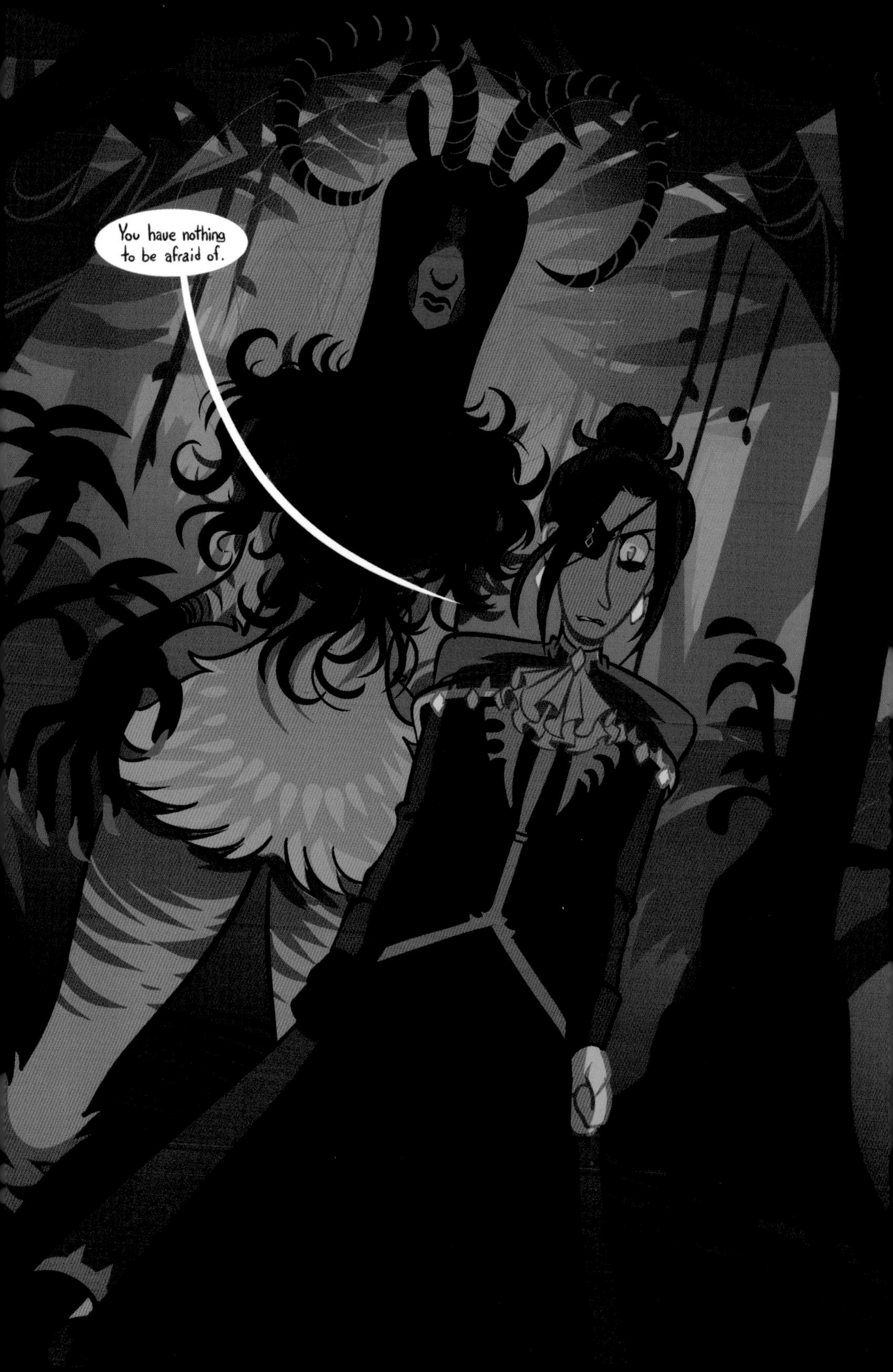
You have nothing to be afraid of.

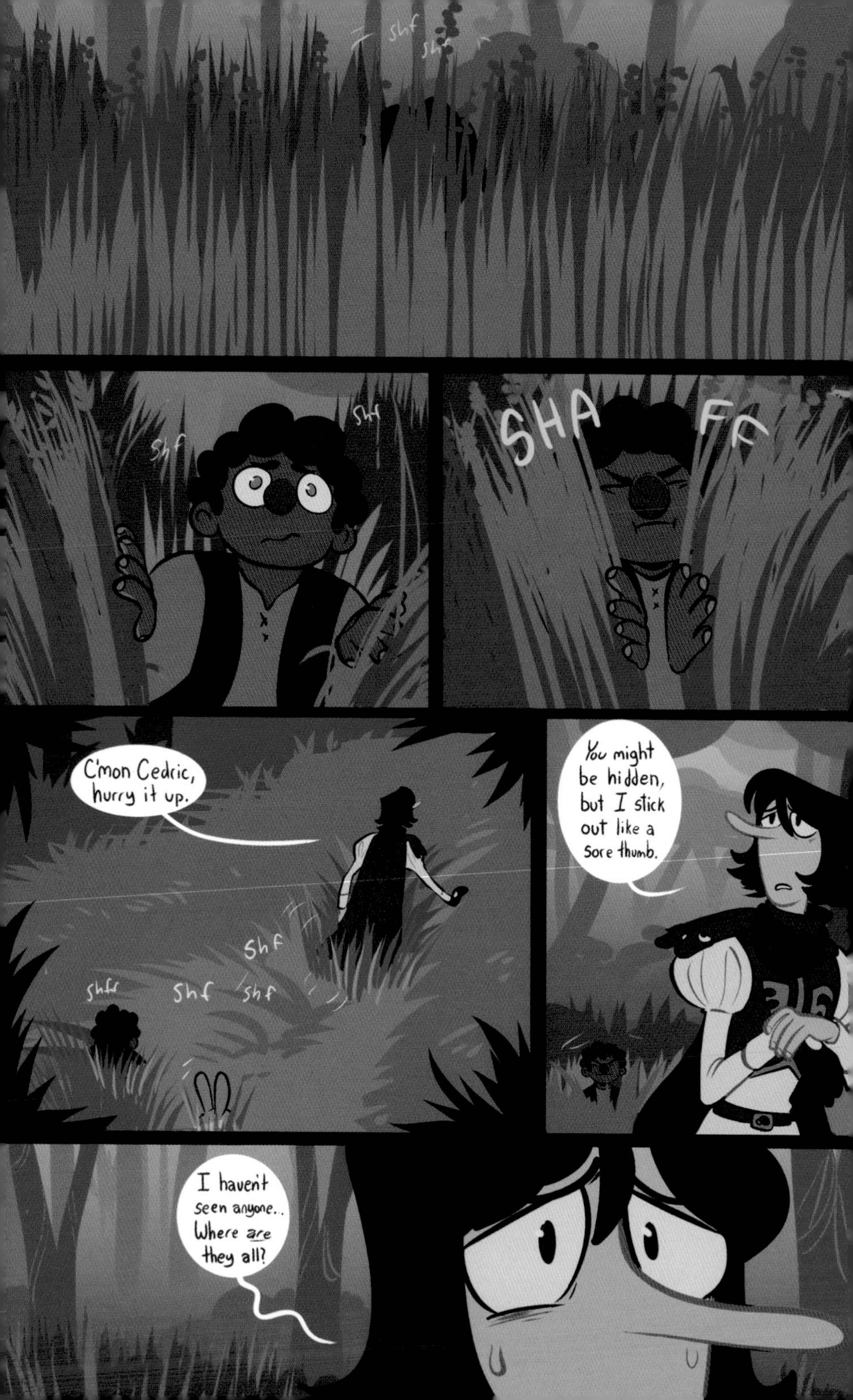
shf
shf
shf
shf
SHA FF
C'mon Cedric, hurry it up.
Shf
shfr
Shf
shf
You might be hidden, but I stick out like a sore thumb.
I haven't seen anyone... Where are they all?

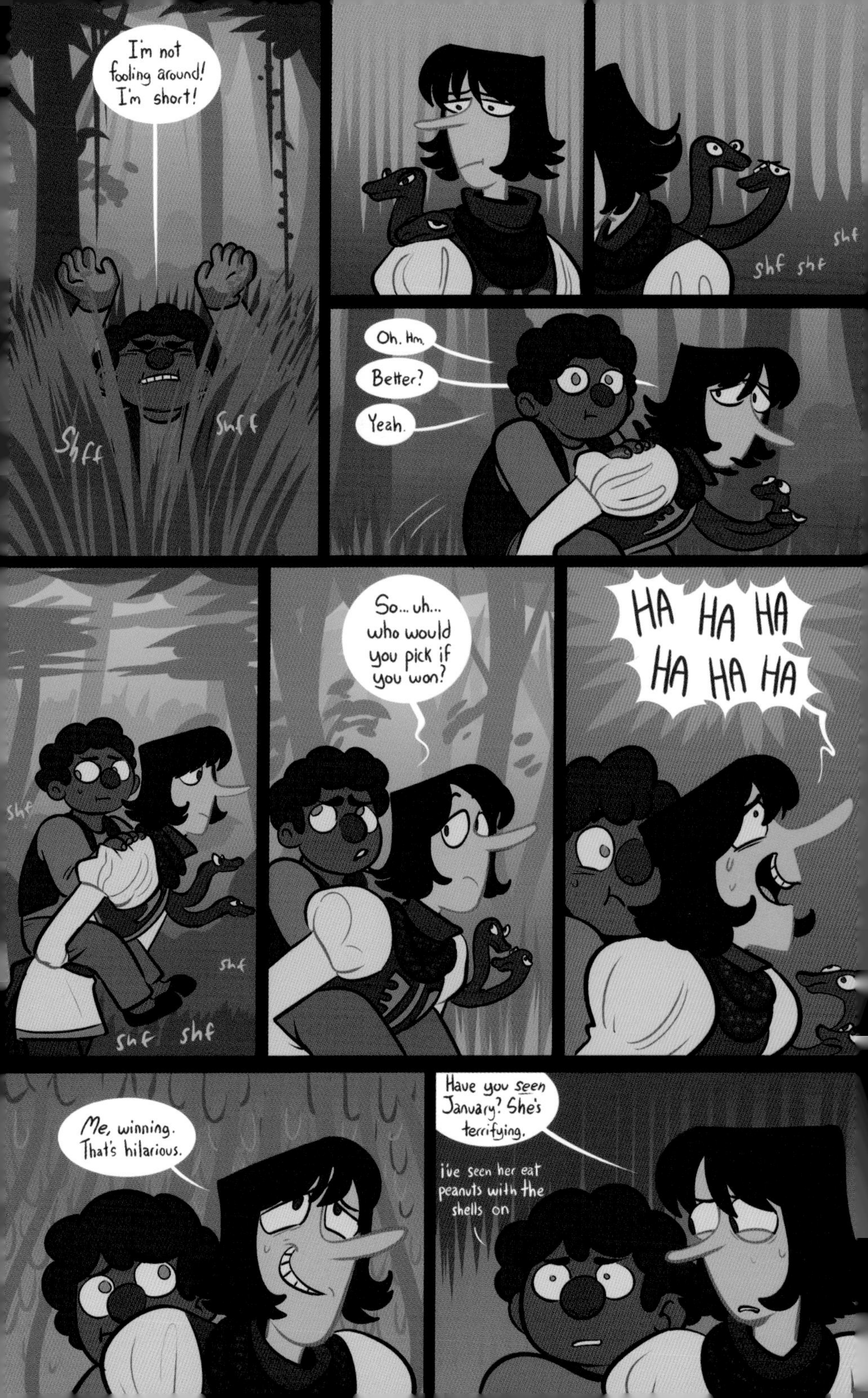

I'm not fooling around! I'm short!
Shff
Shff
shf
shf shf
Oh. Hm.
Better?
Yeah.
shf
shf
shf shf
So... uh... who would you pick if you won?
HA HA HA HA HA HA
Me, winning. That's hilarious.
Have you seen January? She's terrifying.
i've seen her eat peanuts with the shells on

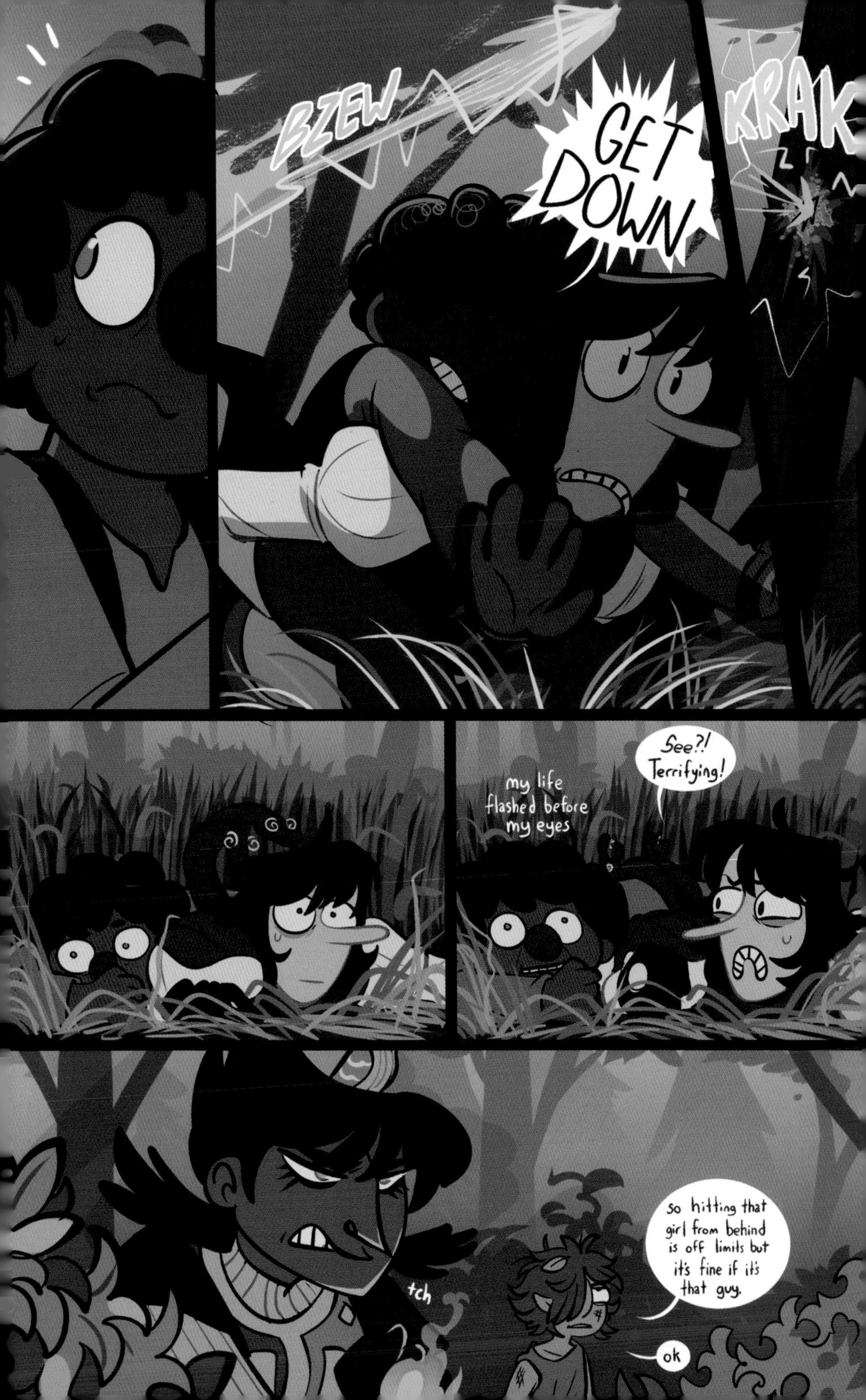
BZEW
GET DOWN
KRAK
my life flashed before my eyes
See?! Terrifying!
tch
so hitting that girl from behind is off limits but it's fine if it's that guy.
ok

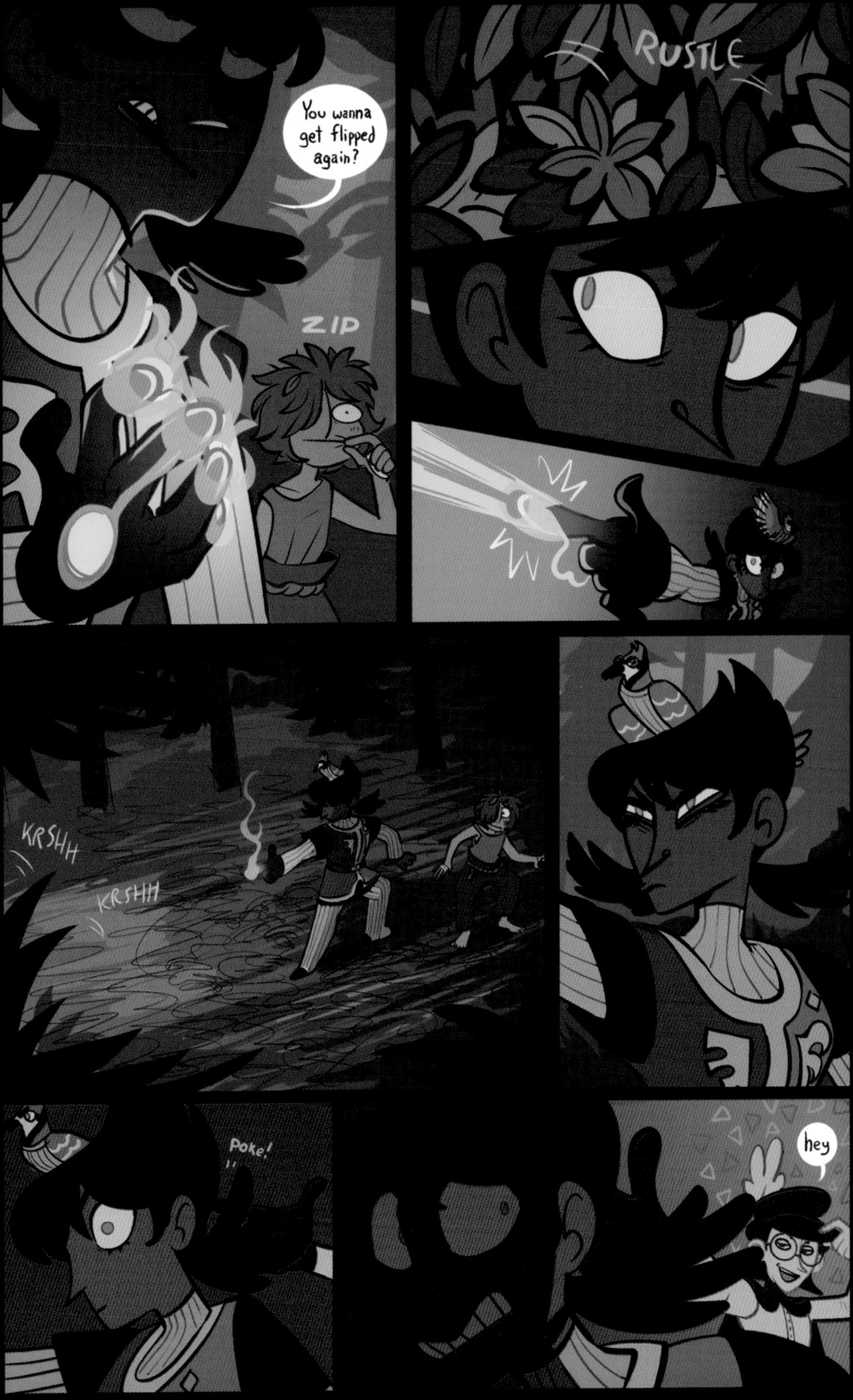
You wanna get flipped again?
ZIP
RUSTLE
KRSHH
KRSHH
Poke!
hey

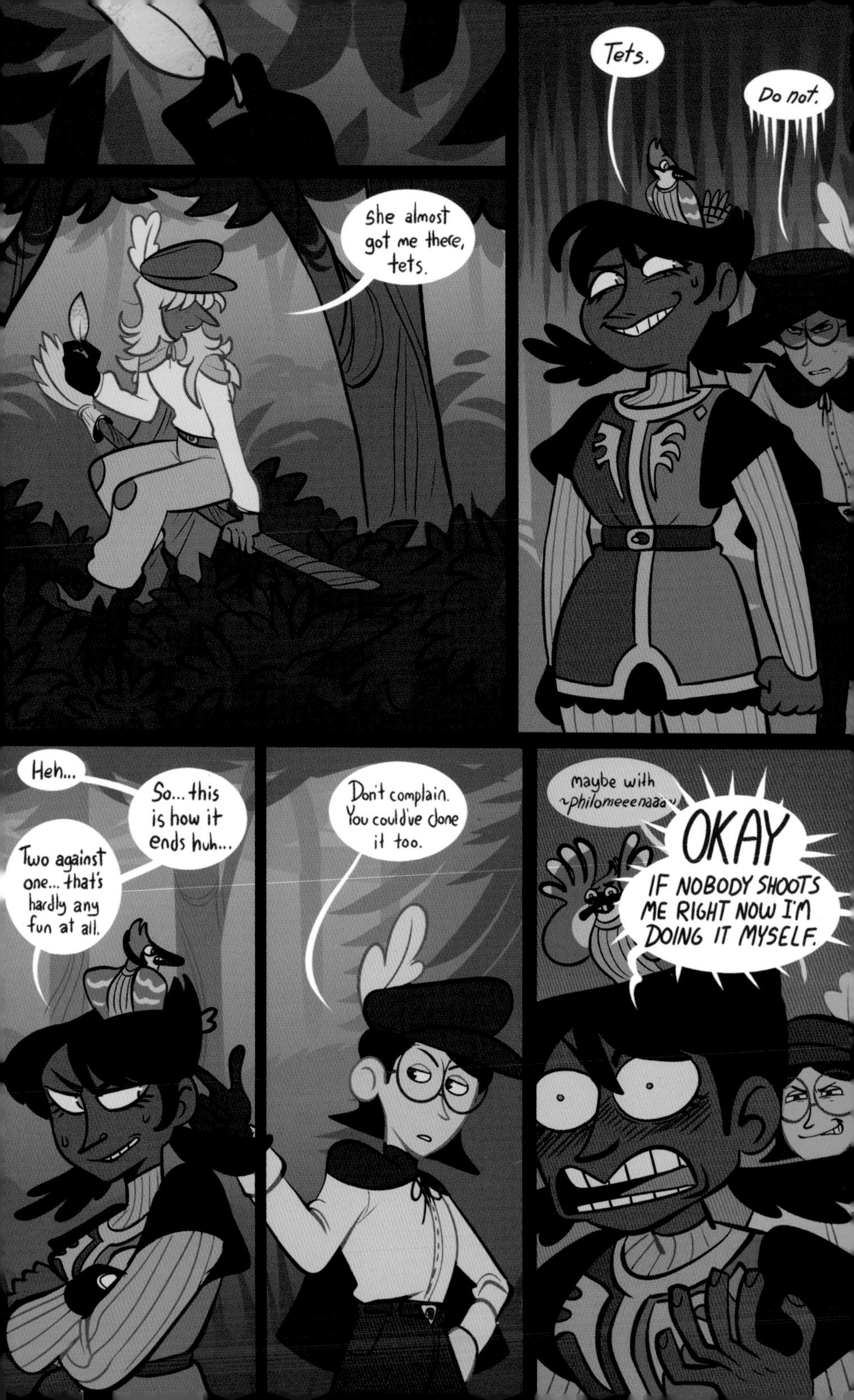
she almost got me there, tets.
Tets.
Do not.
Heh...
So... this is how it ends huh...
Two against one... that's hardly any fun at all.
Don't complain. You could've done it too.
maybe with ~philomeeenaaa~
OKAY
IF NOBODY SHOOTS ME RIGHT NOW I'M DOING IT MYSELF.

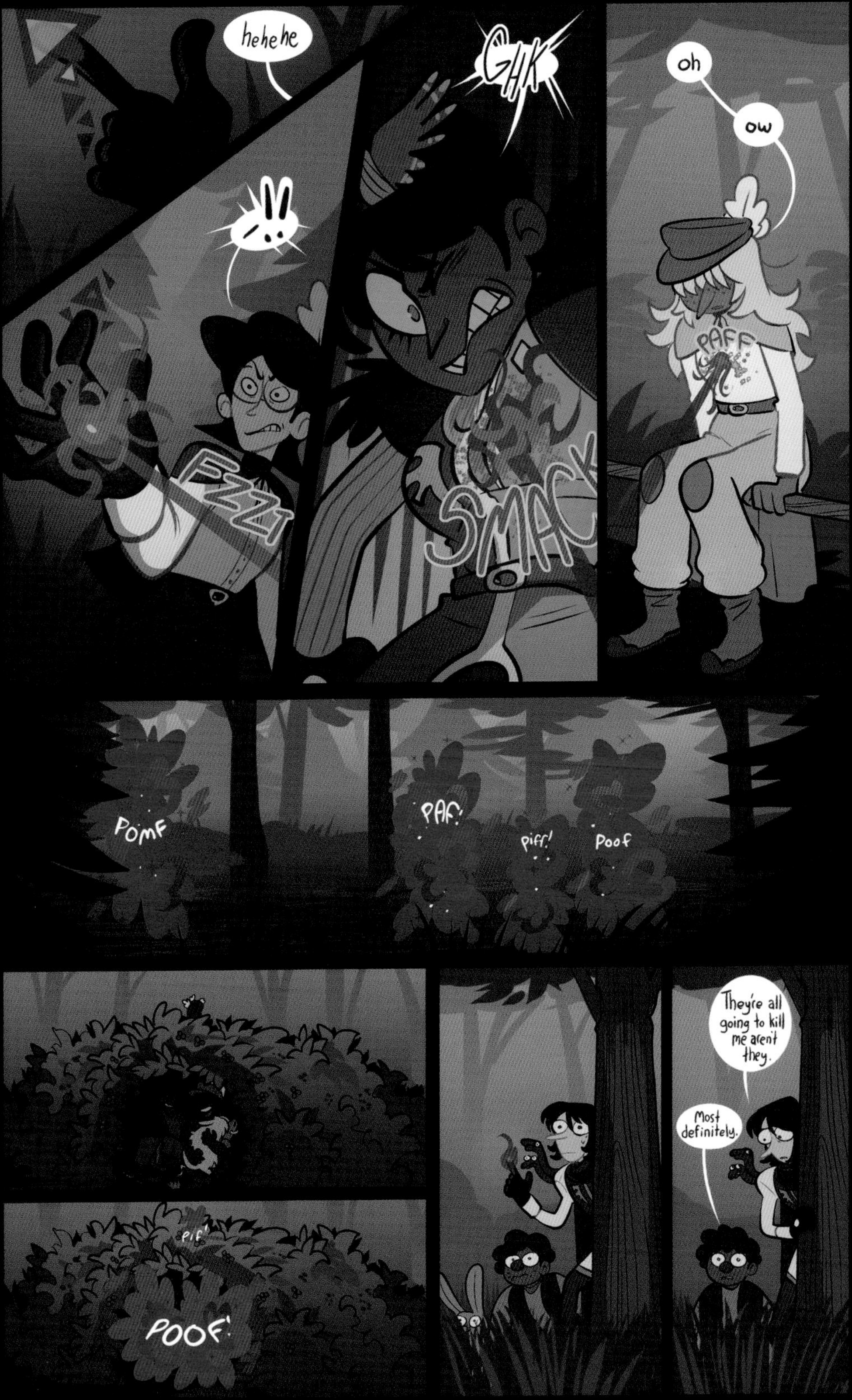

hehehe
FZZZT
GHK
SMACK
oh
ow
PAFF
POMF
PAF!
piff!
Poof
pif!
POOF!
They're all going to kill me aren't they.
Most definitely.

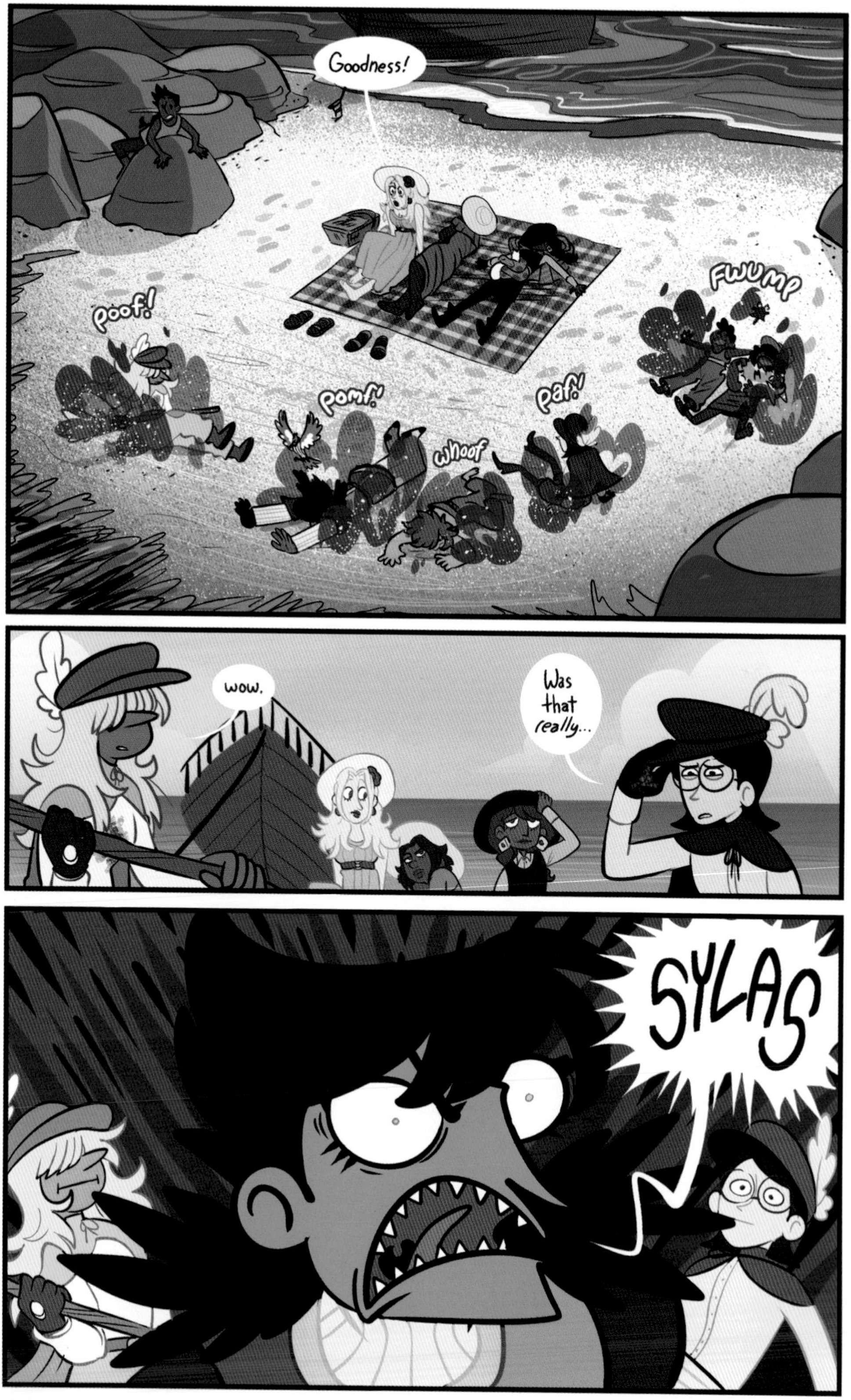
Goodness!
poof!
FWUMP
pomf!
paf!
whoof
wow.
Was that really...
SYLAS

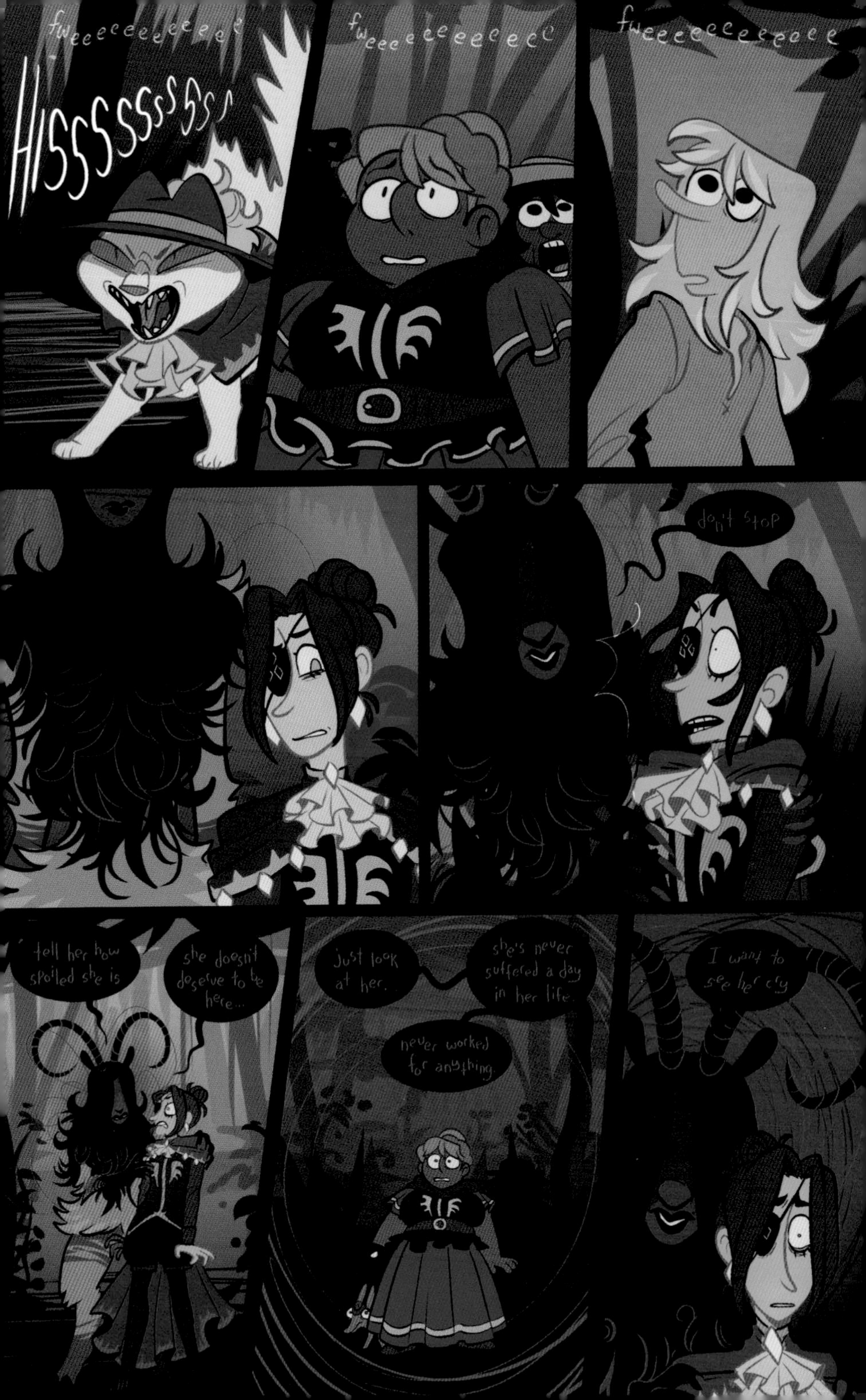
fweeeeeeeeeeee
HISSSSSSSSSS
fweeeeeeeeeeeee
fweeeeeeeeeeeeee
don't stop
tell her how spoiled she is
she doesn't deserve to be here...
just look at her.
she's never suffered a day in her life.
never worked for anything.
I want to see her cry

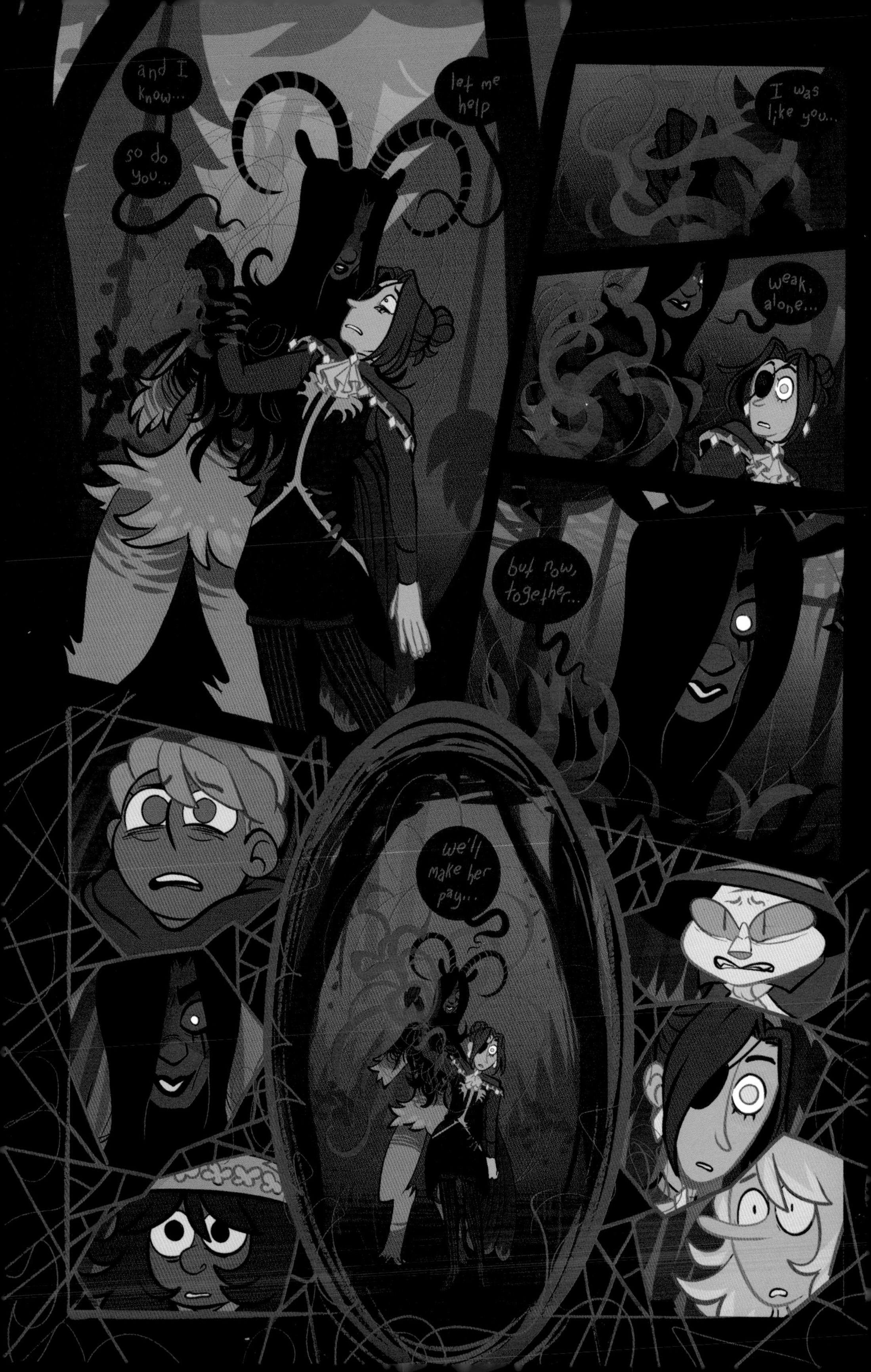
and I know...
so do you...
let me help
I was like you...
weak, alone...
but now, together...
we'll make her pay...

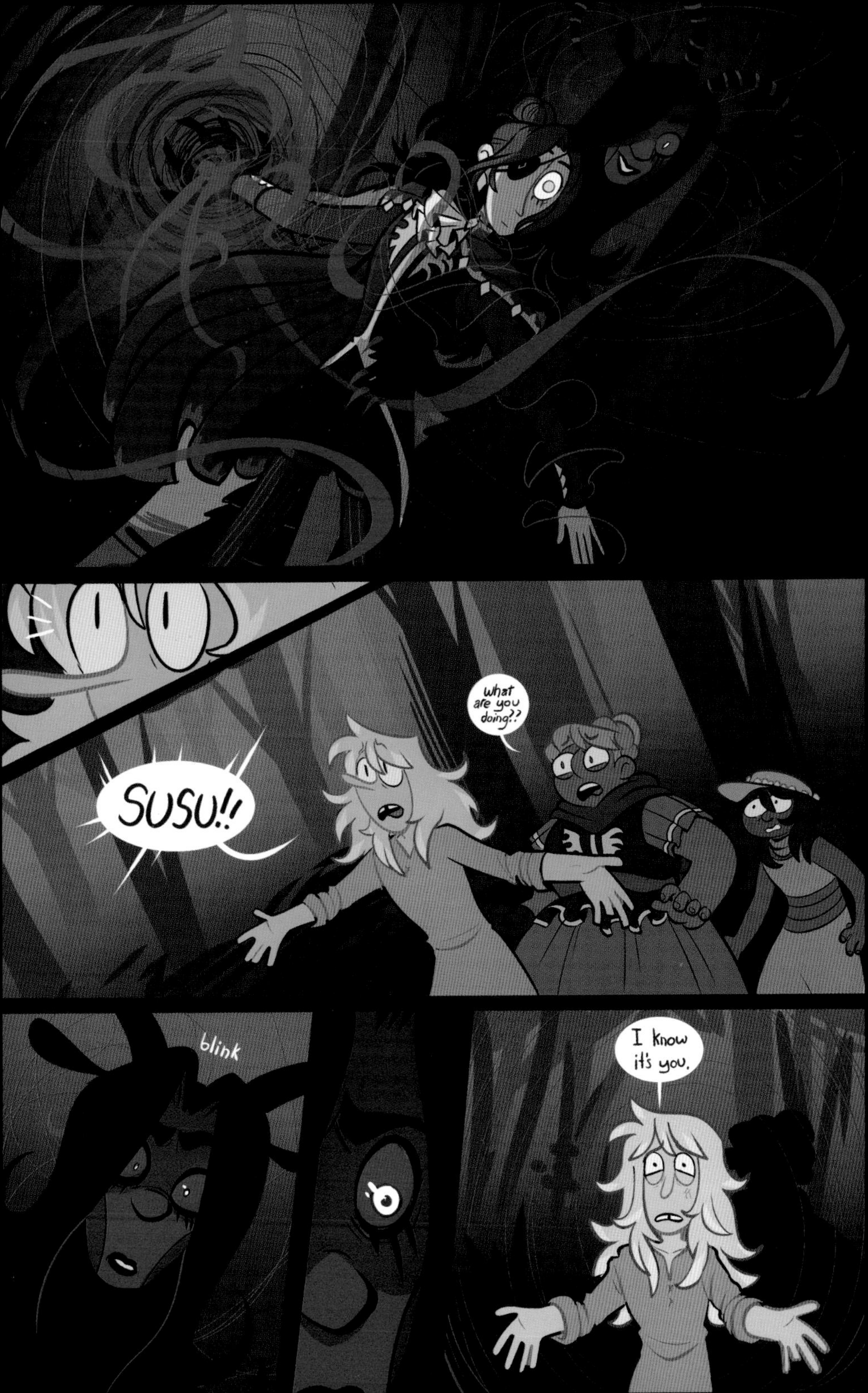
what are you doing??
SUSU!!
blink
I know it's you.

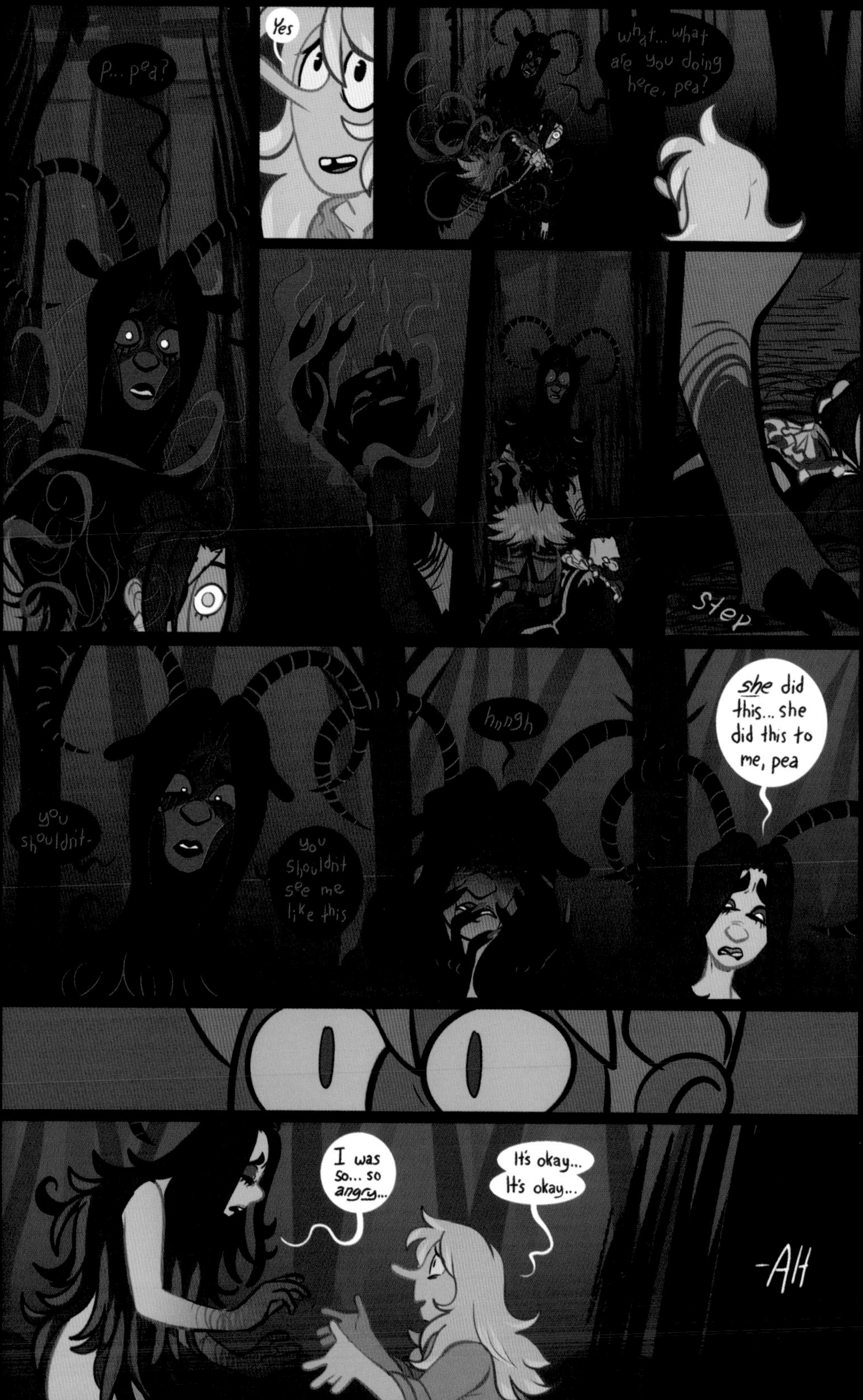

p... pea?
Yes
what... what are you doing here, pea?
step
you shouldnt-
you shouldnt see me like this
hnngh
she did this... she did this to me, pea
I was so... so angry...
It's okay... It's okay...
-AH

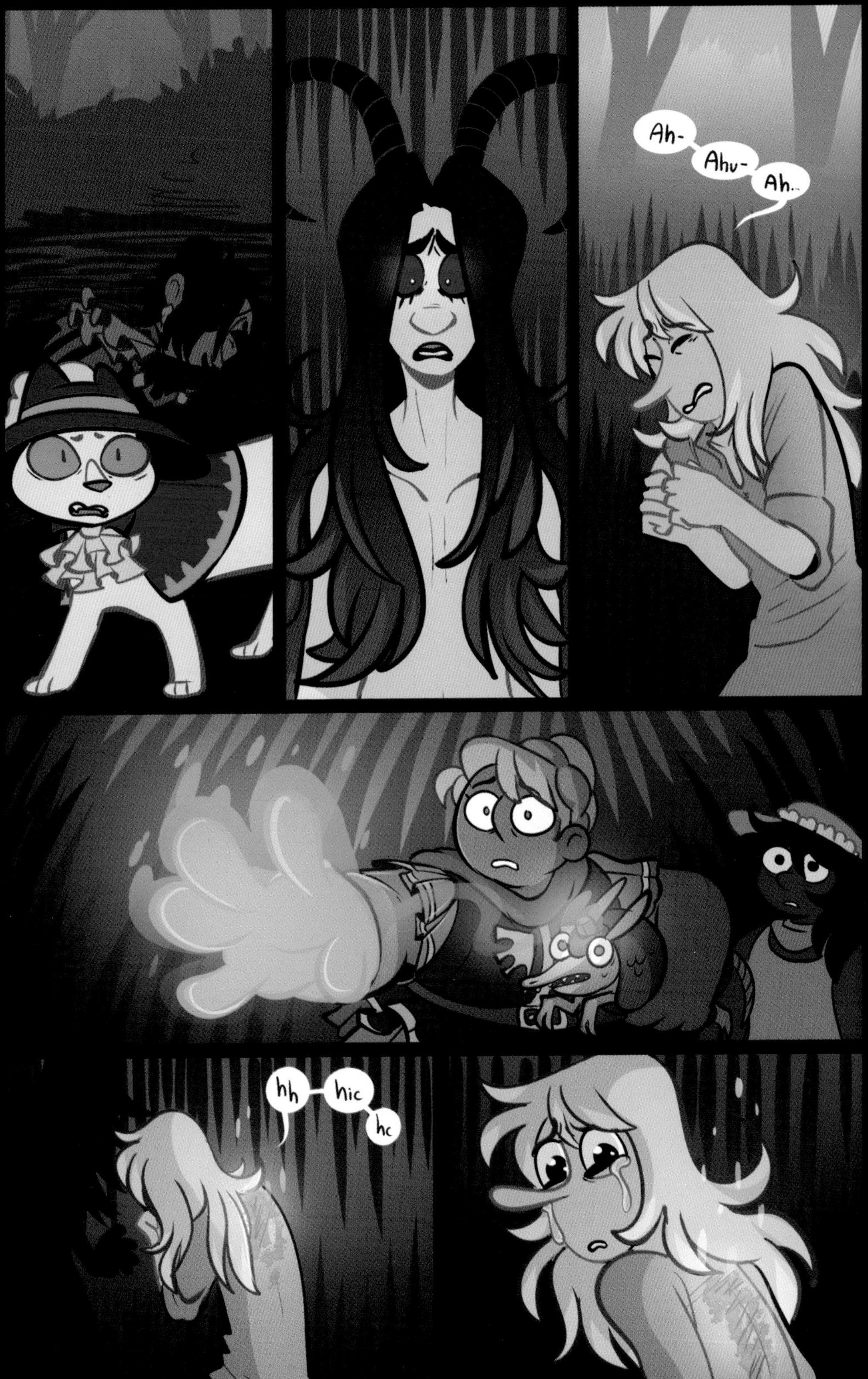
Ah-
Ahu-
Ah...
hh
hic
hc

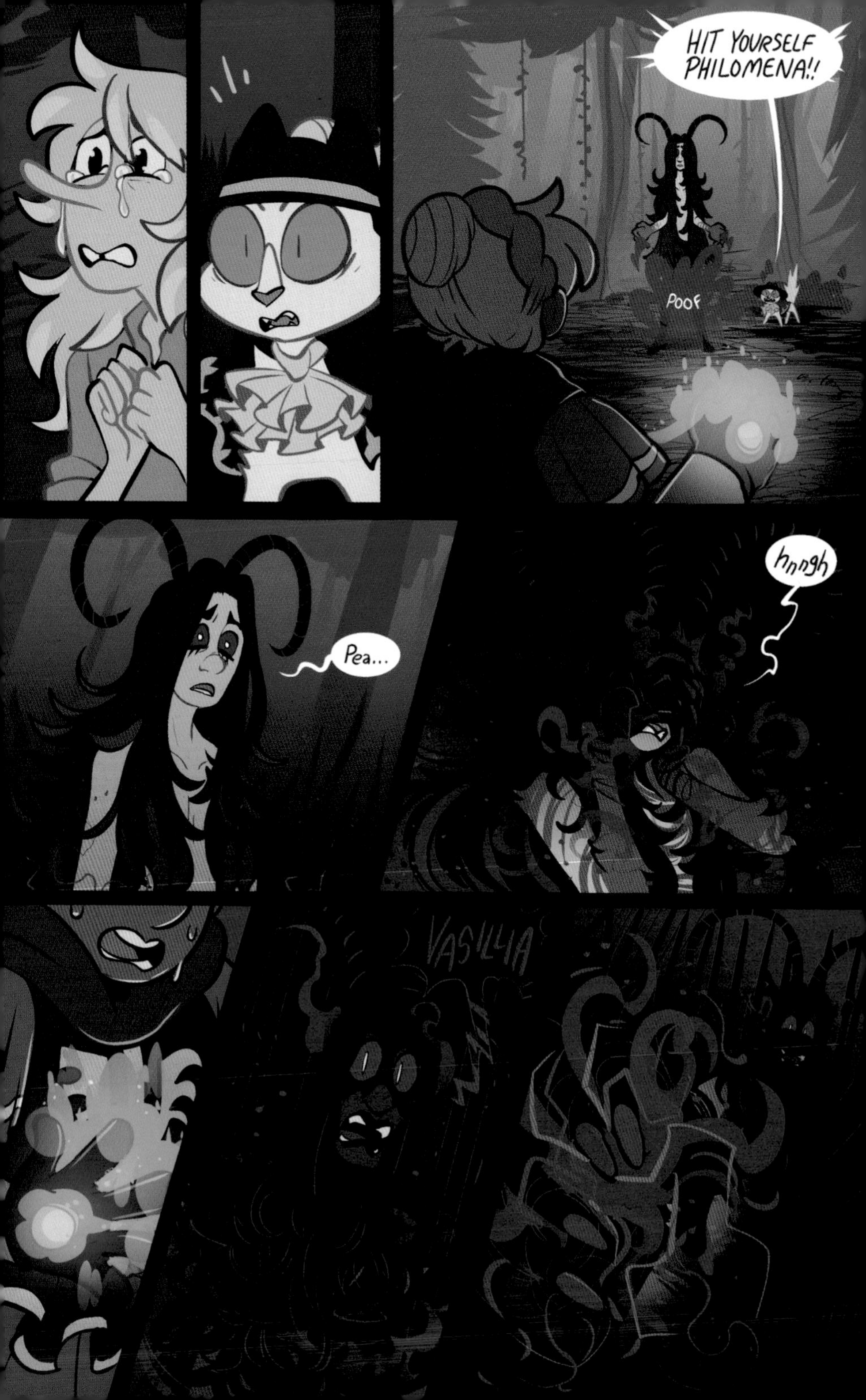
HIT YOURSELF PHILOMENA!!
POOF
Pea...
hnngh
VASILLIA

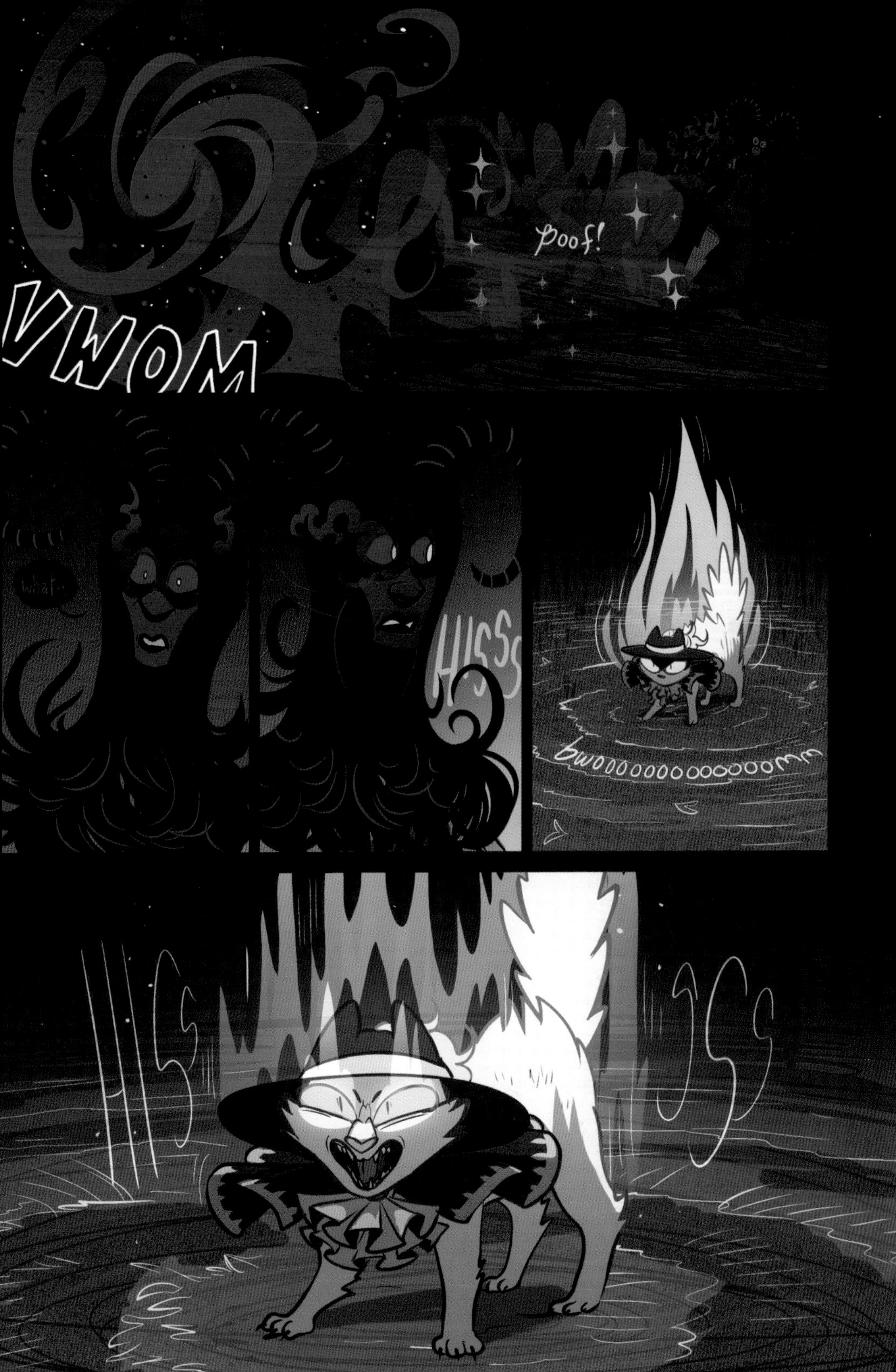
poof!
VWOM
what...
HISSS
bwooooooooooooooomm
HISSSSSSS

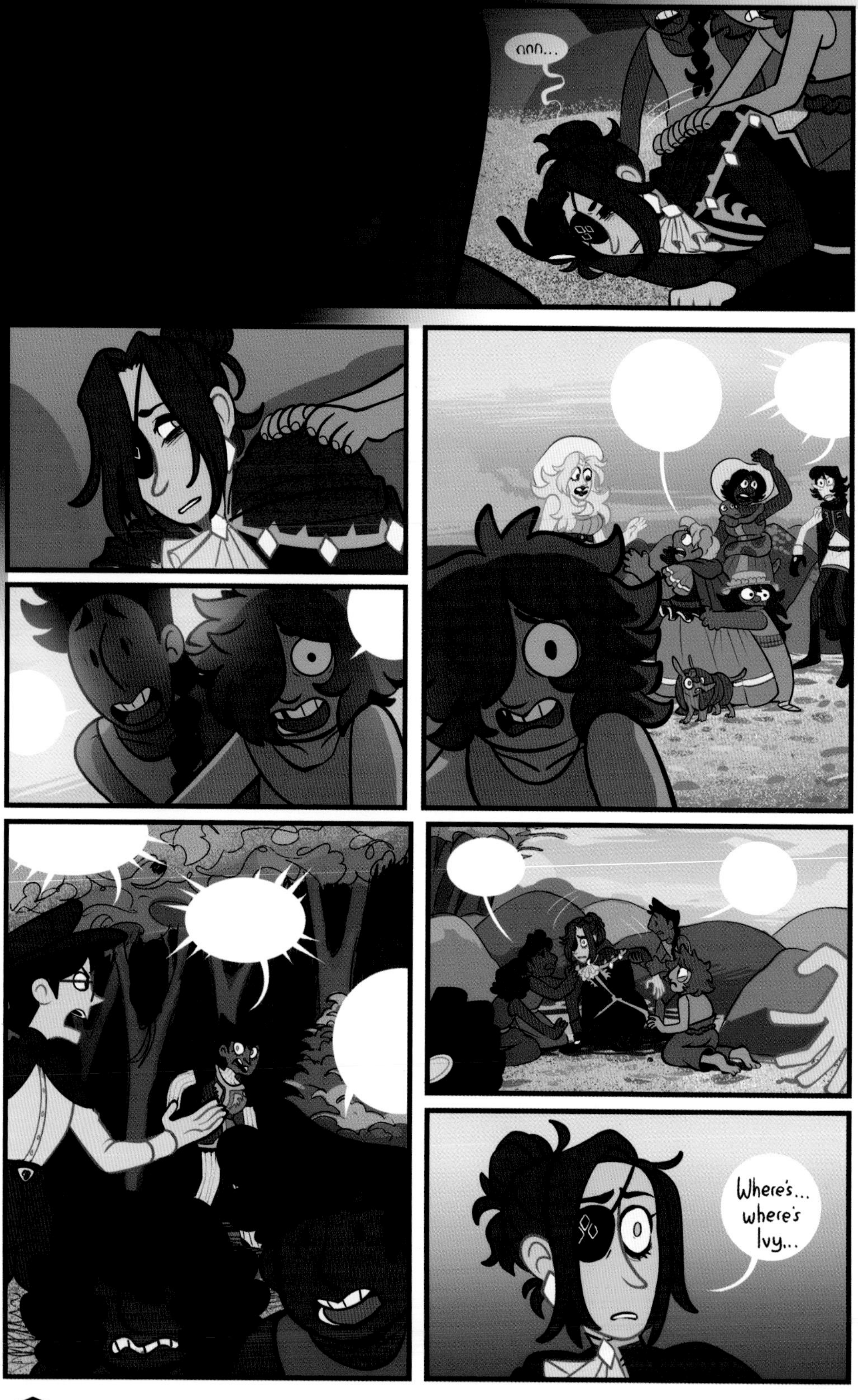
nnn...
Where's... where's Ivy...

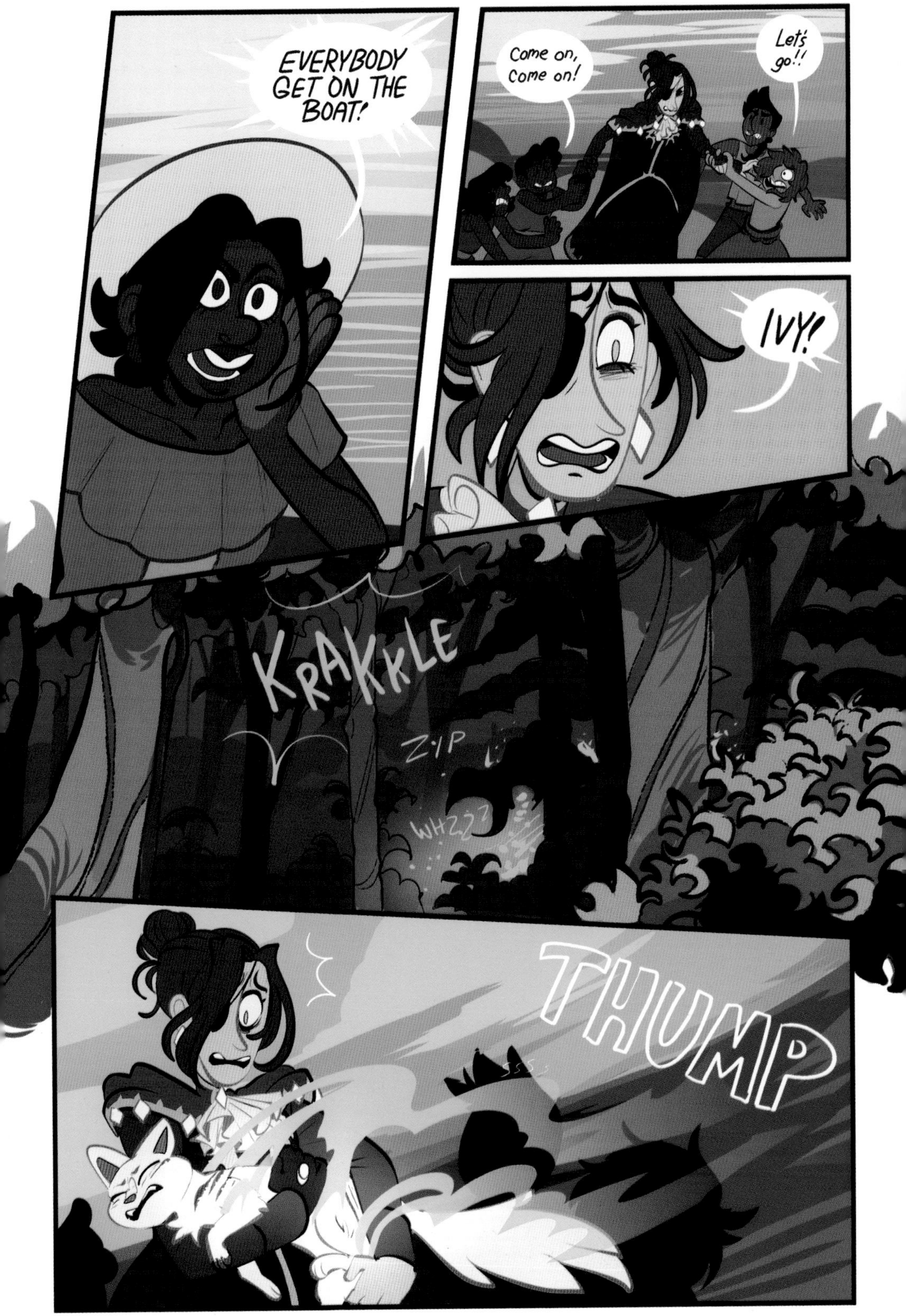
EVERYBODY GET ON THE BOAT!
Come on, come on!
Let's go!!
IVY!
KRAKKLE
ZIP
WHZZZ
THUMP

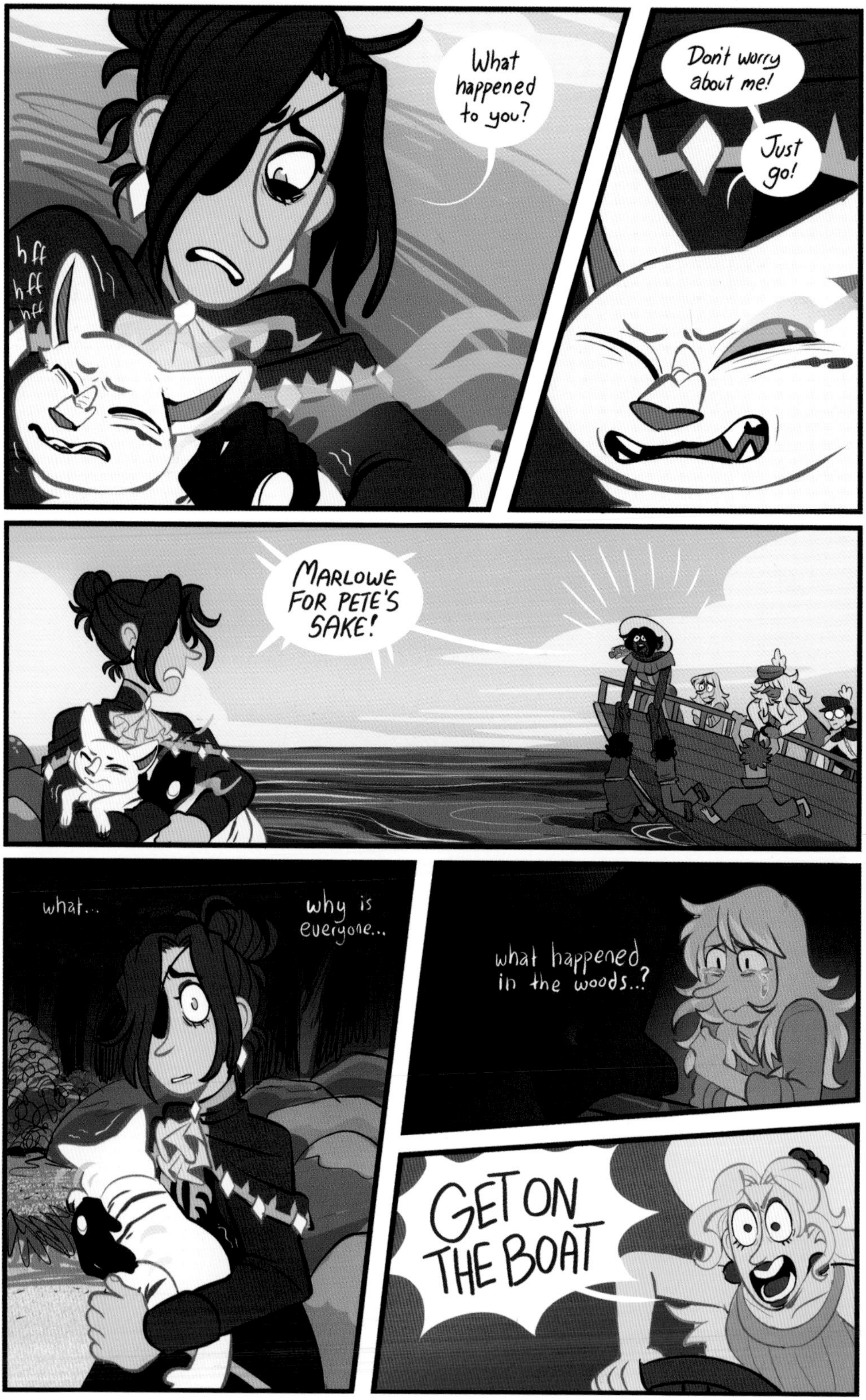
hff
hff
hff
What happened to you?
Don't worry about me!
Just go!
MARLOWE FOR PETE'S SAKE!
what...
why is everyone...
what happened in the woods..?
GET ON THE BOAT

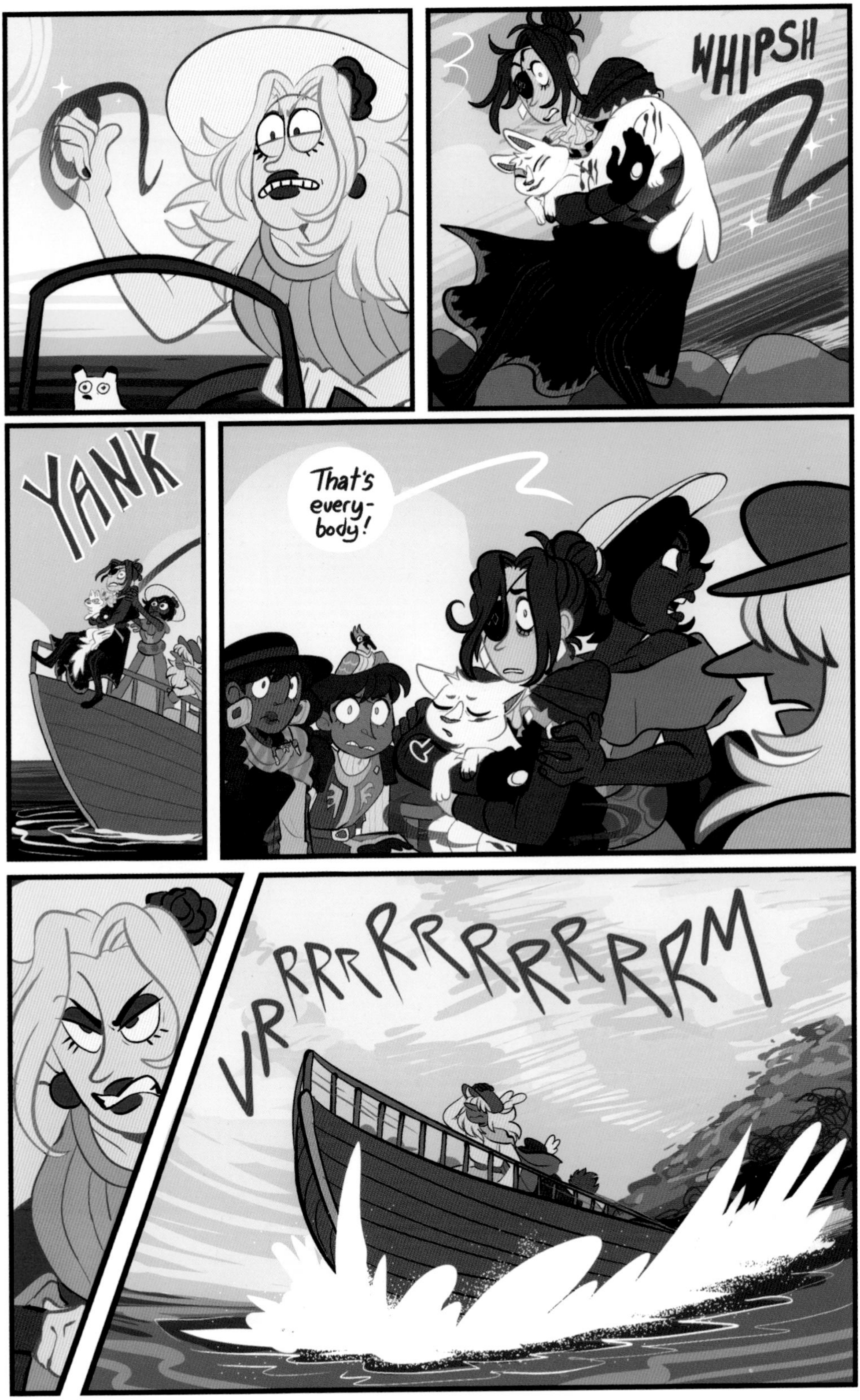
WHIPSH
YANK
That's every-body!
VRRRRRRRRRRRRM

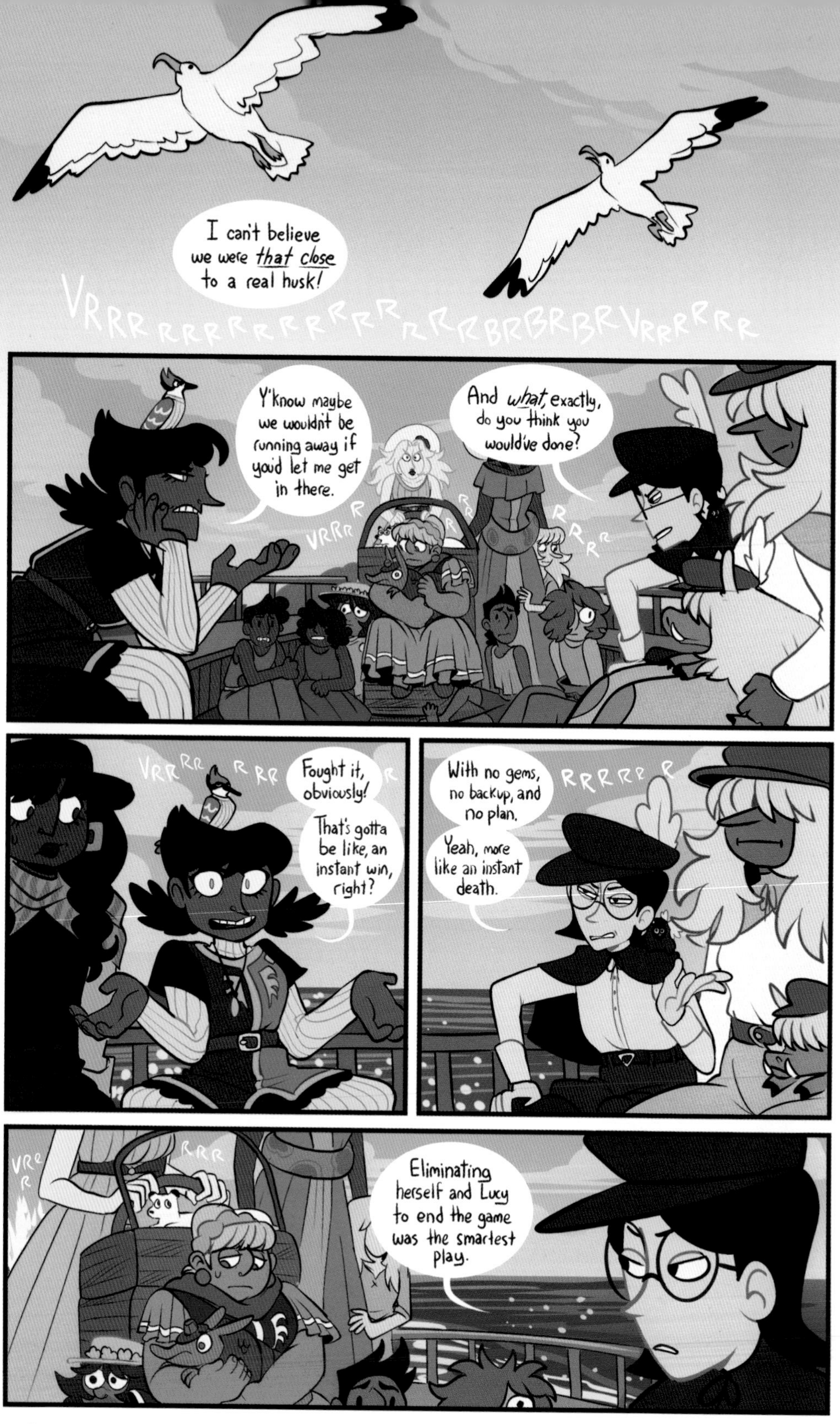
I can't believe we were that close to a real husk!
VRRRRRRRRRRRRRRRRRBRBRBRVRRRRRR
Y'know maybe we wouldn't be running away if you'd let me get in there.
VRRR
And what, exactly, do you think you would've done?
RRRR
VRRRR RRR
Fought it, obviously!
That's gotta be like, an instant win, right?
With no gems, no backup, and no plan.
RRRRRR
Yeah, more like an instant death.
VRRR
RRR
Eliminating herself and Lucy to end the game was the smartest play.

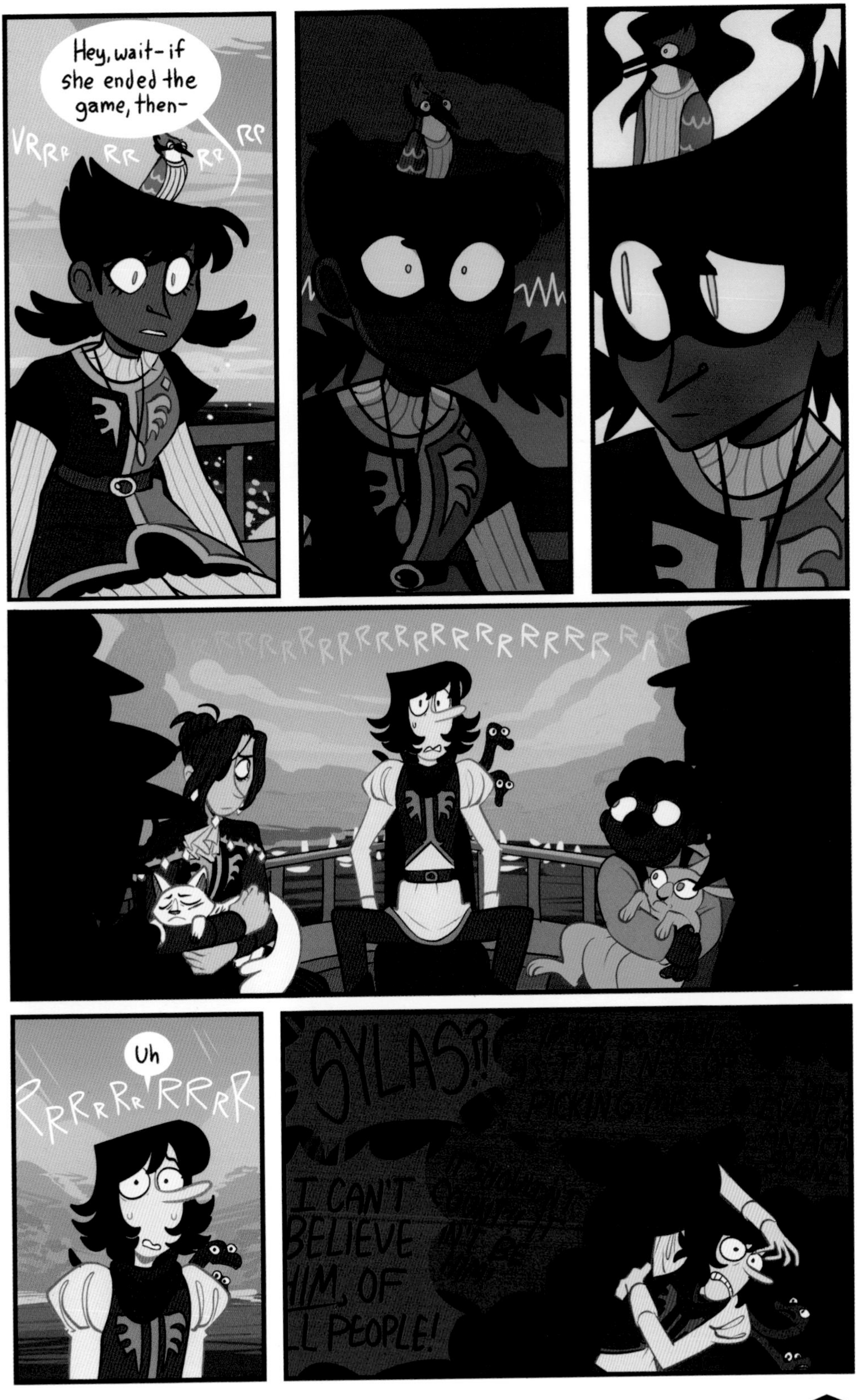
Hey, wait- if she ended the game, then-
VRRR RR RR RP
RRRRRRRRRRRRRRRRR
Uh
RRRRRRRRRR
SYLAS?!
I CAN'T BELIEVE HIM, OF
L PEOPLE!

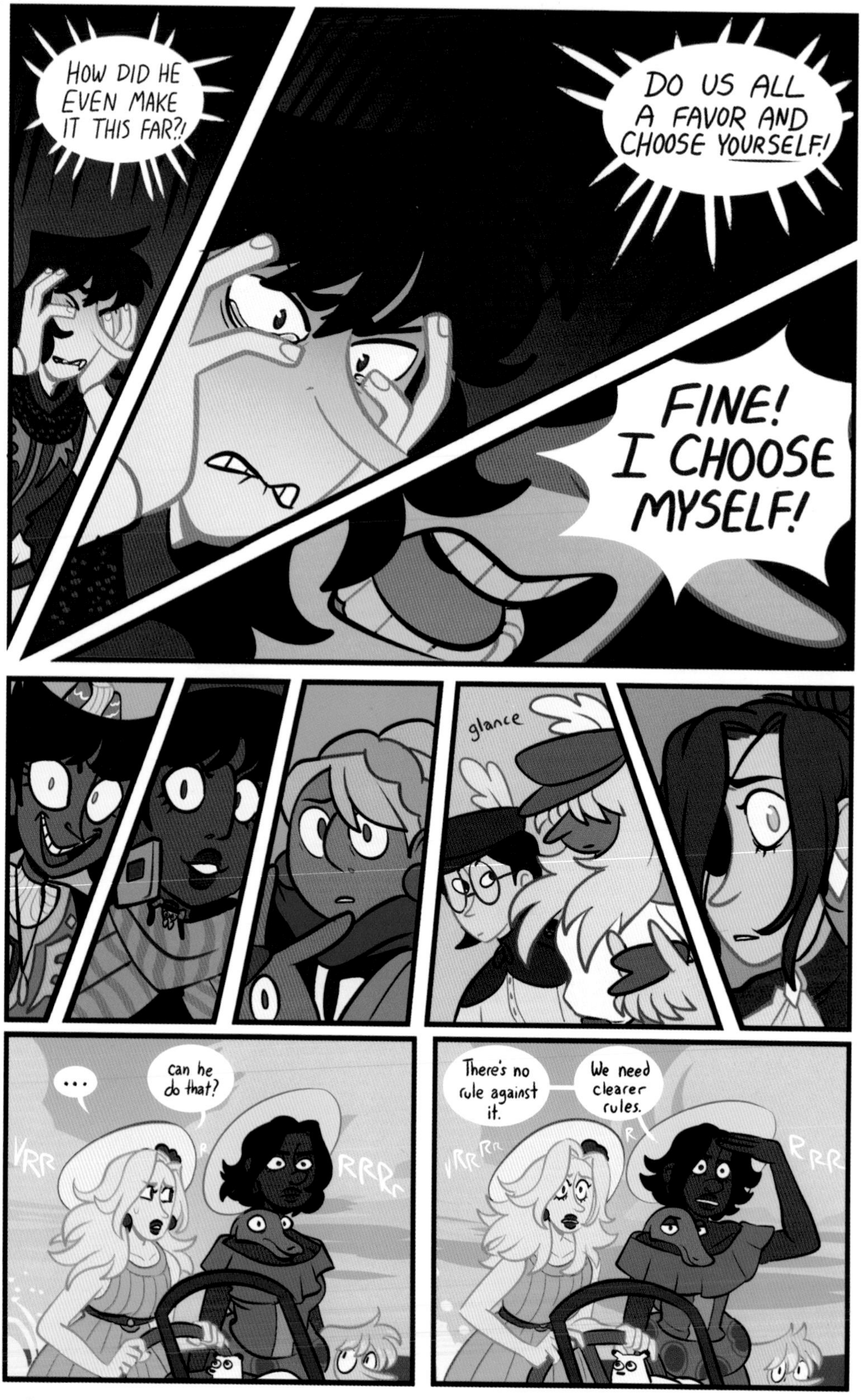
HOW DID HE EVEN MAKE IT THIS FAR?!
DO US ALL A FAVOR AND CHOOSE YOURSELF!
FINE! I CHOOSE MYSELF!
glance
...
can he do that?
VRR
R
RRRr
There's no rule against it.
We need clearer rules.
VRRRr
R
RRR

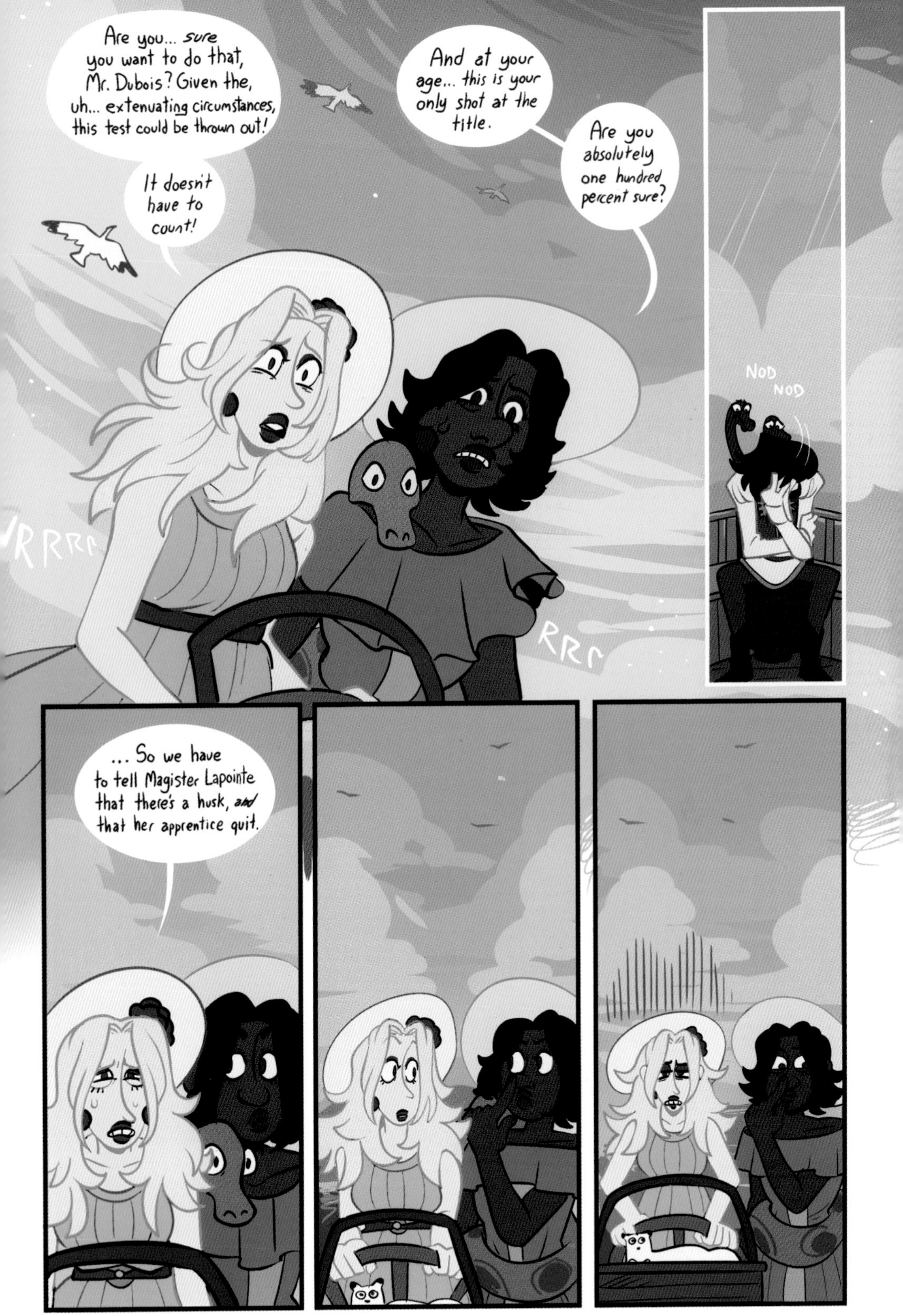
Are you... sure you want to do that, Mr. Dubois? Given the, uh... extenuating circumstances, this test could be thrown out!
It doesn't have to count!
And at your age... this is your only shot at the title.
Are you absolutely one hundred percent sure?
RRRr
RRr
NOD
NOD
... So we have to tell Magister Lapointe that there's a husk, and that her apprentice quit.

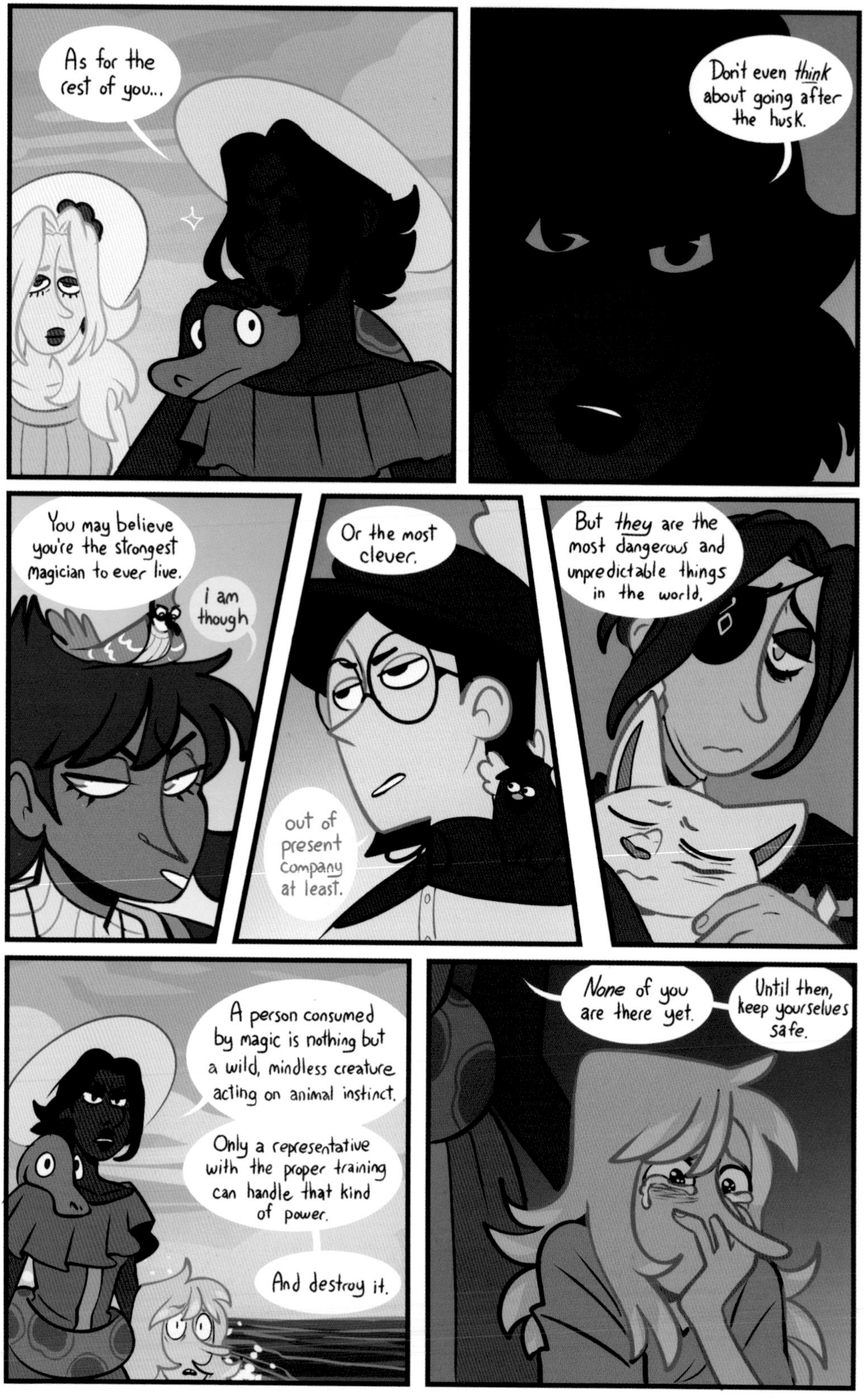
As for the rest of you...
Don't even *think* about going after the husk.
You may believe you're the strongest magician to ever live.
i am though
Or the most clever.
out of present company at least.
But *they* are the most dangerous and unpredictable things in the world.
A person consumed by magic is nothing but a wild, mindless creature acting on animal instinct.
Only a representative with the proper training can handle that kind of power.
And destroy it.
None of you are there yet.
Until then, keep yourselves safe.

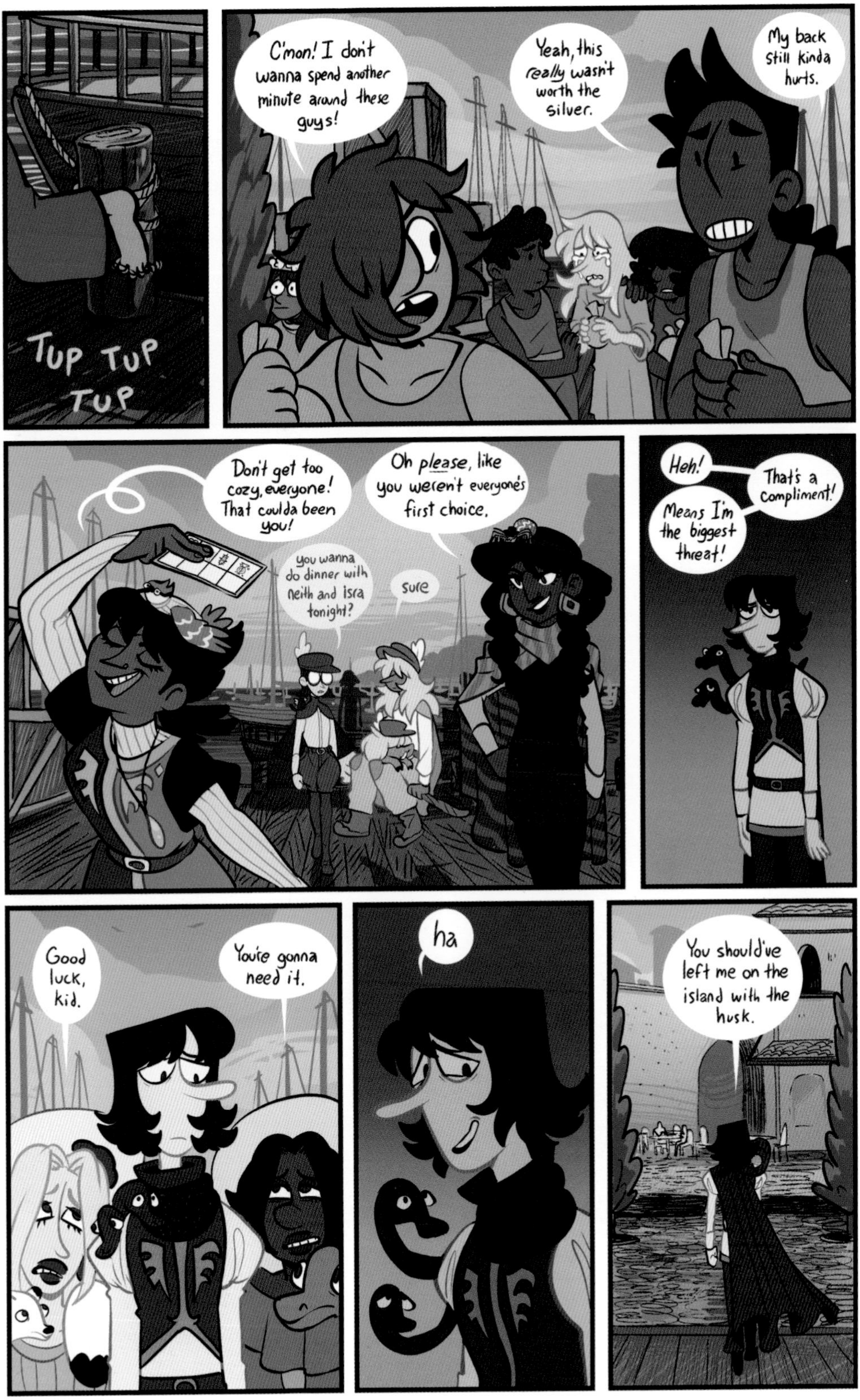

TUP TUP TUP
C'mon! I don't wanna spend another minute around these guys!
Yeah, this really wasn't worth the silver.
My back still kinda hurts.
Don't get too cozy, everyone! That coulda been you!
Oh please, like you weren't everyone's first choice.
you wanna do dinner with neith and isra tonight?
sure
Heh!
That's a compliment!
Means I'm the biggest threat!
Good luck, kid.
You're gonna need it.
ha
You should've left me on the island with the husk.

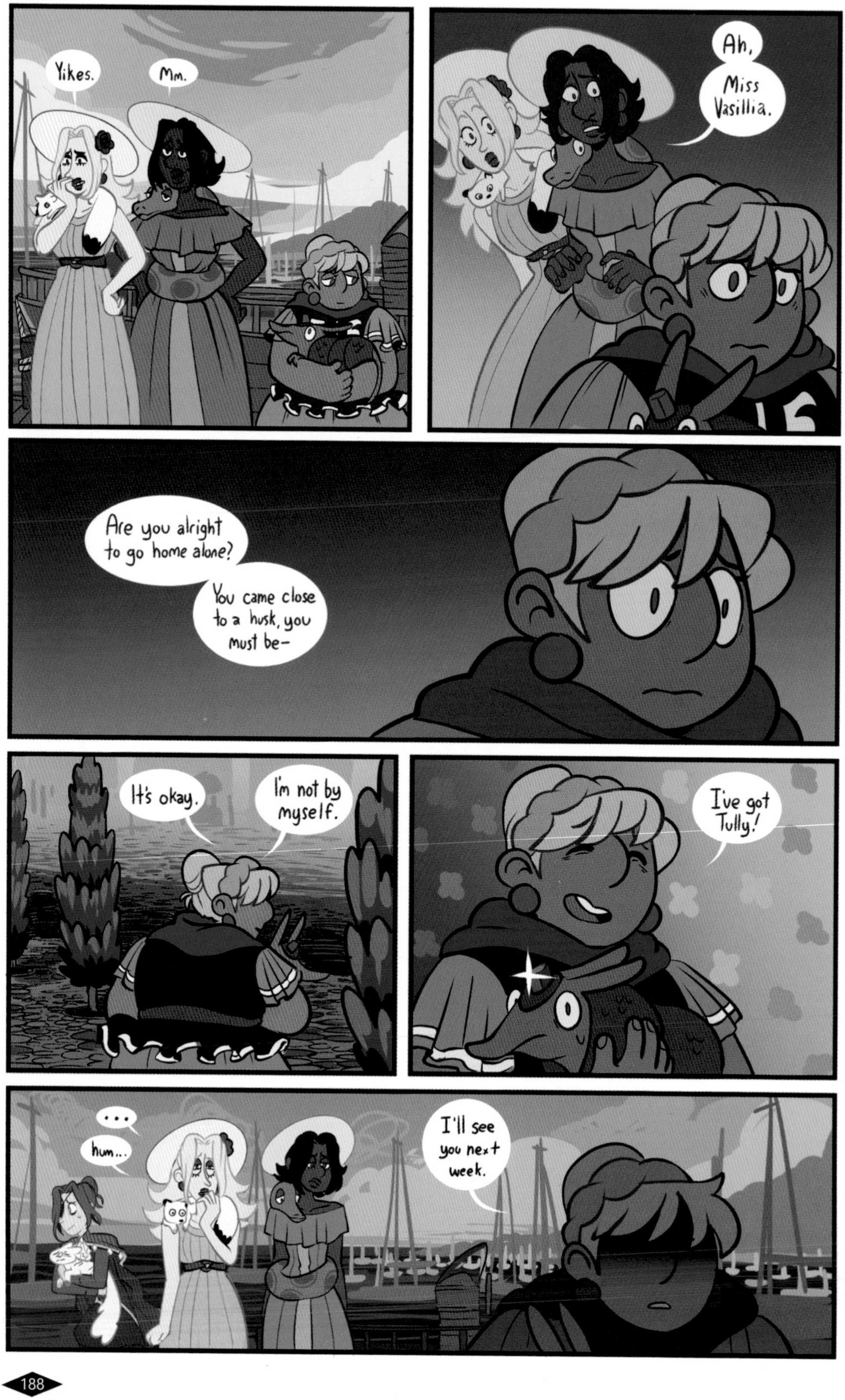
Yikes.
Mm.
Ah, Miss Vasillia.
Are you alright to go home alone?
You came close to a husk, you must be-
It's okay.
I'm not by myself.
I've got Tully!
...
hum...
I'll see you next week.

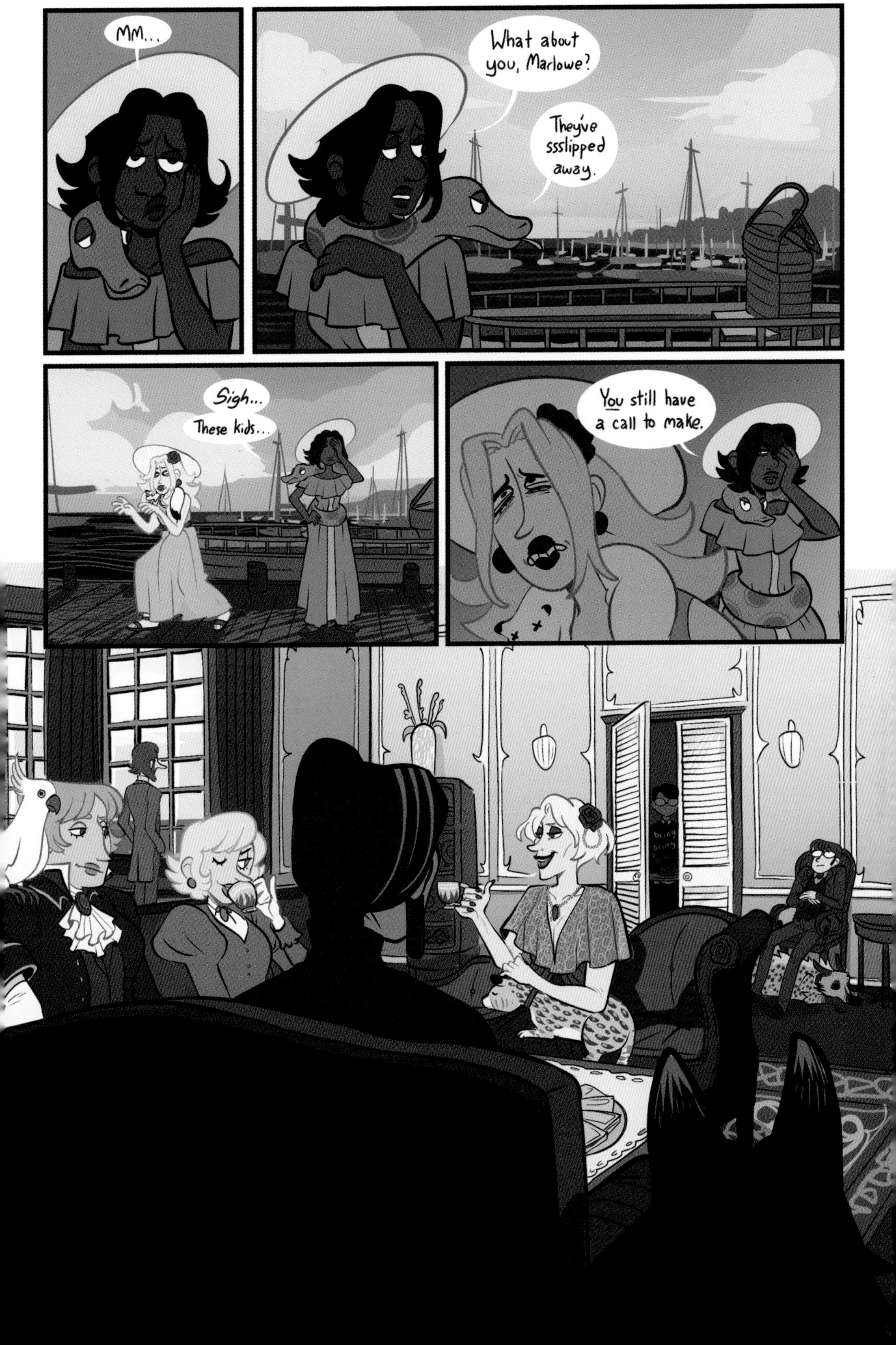
MM...
What about you, Marlowe?
They've ssslipped away.
Sigh...
These kids...
You still have a call to make.

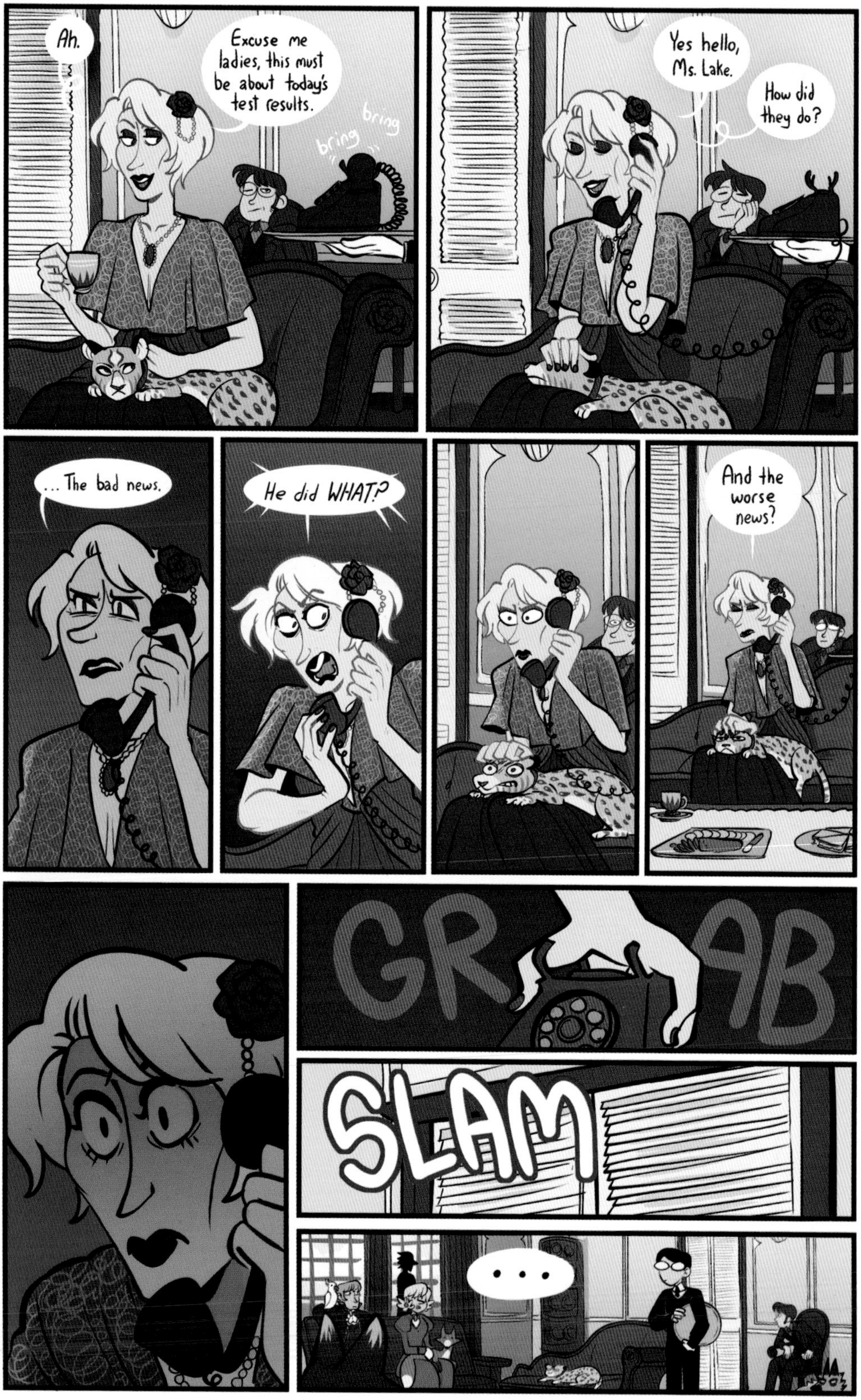

Ah.
Excuse me ladies, this must be about today's test results.
bring bring
Yes hello, Ms. Lake.
How did they do?
... The bad news.
He did WHAT?
And the worse news?
GRAB
SLAM
. . .

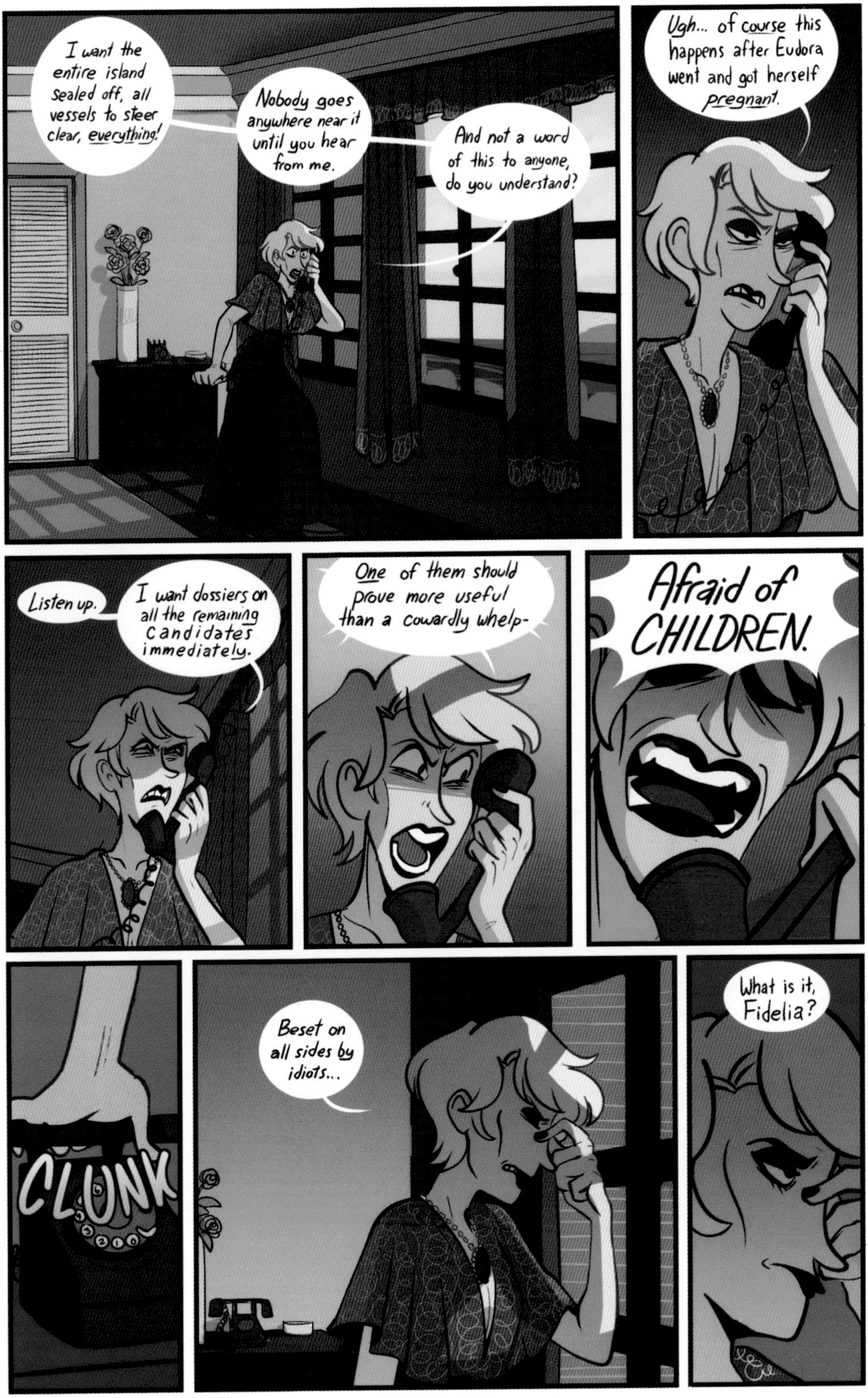
I want the entire island sealed off, all vessels to steer clear, everything!
Nobody goes anywhere near it until you hear from me.
And not a word of this to anyone, do you understand?
Ugh... of course this happens after Eudora went and got herself pregnant.
Listen up.
I want dossiers on all the remaining candidates immediately.
One of them should prove more useful than a cowardly whelp-
Afraid of CHILDREN.
CLUNK
Beset on all sides by idiots...
What is it, Fidelia?

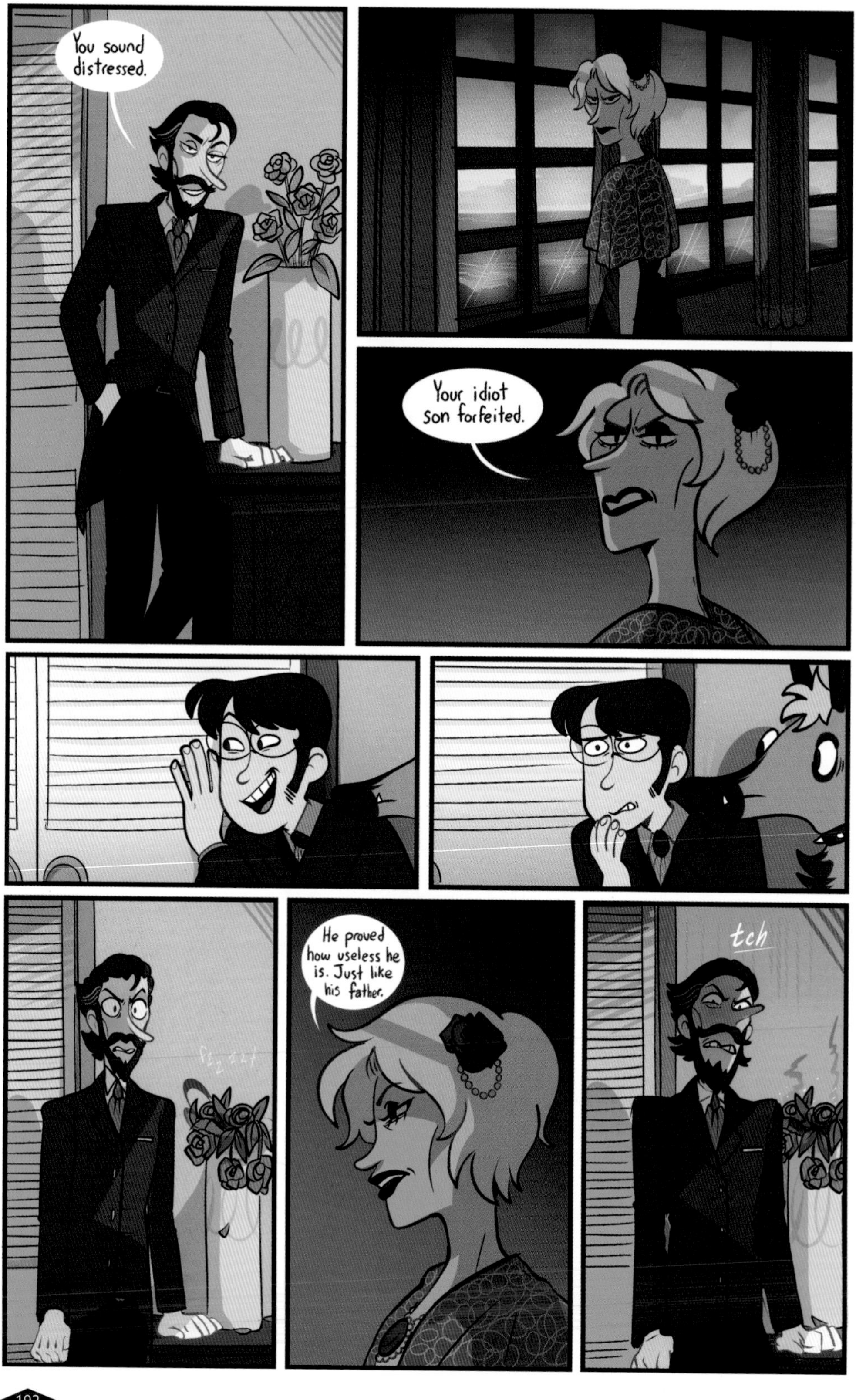
You sound distressed.
Your idiot son forfeited.
fzzzt
He proved how useless he is. Just like his father.
tch

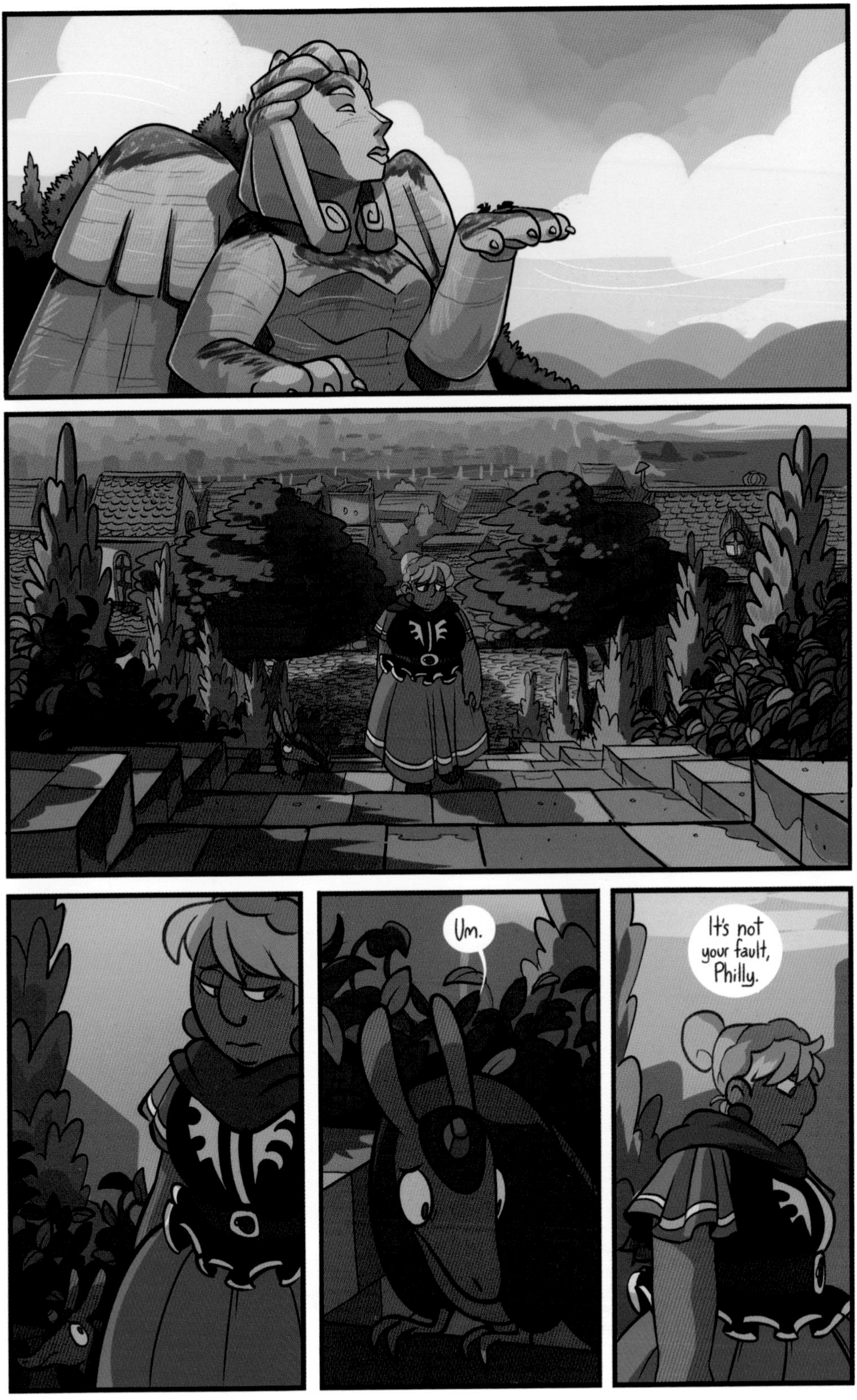
Um.
It's not your fault, Philly.

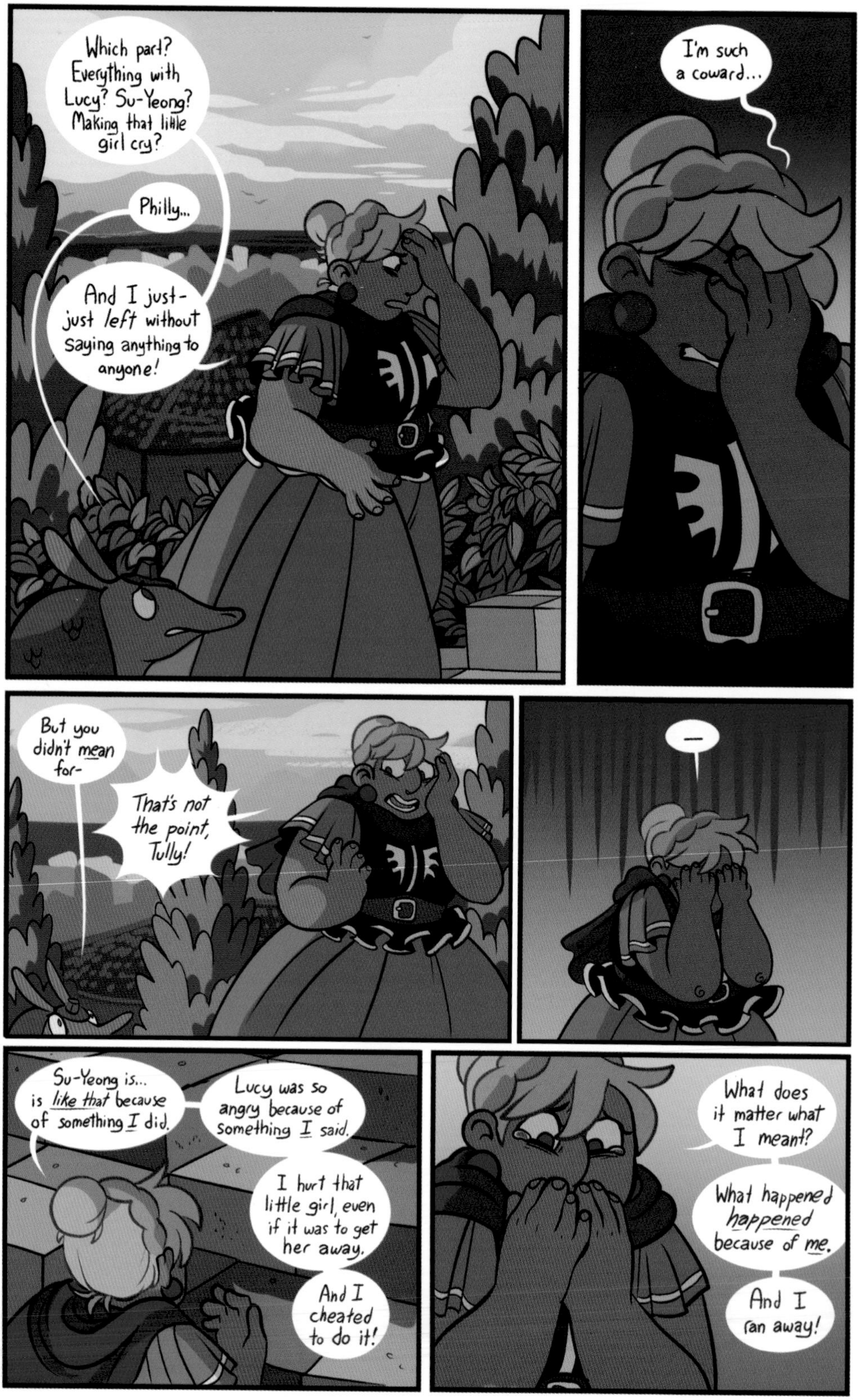
Which part? Everything with Lucy? Su-Yeong? Making that little girl cry?
Philly...
And I just-just *left* without saying anything to anyone!
I'm such a coward...
But you didn't mean for-
That's not the point, Tully!
—
Su-Yeong is... is *like that* because of something I did.
Lucy was so angry because of something I said.
I hurt that little girl, even if it was to get her away.
And I cheated to do it!
What does it matter what I meant?
What happened happened because of me.
And I ran away!

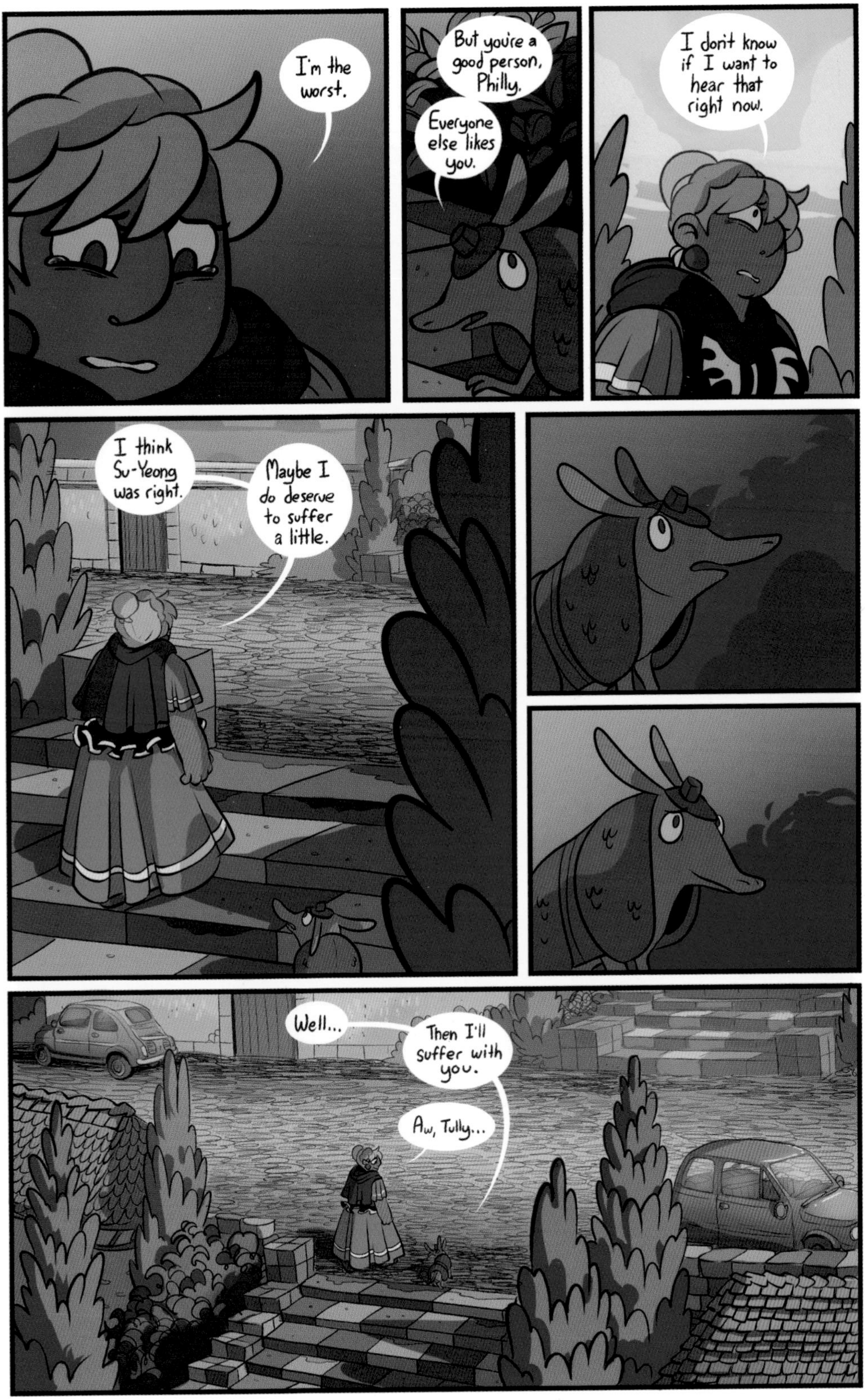
I'm the worst.
But you're a good person, Philly.
Everyone else likes you.
I don't know if I want to hear that right now.
I think Su-Yeong was right.
Maybe I do deserve to suffer a little.
Well...
Then I'll suffer with you.
Aw, Tully...

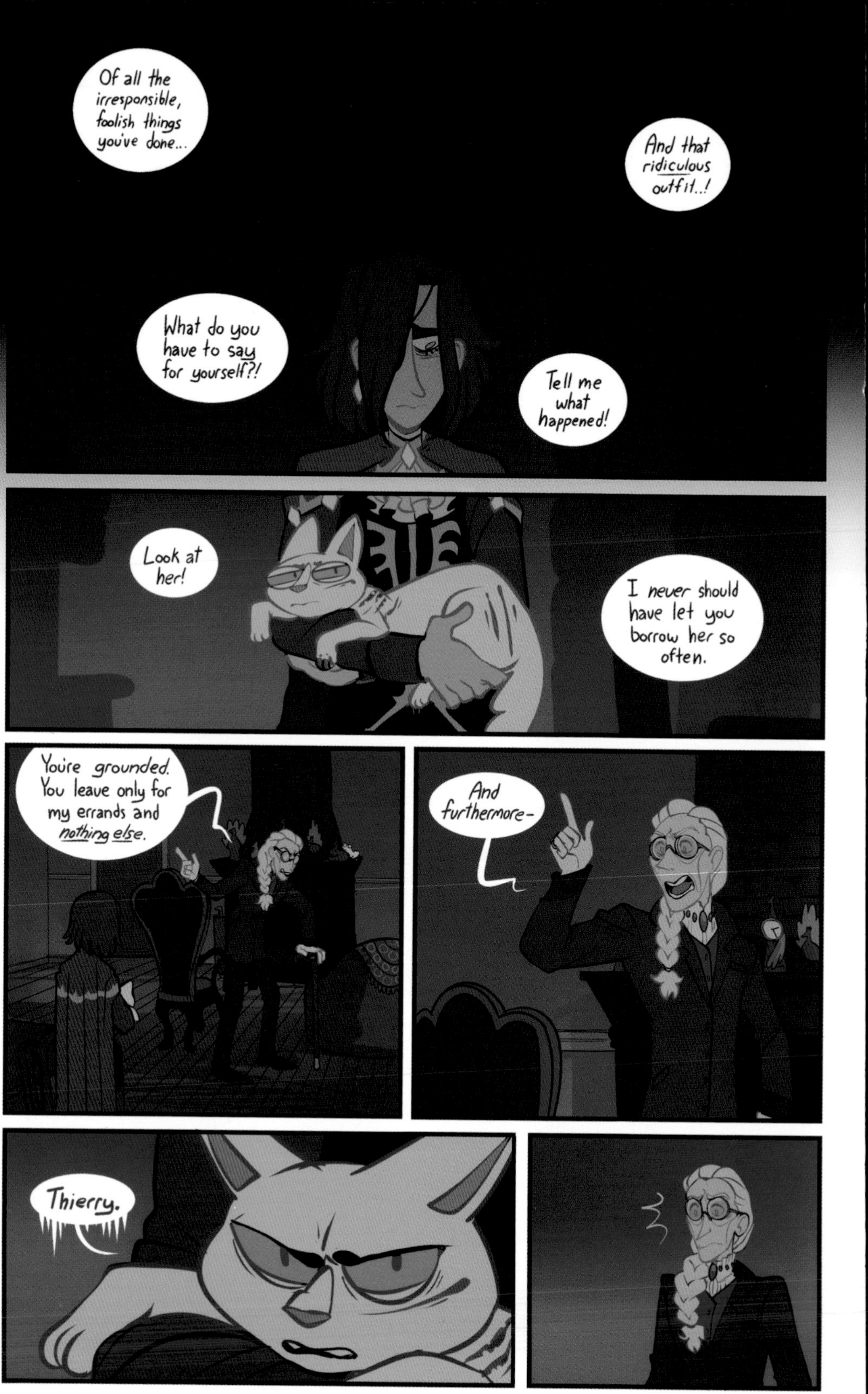
Of all the irresponsible, foolish things you've done...
And that ridiculous outfit..!
What do you have to say for yourself?!
Tell me what happened!
Look at her!
I never should have let you borrow her so often.
You're grounded. You leave only for my errands and nothing else.
And furthermore-
Thierry.

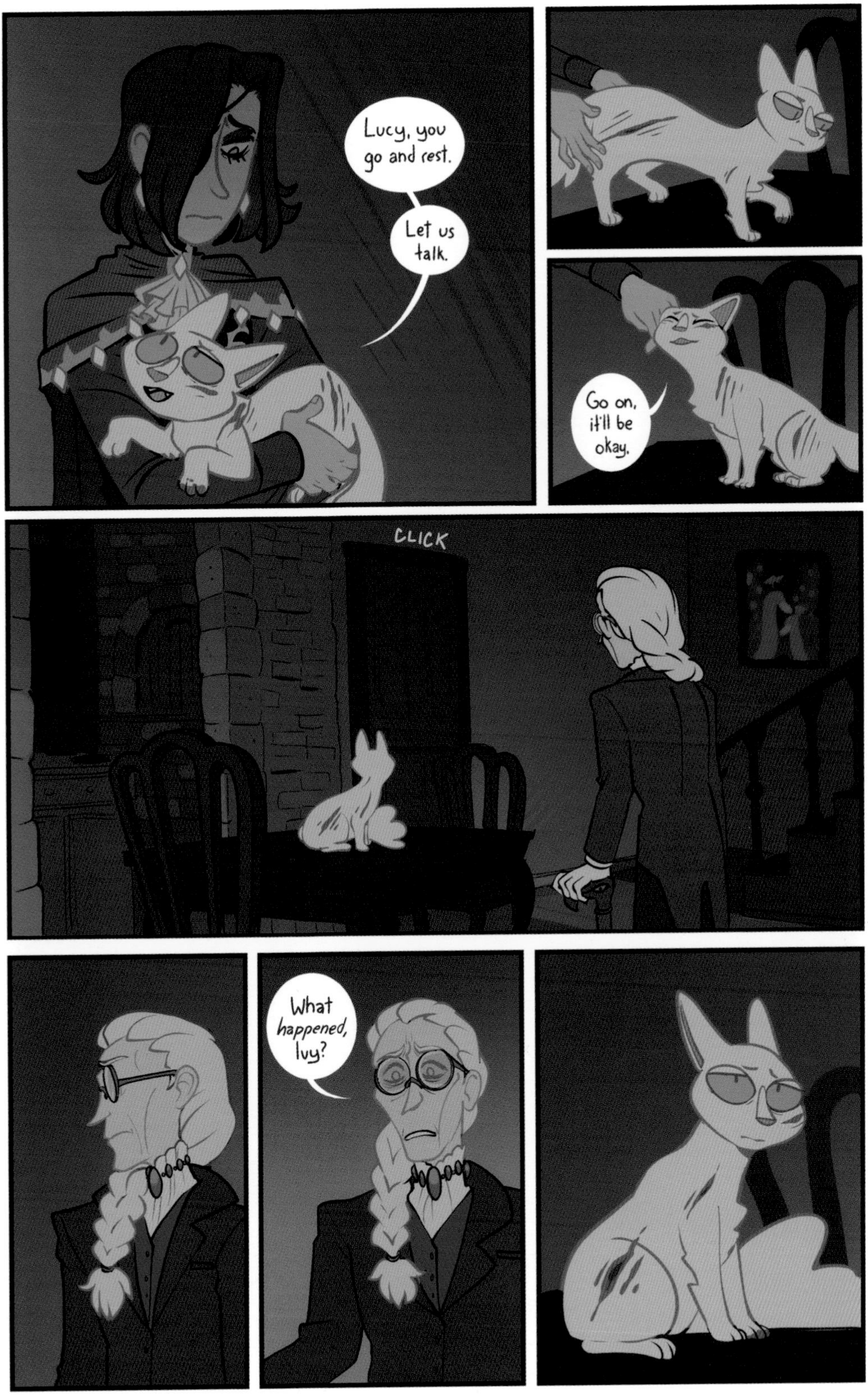
Lucy, you go and rest.
Let us talk.
Go on, it'll be okay.
CLICK
What *happened*, Ivy?

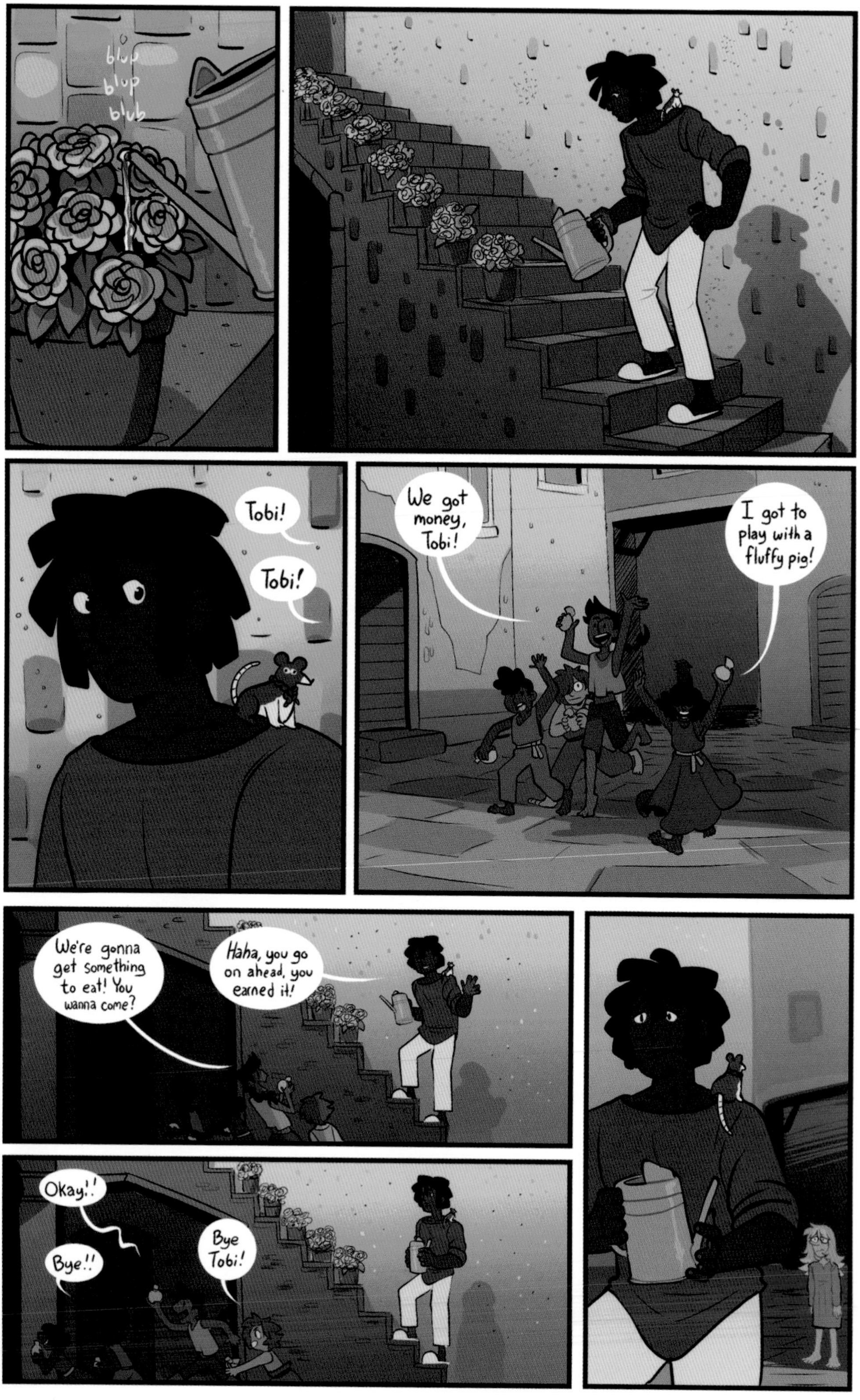
blup
blup
blub
Tobi!
Tobi!
We got money, Tobi!
I got to play with a fluffy pig!
We're gonna get something to eat! You wanna come?
Haha, you go on ahead, you earned it!
Okay!!
Bye!!
Bye Tobi!

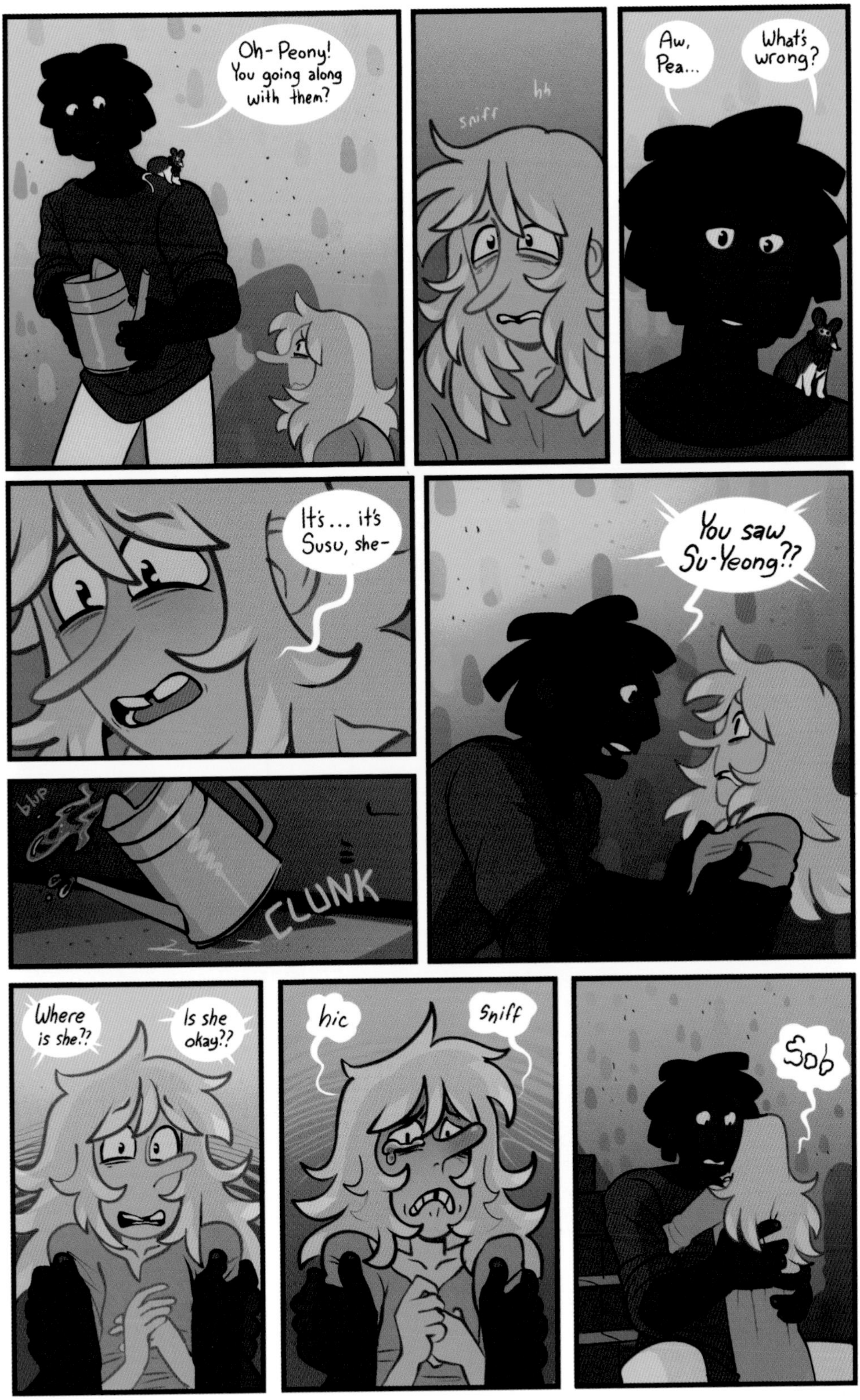

Oh- Peony! You going along with them?
sniff
hh
Aw, Pea...
What's wrong?
It's ... it's Susu, she-
You saw Su-Yeong??
blup
CLUNK
Where is she??
Is she okay??
hic
sniff
Sob

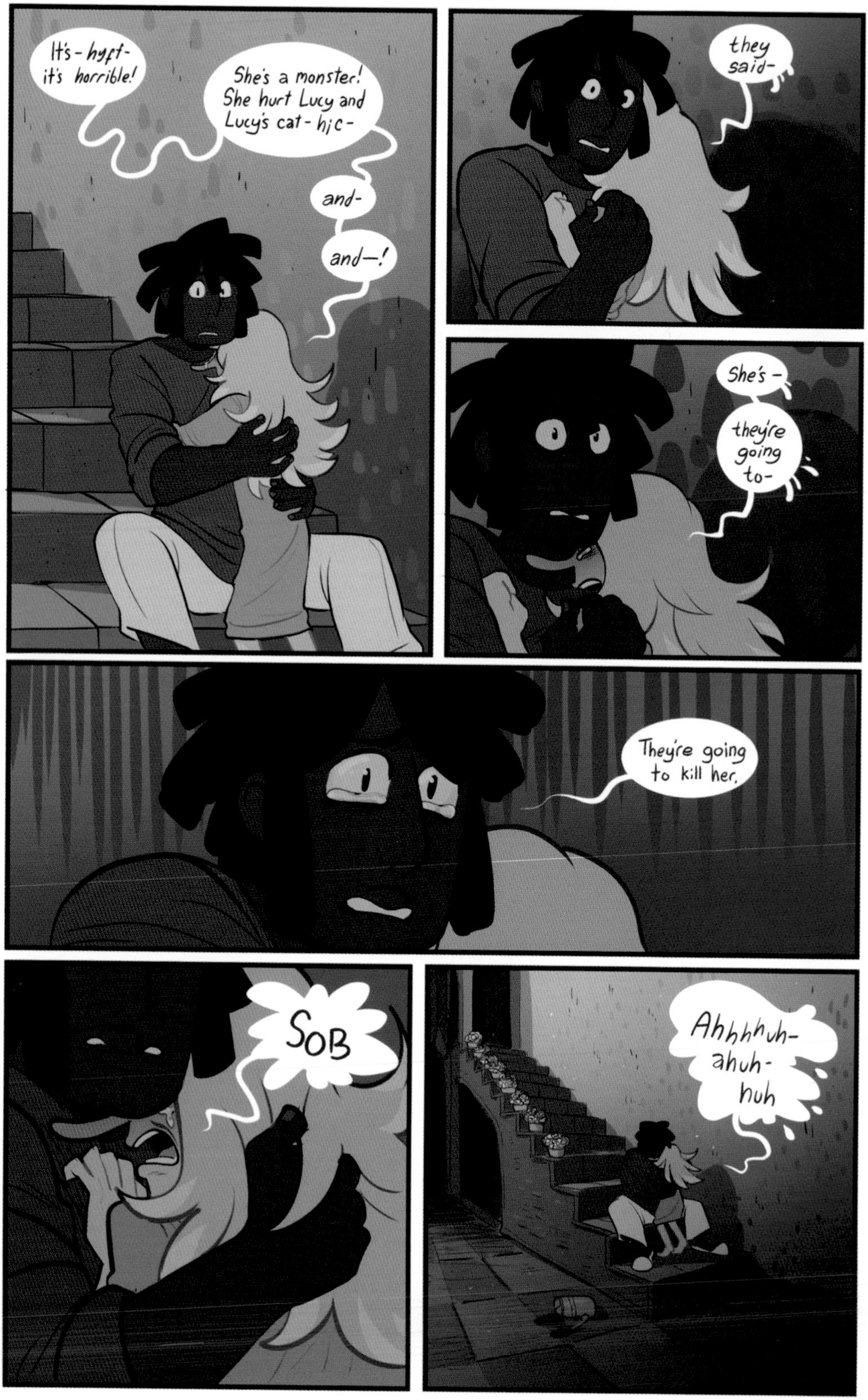
It's - hyft-
it's horrible!
She's a monster! She hurt Lucy and Lucy's cat - hic -
and-
and—!
they said-
She's -
they're going to-
They're going to kill her.
SOB
Ahhhhuh-
ahuh-
huh

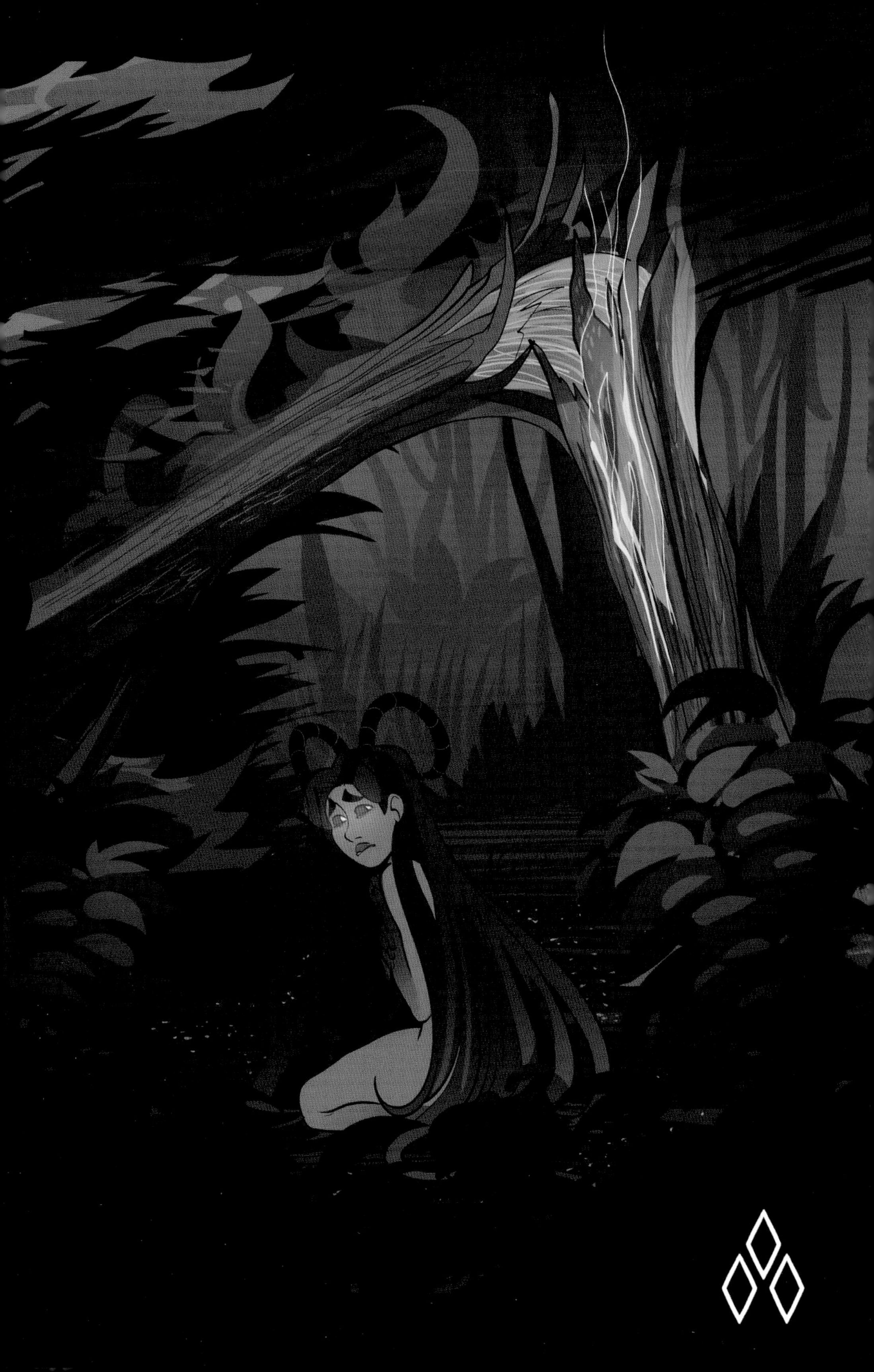

shuffle

Joseph
rt
City Gua
5 Years
2 Years
ra Karim
rket

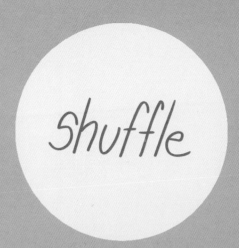

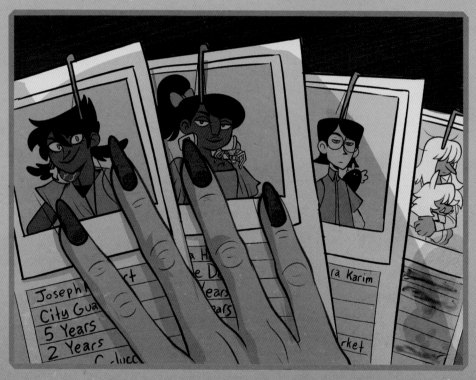

V

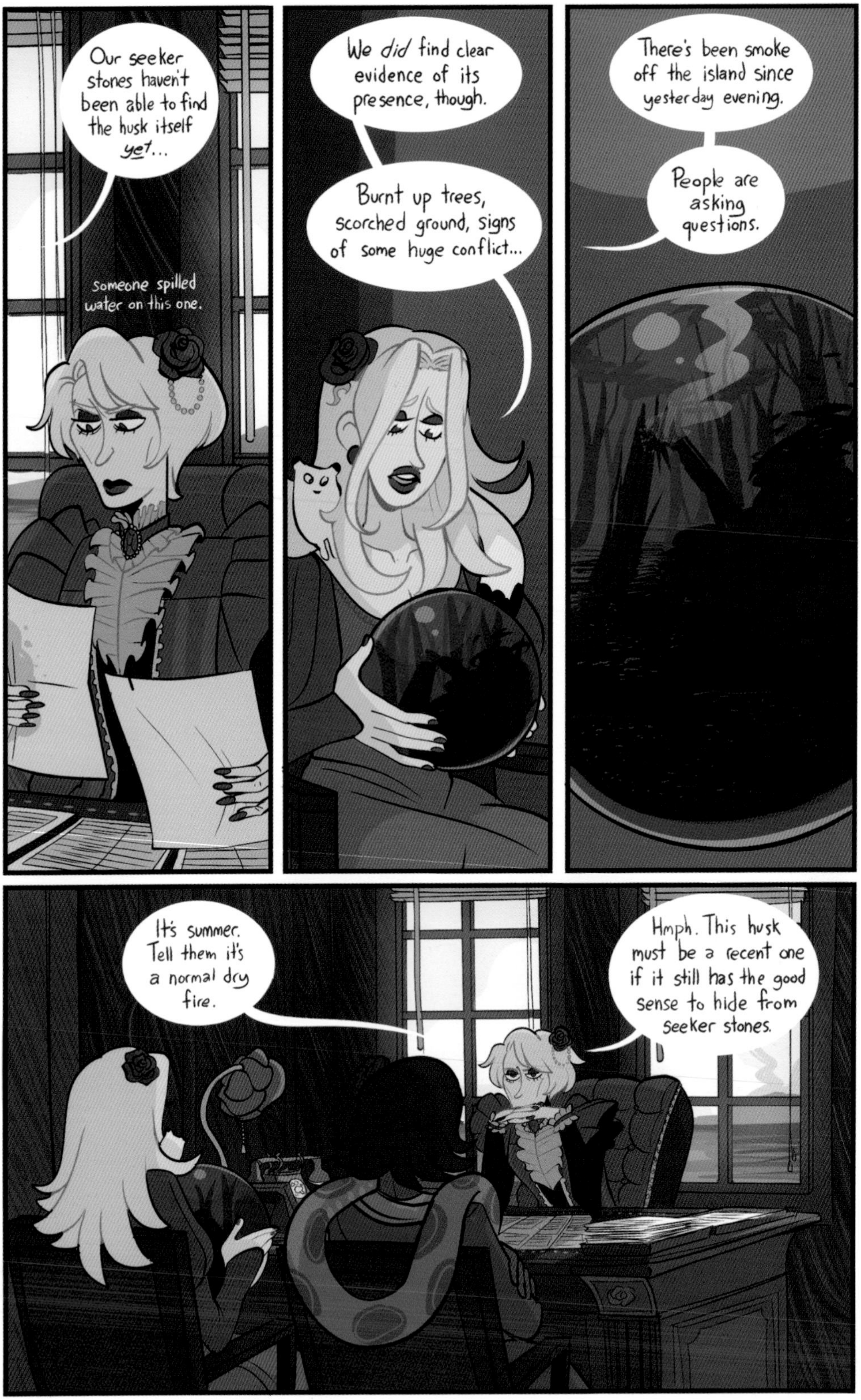

Our seeker stones haven't been able to find the husk itself yet...
someone spilled water on this one.
We did find clear evidence of its presence, though.
Burnt up trees, scorched ground, signs of some huge conflict...
There's been smoke off the island since yesterday evening.
People are asking questions.
It's summer. Tell them it's a normal dry fire.
Hmph. This husk must be a recent one if it still has the good sense to hide from seeker stones.

Keep the seeker stones on the island.

It'll have to show itself eventually.

In the meantime...

Tell me about this contestant.

Nam	Ja
Famil	Bl
F. Nam	Fo
Color	Ag
Gemtype	Aq
Age	16
Y.W.M.	7

1 Mentor Joseph R

January...

She broke my zebra finch's wing.

She was a *very* vocal player in Sylas'...

departure.

I see...

Well.

She has excellent credentials.

Guard apprentices always do well in the position.

Their loyalty to the magistration is invaluable.

ry Singh
jay
ay
rine

She'll do.

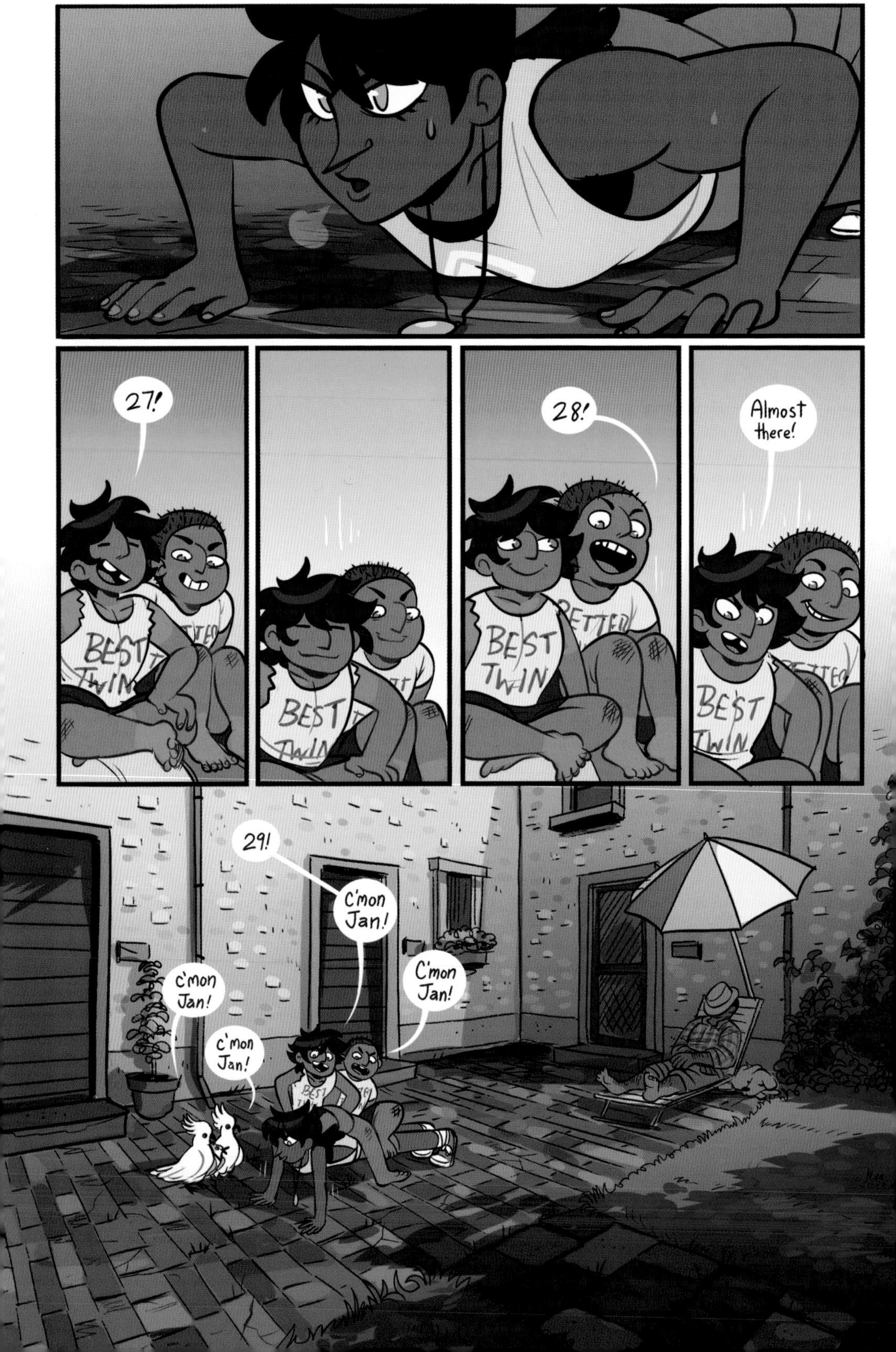
27!
28!
Almost there!
29!
C'mon Jan!
C'mon Jan!
C'mon Jan!
C'mon Jan!

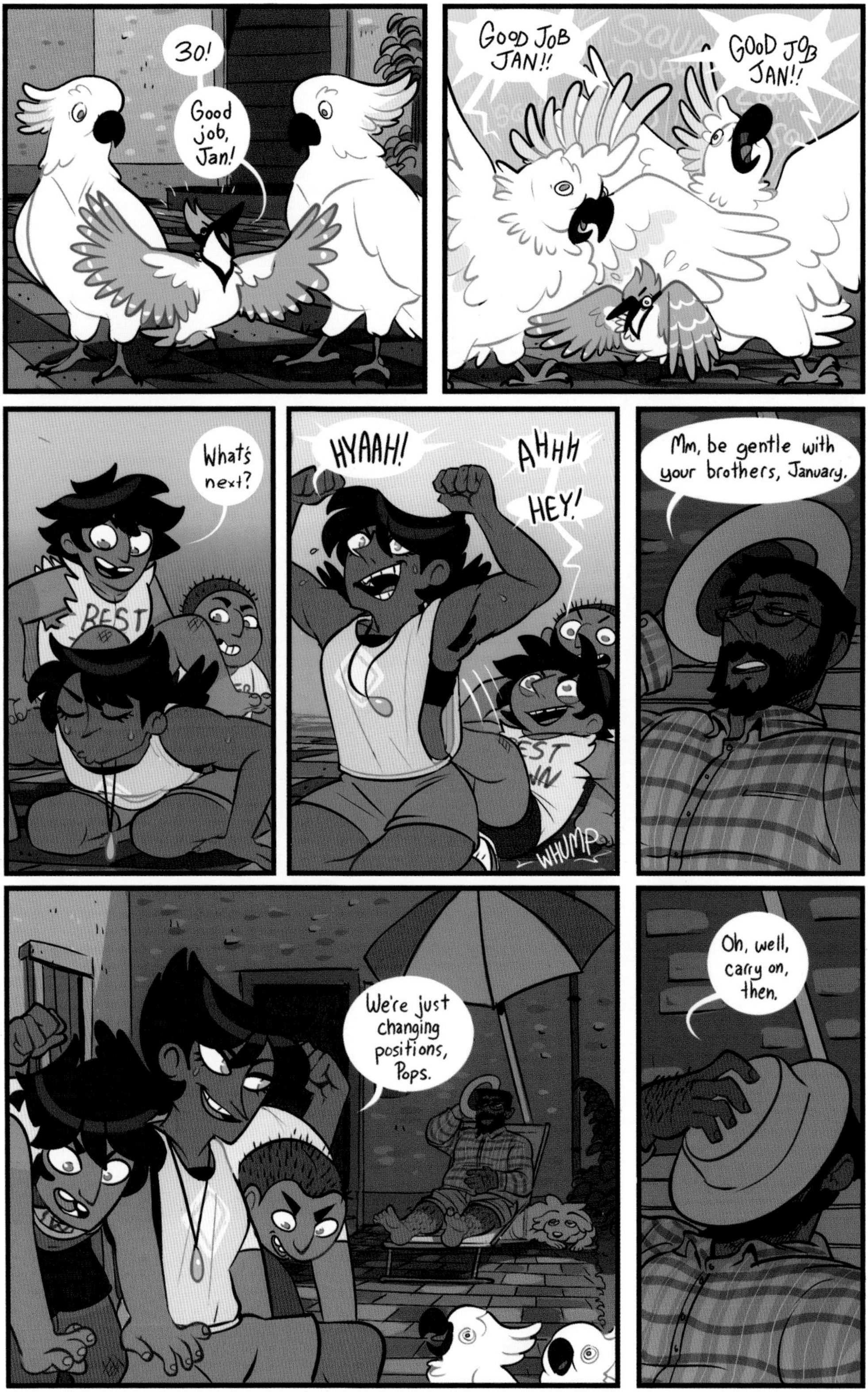
30!
Good job, Jan!
GOOD JOB JAN!!
GOOD JOB JAN!!
What's next?
HYAAH!
AHHH
HEY!
WHUMP
Mm, be gentle with your brothers, January.
We're just changing positions, Pops.
Oh, well, carry on, then.

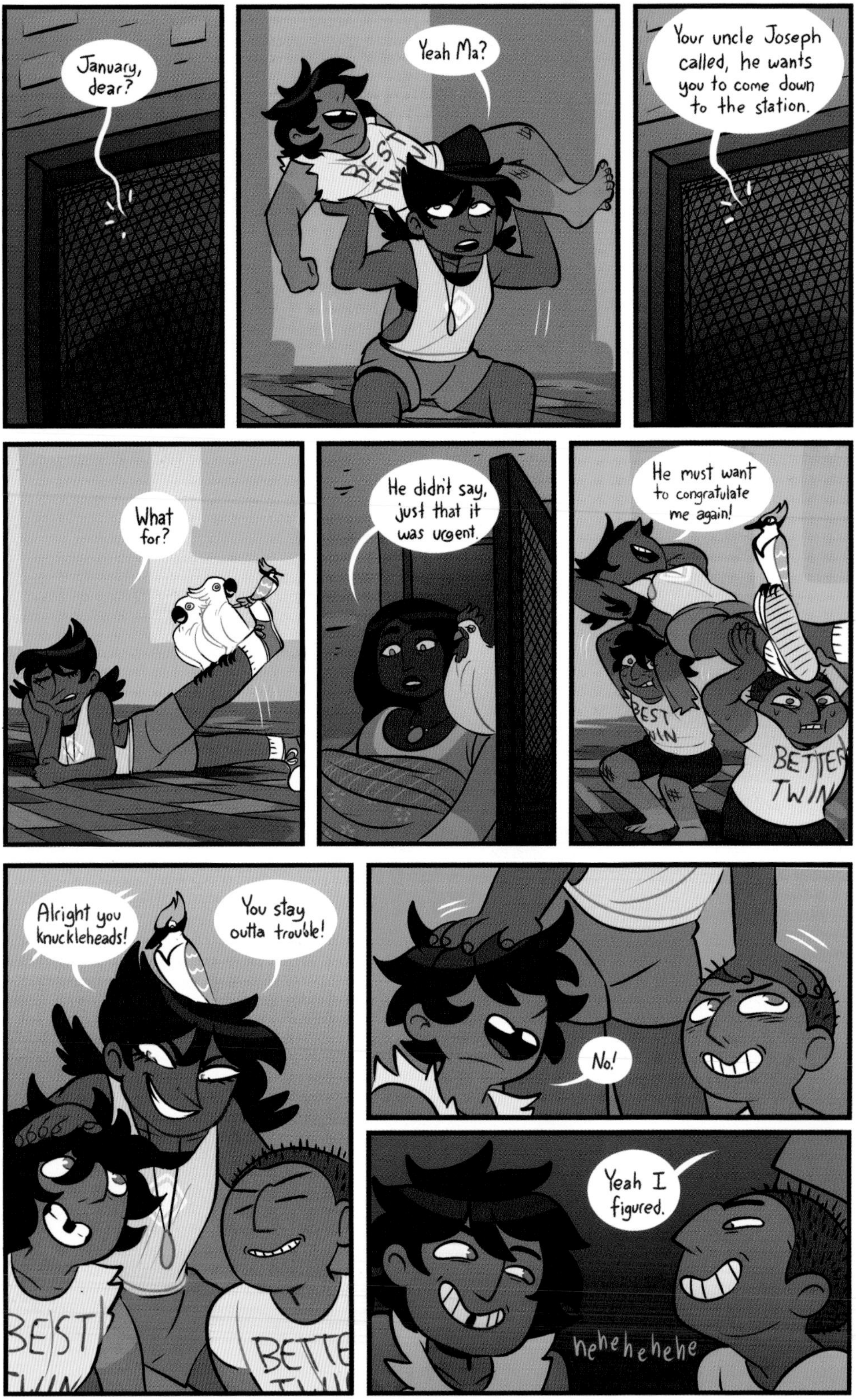
January, dear?
Yeah Ma?
Your uncle Joseph called, he wants you to come down to the station.
BEST TWIN
What for?
He didn't say, just that it was urgent.
He must want to congratulate me again!
BEST TWIN
BETTER TWIN
Alright you knuckleheads!
You stay outta trouble!
No!
Yeah I figured.
hehehehehehe

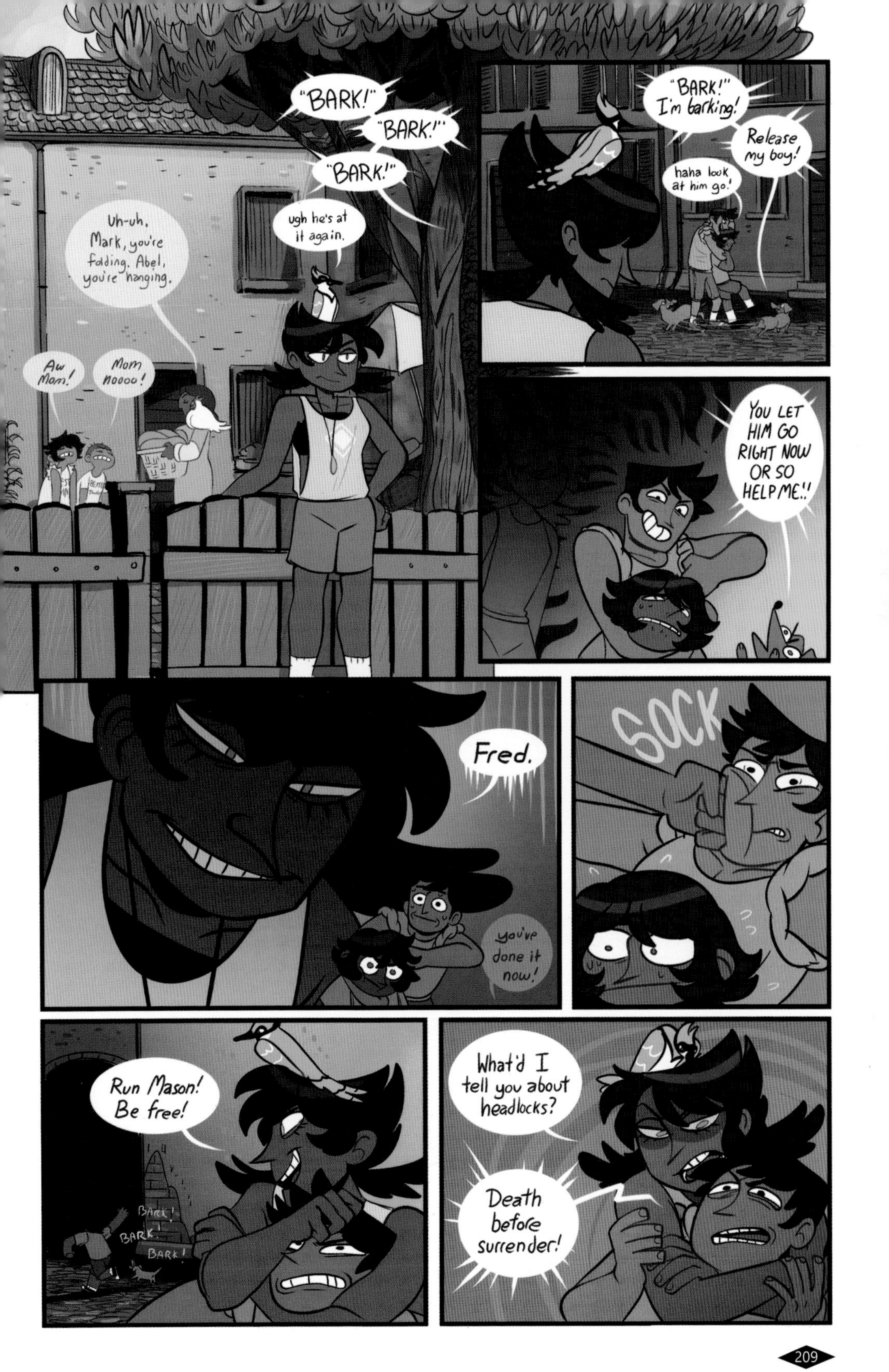

"BARK!"
"BARK!"
"BARK!"
ugh he's at it again.
Uh-uh. Mark, you're folding. Abel, you're hanging.
Aw Mom!
Mom noooo!
"BARK!" I'm barking!
Release my boy!
haha look at him go!
YOU LET HIM GO RIGHT NOW OR SO HELP ME!!
Fred.
you've done it now!
SOCK
Run Mason! Be free!
BARK!
BARK!
BARK!
What'd I tell you about headlocks?
Death before surrender!

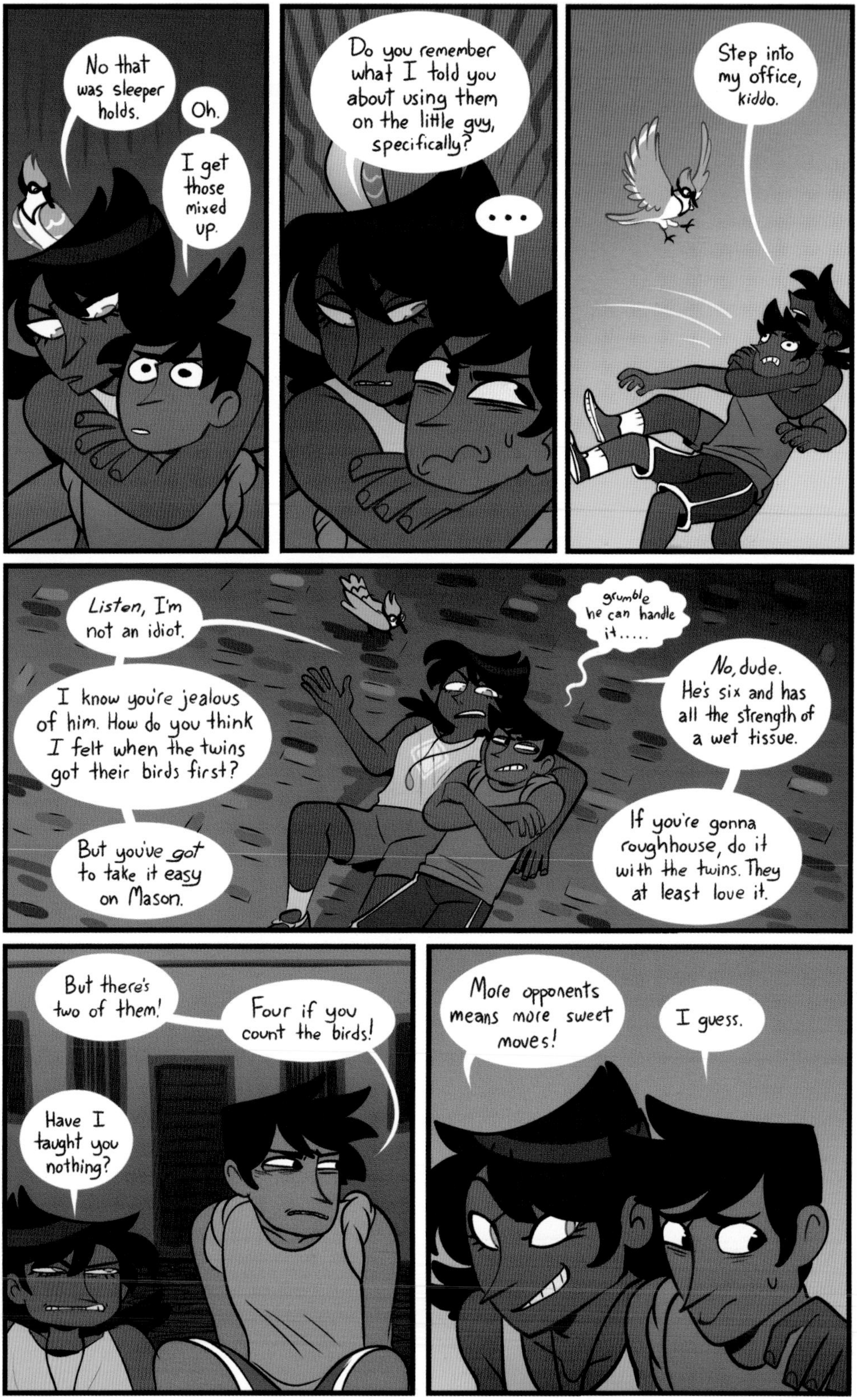
No that was sleeper holds.
Oh.
I get those mixed up.
Do you remember what I told you about using them on the little guy, specifically?
...
Step into my office, kiddo.
Listen, I'm not an idiot.
I know you're jealous of him. How do you think I felt when the twins got their birds first?
But you've got to take it easy on Mason.
grumble he can handle it.....
No, dude. He's six and has all the strength of a wet tissue.
If you're gonna roughhouse, do it with the twins. They at least love it.
But there's two of them!
Four if you count the birds!
Have I taught you nothing?
More opponents means more sweet moves!
I guess.

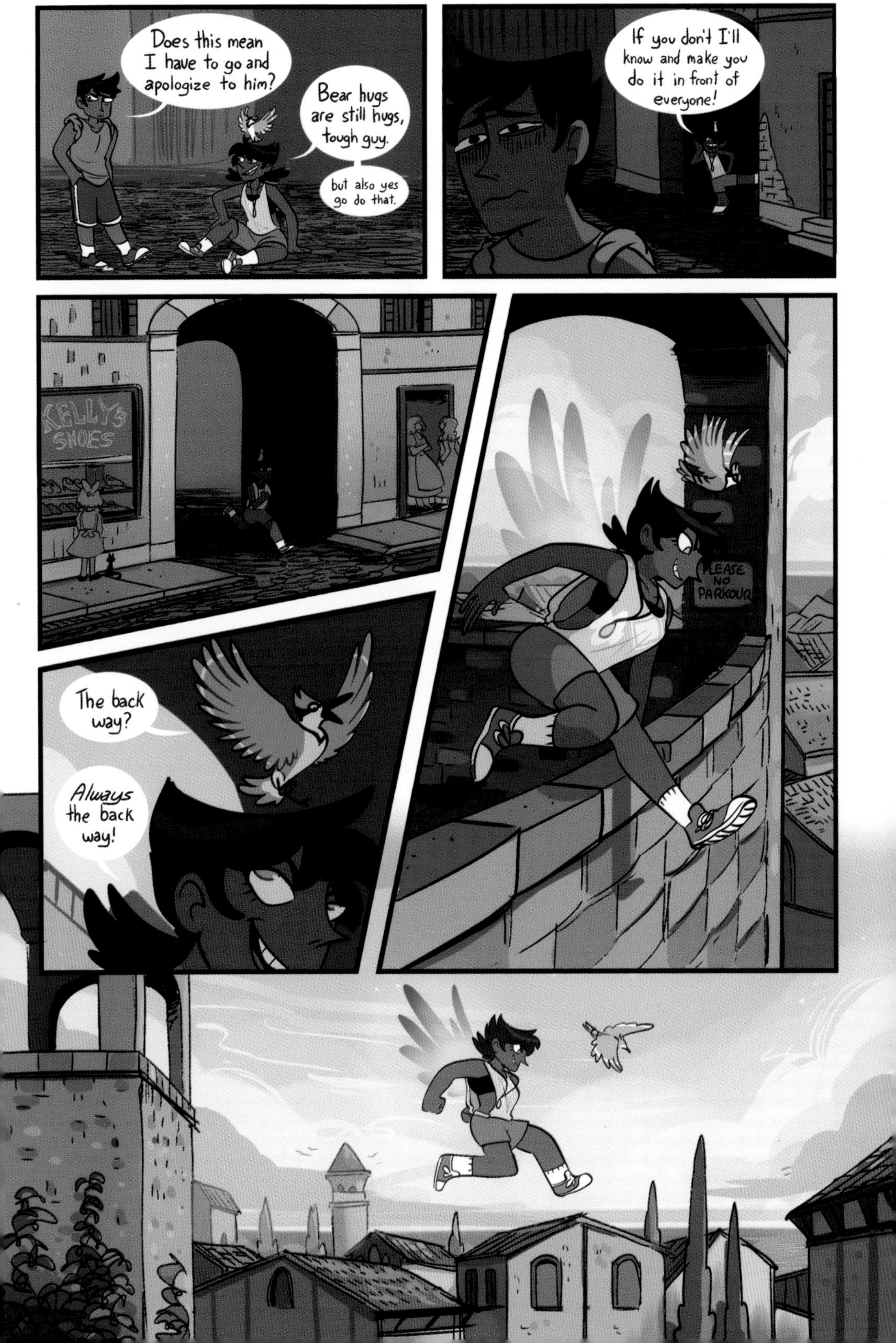
Does this mean I have to go and apologize to him?
Bear hugs are still hugs, tough guy.
but also yes go do that.
If you don't I'll know and make you do it in front of everyone!
KELLY'S SHOES
The back way?
Always the back way!
PLEASE NO PARKOUR

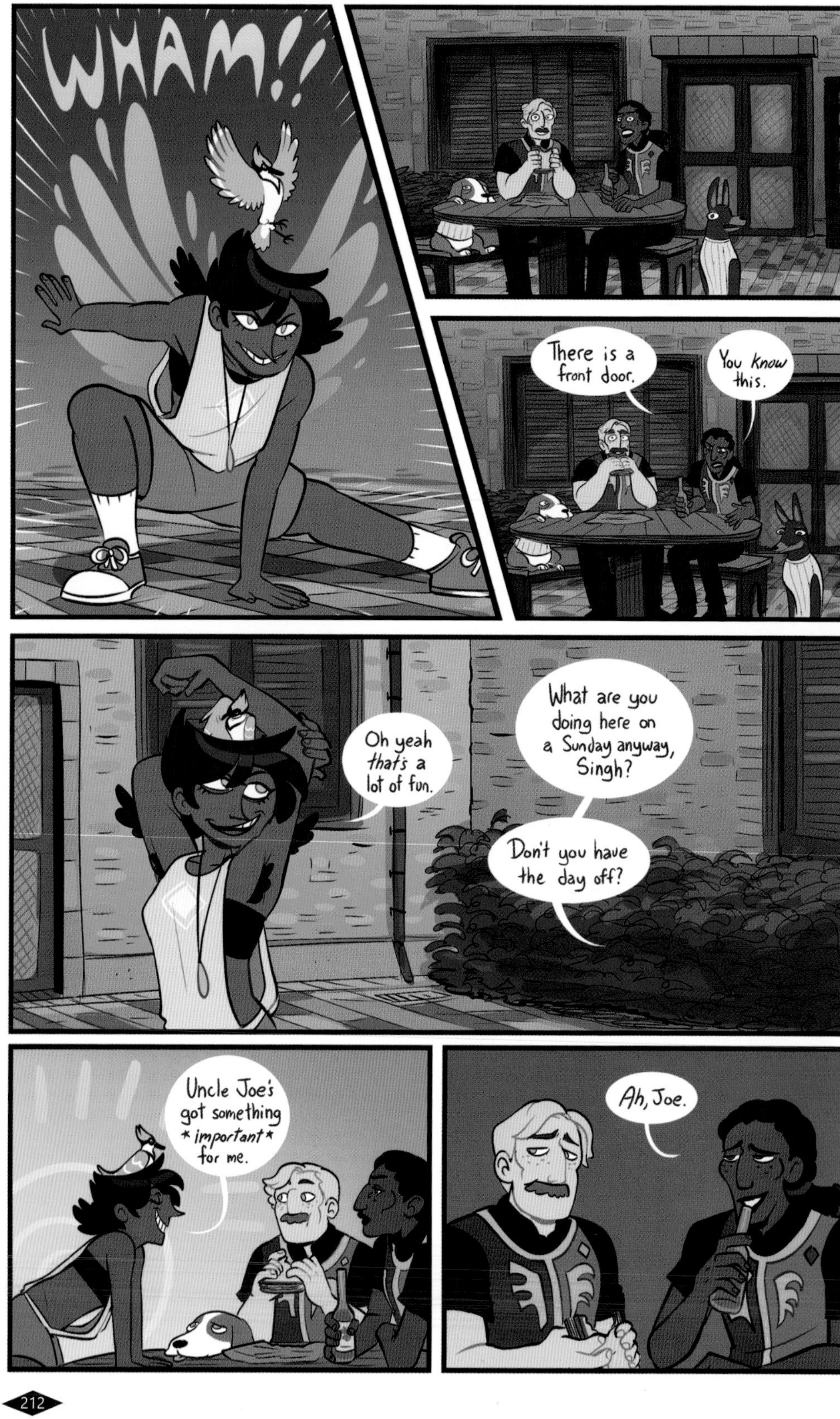
WHAM!!
There is a front door.
You know this.
Oh yeah that's a lot of fun.
What are you doing here on a Sunday anyway, Singh?
Don't you have the day off?
Uncle Joe's got something *important* for me.
Ah, Joe.

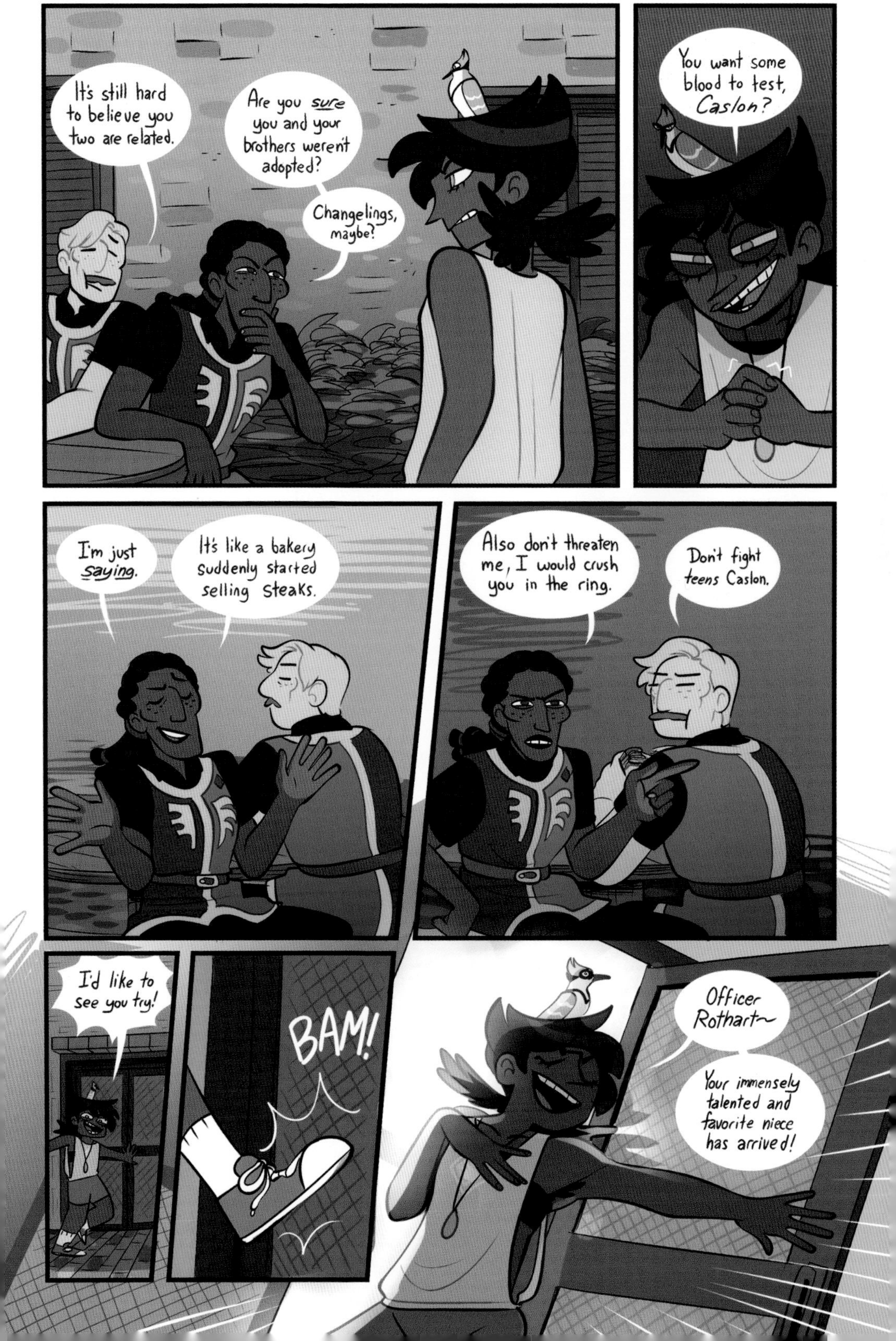
It's still hard to believe you two are related.
Are you sure you and your brothers weren't adopted?
Changelings, maybe?
You want some blood to test, Caslon?
I'm just saying.
It's like a bakery suddenly started selling steaks.
Also don't threaten me, I would crush you in the ring.
Don't fight teens Caslon.
I'd like to see you try!
BAM!
Officer Rothart~
Your immensely talented and favorite niece has arrived!

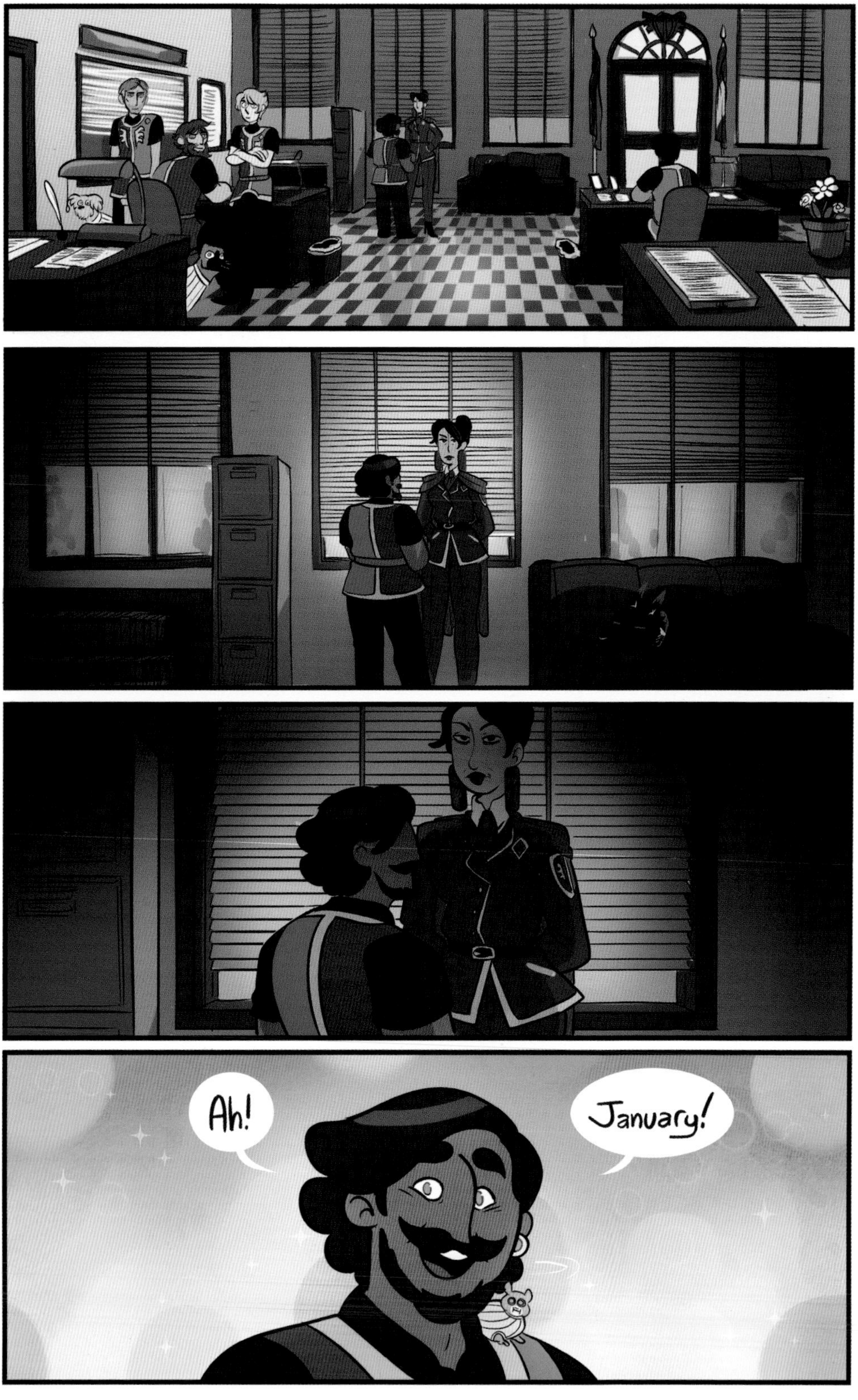
Ah!
January!

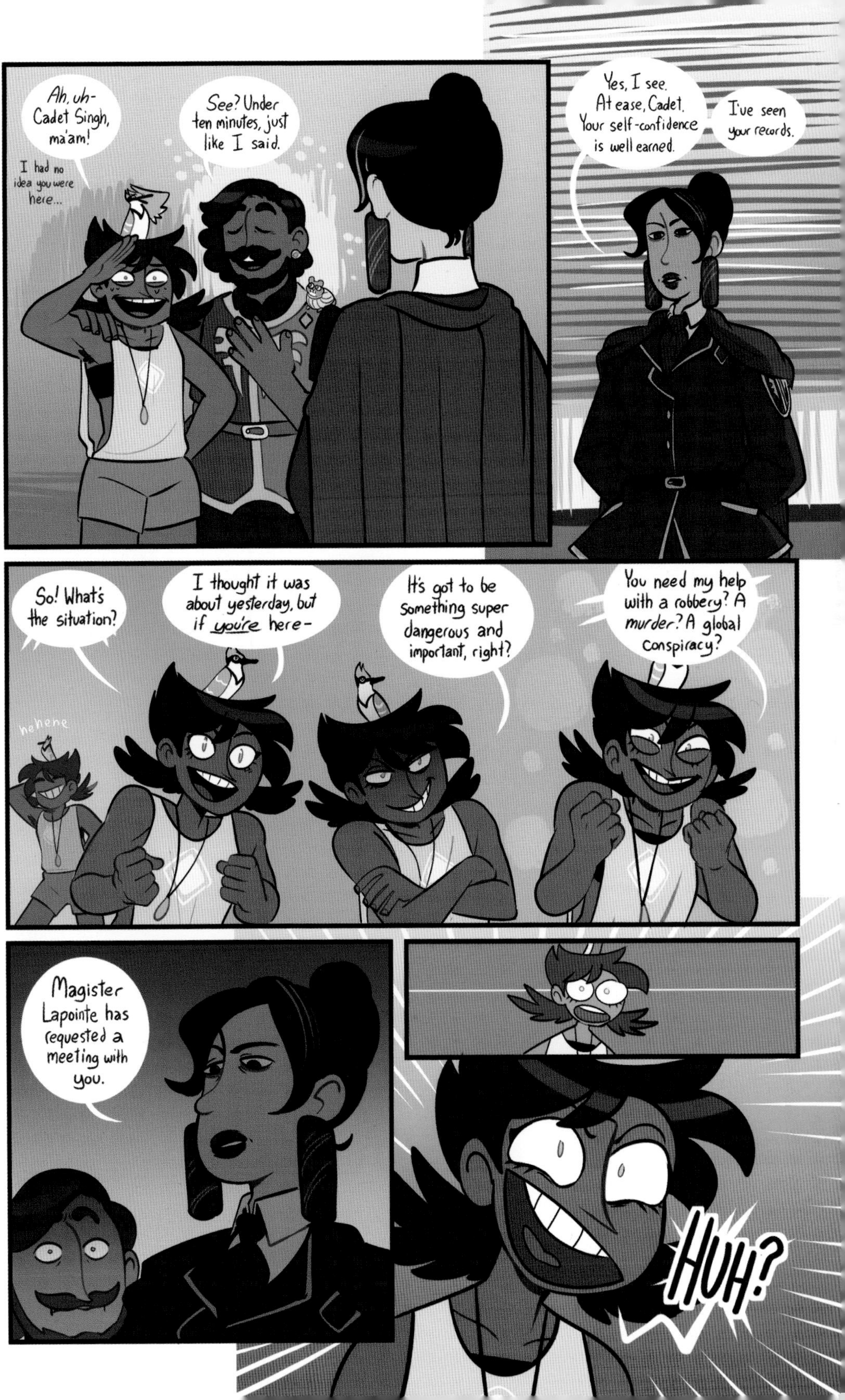
Ah, uh-
Cadet Singh, ma'am!
I had no idea you were here...
See? Under ten minutes, just like I said.
Yes, I see. At ease, Cadet. Your self-confidence is well earned.
I've seen your records.
So! What's the situation?
I thought it was about yesterday, but if *you're* here-
hehene
It's got to be something super dangerous and important, right?
You need my help with a robbery? A *murder*? A global conspiracy?
Magister Lapointe has requested a meeting with you.
HUH?

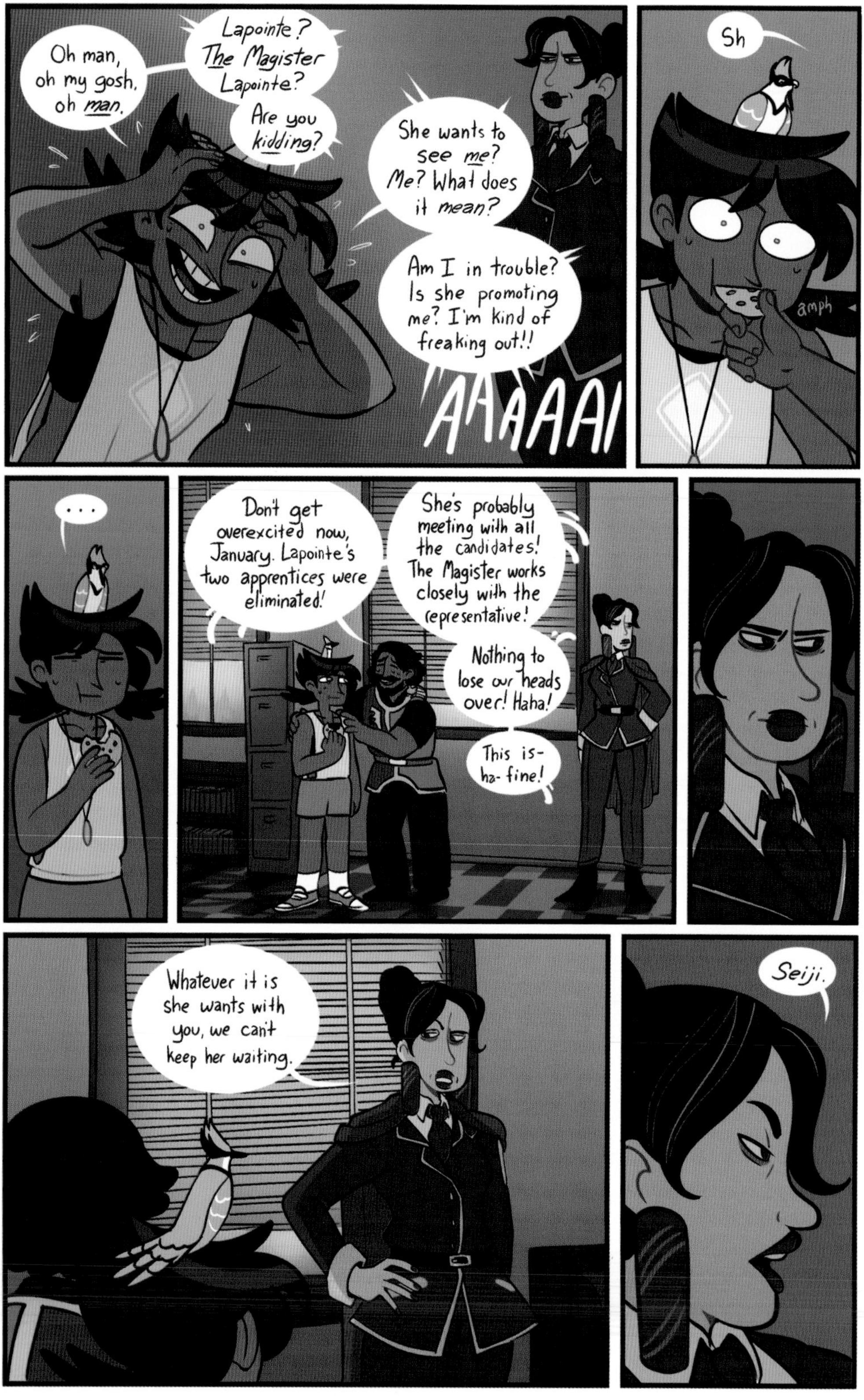
Oh man, oh my gosh, oh man.
Lapointe? The Magister Lapointe?
Are you kidding?
She wants to see me? Me? What does it mean?
Am I in trouble? Is she promoting me? I'm kind of freaking out!!
AAAAAI
Sh
amph
...
Don't get overexcited now, January. Lapointe's two apprentices were eliminated!
She's probably meeting with all the candidates! The Magister works closely with the representative!
Nothing to lose our heads over! Haha!
This is- ha- fine!
Whatever it is she wants with you, we can't keep her waiting.
Seiji.

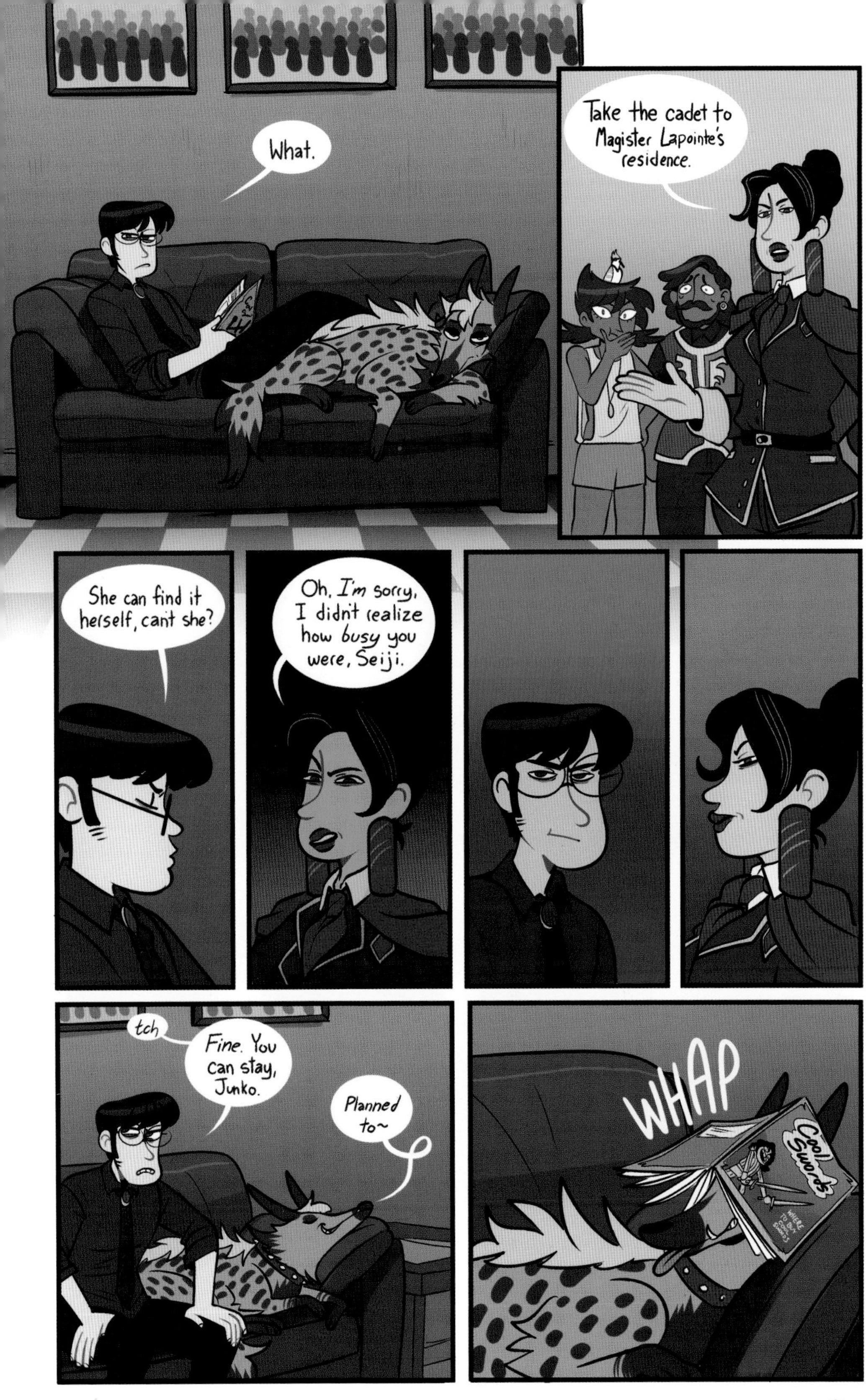
What.
Take the cadet to Magister Lapointe's residence.
She can find it herself, can't she?
Oh, I'm sorry, I didn't realize how busy you were, Seiji.
tch
Fine. You can stay, Junko.
Planned to~
WHAP
Cool Swords
WHERE TO BUY COOL SWORDS

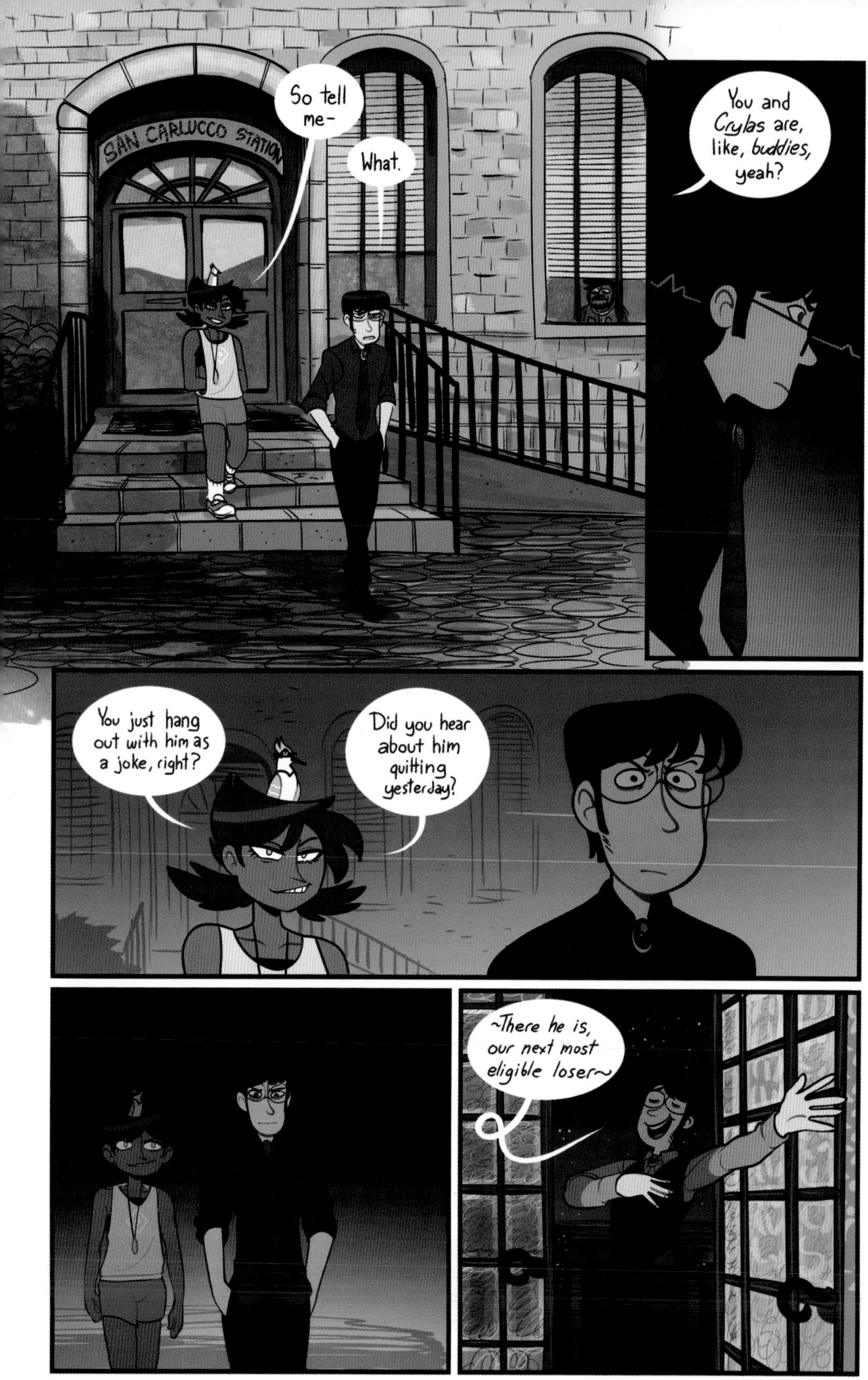
SAN CARLUCCO STATION
So tell me-
What.
You and Crylas are, like, buddies, yeah?
You just hang out with him as a joke, right?
Did you hear about him quitting yesterday?
~There he is, our next most eligible loser~

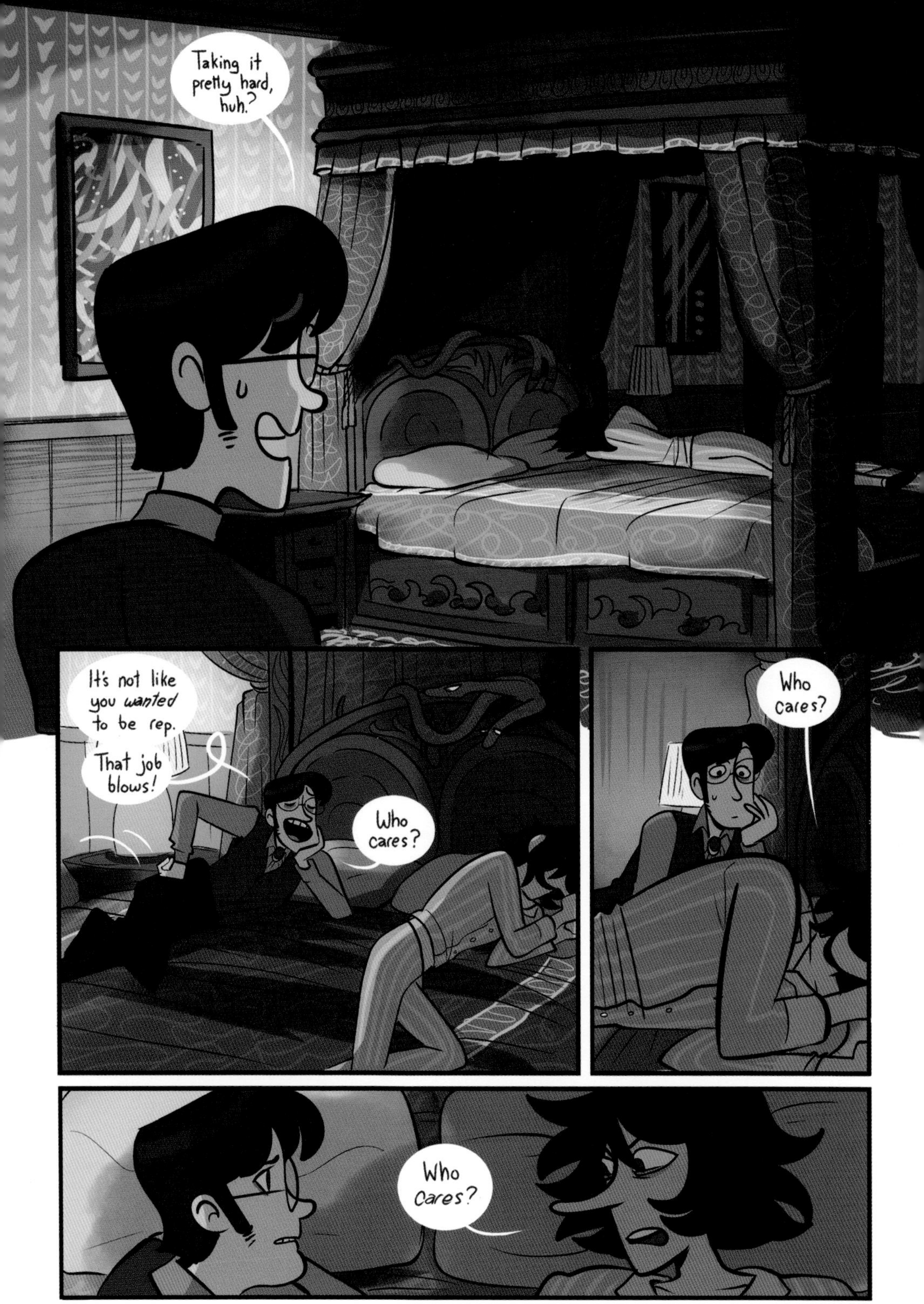
Taking it pretty hard, huh?
It's not like you wanted to be rep.
That job blows!
Who cares?
Who cares?
Who cares?

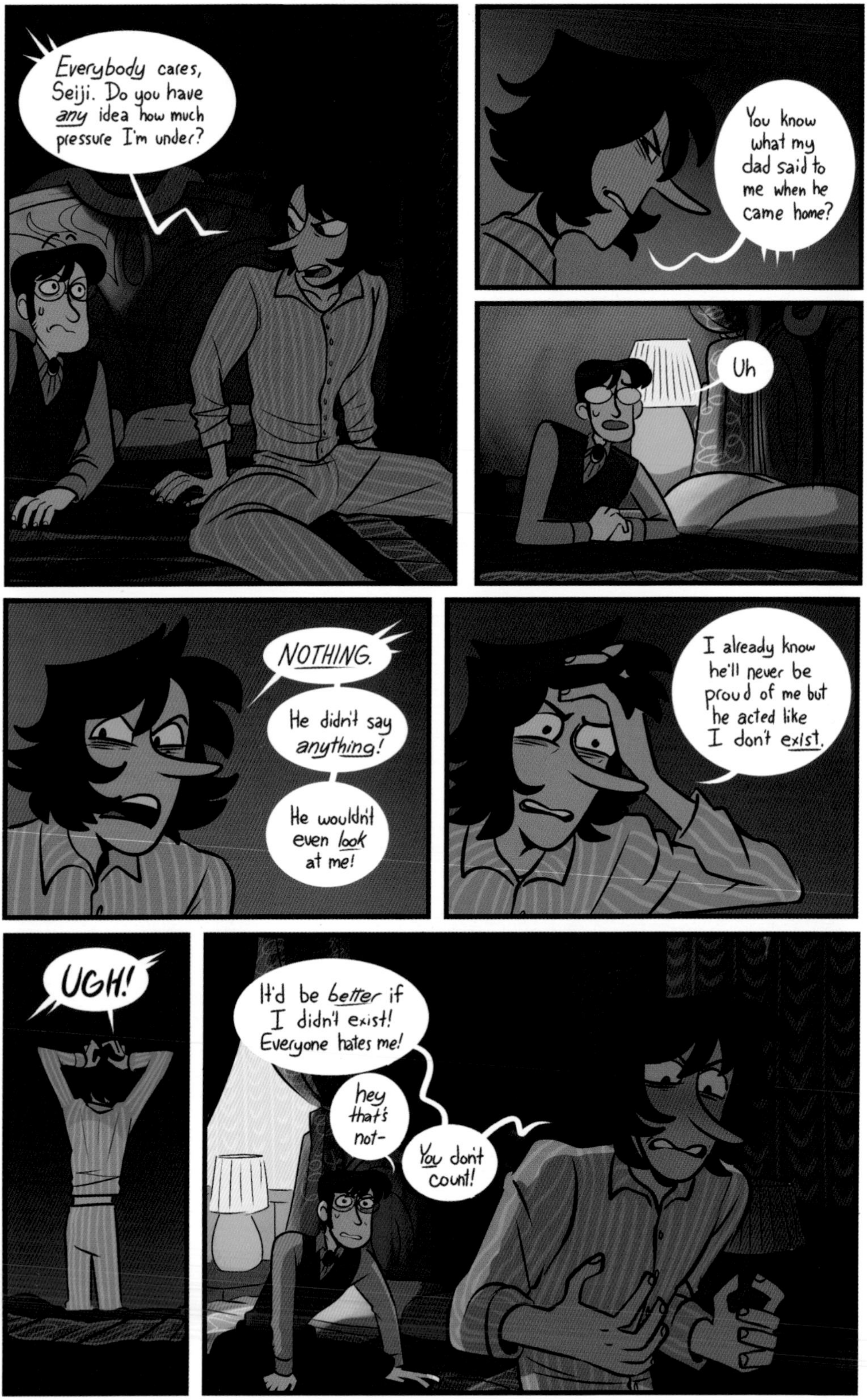
Everybody cares, Seiji. Do you have any idea how much pressure I'm under?
You know what my dad said to me when he came home?
Uh
NOTHING.
He didn't say anything!
He wouldn't even look at me!
I already know he'll never be proud of me but he acted like I don't exist.
UGH!
It'd be better if I didn't exist! Everyone hates me!
hey that's not-
You don't count!

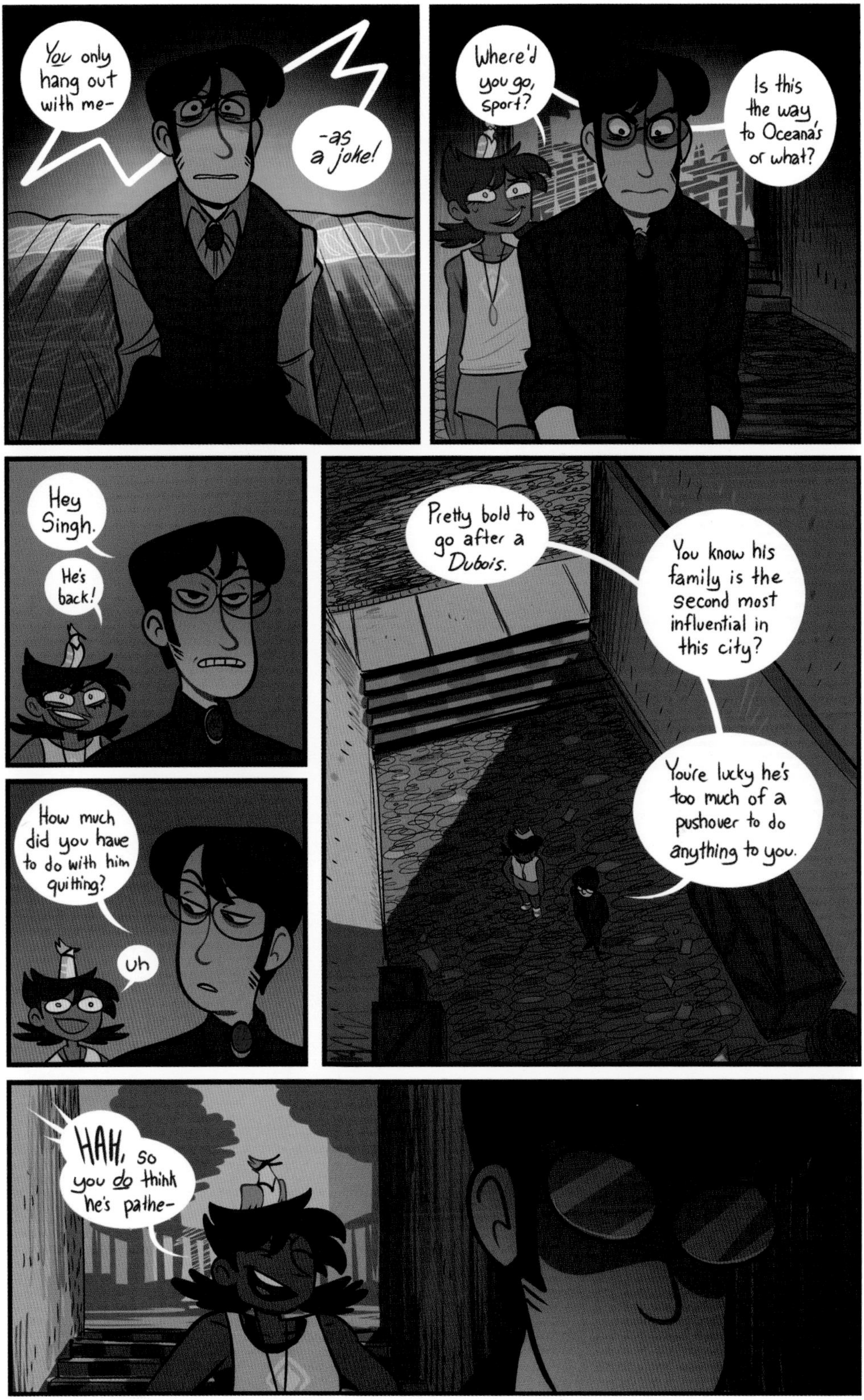
You only hang out with me-
-as a joke!
Where'd you go, sport?
Is this the way to Oceana's or what?
Hey Singh.
He's back!
Pretty bold to go after a Dubois.
You know his family is the second most influential in this city?
You're lucky he's too much of a pushover to do anything to you.
How much did you have to do with him quitting?
uh
HAH, so you do think he's pathe-

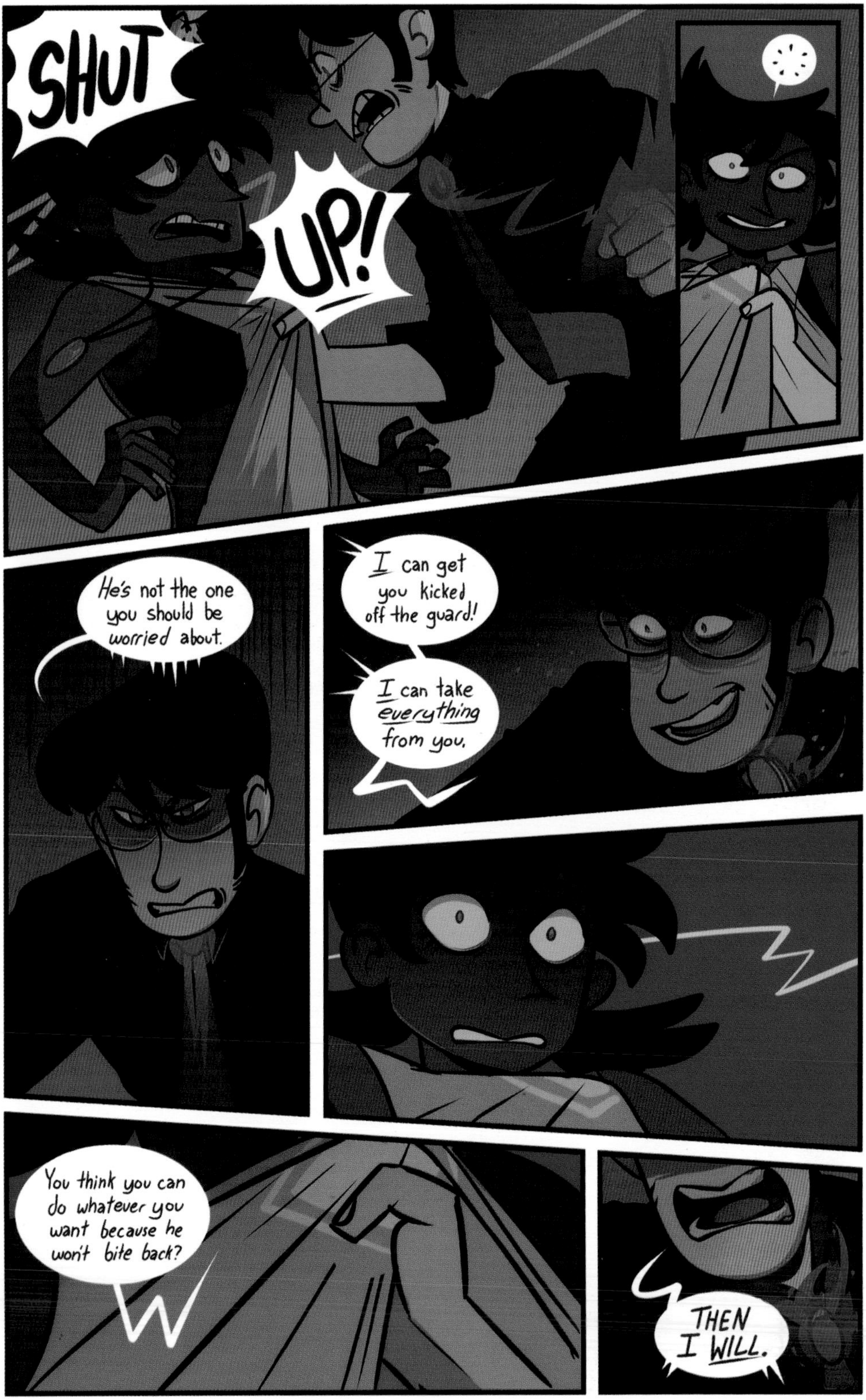
SHUT
UP!
He's not the one you should be worried about.
I can get you kicked off the guard!
I can take everything from you.
You think you can do whatever you want because he won't bite back?
THEN I WILL.

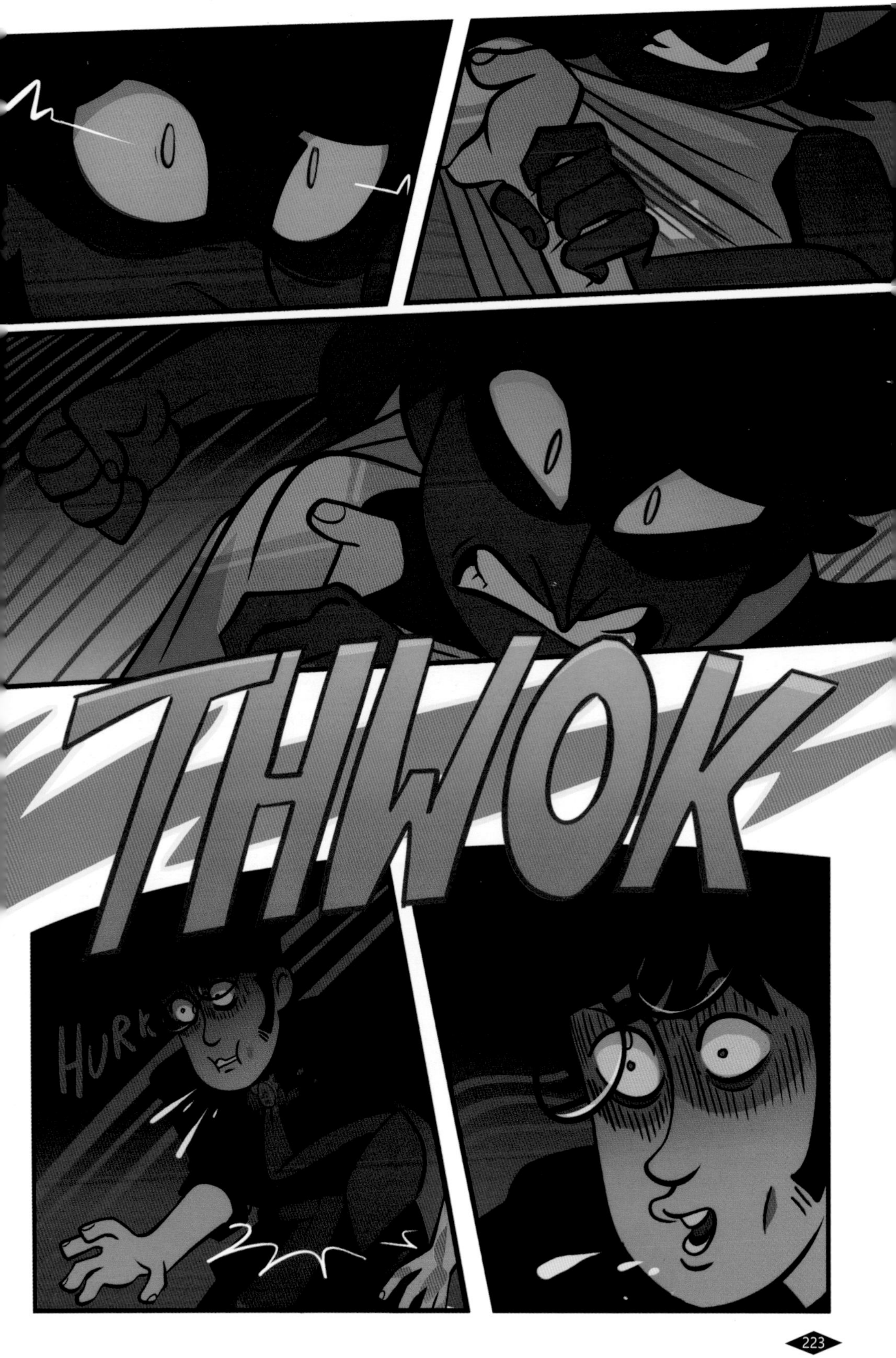
THWOK
HURK

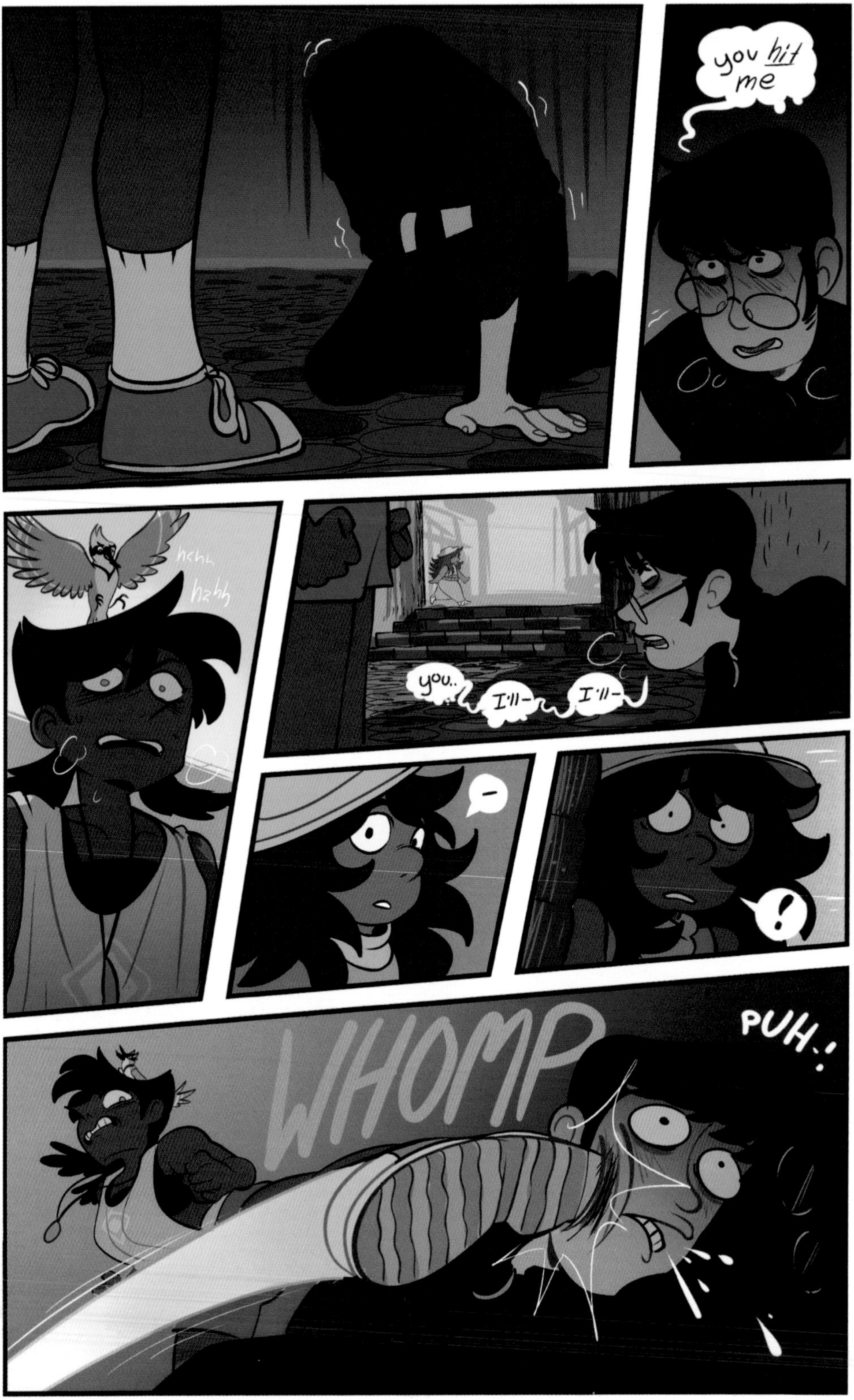
you hit me
hnhh
hnhh
you..
I'll–
I'll–
–
!
WHOMP
PUH.!

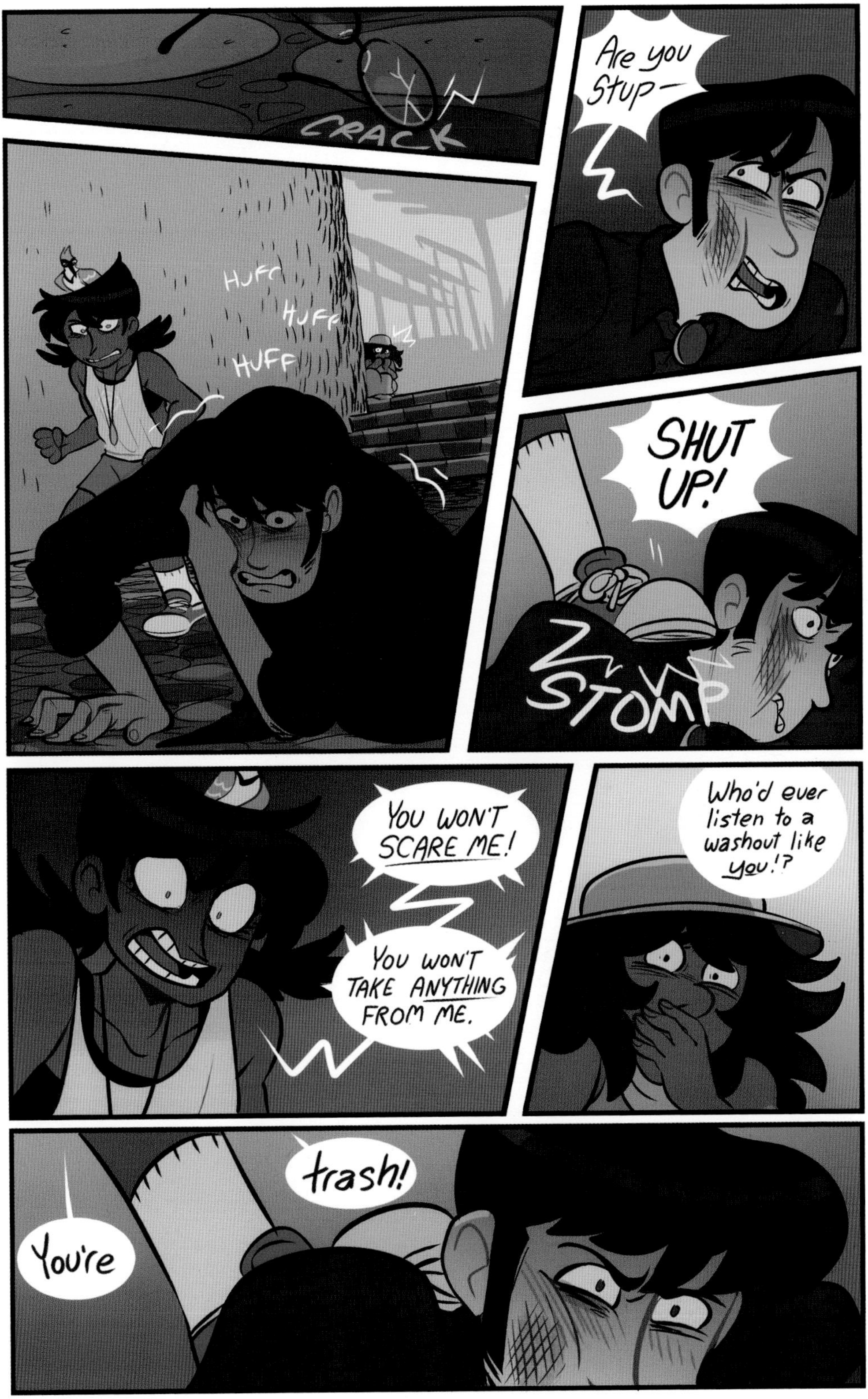
CRACK
Are you Stup—
HUFF
HUFF
HUFF
SHUT UP!
STOMP
YOU WON'T SCARE ME!
YOU WON'T TAKE ANYTHING FROM ME.
Who'd ever listen to a washout like you!?
You're
trash!

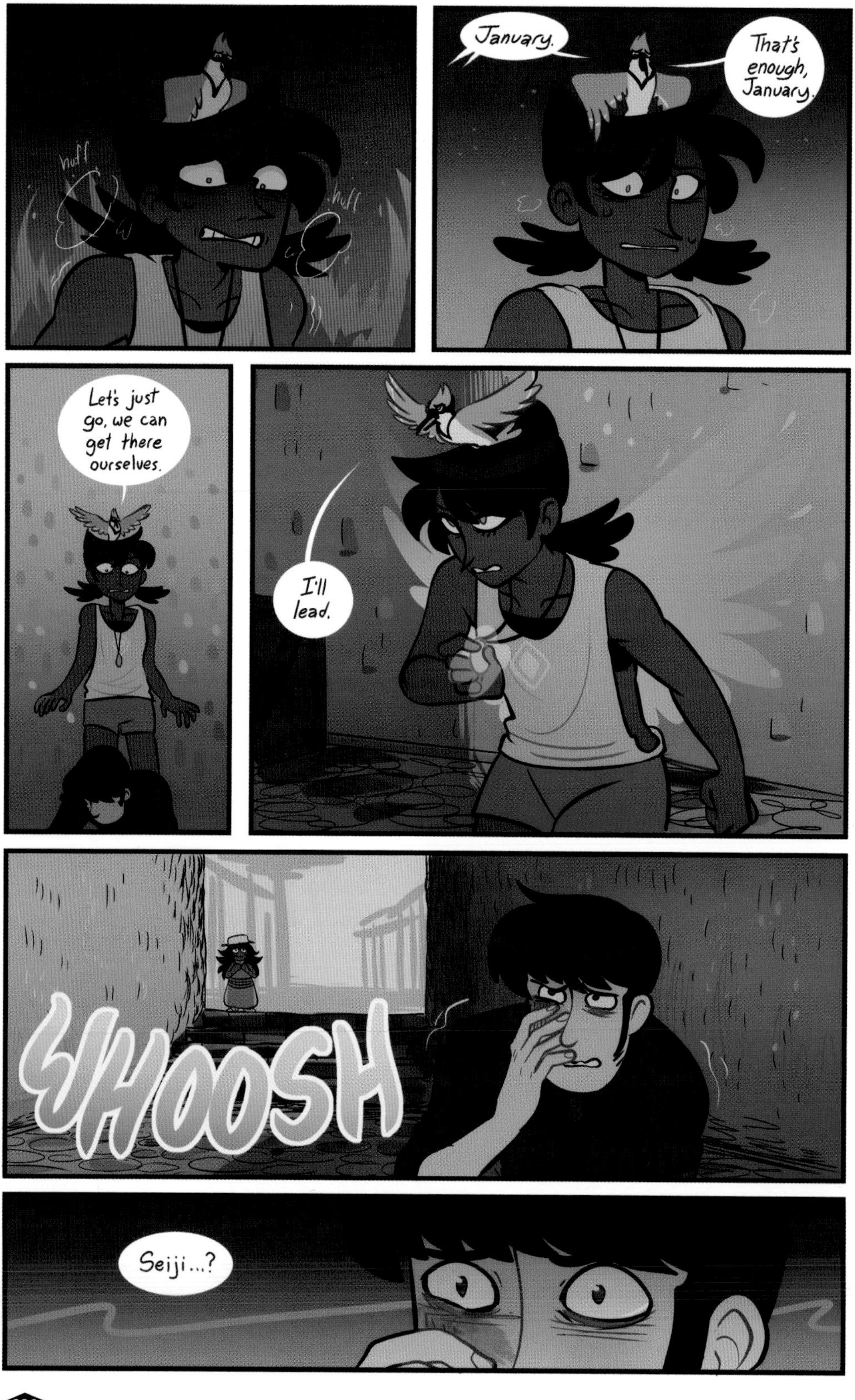
huff
huff
January.
That's enough, January.
Let's just go, we can get there ourselves.
I'll lead.
WHOOSH
Seiji...?

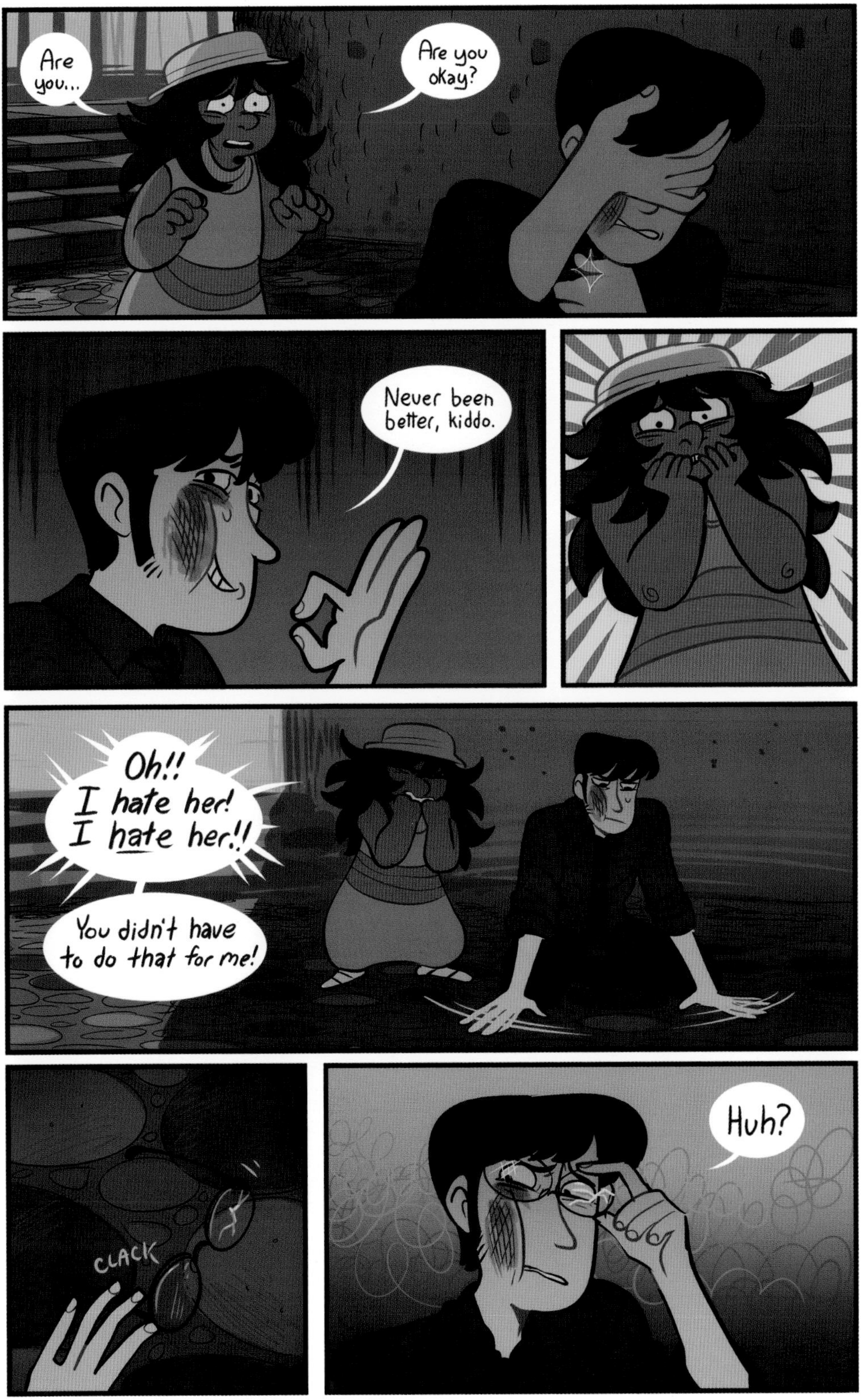
Are you...
Are you okay?
Never been better, kiddo.
Oh!! I hate her! I hate her!!
You didn't have to do that for me!
CLACK
Huh?

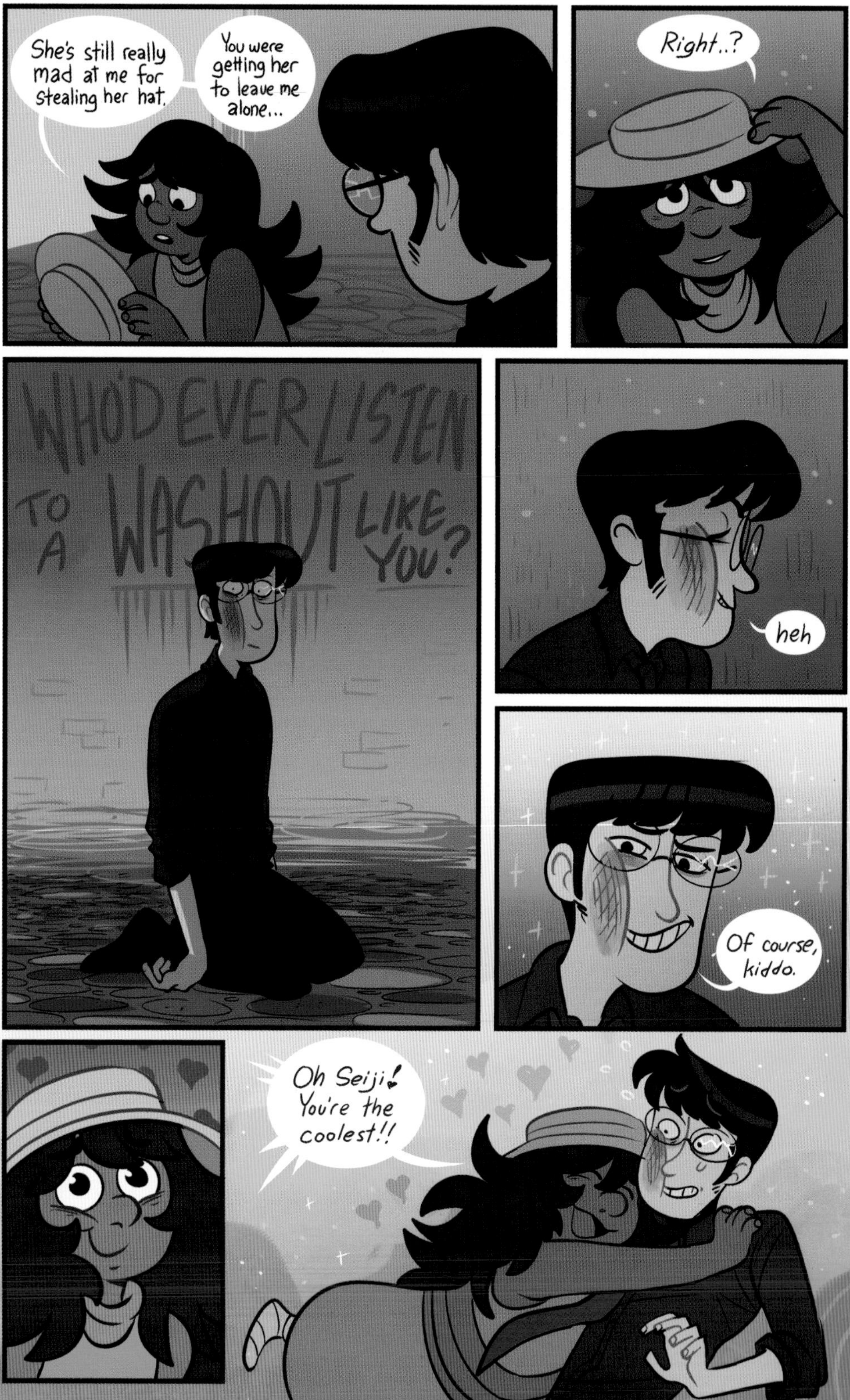
She's still really mad at me for stealing her hat.
You were getting her to leave me alone...
Right..?
WHO'D EVER LISTEN TO A WASHOUT LIKE YOU?
heh
Of course, kiddo.
Oh Seiji! You're the coolest!!

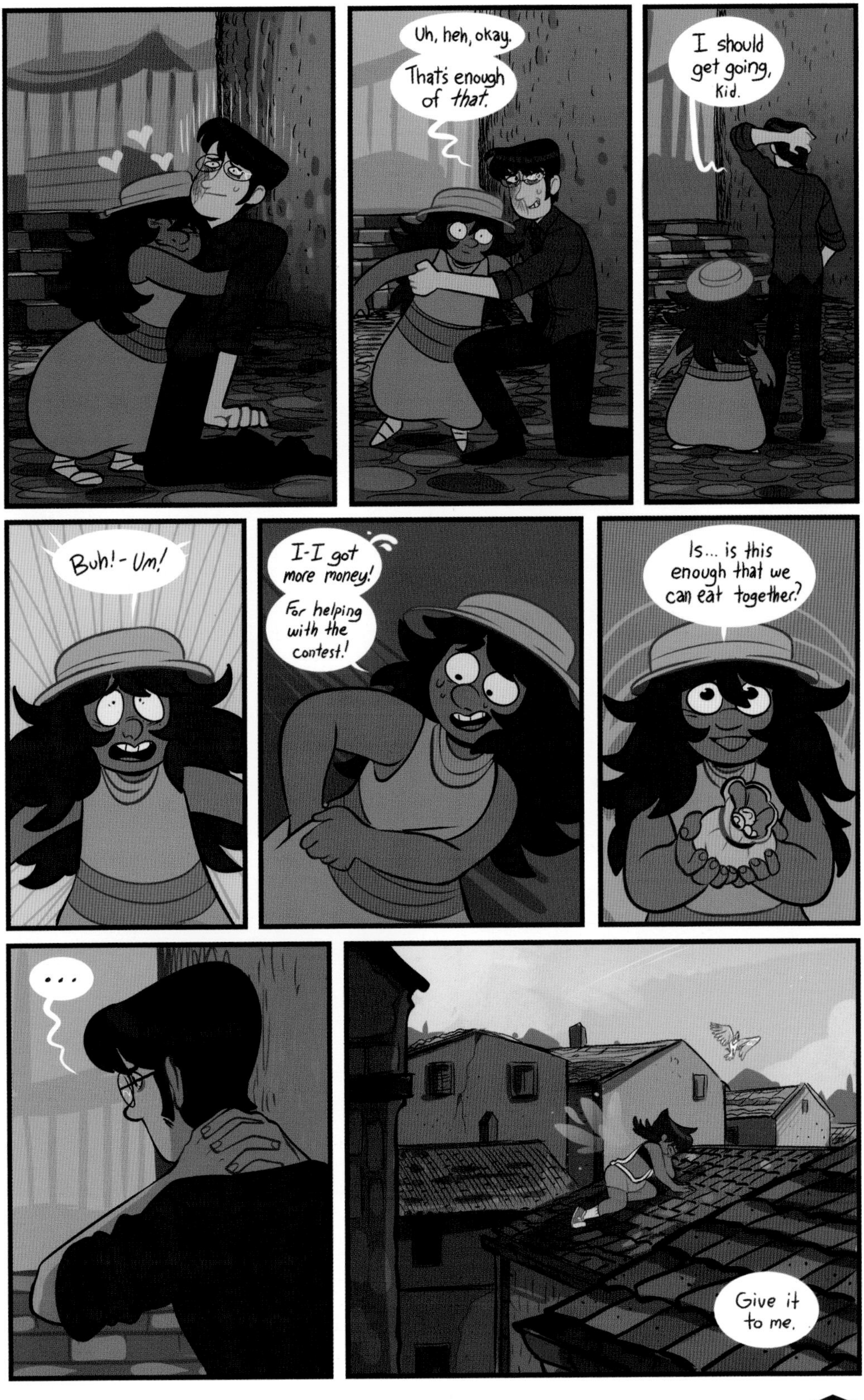
Uh, heh, okay.
That's enough of *that*.
I should get going, kid.
Buh! - Um!
I-I got more money!
For helping with the contest!
Is... is this enough that we can eat together?
...
Give it to me.

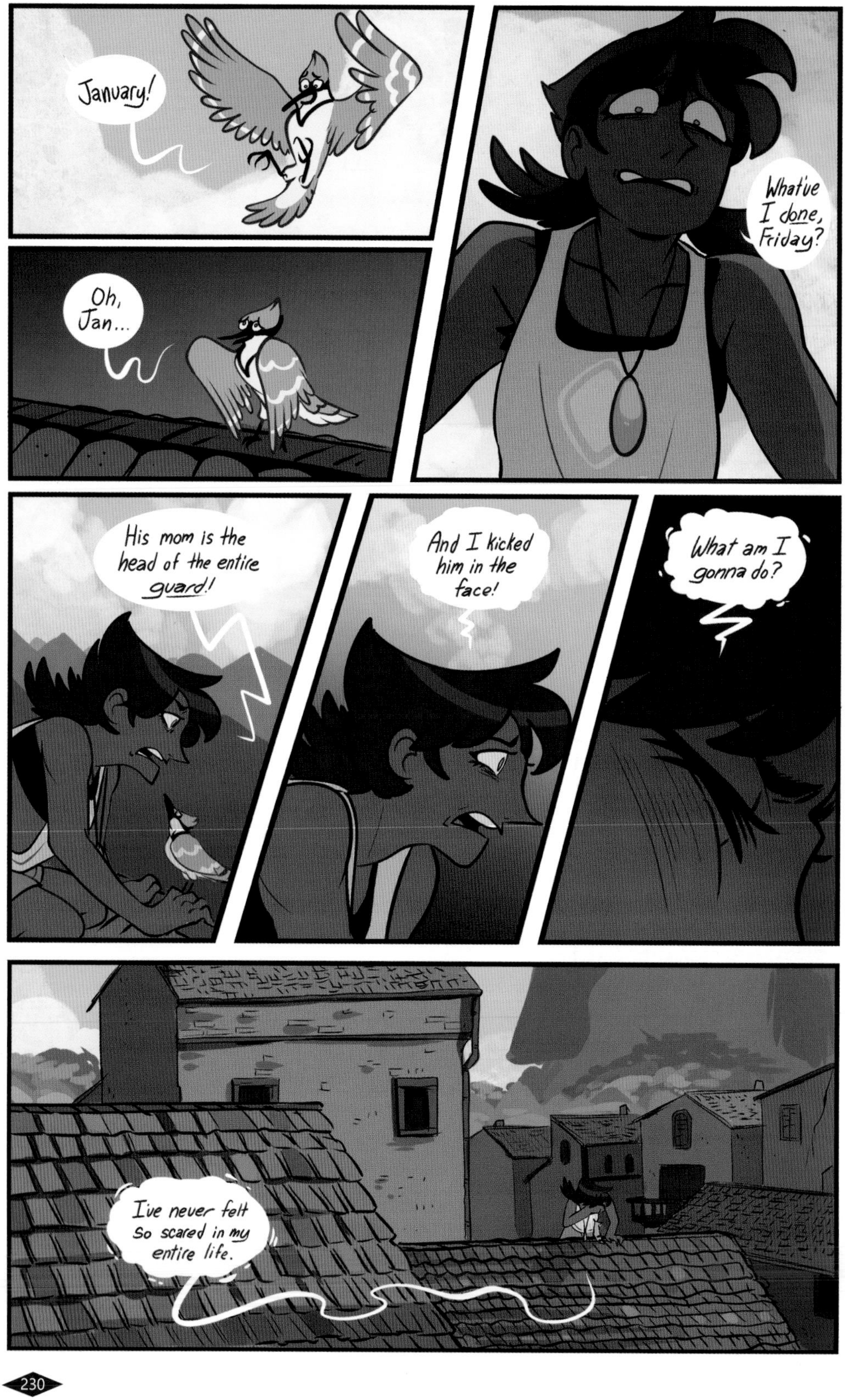
January!
Oh, Jan...
What've I done, Friday?
His mom is the head of the entire guard!
And I kicked him in the face!
What am I gonna do?
I've never felt so scared in my entire life.

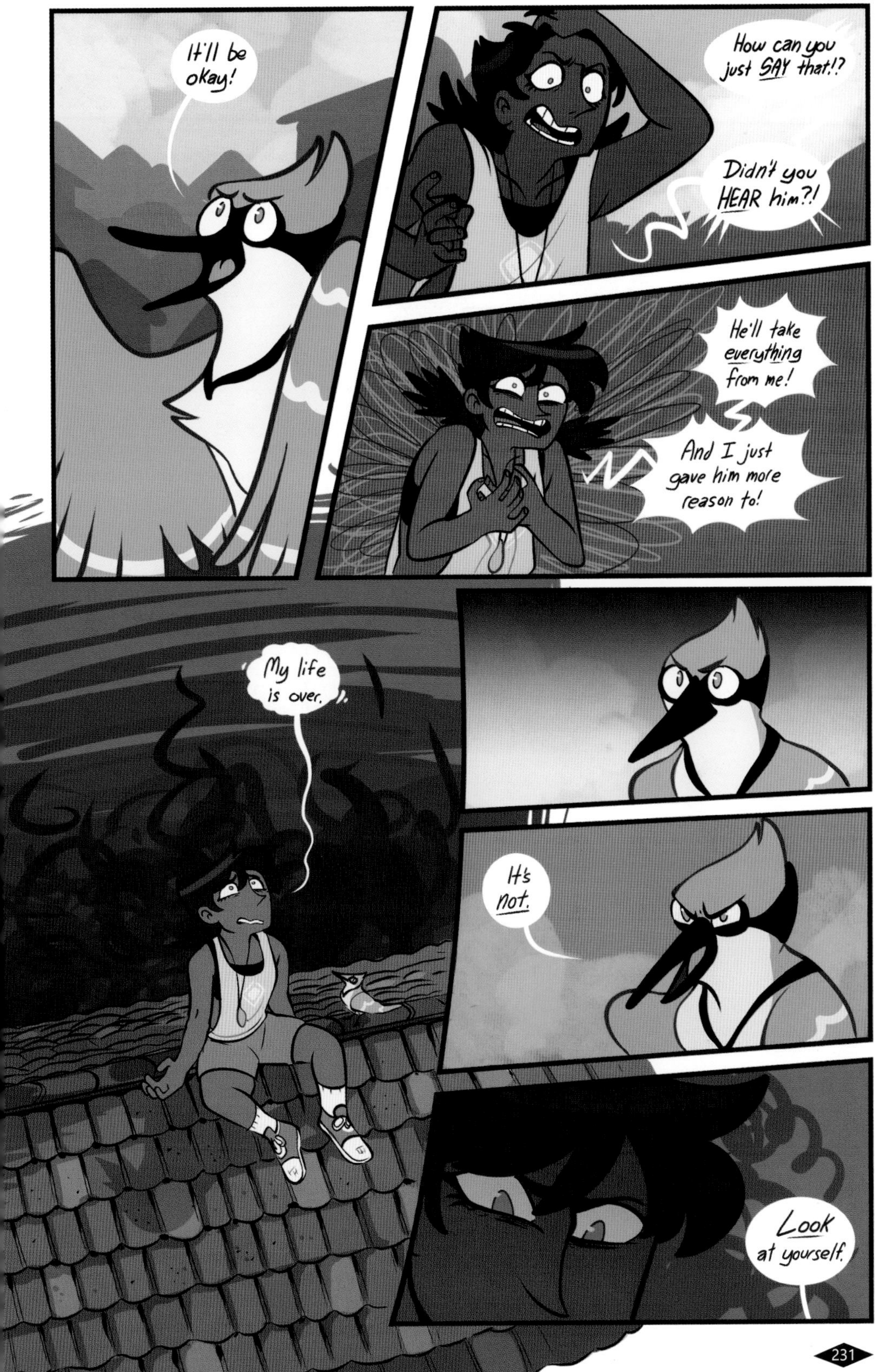
It'll be okay!
How can you just SAY that!?
Didn't you HEAR him?!
He'll take everything from me!
And I just gave him more reason to!
My life is over.
It's not.
Look at yourself.

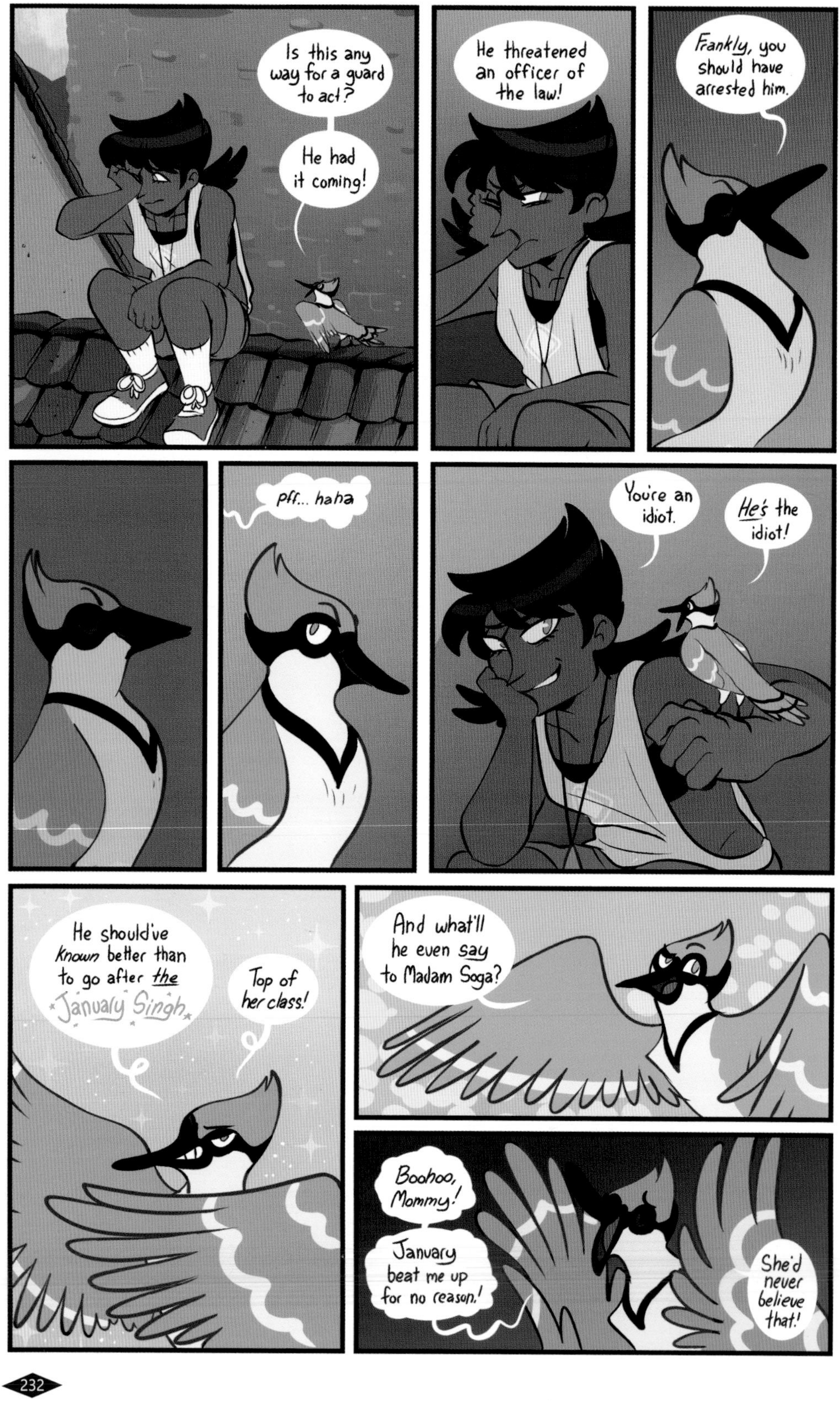

Is this any way for a guard to act?
He had it coming!
He threatened an officer of the law!
Frankly, you should have arrested him.
pff... haha
You're an idiot.
He's the idiot!
He should've known better than to go after the January Singh
Top of her class!
And what'll he even say to Madam Soga?
Boohoo, Mommy!
January beat me up for no reason!
She'd never believe that!

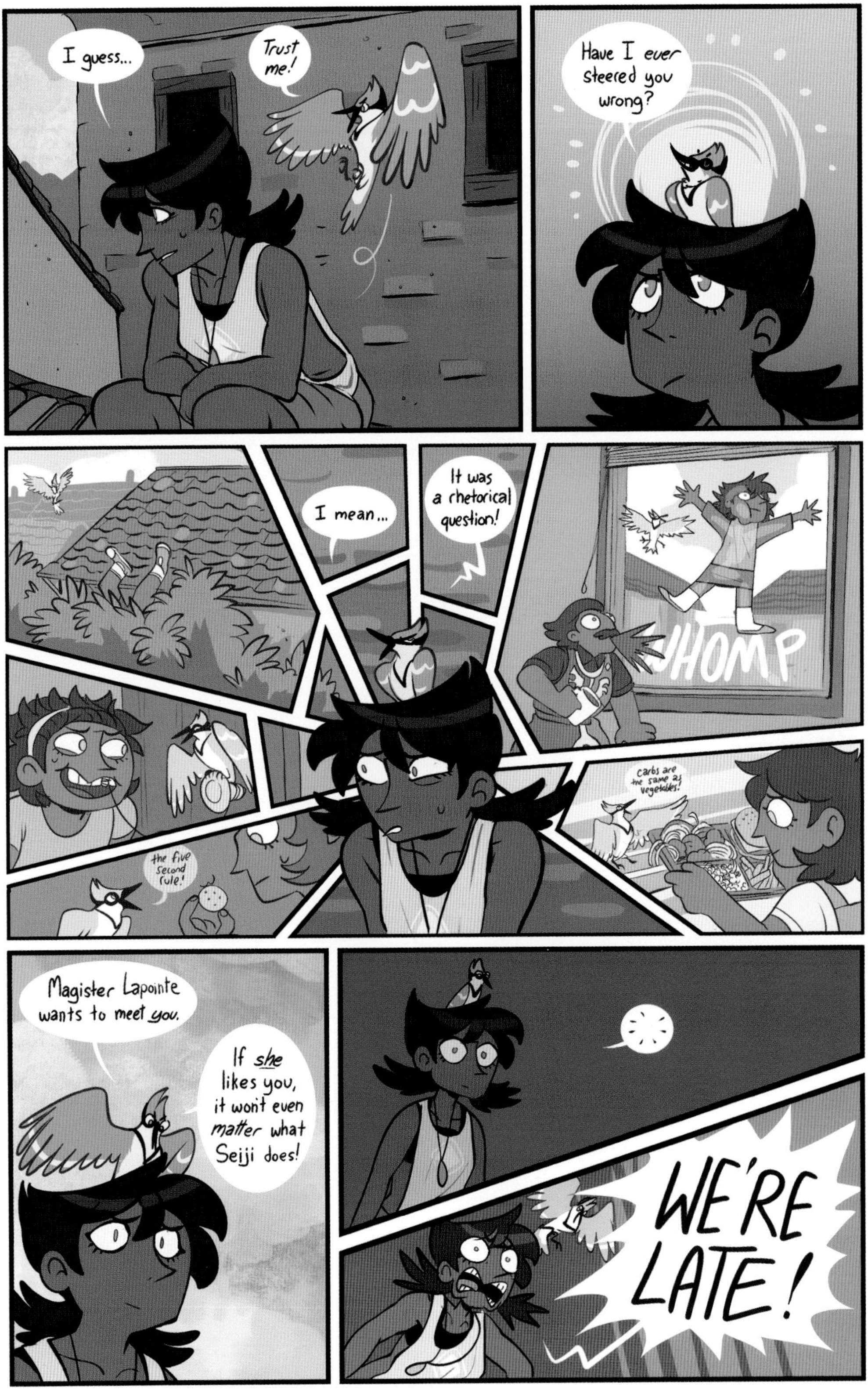

I guess...
Trust me!
Have I ever steered you wrong?
I mean...
It was a rhetorical question!
WHOMP
carbs are the same as vegetables!
the five second rule!
Magister Lapointe wants to meet you.
If she likes you, it won't even matter what Seiji does!
WE'RE LATE!

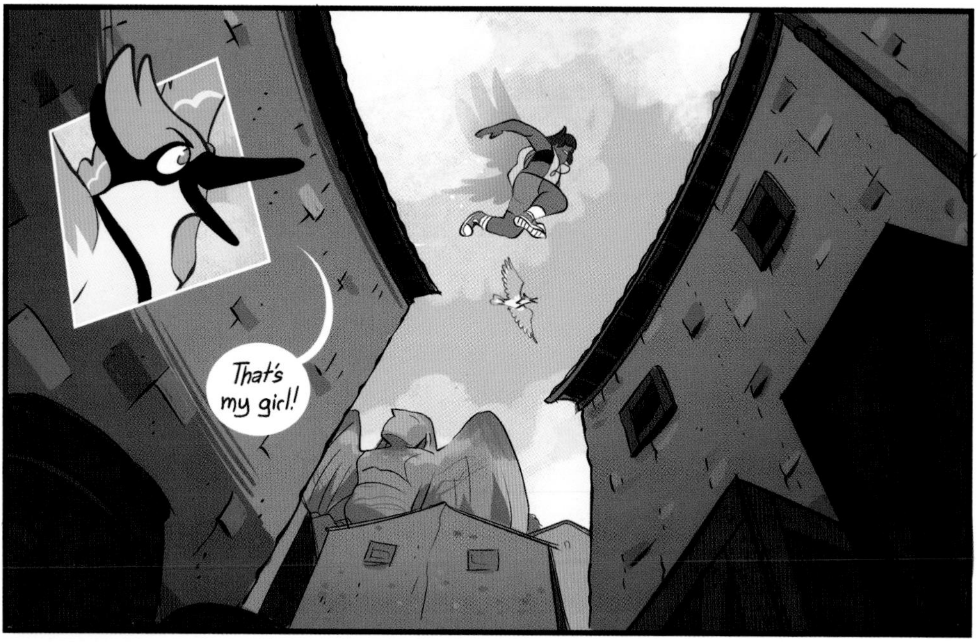
That's my girl!

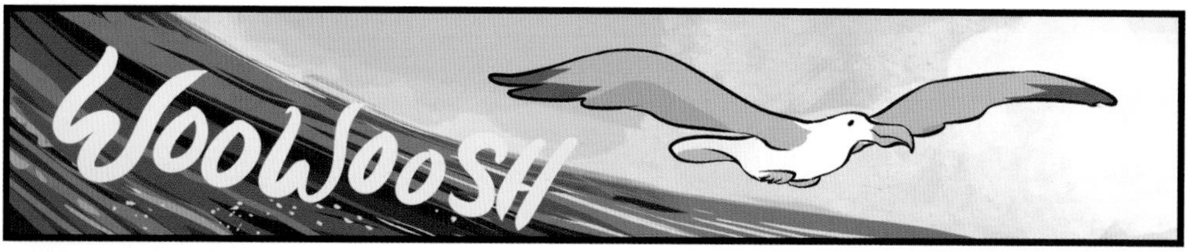
WOOWOOSH

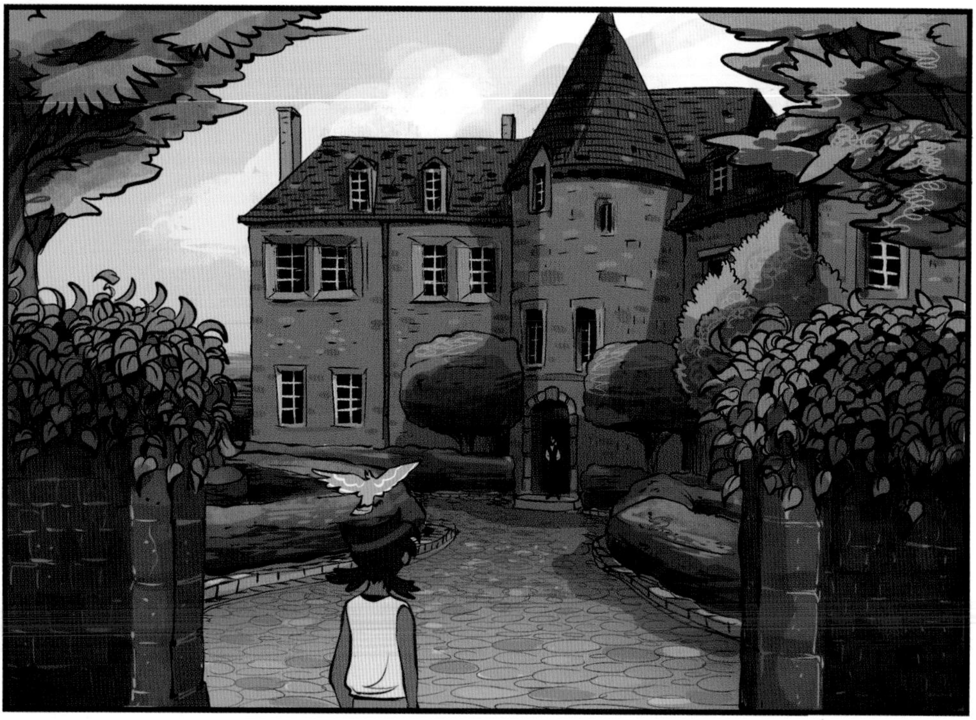

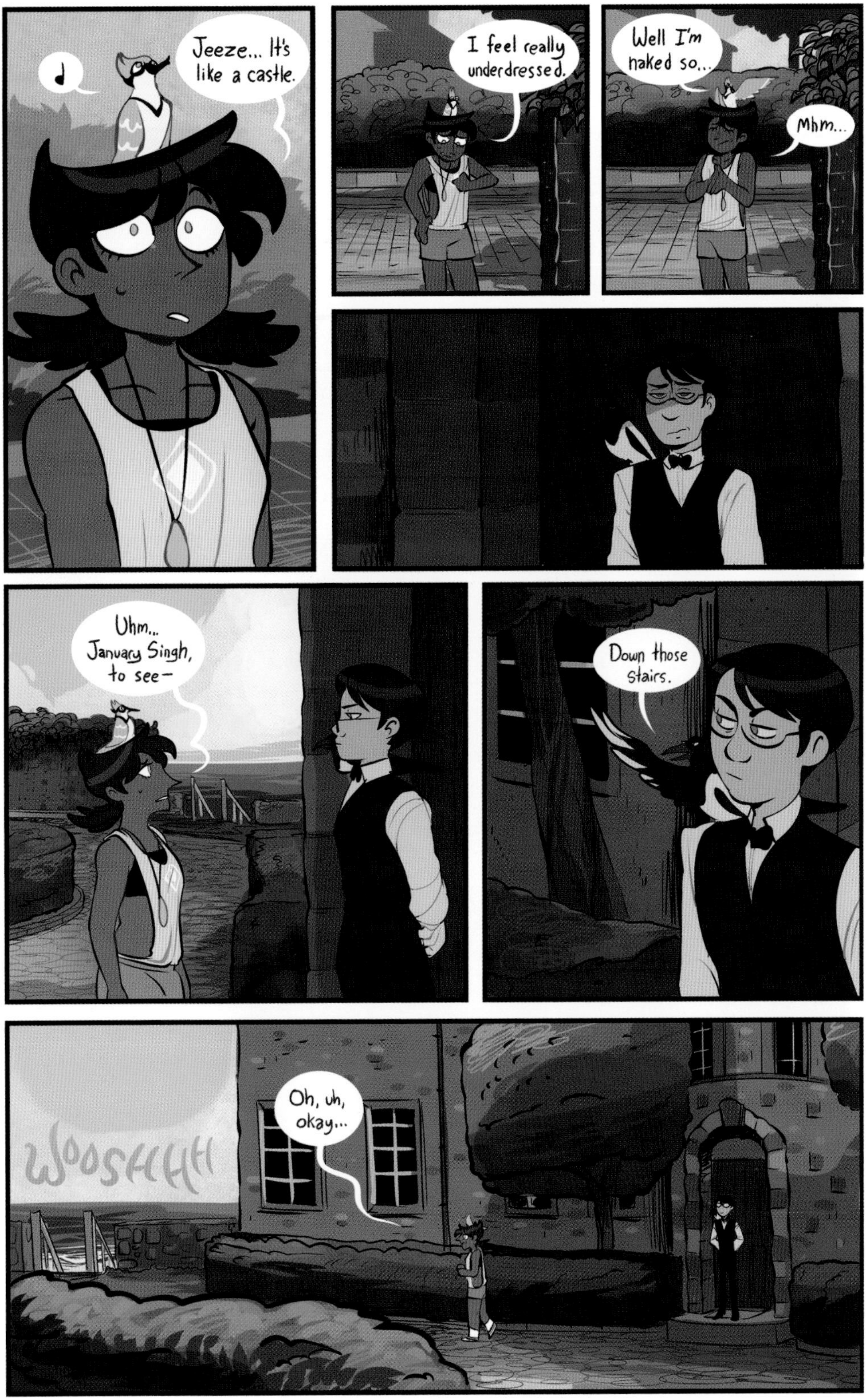

♩
Jeeze... It's like a castle.
I feel really underdressed.
Well I'm naked so...
Mhm...
Uhm... January Singh, to see–
Down those stairs.
WOOSHHH
Oh, uh, okay...

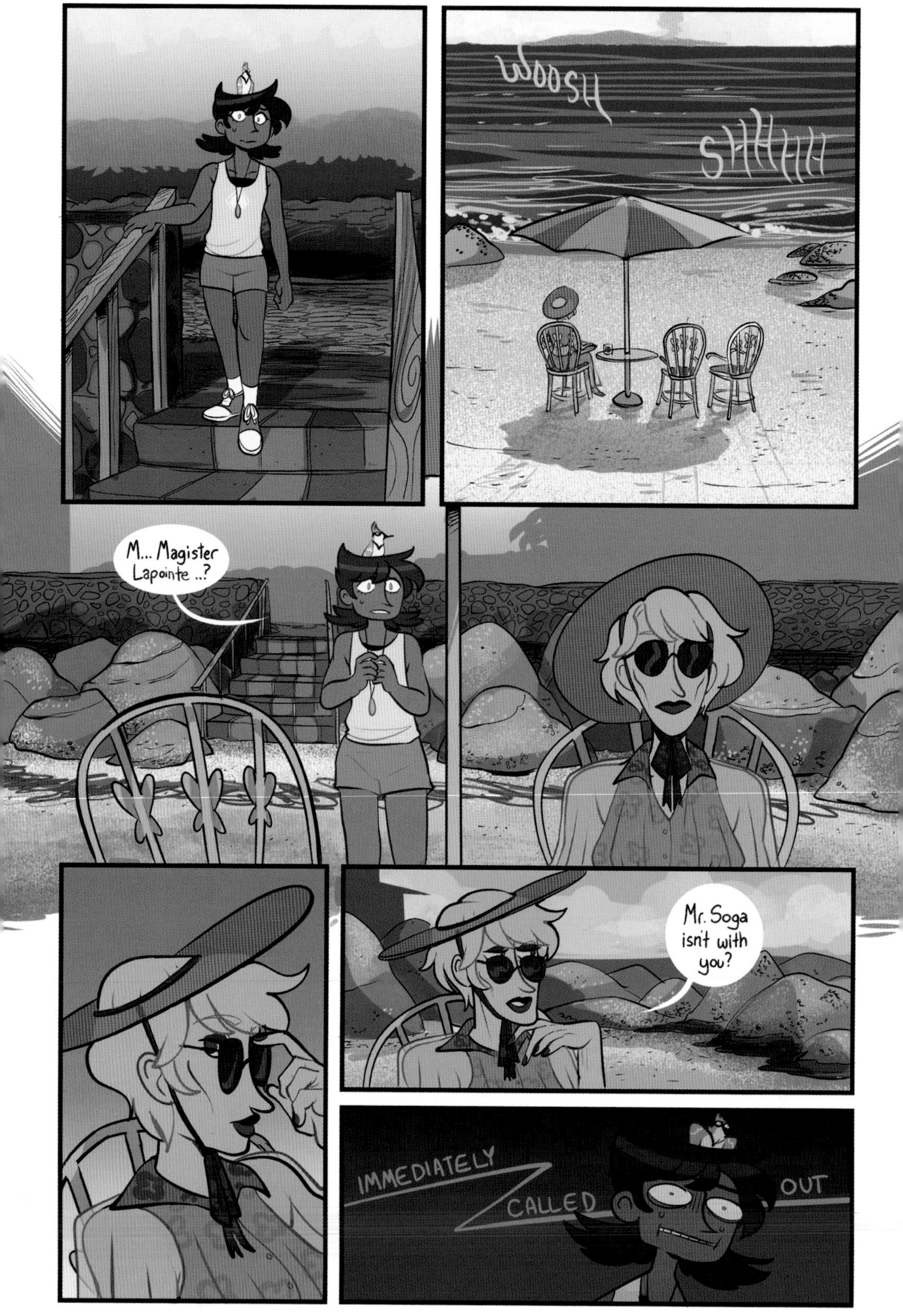
WOOSH
SHHHHH
M... Magister Lapointe ..?
Mr. Soga isn't with you?
IMMEDIATELY
CALLED
OUT

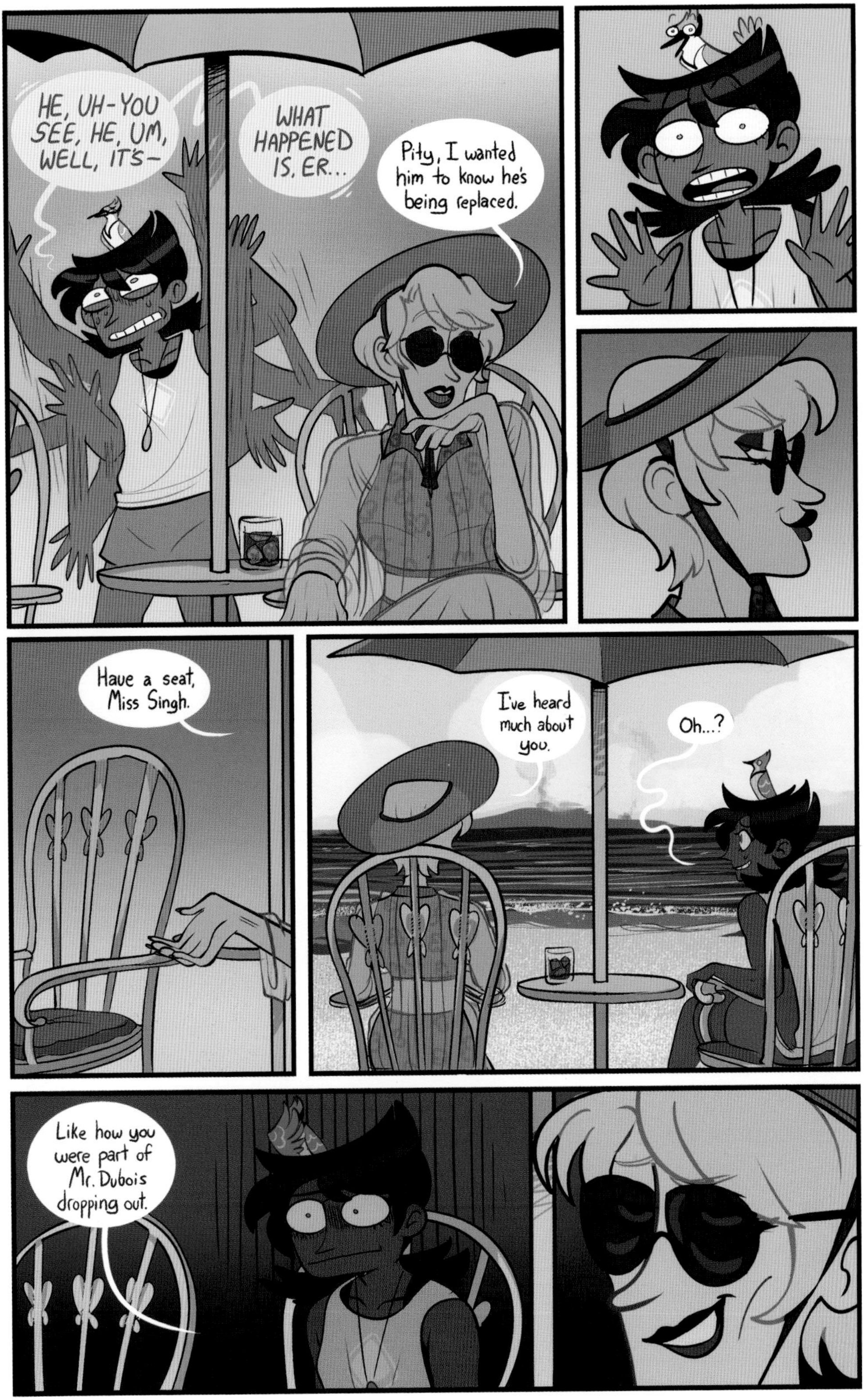
HE, UH-YOU SEE, HE, UM, WELL, IT'S—
WHAT HAPPENED IS, ER...
Pity, I wanted him to know he's being replaced.
Have a seat, Miss Singh.
I've heard much about you.
Oh...?
Like how you were part of Mr. Dubois dropping out.

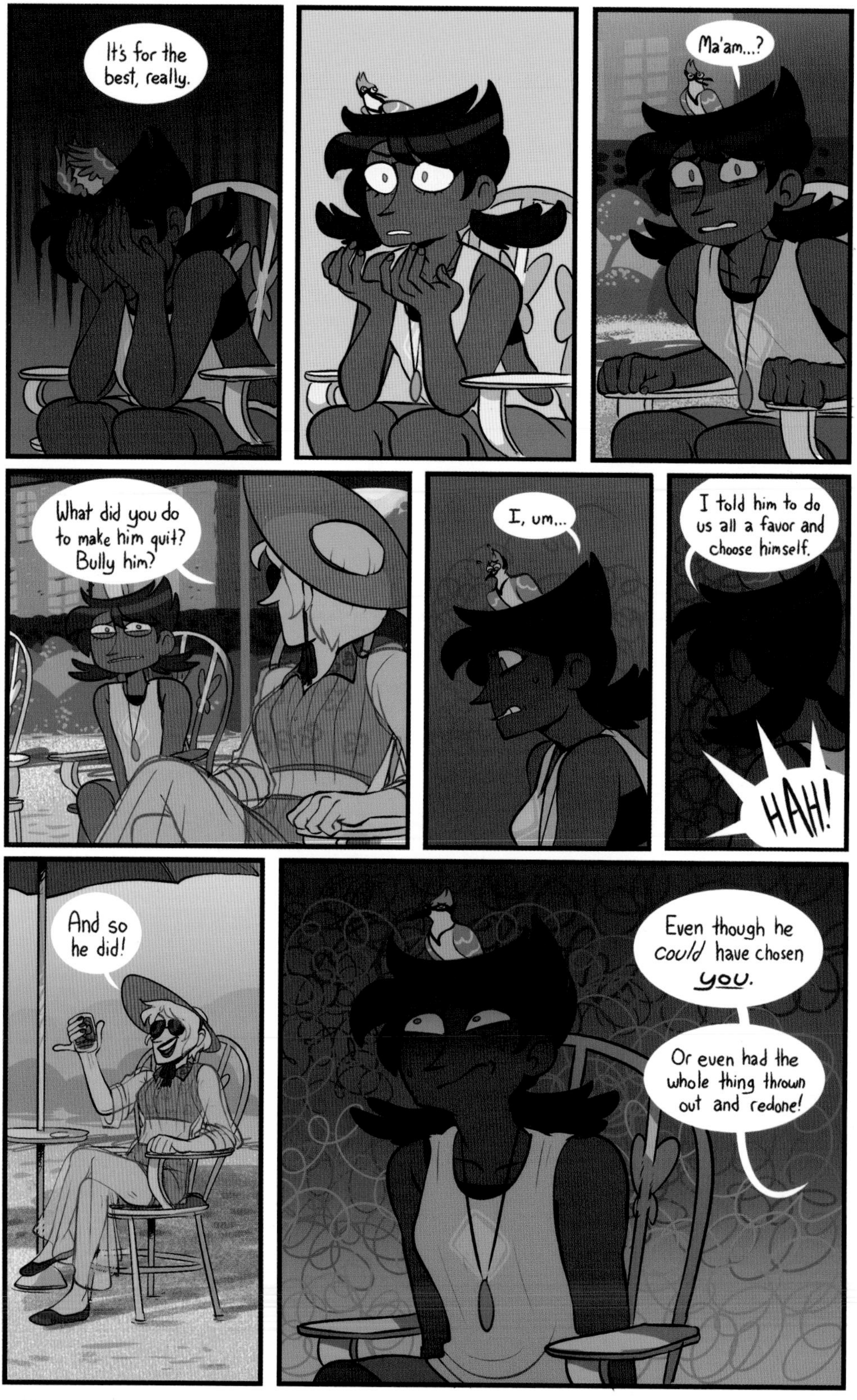
It's for the best, really.
Ma'am...?
What did you do to make him quit? Bully him?
I, um...
I told him to do us all a favor and choose himself.
HAH!
And so he did!
Even though he could have chosen YOU.
Or even had the whole thing thrown out and redone!

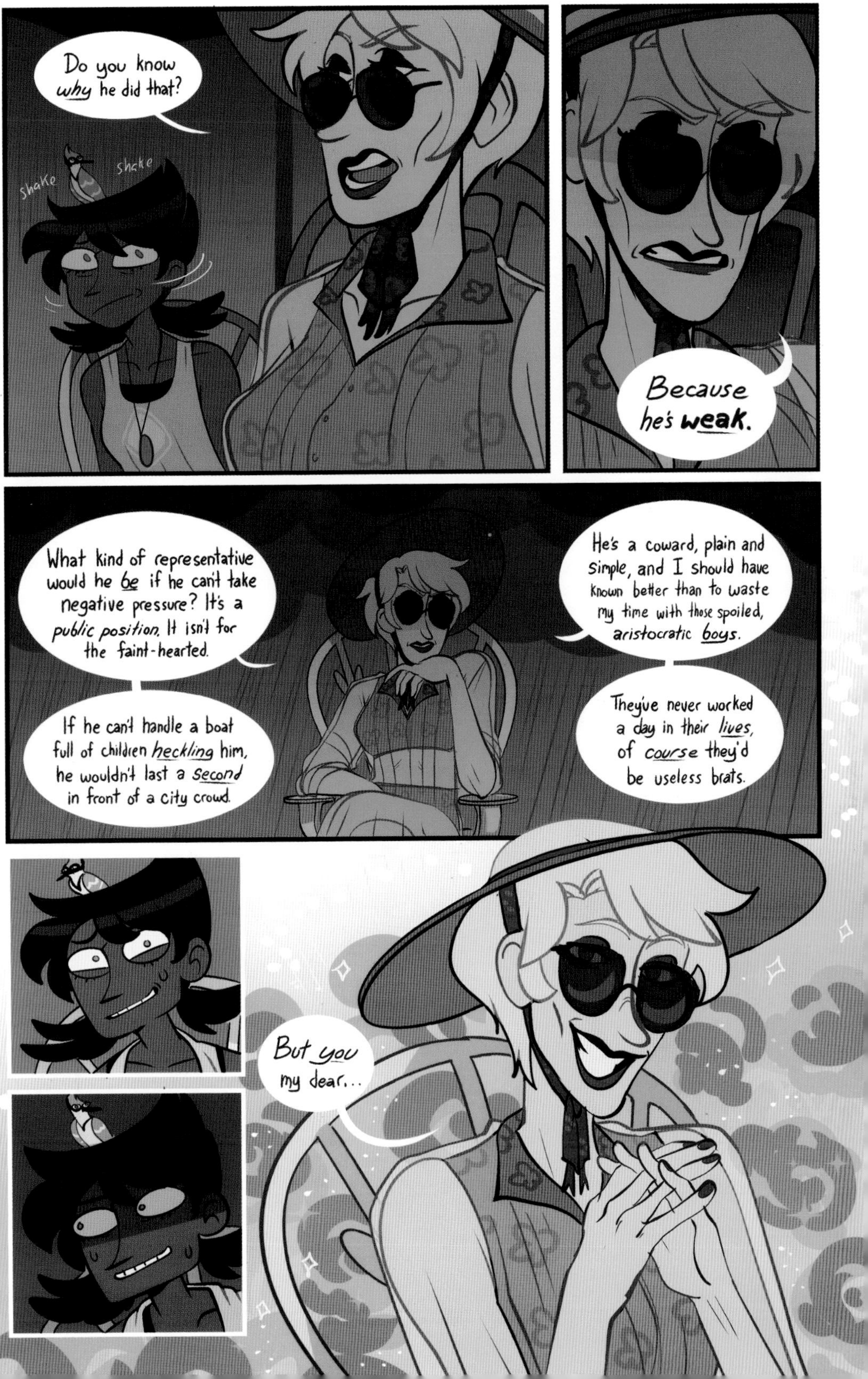
Do you know why he did that?
shake shake
Because he's weak.
What kind of representative would he be if he can't take negative pressure? It's a public position. It isn't for the faint-hearted.
If he can't handle a boat full of children heckling him, he wouldn't last a second in front of a city crowd.
He's a coward, plain and simple, and I should have known better than to waste my time with those spoiled, aristocratic boys.
They've never worked a day in their lives, of course they'd be useless brats.
But you my dear...

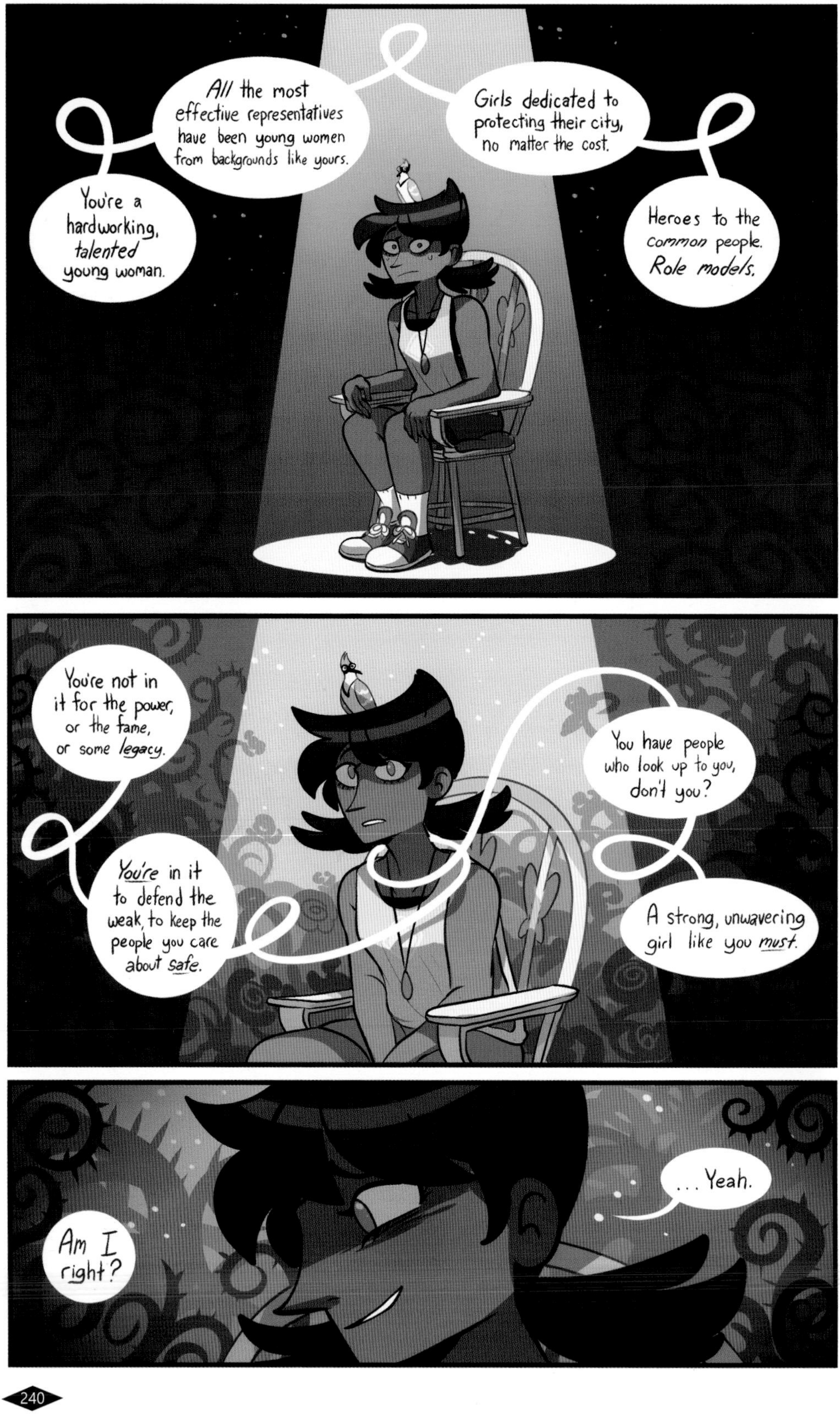

You're a hardworking, *talented* young woman.
All the most effective representatives have been young women from backgrounds like yours.
Girls dedicated to protecting their city, no matter the cost.
Heroes to the *common* people. *Role models.*
You're not in it for the power, or the fame, or some *legacy*.
You're in it to defend the weak, to keep the people you care about *safe*.
You have people who look up to you, don't you?
A strong, unwavering girl like you *must*.
Am I right?
. . . Yeah.

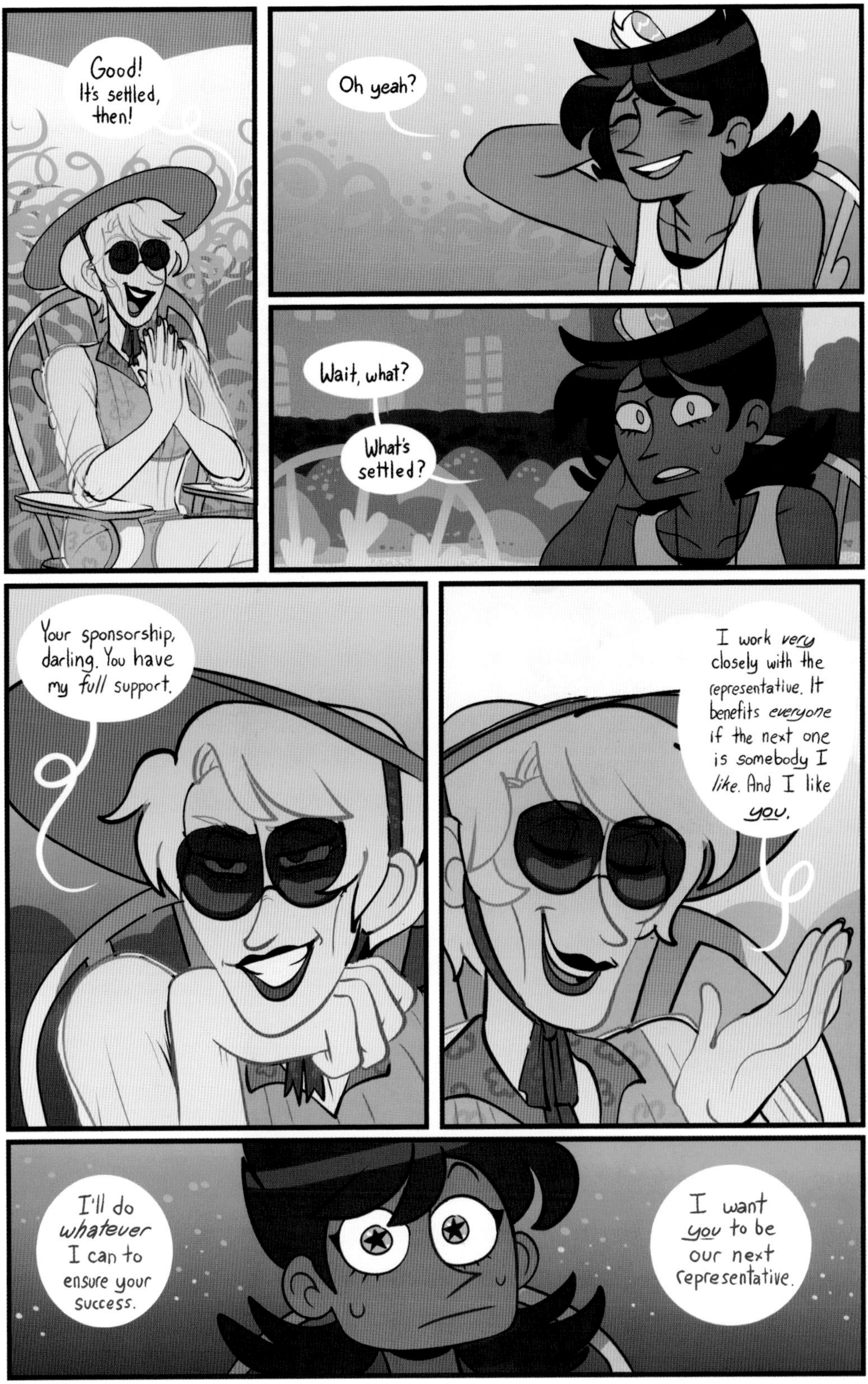
Good! It's settled, then!
Oh yeah?
Wait, what?
What's settled?
Your sponsorship, darling. You have my full support.
I work very closely with the representative. It benefits everyone if the next one is somebody I like. And I like you.
I'll do whatever I can to ensure your success.
I want you to be our next representative.

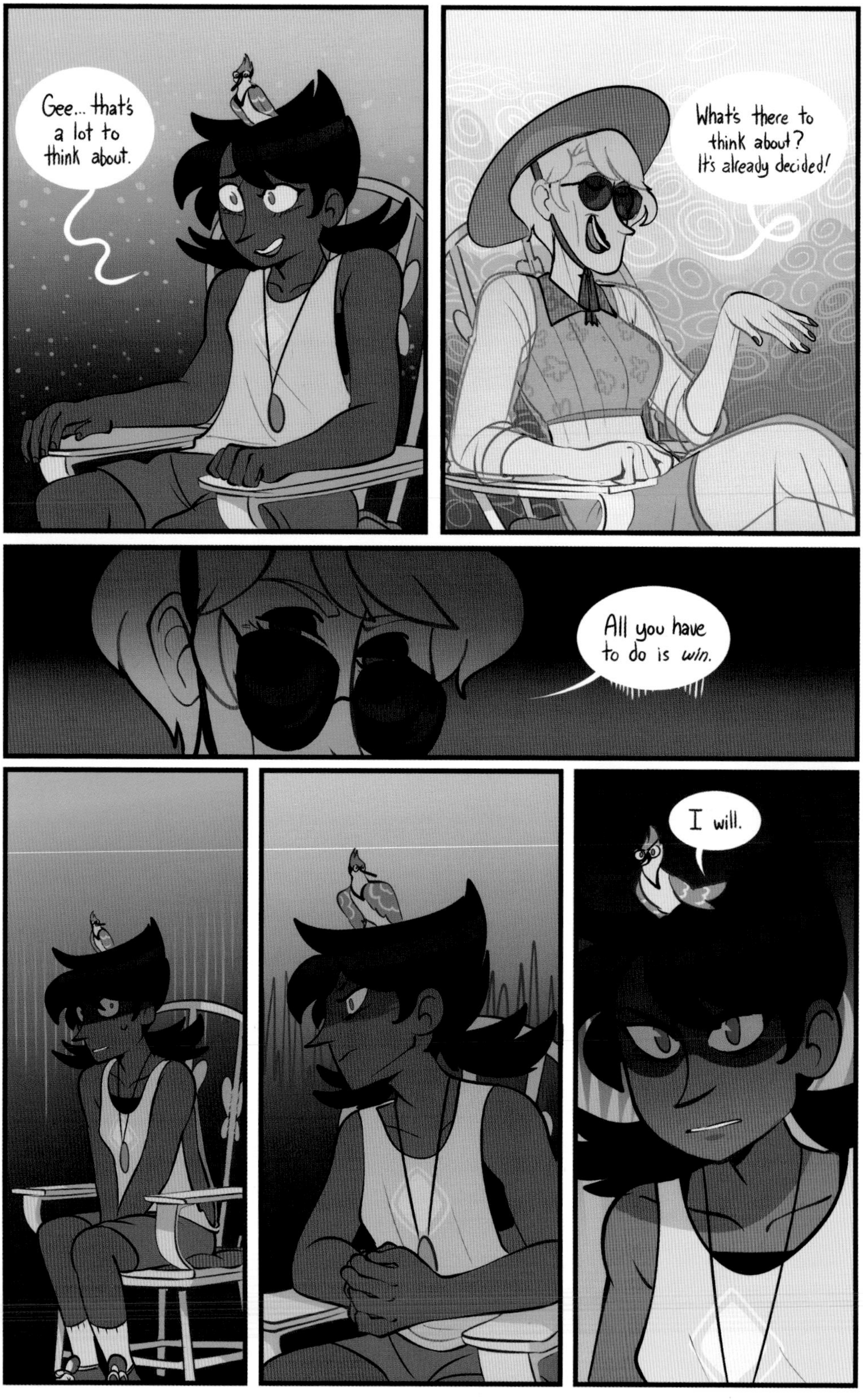
Gee... that's a lot to think about.
What's there to think about? It's already decided!
All you have to do is *win.*
I will.

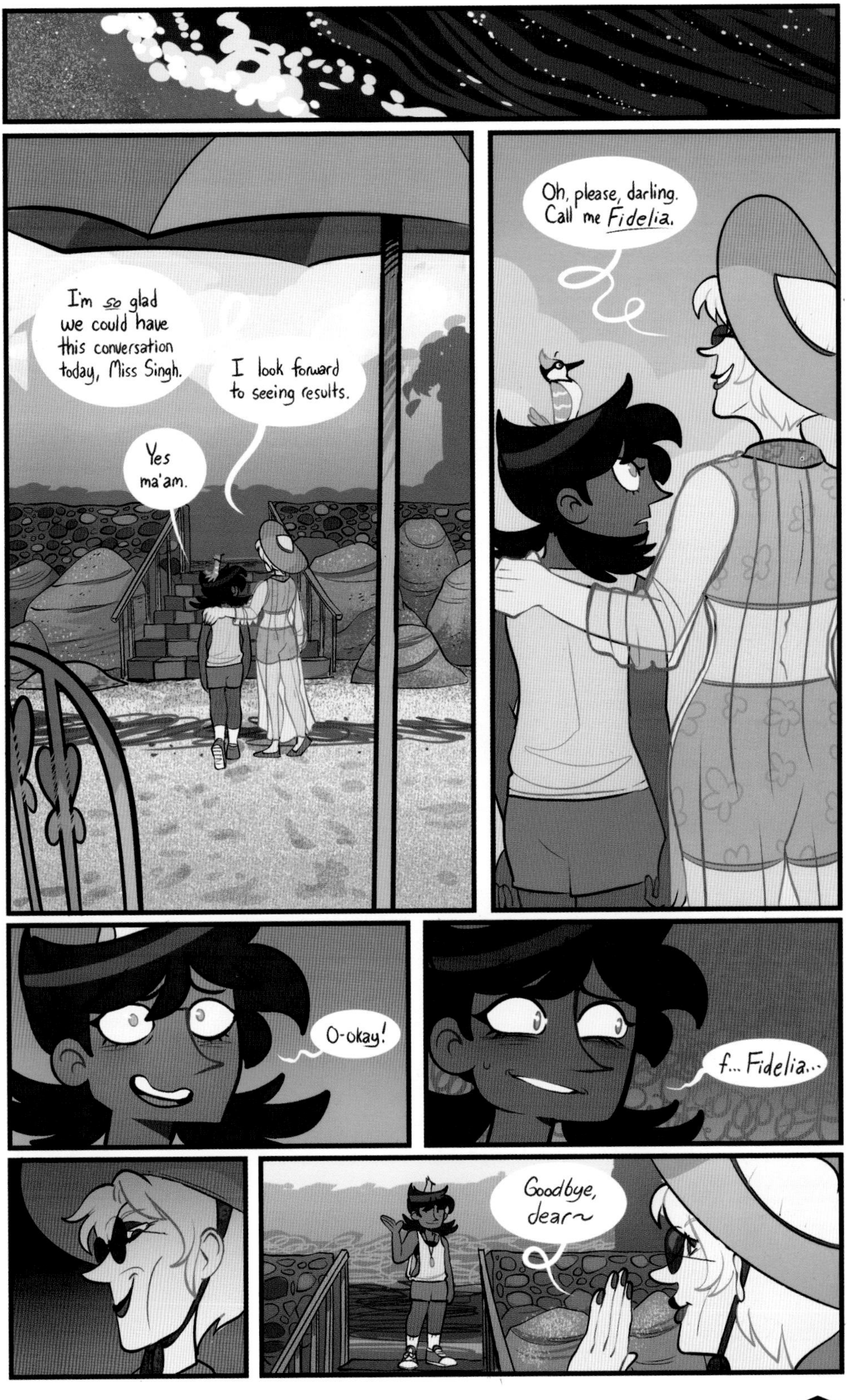
I'm so glad we could have this conversation today, Miss Singh.
I look forward to seeing results.
Yes ma'am.
Oh, please, darling. Call me Fidelia.
O-okay!
f... Fidelia...
Goodbye, dear~

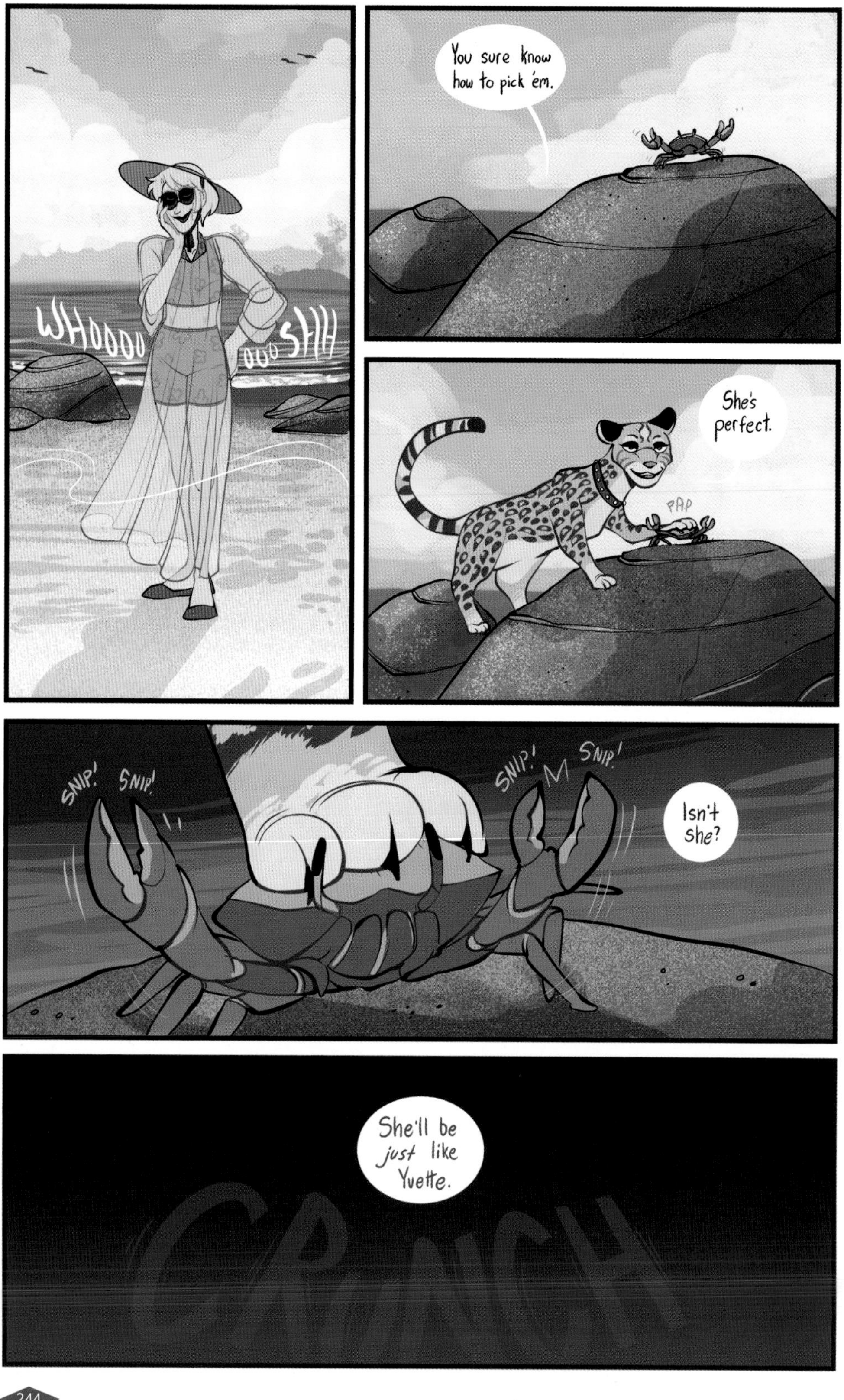
WHOOOOOOOSHH
You sure know how to pick 'em.
She's perfect.
PAP
SNIP! SNIP!
SNIP! SNIP!
Isn't she?
She'll be *just* like Yvette.
CRUNCH

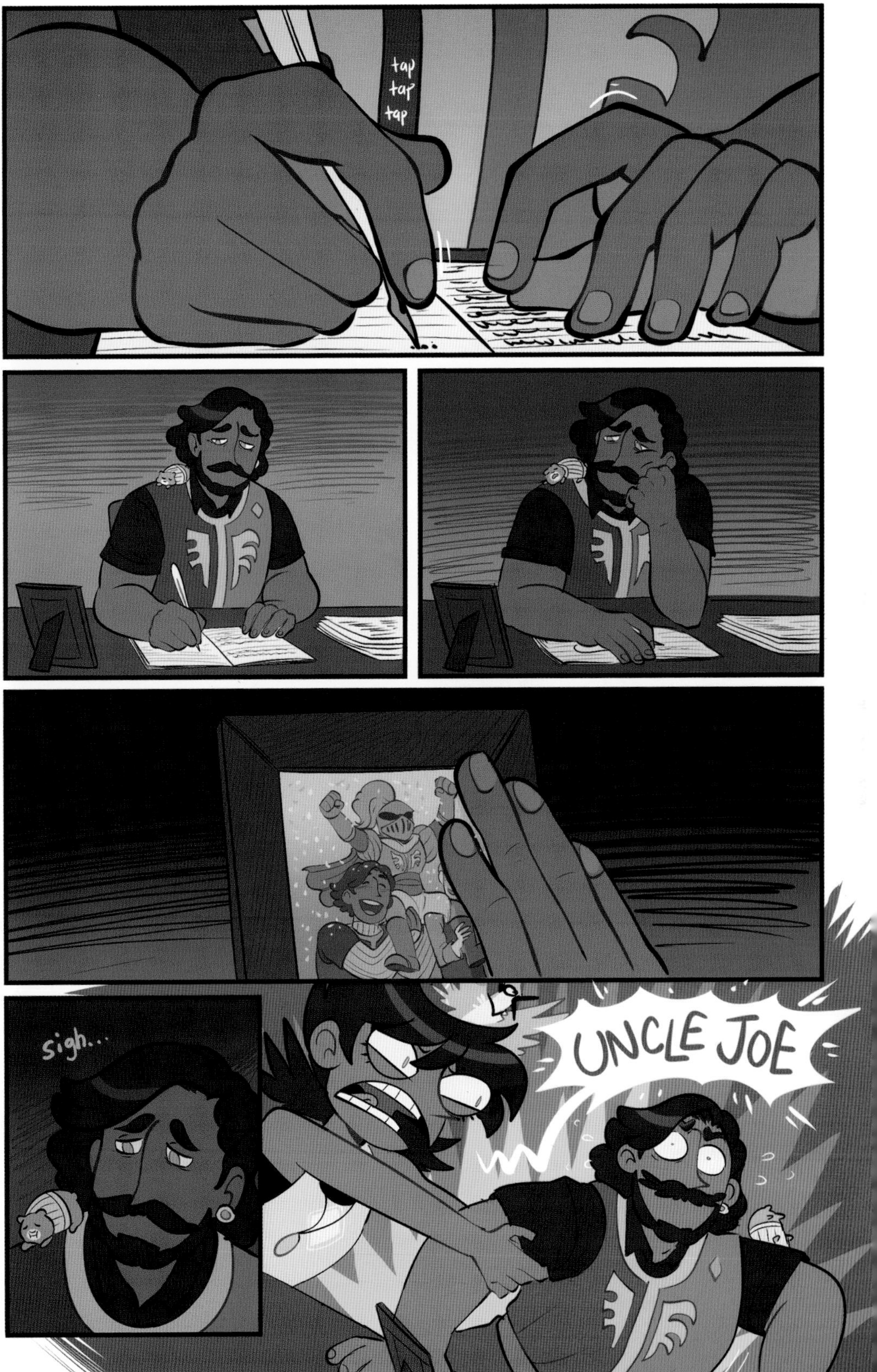
tap
tap
tap
sigh...
UNCLE JOE

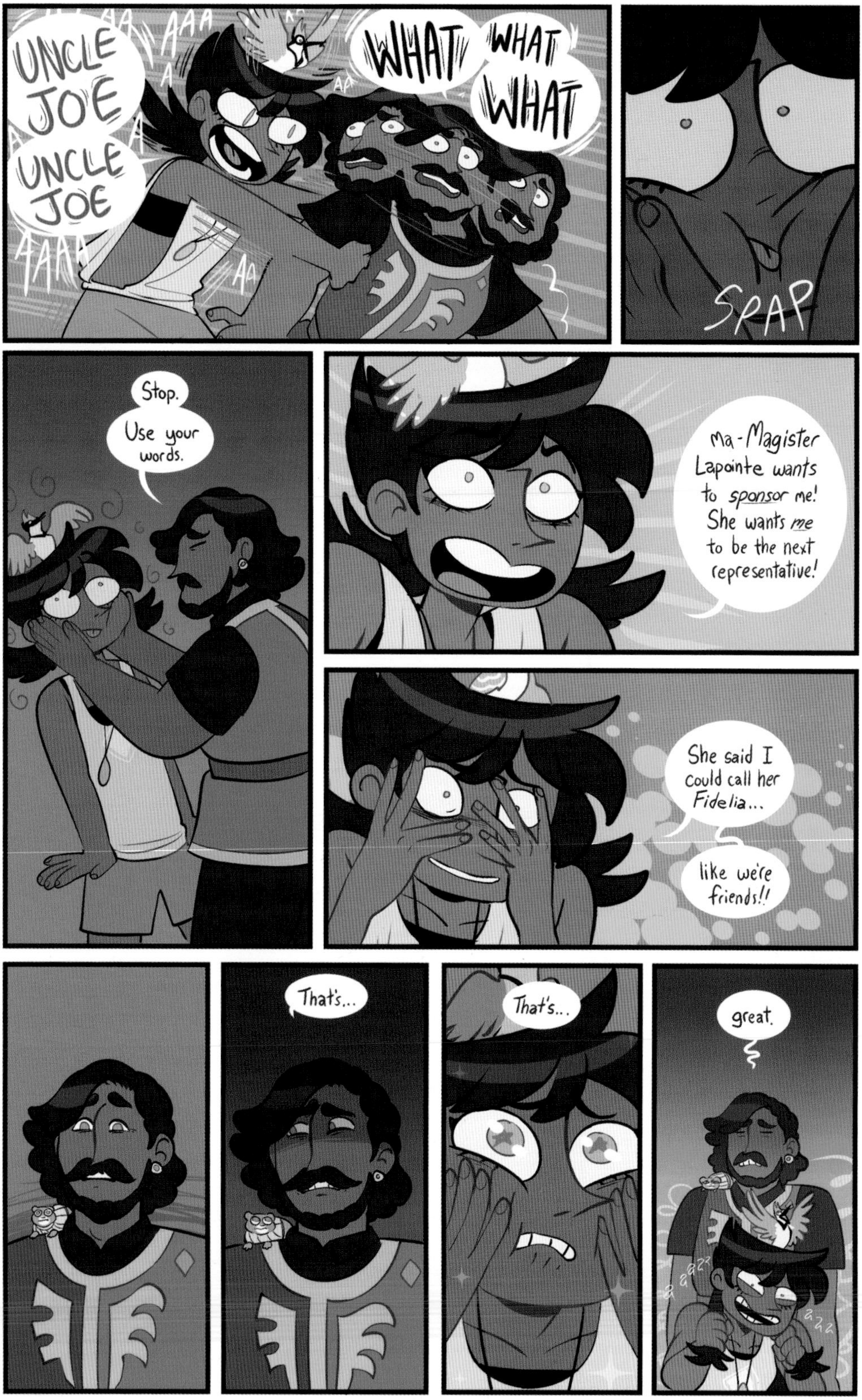
UNCLE JOE
UNCLE JOE
AAAA
WHAT
WHAT
WHAT
SPAP
Stop.
Use your words.
Ma-Magister Lapointe wants to sponsor me! She wants me to be the next representative!
She said I could call her Fidelia...
like we're friends!!
That's...
That's...
great.

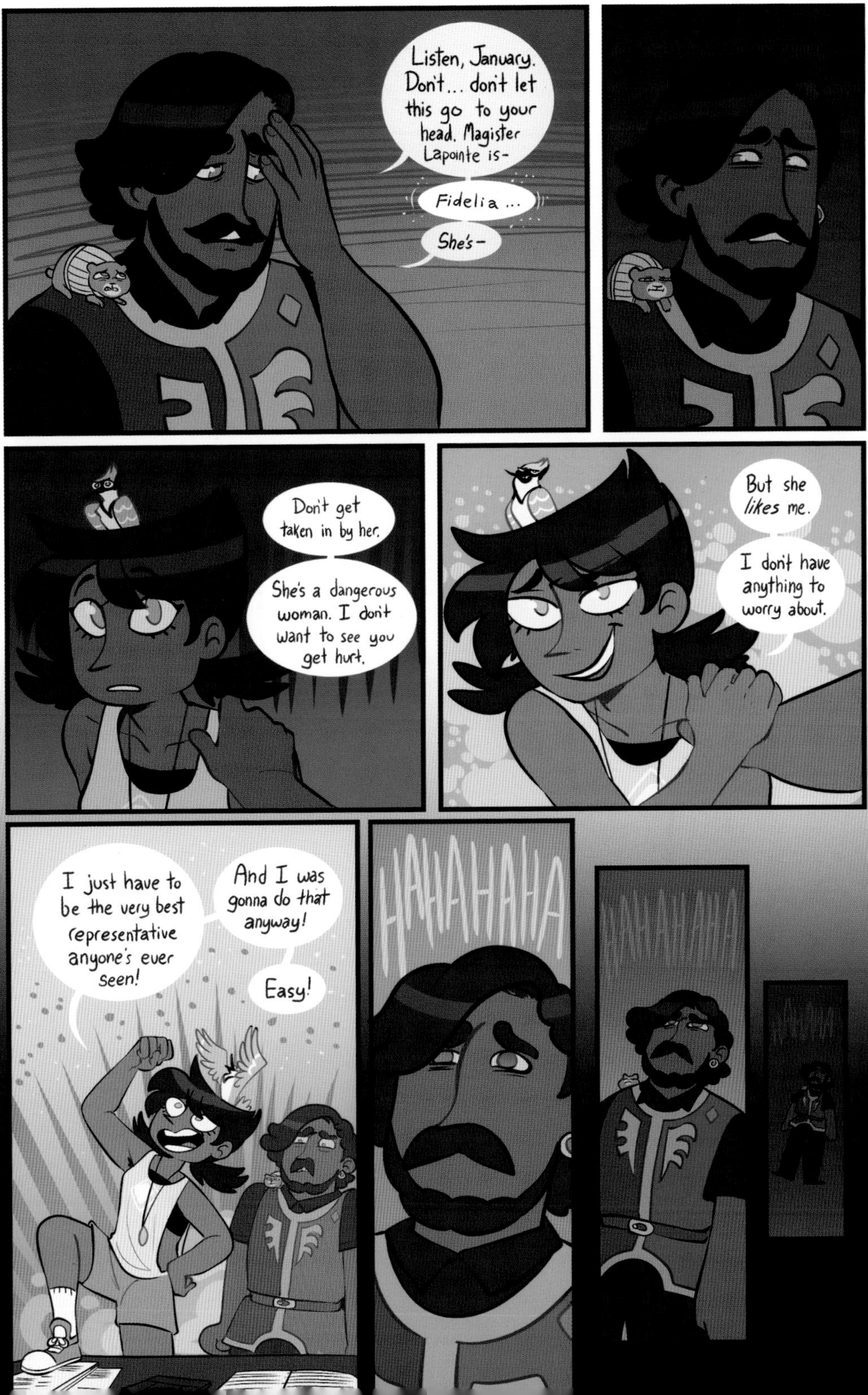
Listen, January. Don't... don't let this go to your head. Magister Lapointe is-
Fidelia...
She's-
Don't get taken in by her.
She's a dangerous woman. I don't want to see you get hurt.
But she *likes* me.
I don't have anything to worry about.
I just have to be the very best representative anyone's ever seen!
And I was gonna do that anyway!
Easy!
HAHAHAHA
HAHAHAHA

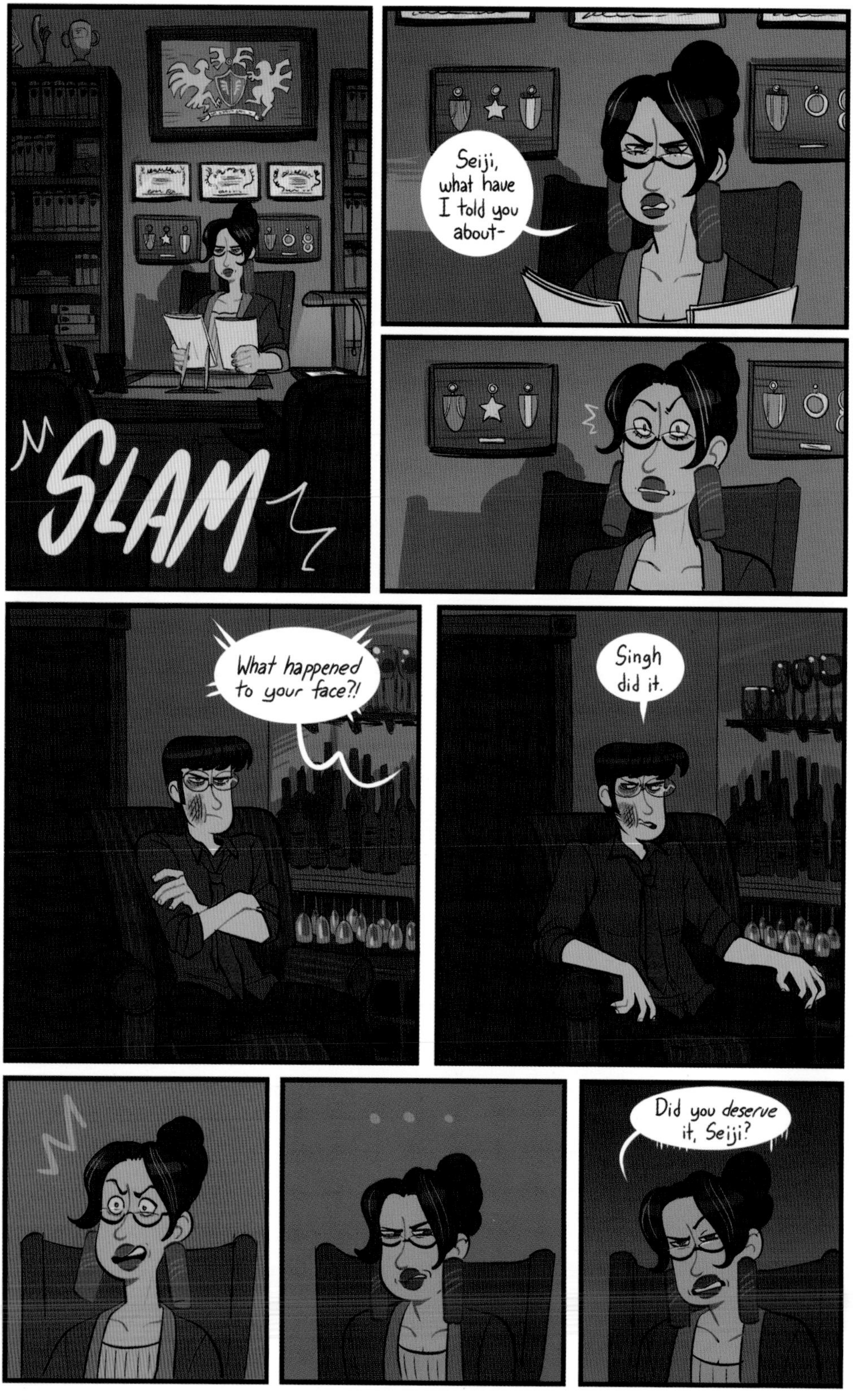
SLAM
Seiji, what have I told you about-
What happened to your face?!
Singh did it.
Did you deserve it, Seiji?

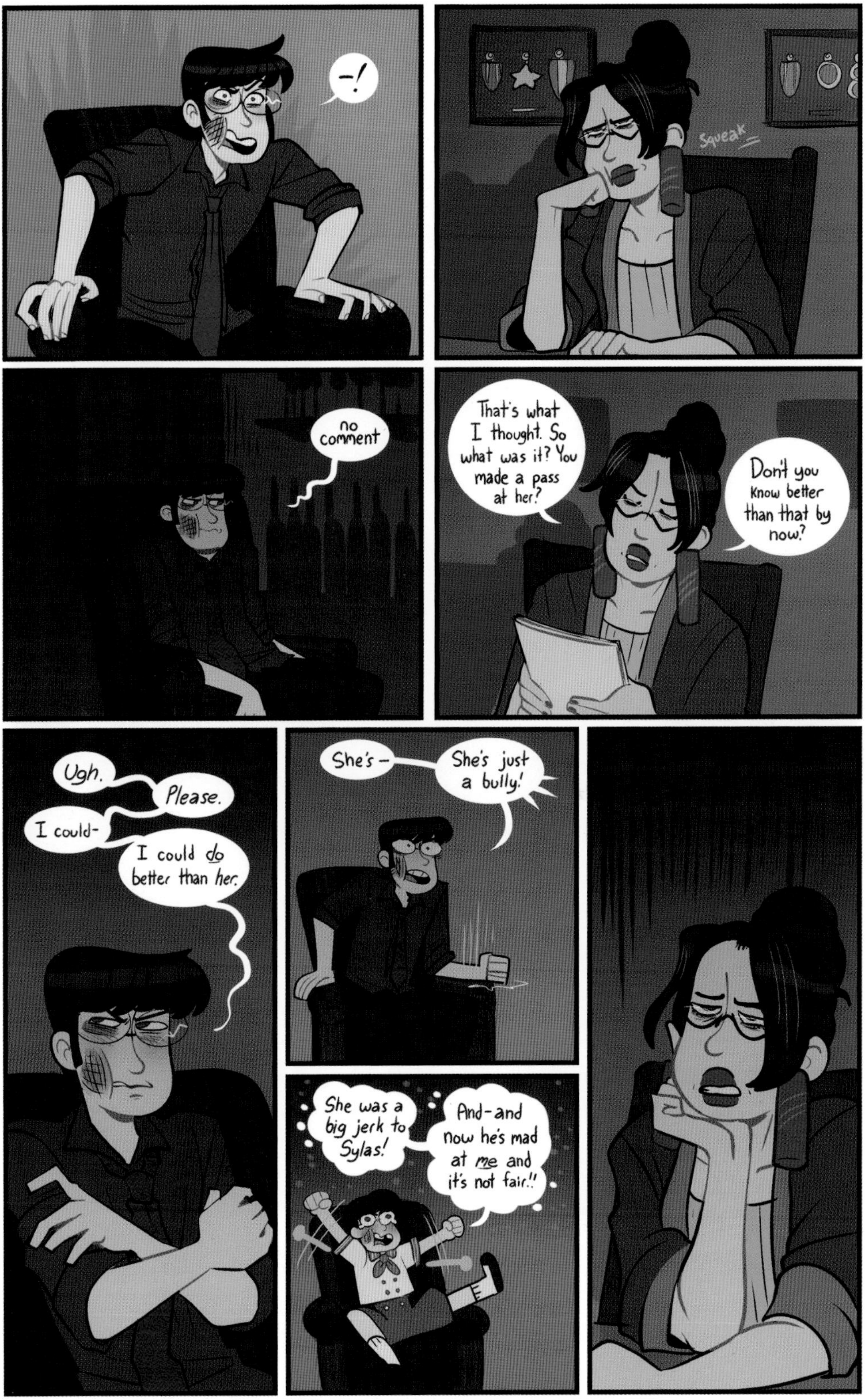
-!
Squeak
no comment
That's what I thought. So what was it? You made a pass at her?
Don't you know better than that by now?
Ugh.
Please.
I could-
I could do better than her.
She's-
She's just a bully!
She was a big jerk to Sylas!
And-and now he's mad at me and it's not fair!!

It's not her fault if your boyfriend's mad at-

BUH- SPUH- HE'S NOT MY BOYFRIEND!!

Seiji, *please.*

You've been following him around like a lovesick puppy ever since you were *kids.* You *begged* to be taught by Lapointe with him.

And now you're telling me you picked a fight with an *apprentice of the city guard* because she was *mean* to him?

I don't have to be a detective to figure it out.

I don't –! I don't have to listen to this!

You never have, why would this be any different?

It's not like I'm your mother who raised you by myself or anything.

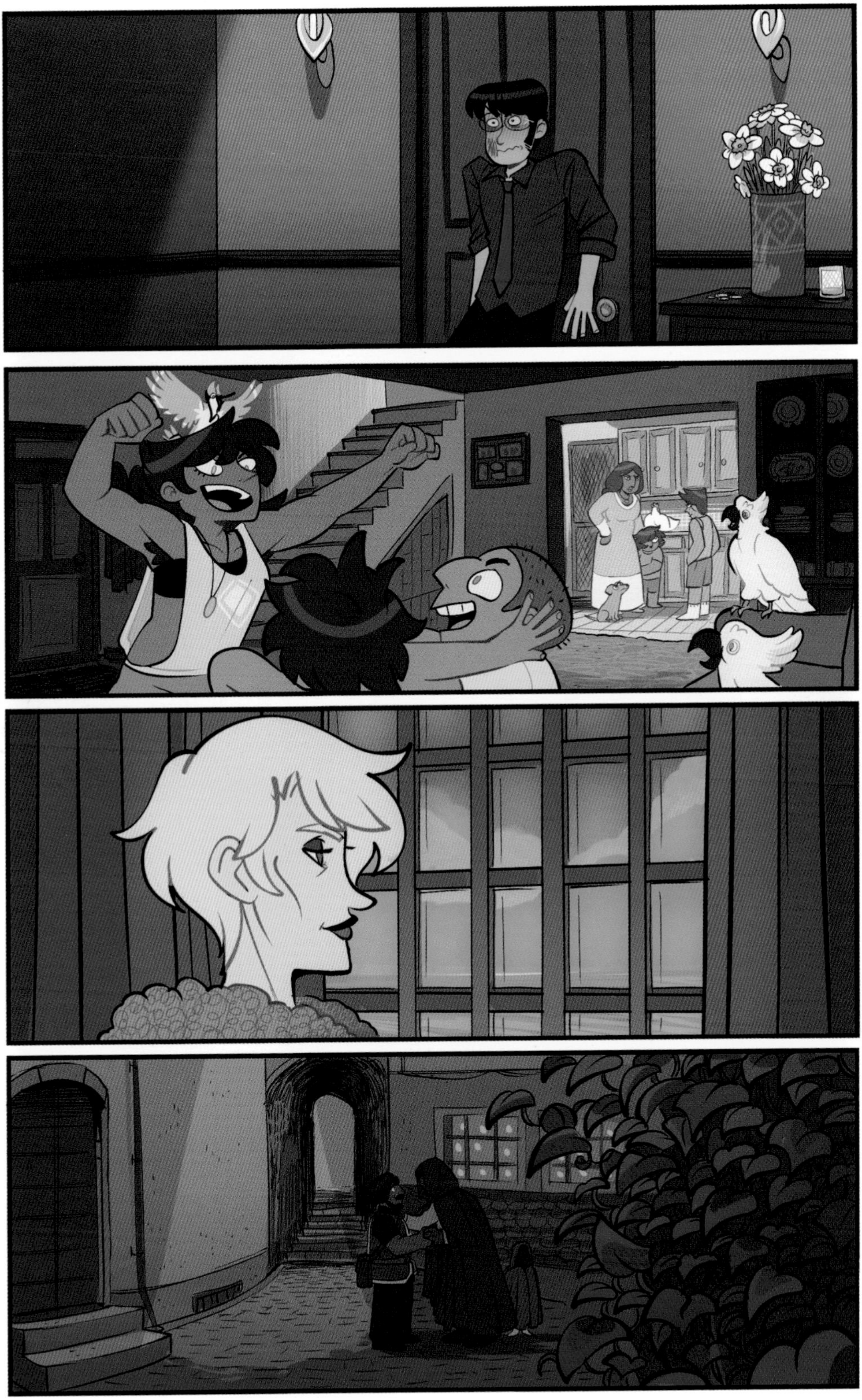

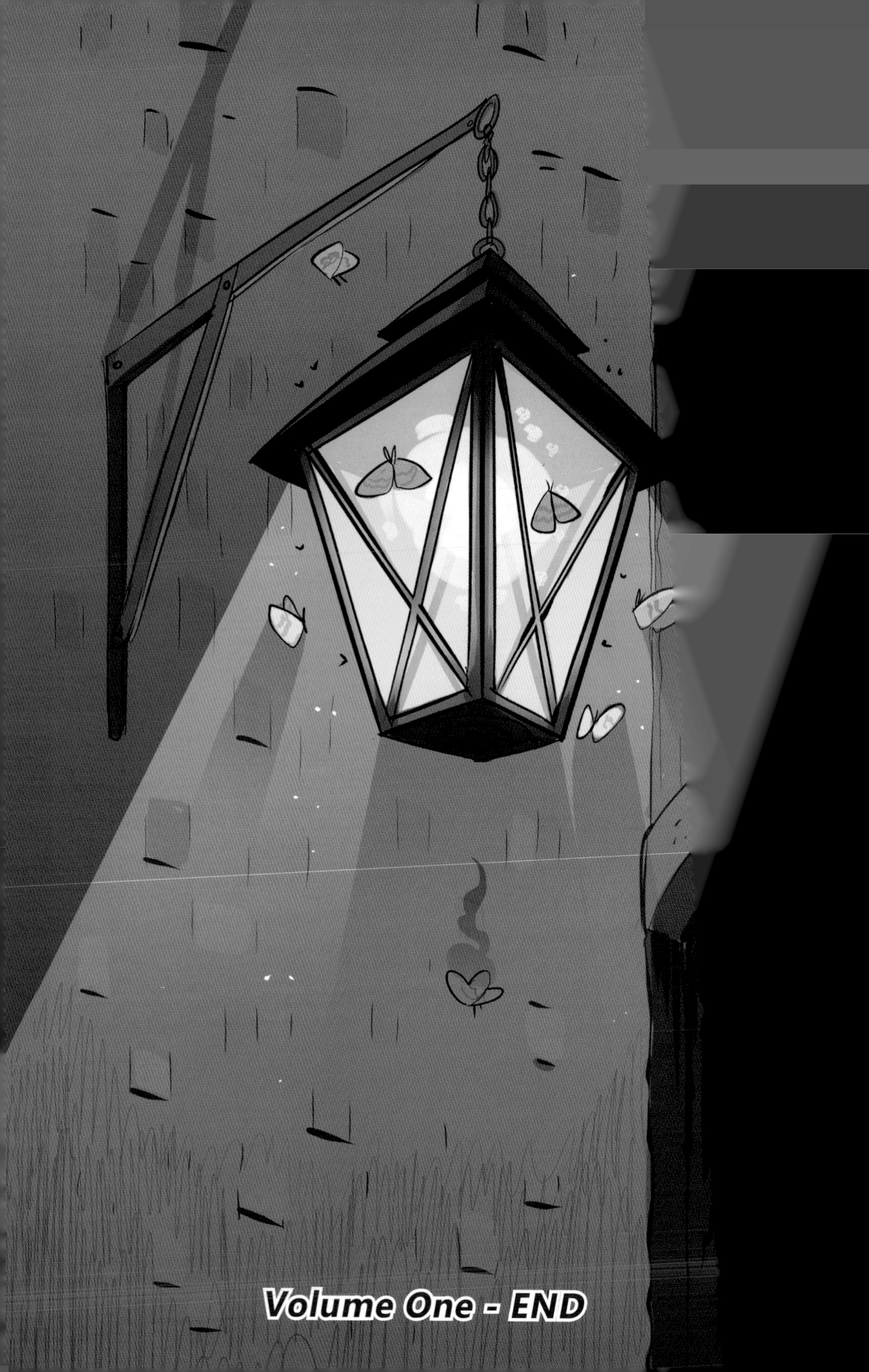
Volume One - END

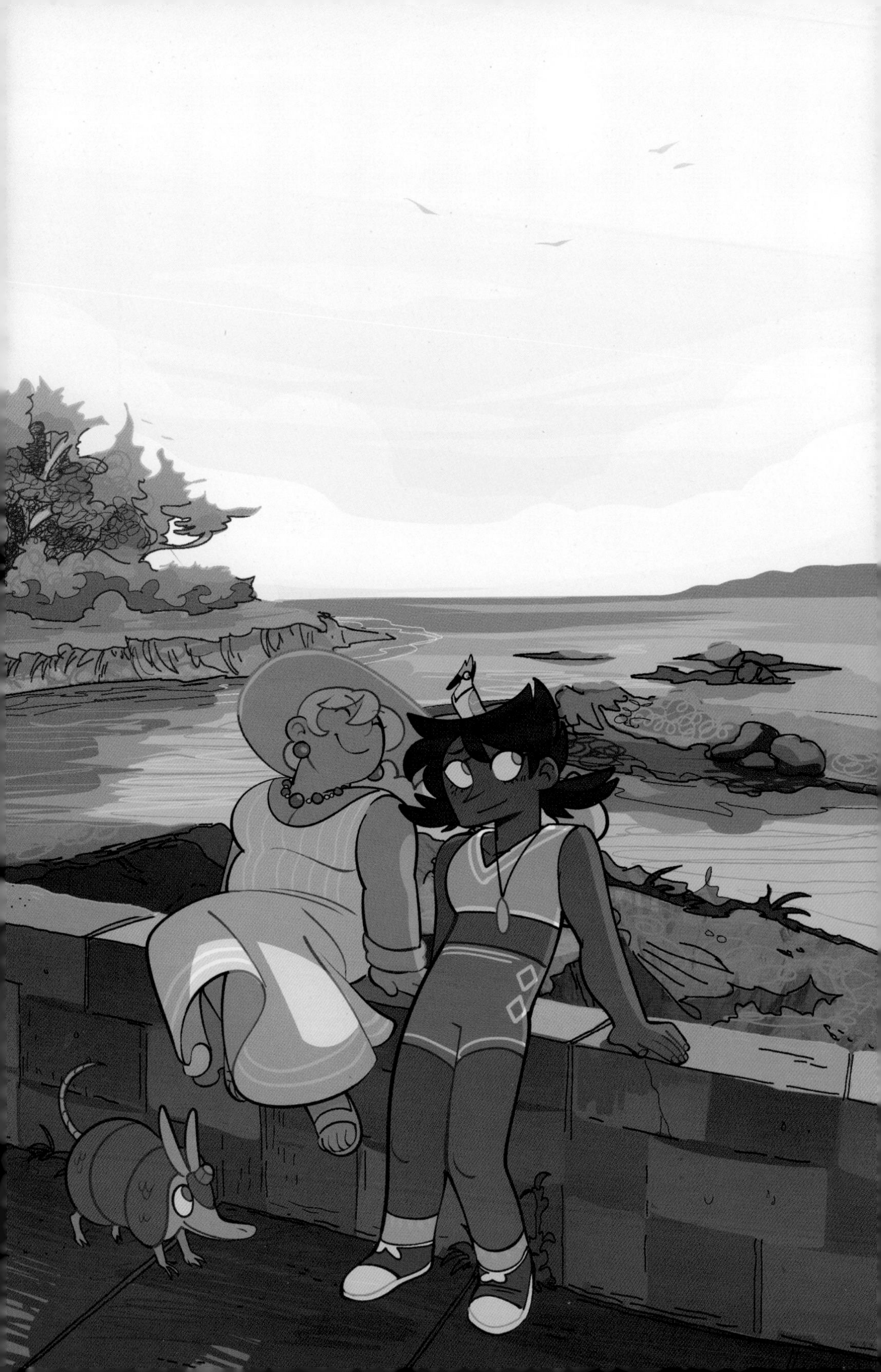

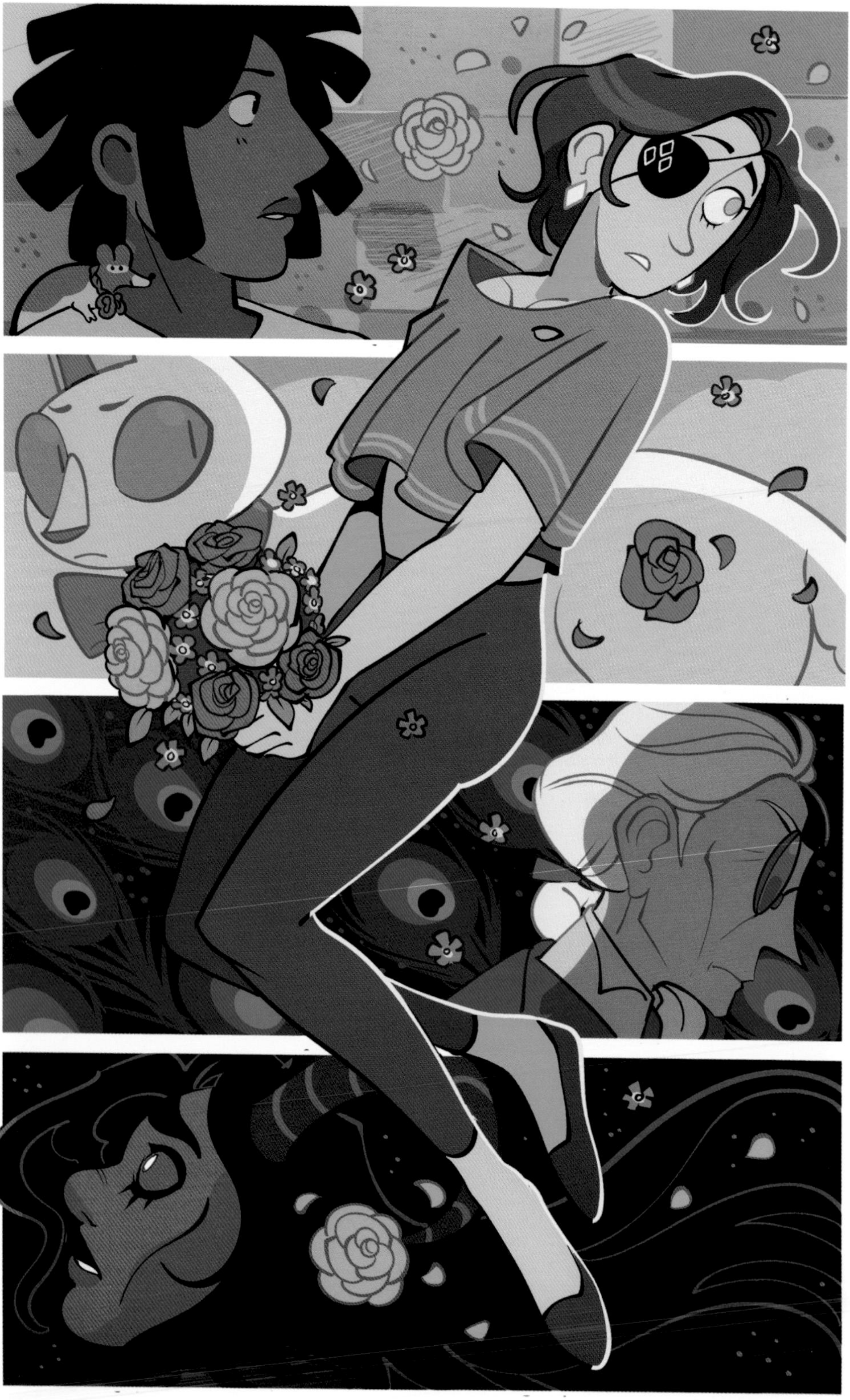